Italy's "Southern Question"

Italy's "Southern Question"

Orientalism in One Country

Edited by
Jane Schneider

Oxford • New York

First published in 1998 by
Berg
Editorial offices:
150 Cowley Road, Oxford, OX4 1JJ, UK
70 Washington Square South, New York, NY 10012, USA

Berg is the imprint of Oxford International Publishers Ltd.

Library of Congress Cataloging-in-Publication Data

A catalogue record for this book is available from the Library of Congress

British Library Cataloguing-in-Publication Date

A catalogue record for this book is available from the British Library

ISBN 1 85973 992 X (Cloth)
1 85973 997 0 (Paper)

Typeset by JS Typesetting, Wellingborough, Northants.

Contents

Contents

Acknowledgments

The authors of this book first gathered in the spring of 1992, at the Graduate School of the City University of New York, to embark on a discussion of the "Italian Southern Question, Representations and Realities." Shaped by several different disciplines – anthropology, history, literature, sociology, political science – and by scholarly traditions on both sides of the Atlantic, they discovered, first and foremost, that they shared a great deal of common ground regarding this problem. The experience led to a conference, held in Tarrytown, New York, in May 1995, where participants presented and worked over formal papers that addressed the emerging common themes. I would like to thank the Wenner-Gren Foundation for Anthropological Research, which not only funded the conference but encouraged the publication of this, the resulting volume, with a small subsidy.

On behalf of the volume authors and Berg Publishers, I also wish to express appreciation to the University Seminars at Columbia University for financial assistance in the preparation of the manuscript for publication. Several of the contributing authors belong to the University Seminar on Studies in Modern Italy, and have presented related material at seminar meetings, benefiting from discussions there. The following colleagues helped the project come to fruition in other ways, from reading drafts of conference proposals or the introductory essay to joining the dialogue in one or another of its several settings: Jeffrey Cole, Vincent Crapanzano, Kate Creehan, and Michael Herzfeld. A perceptive and knowledgeable anonymous reader for Berg made significant criticisms and suggestions. I am grateful to all for their contributions; none, of course, is responsible for the outcome. Finally, thanks are owed to four Italy-bound graduate students of CUNY – Ann Berg, Stanley Davis, Maria Hart, and Christine Tartaglia – who served the conference as rapporteurs and to my daughter, Julia Schneider, who generously donated time and computer expertise to the final preparation of the manuscript.

Introduction: The Dynamics of Neo-orientalism in Italy (1848–1995)

Jane Schneider

In Italy, and in Italian studies, the "Southern Question" evokes a powerful image of the provinces south of Rome as different from the rest of the peninsula, above all for their historic poverty and economic underdevelopment, their engagement in a clientelistic style of politics, and their cultural support for patriarchal gender relations and for various manifestations of organized crime. This tenacious catalogue of stereotypes includes, as well, the notion that southerners, by dint of their very essence, or at least their age-old culture and traditions, possess character traits that are opposite to the traits of northerners. Passionate, undisciplined, rebellious, intensely competitive, and incapable of generating group solidarity or engaging in collective action, they were and are, as the cliché, would have it, unable to build the rational, orderly, civic cultures that, in the North, underwrote the emergence of industrial capitalist society.

This volume is an interdisciplinary effort to understand how and why the forceful rhetoric of North versus South took hold in Italy, becoming an everyday symbolic geography for northerners and southerners alike. In addition, it further addresses the problem of generating alternative representations of the South. The timing is propitious. A regionalist movement rooted in Lombardy and the Veneto, the Lega Nord (Northern League), has challenged national unity through a surprising show of electoral strength in the 1994 and 1996 elections. Although many observers have been reluctant to take seriously the movement's flamboyant, theatrical leader, Umberto Bossi, they have nevertheless been shaken by the unexpected resonance which his anti-southern (as well as anti-immigrant) stance has evoked in the North.

Reminiscent of neo-liberalism in other industrialized countries, the Lega has attacked the national government for over-taxing the productive economy of Northern Italy and then over-spending on welfaristic infusions of capital and social services in the South. Given the inherently corrupt practices of southerners, it is argued, such investments have not transformed, but only reproduced, a backward system. Policy-makers were right, therefore, when in 1992, in the context of Italy's first budgetary restrictions preparatory to entering the European Monetary Union, they terminated a range of programs that dated back to 1950, when the national government launched its "extraordinary intervention" to develop the South (see Clark 1984: 357–60; Ginsborg 1990: 162, 229–30; Levy 1996: 2–3). Bossi has himself gone much further, imagining and preparing for the creation and secession of a mythical northern state he calls "Padania."

The would-be revolution of Umberto Bossi and the Northern "Leghisti" is not the only upheaval in contemporary Italy that renders an exploration of the Southern Question timely. There are, as well, powerful social forces at work in the South – antimafia reform movements opposed to organized crime and its ally, political corruption – whose followers are deeply committed to building the political, cultural, and judicial institutions of southern civil society. Evident since the early 1980s, particularly in the cities, these movements, too, have thrown down the gauntlet to Italy, the nation. Like the Leghisti, their critique singles out for special opprobrium the regime of center-left political parties that governed the country from the end of the war until the first post-Cold War election of 1992. In their analyses, however, the problem with this regime is not that it was permeated by clientelistic practices emanating from the South, but rather that it protected some of the South's most vile criminals – bosses who assumed a dominant role in the international traffics of arms and drugs – in order to hang on to power. The magistrates, intellectuals, and political leaders who have spearheaded the southern reform movements would further remind us that they were active before, and an inspiration to, the "clean hands" anti-corruption prosecutions of the North (prosecutions that developed independently of, even though they have been exploited by, the Lega).

There are many obstacles to Italy's splitting in two. Despite their strong regional focus, both the Antimafia or Rete Party that was founded in Palermo in 1990 and the Lega Nord have national ambitions and pursue strategies for mobilizing support beyond their respective homelands. Meanwhile, the decidedly national electorates of the former Communists, Socialists, and Christian Democrats have been re-channeled into two new parties of national scope – the Democratic Party of the Left and the Forza Italia Party of Silvio Berlusconi (see Levy 1996). And, as Gabriella Gribaudi reminds us in a recent essay, "Images of the South," there remains to consider "all the intermarriages between northerners and southerners, the assimilation into Northern cities of Southern migrants of the 1950s and 1960s, [and] the high number of southerners amongst the Italian ruling class, not only in the ranks of the discredited state bureaucracy" (1996: 85). Yet Gribaudi also notes a recent "marked return to the divisive arguments of the nineteenth century, but with even greater malice . . . rekindling conflicts and channeling hatreds." Although Italy has not seen bloodshed, she warns, the conflict between North and South is "developing in a similar manner to that in Eastern Europe" (ibid.).

A common ingredient in both situations is surely the European Union, which, in the very process of moving toward a single currency and more integrated political economy, has touched off an intense set of debates about belonging: which nation states will be deemed qualified to join which institutions, and in which order or "round." In the former Yugoslavia, the desire to belong to Europe was a powerful motive underlying the separatist strategies of Croatia and Slovenia, whose leaders redefined Serbia as a burden and an embarrassment, complaining that, in the name of brotherly unity, Belgrade was siphoning resources from the more "progressive, prosperous, hard-working, tolerant, democratic . . . in a word, *European*," regions of the country so that the "primitive, lazy, intolerant," *Balkan* regions could "freeload" (Bakić-Hayden and Hayden 1992: 6–8).

It is not altogether beside the point to see in the Northern League an analog to the Croatian and Slovenian moves, or to worry that in Southern Italy the new efforts to build a nationally-resonant civil society may be swamped by other, less democratic and less peaceful, movements. The disparities between North and South in gross domestic product, in receipt of capital transfers as against payment of taxes, and in unemployment, remain dramatically high, and the neo-fascist Alleanza Nazionale Party, having taken up the cause of defending the South from recent moves to dismantle the welfare state, is enjoying a disproportionate expansion in this region (Levy 1996).

Yet another, broader, reason for examining the Southern Question now is that, in today's context of global capitalism, which emphasizes "flexible accumulation" and the unfettered mobility of capital, both large-scale investors and a growing number of social economists and political scientists have focused their attention on regional potentialities, as shaped by regional cultures. In such a climate, there is a kind of urgency to exploring how these cultures become delineated – synthesized in a few images, constructed or defined. Particularly when the definitions are pejorative, one wants to know what might be required for alternative understandings to be articulated and heard. As anthropologist James Carrier has put it, considerable power imbalances affect "the larger uses to which these representations are put and the broader actions that they help motivate, by development agencies, international corporations, . . . governments, the tourist industry, and the like" (1992: 197).

The volume at hand, written from the varied perspectives of history, literature, anthropology, sociology, and political science, addresses these concerns. Several issues are worthy of our attention in this introduction. First, the Southern Question discourse, although in some respects an age-old phenomenon, took on its radical, oppositional contours – North versus South, advanced industrial versus backward agrarian, well-governed "civic" versus clientelistic – in the 1870s to 1890s, after the Unification of Italy, when the contrasts became not only essentialized, but racialized as well. Second, some important contributors to the discourse were and are southerners; stigmatizing the South is not exclusively an activity of northerners and non-Italians. This said, however, a third consideration presents itself: Italians have reified their internal differences in relation to a much wider context for defining difference: the context set by the dominant colonial and neo-colonial powers of the nineteenth and twentieth centuries, the successors of the Spanish and Portuguese empires – England, France, and the United States. Let us begin with this wider context.

Orientalism as Wider Context

Within the northern hemisphere, travellers voyaging from north to south in earlier centuries typically commented on differences of climate and sometimes invented elaborate theories relating climate and topography to the "character" of the peoples they encountered. They also often reacted to the visibility of poverty and squalor in southern city streets. Since they were people of means, they had no doubt learned to screen out such disturbing images in the places they came from, assisted, perhaps, by the fact that in cold climates less of domestic life unfolds outdoors. Grand Tour travellers of the eighteenth century had an added reason to be sensitive. Having studied the classics in England, France and Germany, they made the journey to Southern Italy, as to Greece, in search of an unspoiled antiquity; but the recent histories and societies of the living peoples of these places marred the experience (see Herzfeld 1987: 53–64). Nelson Moe, who has written extensively on the historical and literary background of the Southern Question, has assembled a series of revealing travellers' accounts from the "age before nationalism." In one of them, "the great cities of Italy" are described as "ignorant and corrupt . . . peopled by nothing but lords, valets, and an extremely crude populace." In another, Southern Italy is singled out as a region where "sensation dominates everything . . . Never did a noble thought germinate under this sun . . . they let themselves be carried away by inebriating nature" (quoted in Moe 1994: 7, 23).

Such judgments, many of them expressed in literature, were relatively benign. Apart from being traceable to the quite human experience of "culture shock," to borrow an expression from anthropology, they resonated with what James Fernandez suggests is a Europe-wide "popular cosmology" of North–South oppositions, in which both northerners and southerners see the "other" as different and in some respects morally inferior (Fernandez 1997; see also Campbell and Levine 1968). In addition they had to be weighed against knowledge of a recent past when Renaissance Italy was an economic and cultural center, and a source of political models, for much of Europe. All of this changed, however, when, in the wake of industrial development and colonial expansion, a system of nation-states was consolidated in North Atlantic Europe whose economic and military prowess transcended the standards of the past. As Moe has observed, developmental advances on this scale bestowed a prerogative to define what would be considered civilizational values, and to elevate or demote various peoples in relation to them (Moe 1994: 4). Tellingly, the discourses about who did and did not qualify as civilized gained much of their force from the deployment of simplistic binary categories, for, as Michael Herzfeld notes, by dividing the world into "manichean pairs . . . binarism makes distinctions into entities" and constitutes a "key ordering principle of political inequality" (Herzfeld 1997: 15). There is the further advantage that binary oppositions connect with "popular cosmologies" of difference, for example between North and South.

A particularly powerful instance of the new geopolitics of civilization was, of course, the radically dichotomous discourse on Orientalism. As applied to the Muslim societies of the Middle East, this literary, scholarly, and political tradition both derived from, and justified, the colonial projects of the emergent European powers. In his groundbreaking exploration of the phenomenon, Edward Said noted how the accumulated textual and visual elements contrasting a mystical, sensual, and indolent "East" with a rational, progressive, and modern West were not aimed at the "acephalous" or "tribal" societies of some colonial encounters, but at elaborate centralized states, heirs of past civilizations, which might well have been competitors. By rendering the governments of these states as both archaic and "bad," Orientalist discourse trivialized their role in world history and put forth a vision of a future in which they would be eclipsed by more Western-appearing and westward-tilting regimes (Said 1979). Said also traced how, after the Second World War, Orientalist discourse was reinvented and substantially reinforced in the academic halls of prestigious universities and government circles in the United States, the baton of preeminent economic and military might having crossed the Atlantic Ocean to locate itself in Washington and New York. To quote Herzfeld again, "models of cultural superiority" get established and imposed, initially, by "force of arms and wealth" (1997: 16).

Italy was certainly affected by Orientalism. For, although the imperial powers of the north did not envision the Italian peninsula as a land they had to colonize – its inhabitants were European Christians, after all – it was nevertheless their goal that Italian resources and products circulate freely in international markets, that Italian markets be open to English and French manufactures, and that Italian élites share in and support the world civilizational system that these powers believed it was their prerogative to create. As such they critically scrutinized the divergent polities of the peninsula on the eve of their unification in 1860, much to the disadvantage of the Neapolitan Kingdom of the Two Sicilies that governed the southern region and Sicily. A telling, because widely publicized, indictment was that of William Gladstone, who took up the cause of political prisoners in Naples after the Kingdom repressed the uprising against it in 1848. This Bourbon monarchy, he scolded, was "the negation of God erected into a system of Government" (quoted in Moe 1994: 35). For Gladstone and his contemporaries,

Moe proposes, the way this government treated its prisoners was a "synecdoche for a much larger ensemble of political and ideological problems, ranging from . . . resistance to international free trade to [their] 'abominable' anti-liberal, anti-constitutional doctrines" (ibid.). Meanwhile, the Kingdom of Sardinia in Piedmont, which was to spearhead the Unification, emerged from the turmoil of 1848 embracing the ideals of constitutional monarchy and liberalized trade, winning much higher marks.

Evaluations of Italy emanating from the world centers of military and economic power in the second half of the twentieth century share an uncanny similarity to these pronouncements, replete with the paternalistic rhetoric of the good, or almost good, northern protégé and the bad southern one. An influential example is political scientist Edward C. Banfield's 1958 *The Moral Basis of a Backward Society*, which helped convince policy circles in Cold War America of the urgency of developing and thus transforming the Italian South. In line with the burgeoning research tradition nurtured by sociologist Talcott Parsons at Harvard University, Banfield proposed a direct, causal connection between economic development (as measured by industrial capacity, workers' productivity, and standard of living), and a people's propensity to join voluntary associations and engage in collective projects for the common good. Southern Italian society was backward, he argued, because instead of a civic culture that would promote this sort of collaboration, it had a familistic culture favorable to agonistic separation. Southern Italians acted to further the short-term interests of their respective nuclear families – hardly the common good – and assumed that their fellow citizens were doing the same. Banfield labeled them "amoral familists" and, as Simona Piattoni explains in a later chapter in this volume, he held this ethos responsible for their clientelistic conduct of politics as well.

Thirty-five years later, in 1993, another American political scientist, Robert D. Putnam, produced a second key text in the English language for interpreting Southern Italian "backwardness", *Making Democracy Work; Civic Traditions in Modern Italy*. Based on a twenty-year study of the differences in performance of six regional governments distributed throughout the peninsula, Putnam's book is considerably more systematic and comprehensive than Banfield's. Yet it too constructs an opposition between North and South. Finding that the northern regional governments out-perform the southern ones in their ability to enact and implement policy, Putnam locates their effectiveness in a "civic tradition" of communally oriented city states that stretches "from Rome to the Alps" and can be dated to the Middle Ages. In drastic contrast, the South suffered from medieval times under royal governments at once feudal, bureaucratic, and absolutist (1993: 123).

That Putnam intended the contrast to be not merely a difference of elements, but rather a binary set of forms is suggested by his use of the terms "horizontal collaboration" and "vertical hierarchy" for the governmental institutions of the North and the South, respectively (1993: 124). A deep history, moreover, renders these polarized structures essential: "by the beginning of the fourteenth century, Italy had produced" two (and only two) different "patterns of governance," two different "ways of life." "In the North, people were citizens; in the South they were subjects ... In the North the crucial social, political, and even religious allegiances and alignments were horizontal, while those in the South were vertical. Collaboration, mutual assistance, civic obligation, and even trust ... were the distinguishing features in the North. The chief virtue in the South, by contrast, was the imposition of hierarchy and order on latent anarchy" (1993: 130).

Centuries later, after the collapse of the communal republics and their "re-feudalization," the North, too, succumbed to bad government. "However, among the northern heirs to the communal tradition, patrons, no matter how autocratic, still accepted civic responsibilities," whereas their contemporaries in the South, the Spanish Habsburgs and the Bourbons, "systematically promoted mutual distrust and conflict among their subjects, destroying horizontal ties of solidarity in order to maintain the primacy of vertical ties of dependence and exploitation" (1993: 135–6). The legacy for the North, Putnam argues, was that its citizens would meet the challenges of Italian Unification and subsequent industrial transformation with a "practical reciprocity," a "pragmatic readiness to cooperate," a well-spring of mutual trust, generating all manner of voluntary associations in reinforcement of their civic culture. Quite the contrary for the South, where patron–client networks persisted "as the primary structure of power," even after the appearance of mass parties. Here "civic habits" paled before "the ancient culture of mistrust" and the absence of the practice of mutual assistance sabotaged economic development projects, regardless of how well they were financed.

I note the dichotomous language of the Putnam text (as does Piattoni) because it marks the continuation of the wider, hegemonic context within which debates over the Italian Southern Question of necessity unfold. Rich in data on regional governmental performance measured over time, *Making Democracy Work* is already influential in the policy-making circles of various governing bodies – Italian, European, American – and probably also among private financial analysts (see Tarrow 1996: 389, notes 1 and 4). It certainly works hand in hand with journalistic accounts of Italy's present situation *vis-à-vis* the pending Monetary Union of Europe. Finance ministers of the Northern powers have yet to commit to including this Mediterranean country in the first round of the Union, claiming to doubt the stability of its government and the government's ability to lower its budget deficit. The subtext of the pessimism is suggested by the following *New York Times* headline: "North–South Divide in Italy, a Problem for Europe, Too." In the article so titled, correspondent Celestine Bohlen refers to the division between the rich North and the dependent passive South as the "curse of Italian unity" and warns that the split "augurs ill for Italy as a whole as it tries to put its financial house in order" (*NYT* 1996, Nov. 15).

Given the forcefulness of these images, in which Italy appears dragged down by its southern half, it is tempting to attribute the Southern Question discourse to the expansionist political-economic and cultural projects of North Atlantic Europe and the United States. To do so, however, would be to overlook two critical processes that interacted to produce what might be called a neo-Orientalist discourse *within* Italy itself. Moe has identified these processes as first, the tendency for northern and national élites to displace their anxieties about belonging to Europe onto that part of the country that is geographically and, in their minds, culturally, most distant from the European "core"; and second, the tendency for southern intellectuals and liberal élites to articulate a profound critique of their native society and government, becoming the interlocutors of northerners' negative views (Moe 1992, 1994). These processes – displacement and complicity – illuminate how Orientalism can work within a country to reinforce the wider geopolitical and geo-cultural ambitions of the great powers, creating what an East European specialist refers to as "nesting Orientalisms" (Bakić-Hayden 1995). It is with them in mind that I turn to the specific contributions of this book.

The Genesis of the Southern Question

Within Italy, a discourse about the South emerged simultaneously in many fields, some of which – public policy, statistics, criminology, and literature – are represented in this book. (Others, for example art, music, theater, poetry, and folklore, should be noted.) Taken together, the different fields suggest a rhythm of genesis: only after the Unification of Italy did an image of the South as internally homogeneous and qualitatively "other" become consolidated, displacing a picture of open-ended possibilities in which the region's particular or divergent institutions, laws, and customs were noted but not reified. Our account begins with Marta Petrusewicz's chapter "Before the Southern Question," which not only illustrates this open-endedness, but lays the groundwork for considering the process of southerners' complicity in stigmatizing the South.

Following its independence from Spain in 1734, the Kingdom of the Two Sicilies set out to reform, and then abolish, feudalism. But there were setbacks: first the French Revolution, which made reforms seem dangerous; then the invasion and conquest by Napoleon's armies; and, finally, after the 1815 restoration, the even more terrifying local uprisings of 1848. The period of calm between 1815 and 1848 nurtured widespread activity on the part of Liberal aristocrats and the emergent middle classes, who met in secret, not only in Naples but in the provinces, to plot the end of feudalism. Petrusewicz is interested in how they navigated their political and cultural choices, knowing that their more or less "enlightened" royals had recently been driven out by the French. During this "first" Restoration, and in keeping with Romantic movements throughout Europe, they clung to Enlightenment ideals yet rejected "the blind application of foreign recipes," "the contempt for native customs and institutions," the "remoteness from popular sentiment" of some Enlightenment projects, all the while continuing to measure their country against those that claimed the top places in the new civilizational hierarchy.

Periods of panic and repression disillusioned these "native" reformers, however, and, after 1848, catapulted many of them into prison or exile. In a 1992 essay, Moe reviews the situation of the Neapolitan exiles to Northern Italy who joined the Piedmontese movement for unifying the nation and who then returned to Naples in 1860. Home again, if only temporarily, they felt more contempt for what they found than did the invading Piedmontese army. This, plus their reciprocal admiration for the invader, led them to envision the new nation, Italy, as formed through the imposition of northern institutions and practices, rather than through regional integration. The equivocation, Moe suggests, opened the door for accentuating the deviation of the South from the whole. Petrusewicz amplifies this point. Highlighting not only the exiles' past efforts to transform the southern kingdom from within, but also their enthusiasms, their hopes, and their great caution, she enables us to appreciate how bitter and disappointing political experiences can shape what happens in history. No wonder, she suggests, that some southerners were fully complicitous with northerners in the construction of the Southern Question discourse.

Moe's chapter focuses on the period between 1874 and 1884 when the Southern Question was actually born, and includes a careful reading of the important exile, Pasquale Villari, who settled in Florence in 1848, liked Tuscany, and lived there until his death in 1917 (1994: 219–20). In 1875, his *Lettere Meridionali* launched the school of "Meridionalisti" – authors of field studies and comprehensive treatises that described southern problems for a northern audience over the next several decades. Villari's *Letters*, Moe tells us, were the work of an "agitator." By detailing the shocking social conditions of his homeland, he hoped to shame the predominantly northern liberal élites into changing what had so far been their largely negative and repressive orientation toward the South: impose new taxes, institute conscription, and suppress banditry. In the light of the Paris Commune of 1871, he believed, this élite would want to redress southern poverty and backwardness, if not from a sense of social justice then at least from fear.

In making his case, Villari increasingly assigned Southern Italy a special function in what Moe suggests was a "moral geography" of Italy, condensing all the social ills of the nation into this single region, from crime and dereliction, to banditry and bad government, to oppressive landlords, peasant and urban squalor, and an absent middle class. As a consequence, his moral outrage worked in tandem with – it did not contradict – the reporting of Leopoldo Franchetti, a Tuscan Senator investigating Sicily at about the same time. As Moe makes clear, Franchetti assumed a thoroughly European stance *vis-à-vis* the Italian South, whose peasants reminded him of the "savages" of America, manifesting little of the human desire to improve. In the case of Sicily, northerners would have to impose their modern practices and values on this still-medieval (and gendered) "little sister;" otherwise it would not qualify for membership in European civilization. Moe explores the many sophisticated rhetorical devices through which Franchetti's writings on Sicily amplified difference, for example his stance as a superior outsider continually surprised by the degradation of this foreign territory. Most telling, perhaps, was his adoption of a medical metaphor that invested the North "with all the authority commonly associated with a doctor, while Sicily is reduced to the figure of sick patient . . . unable to make decisions on its own behalf."

Following the Florentine decade that gave birth to the Southern Question, its contours became ever more rigid and essentialized. In a striking instance of this shift, Silvana Patriarca compares the earliest statisticians of the new nation, who recognized variations throughout the peninsula, accounted for them historically, and believed that "good administration" could resolve serious problems, with their successors of the 1890s, who put statistics to work in support of a racialized, evolutionary paradigm. In the latter's hands, North versus South became not only a binary geography, but a geography that was non-relational. Her essay further reveals how the new languages of official surveys, statistics, and positivist social science lent authority to the representation of the South as truly "other" – a representation that became even more pronounced after the Second World War, as the State prepared its "extraordinary intervention" in southern development.

The new languages grew out of the social theory and social engineering that accompanied nation-state and empire building in France and England. The ideas of English Social Darwinist Herbert Spencer, for example, inspired a group of Northern Italians credited with founding the science of criminology in the 1880s and 1890s – Cesare Lombroso, Enrico Ferri, Giuseppe Sergi and others. Mary Gibson's chapter discusses the turn these theorists took toward a racial analysis of regional difference. In their view, England's accumulation of colonies was owed to the Nordic or Aryan genes of its populace. That Italy had as yet no empire – its troops met defeat in Abyssinia in 1896 – was attributable to its genetically ambiguous situation. Although each criminologist resorted to his own distinctive and muddled classificatory scheme, as a group they propagated the idea that southerners carried inferior mediterranean-type genes that threatened to dilute the progressive northerners' European (Alpine, or Aryan, or Celtic) endowment.

Not surprisingly, this mode of analysis had a gendered dimension. Guglielmo Ferrero, a follower of Lombroso, proposed that Southern Italian men were sexually precocious, wasting their lives in the pursuit and enslavement of women, rather than working for the "advancement of society." An Englishman was worth two such men, being less easily distracted and "twice as energetic" (quoted in Noether n.d.: 9). Most pernicious, the new criminologists sought to prove that Calabrian and Sicilian men were predisposed to crime. Remarkably, Gibson points out, the more "congenital Latin decadence" took over as an explanatory framework for southern crime rates, the more analyses grounded in the South's social problems – poverty, illiteracy, a persistent mal-distribution of property – receded into the background, remaining there even as the hard-edged racial determinism of the new discipline of criminology softened into a determinism based on culture.

The turn toward a racial explanation of regional difference in the Southern Question discourse was accomplished for the most part by North Italians, although Alfredo Niceforo, a Sicilian and among the most outspoken racialists, was a noteworthy exception. Buoyed by their supreme confidence in the positivist paradigm inherited from Northern Europe, Lombroso and the group around him would not easily penetrate the continued hegemony of idealism in Neapolitan philosophical circles. Their "science" was also blatantly offensive. Gibson reviews the response of the Sicilian statistician and sociological criminologist, Napoleone Colajanni, who articulated a forceful critique of their assumptions. Yet many southern intellectuals remained complicitous in essentializing the South, rendering it culturally if not racially homogeneous and unchanging. In the last chapter of Part I, Frank Rosengarten takes up Sicily's modern writers – Giovanni Verga, Leonardo Sciascia, and Tomasi de Lampedusa – all important figures in Italian literature, and all deeply ambivalent about the possibility that their homeland could ever "improve."

Living as an expatriate in Milan, the center of Italy's publishing industry and reading public in the late nineteenth century (see Moe 1994: 227–35), Verga, for example, represented the island of his birth as a radical contrast, in which all human relationships, regardless of social class or degree of intimacy, risked being distorted by greed, misery, envy, treachery or petty scheming for advantage. Victimized by an oppressive history, no less than by a torrid and unrelenting sun, Verga's Sicilians struggle in what Rosengarten suggests is a "hierarchy of emotional pain." Even their efforts at revolt for justice and liberation come across as somewhat fraudulent and ineffective, a judgment that anticipated one of the mantras of twentieth-century Southern Question discourse: southerners' "failure to engage in collective action."

Verga's novels of the 1880s might be compared with the 1960s novels of Leonardo Sciascia, whose main intellectual reference point was outside Italy, in Paris. Finding the Enlightenment traditions of France intellectually attractive, Sciascia also depicted Sicily in contrasting terms. Where "enlightened" societies would honor such "impersonal" or universalizing principles as the equality of citizens before the law, his mystery novels and essays focused on Sicilians' manipulative, hidden relationships in public as well as private life. More to the point, as Rosengarten shows, both Sciascia and Lampedusa held fast to the concept of an essential way of being Sicilian – a distinctive Sicilian mentality or culture – whose foremost feature was resignation, a deep, unshakable fatalism about the future. Lampedusa's imposing hero of *The Leopard*, Don Fabrizio, could not have said it more clearly: "In Sicily, it doesn't matter whether one does good or evil: the sin that we Sicilians never pardon is simply that of doing."

All told, these instances of complicity contribute an important dimension to the analysis of the broader phenomenon of Orientalism, whose negative constructions are usually assumed to emanate from outsiders, apprehending the other from a distance. So much is this the case that even the qualifying argument made by recent scholars (for example Carrier 1992; Coronil 1996) that Orientalist discourses are a reciprocal, or dialectical creation, basically means that their promoters, in the process of dualizing and hierarchizing others, also define themselves. Whether employing the categories of occidentalism or of orientalism, "Orientalists" seem mainly to hail from the dominant metropole or center. This may have been true of the racialized version of the Southern Question discourse (with the exception, again, of Alfredo Niceforo), but was not the case for its other aspects. Internally differentiated and already in turmoil as a consequence of Europe-wide and world-wide transformations, Southern Italy inevitably produced its own, internal critics of illiberal institutions. Believing that national unification would further their cause, these critics, moreover, felt no pressure to censor their judgmental thoughts and words.

Southern Intellectuals and Critical Social Theory

By the end of the nineteenth century, Southern Italians were represented in Italy as racial or cultural others whose differences from northerners were intrinsic and for all time. By nature anarchic, undisciplined, and "unsuited to long-term political preparation" (Gribaudi 1996: 78), they were considered to be totally incapable of changing their way of being. Change would have to come, as Franchetti argued for Sicily, from the North. Yet this mode of interpreting the South provoked a counter-discourse, which put forward the political and economic history of the South as an alternative to race and culture in accounting for what was wrong. Articulating this critique at the turn of the century, the Sicilian, Colajanni, introduced a long line of what we might call advocates for the South who have focused on political economy as a counterweight to Southern Question essentialisms. The roster includes several North Italian, European, and American social scientists as well as southerners. The 1960s responses of sociologist Alessandro Pizzorno (see 1971) and anthropologist Sydel Silverman (1968) to the Banfield treatise are exemplary. They looked, respectively, to the South's political-economic marginality) and agricultural organization for structural influences on clientelistic, atomized, and distrustful behaviors.

Within the political economic tradition, there is a compelling argument that the difficulties of the South are rooted in a colonial or near-colonial past. The position is stated with exceptional clarity by political scientist Sidney Tarrow (1996) in his review of Robert Putnam's *Making Democracy Work*. Although lauding Putnam for his and his collaborators' research "endurance and creativity," leading to a convincing portrait of the operations of several regional governments over twenty years, Tarrow takes him to task for ignoring state-building processes and with them the "differential structuring of a public culture." As Putnam himself acknowledges, but "passes over quickly,"

> every regime that governed southern Italy from the Norman establishment of a centralized monarchy in the twelfth century to the unified government which took over there in 1861 was foreign and governed with a logic of colonial exploitation. Nor did southern Italy's semicolonial status suddenly disappear with unification. The region was joined to the North by a process of royal conquest, its fragile commercial sector brutally merged with the North's more flourishing economy, a uniform tax system and customs union imposed on its vulnerable industries, and brigandage rooted out by a full-scale military campaign. Politically, the South's communes and provinces were governed by northern administrators who regarded the region as a *terra dimissione*, and its economy was penetrated by carpetbaggers in search of new markets and raw materials . . . Like the merger of West and East Germany 130 years later, a stronger, richer, more legitimate regime conquered a weaker, poorer, more marginal one, inducting its residents into political life through the tools of patronage, paternalism, and the power of money – and rubbing it in by sending in commissions of experts to shake their heads over their backwardness (1996: 394).

I understand and appreciate this critique, the more so as I recall the path I followed, in the late 1960s, when first beginning to write about Western Sicily, based on fieldwork undertaken there with Peter Schneider. Indeed, my first article, in the *Anthropological Quarterly* of 1969, belaboring social fragmentation through an examination of "non-corporate groups" – cliques, coalitions, patron–client chains – attributed this pattern to an uncertain economy made marginal by Sicily's subordinate position not only within Italy but *vis-à-vis* international capitalism. The argument was developed more fully, and applied to a wider range of issues, in our jointly authored *Culture and Political Economy in Western Sicily* (1976).

Part II of this book explores two Southern Italian intellectuals who were politically engaged with the crisis of the South in the earlier half of this century and whose Marxist formation or exposure, plus their affection for down home, led them to consider these colonial relations in depth. One, Antonio Gramsci, is already widely translated and familiar to English-language readers; the other,

Ernesto de Martino, has been less accessible. Gramsci hailed from Sardinia, de Martino from Naples. A linguist by training, Gramsci influenced the younger de Martino, whose background was in humanist philosophy, anthropology, and folklore. For both figures, the South was above all a class-divided society, whose relations with the North, and with other both ancient and modern civilizations, were differently experienced by – and had different meanings for – peasant, landed, and urban social groups. Both asked what might be the historical role of southern peasants in redressing their own poverty and misery, raising the problem of southern agency as well as northern blame.

Writing about Gramsci, Nadia Urbinati emphasizes his relational understanding of North and South, as mediated by their respective classes. What peripheralized the South was the "historic bloc" or alliance that southern agrarian élites formed with northern industrialists after Unification, especially around tariff policies that presumably advantaged both. Only a corresponding alliance of southern peasants with northern industrial workers could liberate the South – and the nation. It was important, therefore, to evaluate these peasants as historical actors. Did they meet the Marxist criteria for revolutionary class consciousness or were they, as their reputation had it, merely brigands, assassins of landlords, instinctual rebels driven by the "savage passions" of envy, resentment, and distrust? Gramsci broke new ground with his plea that the Italian Left communicate with southern peasants in terms of their common-sense understandings; show respect for their local dialects; look for progressive elements in their folklore; understand their fatalism as situational; find something positive and life-affirming in their passionate sense of justice; and anticipate the emergence of genuine, if untutored, intellectuals from among their ranks. Like the Neapolitan Liberals of a century earlier, who questioned heavy-handed methods of imposing Enlightenment culture on an ill-prepared hinterland, Gramsci understood, as Petrusewicz writes in presenting these Liberals, that "contempt for native customs and institutions" and "remoteness from popular sentiment" risked provoking a counter-revolution.

Yet ultimately it must be questioned how far Gramsci stood outside the Southern Question discourse. His famous essay on the topic of 1926 described the South as *"una disgregazione sociale"* – a great social disintegration. His *Prison Notebooks*, moreover, depicted peasants as frequent generators of "traditional" intellectuals, above all priests and lawyers, but never of "organic" intellectuals, capable of leading their class in revolt. In the alliance he envisioned between southern peasants and northern industrial workers, the workers would take the lead (Gramsci 1971 [1929–1935]: 6, incl. n. 4). Peasants, Gramsci reiterated, in the section on "State and Civil Society," possess a "'generic' hatred (which) is still 'semi-feudal' rather than modern in character, and cannot be taken as evidence of class consciousness," only as "the first glimmer . . . the basic negative, polemical attitude" (ibid.: 272–3).

Gramsci's pessimism about the capacity of southern peasants to act in history highlights a problem with political-economic critiques of culturalist or racialist essentializing. Do they really generate an alternative discourse or do they, rather, operate within, and reinforce, what they seek to criticize? On the one hand, political-economic accounts allow for malleability; the conditions observed are not considered fixed for all time, as if outside history, but as consequences of human action and therefore susceptible to change. On the other hand, however, it is characteristic of these accounts, Gramsci's included, to assume that the crisis of the South is pervasive, overlooking intra-regional variation. Understandings that emphasize relations of colonial intrusion and domination, moreover, locate responsibility for the disturbing phenomena in an external arena, leaving the victims in the passive position of having history done to them rather than making it themselves. In this respect, it is quite fascinating to consider the somewhat different approach of de Martino.

De Martino's anthropological research, begun during the Second World War and lasting into the 1960s, expanded Gramsci's humanizing approach to the peasantry. This conclusion, however, is possible only after considering the author's work in its entirety. Annalisa Di Nola, who provides this volume with such a reading, begins by exposing passages on mourning rituals in Lucania that could easily lead a superficial reviewer to classify de Martino as a "modernization theorist," prepared to separate off peasant cultures from urban cultures – little traditions from great ones – and downgrade the former into backward, pre-literate survivals of an earlier, more primitive time. Di Nola also explores de Martino's reasons for rejecting the usual anthropological inoculation against this way of thinking: namely, cultural relativism. Without hegemonic, Western Enlightenment culture, he held, there would have been no anthropology. At the same time, however, de Martino insisted that anthropologists interrogate the categories they adopted for understanding other peoples. A trenchant critic of both evolutionism and functionalism in anthropology, he challenged concepts like "popular religion" and "survivals" for failing to locate peasants in history. As Di Nola shows, his analyses of ritual celebrations, including most famously, the healing cult of tarantism in Southern Italy, brought out dense entanglements over many centuries between popular practice and world religions, in which historical action went both ways.

Yet although de Martino dignified Southern Italian peasants, rendering them intrinsically rational, and subjects rather than objects of history (see Gribaudi 1996: 82), he believed that a real transformation of their lives would be impossible without the engagement of the hegemonic forces of the nation – the Catholic Church and the industrial bourgeoisie. Whereas Gramsci, the more thorough Marxist, had looked to southern peasants' eventual alliance with northern factory workers as necessary for the liberation of both from precisely these forces, for de Martino the "molding energy" of élite cultures was potentially positive. In accordance with the relational emphasis of his folkloric studies, which insisted on a continuous circulation between élite and popular elements, he envisioned a possible shaping role for northern as well as southern power-holders in resolving southern problems – provided, however, that their approach was humanistically grounded and addressed issues of economic and social justice as well as culture, caveats that had yet to be fulfilled.

In the final chapter of Part II, George Saunders compares Gramsci and De Martino with regard to the counter-intuitive ways that each understood religious beliefs and practices, above all magic, in the rural Mezzogiorno. For Gramsci, popular religion was implicitly and partially oppositional, thanks to the corruption of the southern clerical hierarchy. Yet its oppositional energy could be tapped for reactionary ends by the dominant classes and was, additionally, always in danger of breaking up and dissipating into fragments. The point for him was to get to know popular religion better, so as effectively to change it.

De Martino was marginally more positive, addressing magical practices like the evil eye and conjuring in terms of his philosophy of "the presence" – an existential concept laid out by Di Nola, which refers to how persons maintain both their boundaries and their vitality in a precarious world. Almost like a strategy for coping, magic helped people resolve "crises of the presence," particularly in places such as rural Southern Italy where misery and exposure to a wide spectrum of traumas rendered life more uncertain than usual. Consistently with his criticism of the Catholic Church and the national bourgeoisie for failing to deploy a convincing amount of "molding energy" in the Mezzogiorno, de Martino also, however, drew attention to the society-wide distribution of evil eye beliefs in Southern Italy. At the time of the Kingdom of the Two Sicilies, they pervaded even the royal court. In Saunders's reading, de Martino, here, revealed himself to be still inside the Southern Question's "traditional versus modern" binary oppositions.

Exploring Alternatives

Today we are increasingly aware of Third World scholars who, like Gramsci and de Martino, have struggled with issues of popular culture and political agency, although from the perspective of Europe's actual colonies. Some – the Indian "subaltern studies" group – have found Gramsci to be the most relevant Marxist. Overall their work points up how little independence the popular traditions and values of agrarian Southern Italy had from wider processes of power, whether in actual practice or in the most generous strands of critical theory. We might contrast, for example, Fernando Ortiz, a Cuban ethnographer and public intellectual whose

1940 classic, *Cuban Counterpoint: Tobacco and Sugar*, has recently been reissued. In a new introduction (supplementing that of Bronislaw Malinowski), Fernando Coronil relates the "counterpoint" of the title to Ortiz's understanding that although the world "is forged by the violence of conquests and colonization," there are constant negotiations and conflicts over "defining the West and its Others, white and dark, man and woman, high and low" . . . (Coronil 1995: xiv).

Of significance for our story, Ortiz's first book of 1906 was influenced by the "evolutionary positivist theories" of Cesare Lombroso, who wrote the preface. By 1910, however, Ortiz had shifted from a racial to a cultural paradigm for explaining Cuban "backwardness," later to discard this too for another, double-edged understanding. On the one hand, colonialism – specifically the sugar plantation – was the source of Cuba's problems: on the other hand, Cuban popular music could bridge the otherwise threatening gap between the island and the ruling centers of Western civilization. With this conclusion, Ortiz established "the universal value of African and Afro-Cuban music," while relativizing "European music as the standard accomplishment" (ibid.: xix). In Coronil's words, "if the self-fashioning of sovereign centers entails the making of dependent peripheries, Ortiz celebrate[d] the self-fashioning of these peripheries, the counterpoint through which people turn margins into centers and make fluidly coherent identities out of fragmented histories" (ibid.: iv).

Another relevant contrast with Southern Italy (and with Gramsci and de Martino) is Partha Chatterjee's analysis of Bengal under British rule, which argues that colonized peoples kept aside an inner, spiritual domain through which they nurtured their distinctive nationalisms. The colonial power was not allowed to intervene in this domain, whose language and institutions – mainly of religion, kinship, and community – put up a front of resistance to the Orientalist prejudice that herein lay an archaic, even barbaric "culture," characterized by too many passions and the mistreatment of women. By resistance Chatterjee means detecting the limits, the contradictions, the ideological implications, of Liberal projects to build "civil society," rather than welcoming such projects, or cultivating alliances within them, as de Martino and Gramsci were inclined to do. Not only did the values of civil society, or a "modern regime of power," derive from the specific history and culture of North Atlantic Europe; they had been imposed on India by alien rulers who premised their power on remaining above and apart. To insist on cultural differences with them in the "inner domains" of religion, language, and family life (if not in the "outer domains" of statecraft, economy, and administration) was the colonized's way of claiming historical agency (1993: 28). Again, Gramsci and de Martino envisioned a less disjunctive separation between "colonizers" and "colonized."

For Chatterjee, the contradictions were especially acute in peasant politics. To the British colonists, Indian peasants were ignorant and exploitable, yet at the same time volatile and superstitious, "easily aroused by agitators and troublemakers," a perception that Indian nationalists invariably shared (1993: 158–9). And, indeed, peasant revolts were numerous, targeting such foci of authority as the police station, the landlord's rent-collection office, and the moneylender's house, "wrecking, burning, eating, and looting" what they could (1993: 162–3). Chatterjee seems more optimistic than Gramsci regarding this pattern of revolt. For him, the principle of community is a unifying feature of peasant consciousness (distinct from the individual preferences and interests of middle-class consciousness). Neither homogeneous nor egalitarian, communities nevertheless fostered alliances that grew out of the mutual bonds and obligations of propinquity and kinship – bonds that bourgeois "rationality" could not abide (1993: 165–7). In the South of Italy, by contrast, fragmentation and lack of trust characterized peasant communities, even in the evaluations of the native revolutionaries.

The writings of Third World scholars like Ortiz and Chatterjee presuppose positions or arguments that, if they were applied to the Italian South, would lead one to seek out unsuspected domains of autonomy, hidden well-springs of opposition to the industrial capitalist civilizational system and its multiple, nested, Orientalist discourses. That these arguments were not produced by Southern Italian intellectuals is consistent with a fundamental feature of regional difference in Italy: until the present moment, and possibly even now, it is remarkably devoid of regional-nationalisms – that is, regional identities mobilized in support of separatist political goals, whether ethnic, religious, or linguistic. Except for a brief and rather easily coopted moment of Sicilian separatism at the end of the Second World War, identity movements have been remarkably absent from the Italian scene (see Levy 1996; Lyttelton 1996; Herzfeld n.d.), even though – or perhaps because – Italy, the nation, was only for a while, under fascism, subjected to an energetic nationalist push for uniformity in language and culture – a point I return to below.

Meanwhile, because the intellectuals who were the strongest advocates for Southern Italian peasants found their uprisings to be anarchic and immature, and their cultural practices archaic, the historical conjuncture in which the South was both more agrarian than urban and the site of ongoing peasant attacks on landlords and tax collectors, did not produce a lasting or deep critique of the Orientalist mode of representing these rural folk. It has taken both a transformation of southern society, in which peasants have given way to other classes, and the emergence of new cohorts of intellectuals for whom the revolutionary potential of the peasantry is no longer a relevant issue, to arrive at challenging alternatives. Part III introduces a small sample of the many contemporary Southern Italian scholars, writers, and political actors who are currently engaged in addressing, breaking down, and seeing beyond the powerful processes of regional stereotyping that have trapped even the best-intentioned advocates for the South up to now.

The first essay by John Davis summarizes the work of several young historians whose research exposes established interpretations of the economic "failure" of the Mezzogiorno as over-simplistic. They criticize, in particular, the past neglect of genuine growth in the production and export of value-added cash crops and processed foods. Attending to the distribution, and the ups and downs, of orchards, gardens, and vineyards, one discovers that even the latifundia were less feudal and more commercial, less monocultural and more varied, than their image; that the above-noted "historic bloc" of southern landowners and northern industrialists was opposed by – and devastating for – *some* of these landowners; that the 1880s marked a turning-point in the structuring of *international* markets that harmed South Italian producers; and that, given these producers' precarious integration into world markets, their tendency to rely on short-term, multi-sectoral investment strategies should not be criticized but admired. In support of this research direction, we might add that the 1880s was the point at which the Italian South and Sicily became massive exporters of people. Precisely as the Southern Question took its turn toward a racialized essentialism, Italy, the nation, began to encourage the exodus of millions of its southern inhabitants (see Schneider and Schneider 1996).

Citing recent historical research on social and political formations in Northern Italy, the Davis essay also opens up a new perspective on clientelism in the South. Southern élites are shown to have been historically much more vulnerable than their northern counterparts to upheaval in the countryside, and to have sought out state protection to keep their peasants at bay. Conversely, the Italian state, always relatively "weak" in the South, "played on and indeed perpetuated factional rivalries and divisions" among these élites, becoming thereby "an important agent of political fragmentation and disunity." That this reciprocal conditioning has now ended makes sense of Carlo Trigilia's impressive case for the growth, since 1980, of an ever richer associational life, both cultural and political, in Southern Italy (Trigilia 1995; see also Tarrow 1996: 392).

Similar issues are addressed by Simona Piattoni in her chapter on the micro-politics of small, sub-regional zones within the region called "South." Piattoni is especially insistent on the reality of "many souths," so much so that, in her view, one must even look closely at the pervasive southern practice of clientelism in politics, disaggregating this stereotype for its possibly different meanings and manifestations in different times and places. Personalistic or patron–client relations are not the simple sign of backwardness that Banfield and Putnam would have us believe; nor are the centers of industrial capitalism devoid of them – witness the scandals surrounding influence-peddling and political-party financing in Northern Italy (and the United States) today. Rejecting constructions of the South as homogeneous, and culturally and socially distinct from an equally homogeneous North, Piattoni ingeniously argues that some patrons, in competing for clients, contribute to the development of a civic culture with salutary consequences for economic growth, and that this has demonstrably happened in some of the micro-regions of the South. We are reminded of Caroline White's 1980 ethnography of two contrastive South Italian towns of the Fucino Basin, which, although neighbors, had strikingly different political cultures (White 1980).

In their chapter, Peter and Jane Schneider discuss how, in the 1960s, Leonardo Sciascia, the grand fatalist, ironically was considered, and considered himself, a leading Sicilian intellectual in social and political movements that would curtail the influence of the mafia. They compare that epoch with the 1980s, a decade during which antimafia activists in Sicily as well as Italy came to see the novelist as very nearly a traitor to their cause. Sciascia, meanwhile, had accused these activists of riding roughshod over "ways of being Sicilian." This dispute, which was far from resolved when Sciascia died at the end of the decade, is a poignant instance not of inertia – of the failure of collective action – but of its risks. Social solidarity is undermined, not by an inherently agonistic *culture*, but rather by the complexities of confronting an institution – the mafia – whose history has been one of aggressively embedding itself both in the regional society and in national politics. There is no one way to be against it. A few contemporary antimafia activists draw parallels between the last twenty years of mafia history and the Nazi regime in Germany (for example, Siebert 1994). Sciascia, his antimafia reputation notwithstanding, took an opposite stance: in defending Sicilian culture against the "mafia of the antimafia," he seemed to be saying, "we have so far avoided fascism here but I see it on the horizon."

The last chapter of Part III is offered by Robert Dombroski, who analyses the de-territorialized characters and situations in the writings of two contemporary Sicilian novelists, Vincenzo Consolo and Gesualdo Bufalino. According to Dombroski, they locate Sicily fully within the orbit of today's "postmodern" spaces, not radically apart from, indeed a beacon for, an increasingly global swirl of cultural elements. Reminiscent of de Martino's discoveries, the elements are shown to derive not from past marginality or barbarism, but from Sicily's historic location at the crossroads of civilizations. The trope of fatalism, so easily assimilated to rurality, tradition, and pagan superstition – to a model of the island as a mystery, a land that missed the Enlightened sweep of progress – gives way to images of a highly cosmopolitan, if fragmentary, series of engagements taking place over hundreds of years. Meanwhile, Western technological and scientific culture is depicted as propagating exploitative, imperialist, and consumerist relations that efface not past "traditions" but past civilizational histories, even cementing over their splendid architectural bequests to future generations. Cutting across and breaking up the unilinear narrative of southern backwardness, this kind of writing constitutes a provocative challenge.

It is salutary, in deconstructing an Orientalist discourse like the Southern Question, to recognize the extent to which its mirror image – the Occidentalism against which it is dialectically depicted – claims a progressive trajectory, an imagined direction for history, in which humans strive to create free, democratic, economically developed and prosperous "civil societies." What if, as Hermann Rebel heuristically asks of eighteenth-century Austrian history, we imagine a different ending, such as the terrible episodes that unfolded in Europe during and between the two world wars (see Rebel 1991). In this respect, it is significant to discover that Putnam's text has only three very brief references to fascism – references couched dismissively as the "Fascist interlude" (1993: 19) or "parenthesis" (ibid.: 233, n. 91). Nor does he acknowledge any redeeming virtue in southerners' tendency to take the National Fascist Party less seriously than did their northern compatriots (above all in the North's "most civic regions, such as Emilia Romagna . . .": 1993: 97). As a coda to Michael Blim's concluding essay, in Part IV, this volume presents Mariella Pandolfi's reflections on the problem of failed nationhood in Italy – reflections that take account of the Fascist regime, including its commitment to avenge Abyssinia, and consolidate Italy's tenuous assertions over Libya, Eritrea, and Somalia.

Acknowledgments

In addition to my colleague Vincent Crapanzano, several authors in this volume read, and commented on, earlier drafts of the introductory essay. I benefited, in particular, from the suggestions of Annalisa Di Nola and Silvana Patriarca, from long conversations with Silvana and Nelson Moe about the issues surrounding "Orientalism" in Italy, and from Nelson's generous sharing of his own research and insights on this topic. I am also much in debt to Peter Schneider for a careful and critical reading and for suggesting the concept "neo-Orientalism".

References

Bakić-Hayden, Milica (1995) "Nesting Orientalisms: The Case of Former Yugoslavia," *Slavic Studies* **54**: 917–31.

Bakić-Hayden, Milica and Hayden, Robert M. (1992) "Orientalist Variations on the Theme 'Balkans': Symbolic Geography in Recent Yugoslav Cultural Politics," *Slavic Review* **51**: 1–15.

Banfield, Edward C. (1958) *The Moral Basis of a Backward Society.* Chicago: The Free Press.

Bohlen, Celestine (1996) "North–South Divide in Italy: A Problem for Europe, Too," *New York Times*, November 15.

Campbell, Donald T. and Levine, Robert A. (1968) *Ethnocentrism, Theories of Conflict, Ethnic Attitudes and Group Behavior.* New York: John Wiley.

Carrier, James G. (1992) "Occidentalism: The World Turned Upside-Down," *American Ethnologist* **19**: 195–213.

Chatterjee, Partha (1993) *The Nation and its Fragments: Colonial and Postcolonial Histories*. Princeton, NJ: Princeton University Press.
Clark, Martin (1984) *Modern Italy, 1871–1982*. London and New York: Longman.
Coronil, Fernando (1995) "Introduction to the Duke University Press Edition" of *Fernando Ortiz, Cuban Counterpoint: Tobacco and Sugar*, pp. ix–lvii. Durham and London: Duke University Press.
—— (1996) "Beyond Occidentalism: Toward Nonimperial Geohistorical Categories," *Cultural Anthropology* 11: 51–87.
Fernandez, James W. (1997) "The North–South Axis in European Popular Cosmologies and the Dynamic of the Categorical." *American Anthropologist* 99: 725–8.
Ginsborg, Paul (1990) *A History of Contemporary Italy: Society and Politics 1943–1988*. London: Penguin Books.
Gramsci, Antonio (1971) *Selections from the Prison Notebooks*, edited and translated by Quintin Hoare and Geoffrey Nowell Smith. New York: International Publishers. [Orig. 1929–1935.]
Gribaudi, Gabriella (1996) "Images of the South." In David Forgacs and Robert Lumley, eds, *Italian Cultural Studies: An Introduction*, pp. 72–88. Oxford and New York: Oxford University Press.
Herzfeld, Michael (1987) *Anthropology Through the Looking-Glass: Critical Ethnography in the Margins of Europe*. Cambridge and New York: Cambridge University Press.
—— (1997) *Cultural Intimacy: Social Poetics in the Nation-State*. New York and London: Routledge.
—— (n.d.) "Ethnographic and Epistemological Refractions of Mediterranean Identity." Unpublished paper.
Levy, Carl (1996) "Introduction: Italian Regionalism in Context." In Carl Levy, ed., *Italian Regionalism: History, Identity and Politics*, pp. 1–33. Oxford and Washington, DC: Berg.
Lyttleton, Adrian (1996) "Shifting Identities: Nation, Region and City." In Carl Levy, ed., *Italian Regionalism: History, Identity and Politics*, pp. 33–53. Oxford and Washington, DC: Berg.
Moe, Nelson (1992) "'Altro che Italia!'. Il Sud dei piemontesi (1860–61)," *Meridiana; Revista di storia e scienze sociali* 15: 53–89.
—— (1994) *Representing the South in Post-Unification Italy, c. 1860–1880*. Unpublished doctoral dissertation, The Johns Hopkins University. (Forthcoming as *Imagining the South: Italy Between Europe and Africa*.)
Noether, Emiliana (n.d.) "Race is Destiny: Latin Decadence in *Fin-de-Siècle* Italian Positivist Thought." Unpublished paper.
Pizzorno, Alessandro (1971) "Amoral Familism and Historical Marginality." In Mattei Dogan and Richard Rose, eds, *European Politics: A Reader*. Boston: Little Brown.

Putnam, Robert D. (1993) *Making Democracy Work; Civic Traditions in Modern Italy*. Princeton, NJ: Princeton University Press.

Rebel, Hermann (1991) "Reimagining the Oikos: Austrian Cameralism in its Social Formation." In William Roseberry and Jay O'Brien, eds, *Golden Ages, Dark Ages: Imagining the Past in Anthropology and History*. Berkeley and Los Angeles: University of California Press.

Said, Edward W. (1979) *Orientalism*. New York: Vintage Books [Orig. 1978.]

Schneider, Jane (1969) "Family Patrimonies and Economic Behavior in Sicily," *Anthropological Quarterly* **42**: 109–29.

Schneider, Jane and Schneider, Peter (1976) *Culture and Political Economy in Western Sicily*. New York: Academic Press.

—— (1996) *Festival of the Poor: Fertility Decline and the Ideology of Class in Sicily, 1860–1980*. Tucson: University of Arizona Press.

Siebert, Renate (1994) *Le Donne, La Mafia*. Milan: il Saggiatore.

Silverman, Sydel (1968) "Agricultural Organization, Social Structure, and Values in Italy: Amoral Familism Reconsidered," *American Anthropologist* **70**: 1–20.

Tarrow, Sidney (1996) "Making Social Science Work Across Space and Time: A Critical Reflection on Robert Putnam's *Making Democracy Work*," *American Political Science Review* **90**: 389–97.

Trigilia, Carlo (ed.) (1995) *Cultura e sviluppo. L'associazionismo nel Mezzogiorno*. Rome: Donzelli.

White, Caroline (1980) *Patrons and Partisans*. Cambridge and New York: Cambridge University Press.

Part I

The Genesis of the Question

1

Before the Southern Question: "Native" Ideas on Backwardness and Remedies in the Kingdom of Two Sicilies, 1815–1849

Marta Petrusewicz

Recently, a historian wrote that "the Southern Question was not born with the political unification of Italy; it had its roots in the history of the Mezzogiorno" (De Rosa 1993: v). But this is an unusual position. For most scholars today, the "Question," understood as a global representation of the Mezzogiorno's people and heritage, was born after 1860, in the wake of the Risorgimento. The arguments are mainly about what there was in the process of Unification that caused the "Question" to crystallize as a discourse. Some scholars, following the well-known thesis of Emilio Sereni (1974), claim that, by broadening the market, unification simply exposed what was already there – namely the structural "backwardness" of the southern economy. Others, in the Gramscian tradition, see Unification and its aftermath as having provided an opportunity for southern agrarian conservative interests to strike a mutually advantageous alliance with northern industrialists; this so-called "historical bloc" in turn caused the economic dualism that condemned the South to the role of a permanent periphery. Yet others, influenced by the dependency school, interpret unification as straightforward colonization. In one, economically-oriented, version of this scenario, northern colonizers forcibly destroyed the existing industries of the South in order to turn the Mezzogiorno into an outlet for northern commodities and a source of cheap and compliant labor. In a second, more political version, the emphasis is placed on the "conquest of the South," the conqueror overthrowing, *manu militari*, a legitimate southern dynasty and pillaging the territory that was defeated.

It is not only that scholars have generally located the origins of the "Southern Question" in the Risorgimento. Until recently, its dominant representation has been composed of economic, social and political elements measured against broad Enlightenment-inspired criteria of progress or development. The result was a series of narratives, at times romantic, at times merely condescending, of failure: the failure or betrayal of the intellectuals; the failure of the popular classes to understand the terms, forms, and directions of collective action; the failure of developmental institutions, from the late-eighteenth-century Cassa Sacra to the Cassa per il Mezzogiorno after the Second World War; the failure of self-government and autonomy. From the beginning of the 1980s, however, in the political climate generated in part by the Northern League movement of Umberto Bossi, the Southern Question has been rephrased as a cultural and emotional one. It has become the Question of the North as much as of the South – an issue that seems to produce more anxiety in the North than in the South.

Meanwhile, southern historians and social scientists – the "new meridionalists" – have begun to challenge this frozen image, questioning the very concept of the "South." Numerous studies have shown that there was not one South, nor even two, as in Manlio Rossi Doria's famous "l'osso e la polpa," but many. And, whereas earlier the issue of poverty loomed large among the southern problems that scholars felt compelled to address, today other concerns have taken over, namely uncertainties surrounding law, and the rights, duties, and obligations of citizens. At the same time, social and intellectual historians and literary critics have studied the very idea of the South as a social construction.[1]

In this chapter, I propose to contribute to the current debate in the following ways. First, I explore the cultural climate prevalent in the Neapolitan Kingdom of the Two Sicilies, also called the Kingdom of Naples or the Neapolitan Kingdom, before the "Southern Question" was articulated, and in particular the southern perception of this country's backwardness and possible remedies. Second, I re-examine the chronology of the Question, proposing the year 1848 as the critical moment in its emergence. Third, I suggest that Southerners themselves played a leading role in constructing the South as a Question. The discussion focuses on the ideas that were prevalent among intellectuals and in what we might call public opinion in the Kingdom, and on the social practices that helped to disseminate these ideas internally before 1848, and in exile afterwards. I concern myself here only with the discourses of the broadly defined southern intelligentsia, and shall not discuss their implementation. Nor shall I examine 'popular' representations of the country's condition.

The culture of the southern intelligentsia had its roots in the 1700s. Some aspects of the Neapolitan Kingdom's eighteenth-century history help to clarify this background. Unlike many other political entities of the Italian peninsula, the Kingdom of Naples was a sovereign state, having achieved independence from Spain in 1734. No longer a vice-royalty, it was governed stably by one dynasty, which rapidly became "neapolitanized." The passage from vice-kingdom to kingdom meant the possibility of pursuing an autonomous foreign policy, of exploring and expanding new commercial opportunities, and of dealing with the Papacy from a position of strength. On the domestic front independence meant a lessening of burdensome fiscal pressures and the possibility of breaking with the Spanish court tradition, in which corruption, violence, and intrigue were integral aspects of rule.

Although the new Kingdom remained within the Spanish sphere of influence, its independence gave considerable impetus to administrative and economic reforms.

Many attitudes and innovations of the new age had been anticipated by the Spanish and Neapolitan reformers of the seventeenth century, but had received scant attention in their day. Now, in the climate of a remarkable recovery and a widespread effort to improve the material conditions of the country, royal councilors and men of letters read their predecessors' works assiduously, had them republished, and experimented with putting their ideas into effect. The minister Bernardo Tanucci's attempts at reform, with all their limitations, were remarkably coherent, aimed at restricting feudal privilege, restructuring public finance and taxation, reorganizing the prison system, and reducing the wealth and power of the Church. He successfully carried out the formation of a modern cadastre, reorganized the *annona* system, negotiated a Concordat with the Papacy, and expelled the Jesuits. In European eyes, Naples, although still believed to be surrounded by a countryside of exotic *barbarie*, was one of the more important cultural capitals. The splendid San Carlo theater was built in this period, art and music flourished, and the first archaeological excavations at Herculaneum and the discovery of Paestum took place. And what was of particular significance was that intellectuals began meeting and conversing in salons.

The young king Ferdinand, who reigned from 1759 (through Tanucci) to 1825, was eager to build up the strength of his state and make a name for himself. Although personally not well educated, he saw himself as a member of that vigorous cohort of "enlightened despots" that included his own father, Charles III of Spain, Frederick II of Prussia, and Joseph II of Austria. Like those monarchs, Ferdinand was at once a political conservative and a committed modernizer. Unwilling to concede a constitution, he nevertheless sought to improve the economic and social conditions of the kingdom. He encouraged industry, commerce and innovation, and attempted a fiscal reform. The Cassa Sacra, created after the huge earthquake in Calabria in 1783 to expropriate and sell ecclesiastical lands, was an attempt at a quite radical land reform that involved the redistribution of the Church's wealth and the curtailing of baronial privileges. In the end, though, the Cassa Sacra was a deceptive façade, like the contemporary villages of Potiomkin, behind which the old regime remained intact. By 1789 the French Revolution and the attendant regicide had generated the "great fear" that afflicted monarchies everywhere, and Ferdinand's program of reforms was abandoned and even reversed. Enlightened despotism, as Benedetto Croce once said, threw off the cloak of the enlightenment and remained just despotic.

And yet, while his reforming spirit lasted, Ferdinand sought the opinions of scholars, courted their approval, and tolerated critical writings so long as they did not question the institution of dynastic monarchy. And the intelligentsia responded enthusiastically. For example, poets and scholars acclaimed the San Leucio royal manufacturing complex, an experimentation in "harmonious," almost utopian, industrialization; the poet Eleonora Fonseca Pimentel even wrote an "Ode" to it. Meanwhile, the University of Naples was revamped, creating the first chair of political economy in continental Europe, which went to the noted economist, Antonio Genovesi. It was a period of intellectual giants whose writings made the Neapolitan Enlightenment famous in Europe.

One of the main questions pondered by these "public intellectuals" was the backwardness of the Neapolitan Kingdom. Despite their different theoretical and political perspectives, there emerged a common catalog of evils that were argued to be hampering the country's progress. Its main points were widely publicized. First, the feudal institutions of primogeniture and entailment, and the ecclesiastical institution of *mainmorte*, were faulted for immobilizing huge tracts of land, preventing the formation of a land market. Second, the iniquity of the fiscal system burdened and stifled the entrepreneurial and laborious classes while favoring parasites. Third, baronial jurisdiction, never just, was made even more unfair and arbitrary by the indifference of its absentee administrators. Fourth, the ambiguity of the land tenure system, and in particular, the absence of clearly defined private property in land, made agricultural improvement impractical. Fifth, the poverty, ignorance and superstition of the peasants hampered social and economic "improvement".

Thus articulated, the catalog was not, however, a specifically *southern* question, but a question of "normal backwardness," common to most of Europe, its various elements applying, *mutatis mutandis*, to many other countries. Moreover, the Neapolitan intellectuals who drew up the list relied upon the same pool of references that enlightened reformers were turning to everywhere. Throughout eighteenth-century Europe, reformers attributed social and economic evils to one structural cause, feudalism, and argued that, if progress were to occur, feudalism would have to be abolished.

These eighteenth-century ideas, and the actions they inspired, constituted the collective cultural memory of the Neapolitan intelligentsia of the century to follow. But the younger generation was drastically separated from its enlightened *maitres à penser* by the experiences of the period 1799–1815: revolution, civil war, foreign rule, and more than one defeat. The year 1799 had been a revolutionary year in Naples, and numerous students of the great masters – for example Vincenzo Cuoco, who was to author a rich essay on the Neapolitan Revolution of 1799, an invaluable source for future scholars (Cuoco 1913 [1800]) – participated in both the revolutionary activity and the Parthenopean Republic that overthrew the monarchy. This group directly experienced the collapse of national institutions, the flight of the monarch, the misinterpretation of their Republic's goals, the terrible "God and King" popular crusade against the Republic, and the eventual massacre of the "Jacobins" at the hands of the Neapolitan *lazzari*. Victims of the mob's rage, they lived through or witnessed cruel and semi-legal trials, mass executions, prison, and exile. In 1806, after the French kings, Joseph and then Murat, had been installed in Naples by Napoleon's troops, the survivors returned, committed to supporting the alien monarch in *his* modernizing effort. There followed the "happy decade," at the end of which the Bourbon Kingdom of Naples was restored, forcing this intelligentsia into exile yet again. The result was a decimated generation, wounded and humiliated, its members burdened with a sense of responsibility for having been witnesses and accomplices to the surrender of Neapolitan sovereignty before the generals of foreign armies. The burden was heavy even when the invader represented Reason. Considering themselves "patriots," they had, after all, given in to French demands. According to one of the most interesting of them, Cuoco, they had thereby rendered their revolution "passive." Furthermore, they had to endure a restoration as passive as the revolution.

From those experiences came a new way of thinking, which flourished during the Restoration. The post-Napoleonic intelligentsia did not reject the *problematique* of the cohort of the revolution, but did challenge many of their founding ideas, methods, and political choices. Their main attack was directed at the universalism of the Enlightenment, the idea of the blind application of foreign recipes, contempt for native customs and institutions, and remoteness from popular sentiment.[2] Yet another generation, influenced by romanticism like its contemporaries in other parts of Europe, searched for local traditions, spirits of the local territory. Rediscovering their own national past, they found inspiration in their Neapolitan forebear, Gianbatista Vico, who had held the chair of rhetoric at the University of Naples in the early 1700s. Vico's *Scienza Nuova* was prescient in arguing for an approach to historical studies that took different societies on their own terms, rather than in terms of universalizing categories like "human nature." The new "romantic generation," if we can refer to them thus, initiated programs of local action, making use of new regional forms of sociability and communication such as associations and journals. Their emphasis on "localism" made them influential in the provinces. All told, the new way of feeling, thinking, and relating helped, as it spread, to form a middle-class "opinion," increasingly focused on organizing and inhabiting what might be called a "civic" space.

The period 1799–1815 changed not only the *Weltanschauung* of the intelligentsia but also of the country. "Murat fell in 1815; but the laws, usages, opinions, and hopes which had been impressed on the *popolo* for ten years, did not fall with him" – thus wrote Pietro Colletta (1967 [1834] book VIII: 701), himself a protagonist of the "decade." Most importantly, feudalism had been abolished. Although the Bourbons returned to the throne in 1815, they did not, and could not, restore feudal institutions. On the contrary, bound by treaties and advised by common sense, Ferdinand maintained as much of the administrative and institutional structure, and as many of the appointments, of the "decade" as possible.

The fact that he made no attempt to reinstate feudalism, which had for so long been considered the primary obstacle to any successful reform, conferred upon the Restoration regime a character of its own, different from that of the *Ancien Régime*. This second restoration was also less radical and less vengeful than the first, the absolutism of the years 1815–1848 being considered generally mild. For example, freedom of the press and of expression was broad, even if punctuated by periods of aggressive censorship. Moreover, although secret societies were banned by law, this stricture on free association was more effective against the reactionary *Calderari* than against the better-organized progressive or radical *Carbonari*. Similarly, Ferdinand signed a new Concordat with Rome; but its most restrictive stipulations (such as the power to censor or suppress any books or journals deemed heretical) were not enforced. The King was a reactionary, but not a fanatic. More like Louis XVIII than Charles X, he favored at least some form of modernization.

The main bone of contention between the throne and the intelligentsia was the question of the constitution and of representative government. Between 1815 and 1848 there unfolded a succession of promises and negotiations, another revolution, concessions, abrogations, repression and forgiveness. In 1815 the intelligentsia, as ignorant as everyone else about the terms of a secret treaty with Austria, were persuaded that it would be easy to obtain a constitution from Ferdinand: after all, he had conceded one in Sicily; his hostile wife, Maria Carolina, was dead; his prime minister, Luigi de' Medici, was a modernizer; and the king had already made a conciliatory gesture by sacking the rabidly reactionary minister of the police, the Prince of Canosa. Through renewed revolution, a constitution was in fact granted in 1820, along with a parliament and a reformist government. The intellectuals who thereby trusted the king were bitterly disappointed when, only a year later, he called for an Austrian invasion, abrogating the new constitution and giving the reinstated Canosa a free hand in the persecution of the *Carbonari*.

This counter-revolution provoked a collective depression made worse by economic and fiscal difficulties. The gloomy mood did not last long, however, as hope returned in 1825 when Ferdinand died. His successor, Francis I, was weak and allowed the corrupt court *camarilla* to rule the country. Nevertheless, he dismissed Canosa, brought back de' Medici and, above all, had the sense to die quickly. Young Ferdinand II's accession to the throne in 1830 was greeted with enthusiasm. He had a clear idea of his program: no representative government, but a serious effort to modernize the state and society. As he himself put it in a letter to his uncle Louis Philippe: "With the help of God, I will give my people prosperity and the honest administration which is their right, but I will be king, alone, and always" (quoted in Di Ciommo 1993: 21). Although never considered friendly to intellectuals, Ferdinand captured their hope. Significantly, he also brought the exiles back and, granting them amnesty, he carried out a true administrative transformation. By initiating railroad construction, moreover, he encouraged the development of industry and banking.

The cultural and intellectual climate was extremely lively. Naples swarmed with students coming from all parts of the country. Luigi Settembrini, who came to the city in 1828, remembered his fellow students in these words: "the young, except for a very few, are all good, with open hearts; prone to every beautiful and generous action, they have an instinct for good, and I found them all liberals" (1934 [1893]: 265). The prestige of the University was declining, but a multitude of new public and private schools, institutes and academies that had mushroomed during Murat's time continued to thrive. In a postscript to Francesco De Sanctis' *La giovinezza* — another valuable firsthand account of this history — Pasquale Villari remembered that "thousands of young people came to Naples, pursuing their professional studies in the many private schools that had emerged because the University existed in little else than name and none to speak of went there" (Villari 1961 [1888]: 336). According to historian Alfredo Zazo, some 800 private teaching institutions existed in the kingdom, in Naples and in the secondary centers of Foggia, Teramo, Lecce, Altamura, Salerno, Cosenza, and Tropea (1927: 202ff.).

Many of the private schools were run by the most illustrious members of the Neapolitan intelligentsia, such as De Sanctis, the great economist Antonio Scialoia, historian Francesco Trinchera, jurists Pasquale Stanislao Mancini and Silvio Spaventa, and Aurelio Saliceti. Years later, in *La giovinezza*, De Sanctis painted an extraordinary portrait of private education in Naples in that period: it was free, liberal, and original (De Sanctis 1961 [1888]). His own school was self-governed in the spirit of a Proudhon-like anarchy, a "small self-contained society, without rules, without discipline, without any authority of command, moved by sentiments of duty, value, and reciprocal respect" (ibid.: 293). The various institutes actively sought out talented youth from the provinces, attracting them with fellowships, free admissions, and competitive "incentive awards." Although upper-class provincial youth had always gone to Naples to study, now, in Pasquale Villari's words, "students were arriving by the thousands," above all the offspring of provincial gentry, lawyers, and even occasionally artisans. Giuseppe Massari, son of a civil engineer from Taranto and a future Risorgimento leader, and Antonio Scialoia, son of an inspector of public security and later an important economist and a member of the 1848 government, were able to study in Naples thanks to such scholarships. One of the most influential of the new institutions, the school founded and administered by the Marquis Basilio Puoti, was free and open to all young men of talent, regardless of their social class or economic circumstances. De Sanctis, who had been Puoti's pupil, remembered that some of the most "cultivated and esteemed men of the city" were associated with the school (Villari 1919 [1888]: 310–11).

In addition to the traditional disciplines of law, medicine, the military arts, and philosophy, there were new popular pursuits such as Italian, political economy, history, engineering, and architecture. The students seemed imbued with the romantic spirit without necessarily knowing what romanticism was. Engrossed in stories, novellas and novels, fantastic and sentimental, they were attentive to all manner of "rumor" from Lombardy. With or without the encouragement of their teachers, they devoured French literature: Mme de Stael, *La Nouvelle Heloise* by Rousseau, Chateaubriand's *Martyrs*, all the novels of D'Alincourt, Victor Hugo, and Alphonse de Lamartine, *Matilde* by Cottin. In addition to the *Divina Commedia*, they read Manzoni and Hegel, and the tragedies of Vittorio Alfieri and William Shakespeare.

The world of the fine arts was also vibrant. Naples was alive with artists, art students, and visitors and distinguished foreigners such as the Russian Silvester F. Scedrin and Francis Hayez. The domination of the classicist Academy of Fine Arts was successfully challenged by the fresher School of Posillipo of Pitloo, Gigante, and their pupils, and by such "revolutionary" romantics as Giuseppe Mancinelli. The Court actively patronized artists through exhibitions and royal commissions: in 1825, Francis I instituted an annual exhibition modeled on the French *salons*. Private patronage followed the royal example, with purchases, commissions, and fellowships for art students (Picone Petrusa 1993).

The salons of wealthy intellectual patrons were important in the liberal circles of Naples, particularly during times when intensified censorship threatened literary and even theatrical life. The salons of the patrician houses were known as *case* (sing. *casa*): the *casa* Guacci-Nobile, *casa* Poerio, *casa* De Thomasis, *casa* Ferrigni-Pisone, *casa* Troya, *casa* Ricciardi. Many of the *case* counted scholars and authors among their family members, for example, the De Thomasis, Poerio, and Ricciardi. The already mentioned *casa* Puoti combined the salon's function with that of a true free school for the teaching of Italian, and attracted a whole world of teachers and literati. Puoti's school was undoubtedly archaic in its dedication to the cult of the Trecento and its rejection of modern literary trends, but its members were serious philologists who produced lexical and grammatical studies, classics, commentaries, and translations. As De Sanctis wrote, they liberated culture from having been "mortgaged to the seminary" (1961 [1888]: 290).

These were years of the strong politicization of the cultural world; but politics was often mediated by culture. The *case* were generically liberal but inoffensive; they did not threaten the monarchy in a serious way. The artists, also liberal, felt obliged to the regime for its favors. The students, generally more radical, "conspired" and held secret meetings, but their discussions were indirect, focusing on the writings of Colletta, Berchet, Gioberti, and Niccolini, and on the debates then going on in the parliaments of London and Paris. Having already encountered the network of progressive secret societies, the *Carboneria*, in the provinces where they originated, these students naturally associated with the *Carbonari* in Naples. Yet their conspiracies consisted mainly in some plotting, in recitations of inflamed poems, and in hanging out in the cafés. This said, it is important to realize that political passion was building. On 15 May 1848, it became manifest when the schools took to the streets; when, as Villari wrote, soldiers' bullets scattered De Sanctis' students "through the streets, houses, and barricades" (1961 [1888]: 347).

"Life in the provinces," wrote Raffaele De Cesare, "was of a marvelous monotony" (1969 [1873]). Still, in these years it seemed much less boring and monotonous. The activities of the *Carboneria*, which had begun to intensify during Murat's reign, continued during the Restoration and made the climate of the provincial towns lively and exciting. General Guglielmo Pepe recounts in his *Memorie* how in 1820, working through the networks of the *Carboneria*, he put together a rebel army in just a few weeks (Pepe 1846). The *Carbonari* – radical, anti-clerical, anti-Bourbon – were the heroes of the provincial youth. Luigi Settembrini, an affiliate of the Puoti school, remembers being offered a tricolor cockade in 1820 on his way to church – "I was a *Carbonaro* at the age of seven." The four brothers Palizzi, later to be eminent painters and participants in the 1848 revolution, grew up in the small town of Vasto in the Abruzzi. Vasto's local hero and its model of all virtues was a *Carbonaro*, Gabriele Rossetti – poet, patriot, and exile, whose sacred poem "Iddio e l'uomo" was on the Pope's *Index* of forbidden books. He was also the future father of the writer Christine and the painter Dante Gabriel. The poet's elder brother, Antonio, was Vasto's barber and himself a poet, too, who authored popular couplets mocking the government's fiscal policies.

In the provinces, the romantic mood was overwhelming. Young people read Mme de Stael, Walter Scott, and Alessandro Manzoni. They also wrote and published their own work. The review *Il Calabrese*, the aggressive voice of Calabrian romanticism, included the contributions of the best young writers, poets, and journalists, whose poems, ballads, tragedies, and novellas were intensely romantic. So was the review's engagement with history, folklore, popular traditions, "rumanze," "impressioni," archeology, new philosophy and psychology. An anecdote can illustrate the diffusion of these romantic references. During a trial in Catanzaro, the prosecutor accused the defendant of being "more daring than the *Innominato di Manzoni*." The year was 1835!

There were other vehicles of cultural discourse in the provinces, including literary and artistic cafés and private circles. An important role was also played by boarding schools and *collegi*, which were part of the university system, such as the Collegio Italo Greco in San Demetrio Corone, and by many private schools of law in the towns and cities. Then, there was the theater. The Teatro Real Ferdinandeo of Cosenza, for example, staged as many as ten operas per season: in 1845 it performed operas by Donizetti, Pacini, Paisiello, and Verdi. There were other opera theaters in the Calabrias: the Real Teatro Borbonico in Reggio Calabria, the Real Francesco in Catanzaro, the 'Comunale' in Castrovillari. The drama season, although it was shorter, included plays by Alfieri, Marenco, Goldoni, and Dumas.

In the early nineteenth century, wealthy young people traveled in Italy and in Europe. In 1827 Giuseppe Ricciardi, aged twenty, went with his family on a year-long *bildung* tour, during which he met everybody who was somebody in the world of intellect and art: for example, Manzoni, the group surrounding the Florentine journal, *Antologia*, and even Lamartine, then secretary of the French mission in Turin. Through the journal he also encountered the Neapolitan exiles Gabriele Pepe, Giuseppe Poerio, Matteo Imbriani, and Pietro Colletta (Ricciardi 1860).

Provincial youths also involved themselves in many conspiracies (in 1834, *Giovine Italia* was founded in many towns simultaneously). This often led to arrests, trials, and prison sentences, and also to occasional executions. The infamous Vallone di Rovito near Cosenza was the site of executions by beheading or firing-squad of the young followers of De Matteis in 1821, of De Liguoro in 1837, of the Cosenza democrats in 1843, and of the Bandiera brothers in 1844. Experiences of prison, exile, flight, and even death added further romantic zest to the conspiracies.

Repression, however, was neither a continuous nor a universal occurrence. In "normal" times there was plenty of room to express ideas and opinions. One of the avenues was the press. The local press flourished, and non-Neapolitan journals and reviews were widely circulated. Many apparently specialized journals, such as the *Giornale Agrario* or the *Annali Universali di Statistica*, enjoyed a broad readership because of their treatment of themes of general interest. Neapolitan literary reviews appeared, as did legal journals, for example Pasquale Stanislao Mancini's *Biblioteca*, which promoted the new juridical culture. All the associations and professional organizations of the Kingdom, as well as the political and literary movements, published some kind of a periodical literature. The influential journal, *Il Progresso delle scienze, delle lettere, delle arti* was founded in 1832 and edited for some time by Giuseppe Ricciardi, playing the role in Naples that *Antologia* played in Florence. When the latter was closed, in fact, *Il Progresso* was the most serious candidate to take its place.

Although Ricciardi was a radical, the journal was liberal and pluralistic, encouraging a diversity of approaches. It incorporated four political generations: the "generation of '99," then in their sixties; that of the "decade;" that of "the constitutional period;" and, lastly, the romantic one, some of them under twenty years of age. Political views encompassed the positions of the radical and republican Ricciardi, the conservative and municipalist Luigi Blanch, and the Catholic and moderate Luigi Dragonetti. Serious scholars and academics, past and future political figures – all collaborated with *Progresso*. There were also several left-wing journals: *Le Charivari des deux Siciles*, a moderate republican paper close to the French *Le National*; the radical and democratic *Caffè di Buono*, named after the meeting-place of the out-of-town students; *Mondo vecchio Mondo nuovo*, an example of the newly emerging critique of capitalism; and *Inferno*, which advocated a Constituent Assembly and universal male suffrage.

This spectrum of interests and political inclinations was replicated in the provincial press. The romantic vanguard's *Calabrese*, founded in Cosenza in 1842 by Saverio Vittari and Francesco Scaglione, would breed future Risorgimento protagonists. *Il Gran Sasso d'Italia*, published in Teramo and Aquila, was founded and directed by Ignazio Rozzi, a professor and well-published agronomist, and was dedicated mostly to social and economic problems. The *Annali della Calabria Citeriore* of Cosenza pursued similar concerns; its founder and director was Luigi Maria Greco, a well-known historian, classicist, and conservative social critic. *Statistica letteraria del Regno delle Due Sicilie*, edited by Carlo De Ribas, was more eclectic, as was the *Giornale di Statistica*, founded in 1835 in Palermo by two young and brilliant liberal economists, Francesco Ferrara and Emerico Amari. Finally, there was a plethora of local journals: *Fata Morgana, Il Lucifero, Il Pitagora, Il Rustico*, and so on (Zazo 1920).

Although these journals can be viewed as belonging to the vast arena of enlightened opinion, there were differences among them. Some were outright in their militancy, for example, Girolamo de Rada's *La bandiera albanese*, which in 1848 was renamed *L'Albanese d'Italia*, its name announcing its program. De Rada was a poet, student, and apostle of the cause of Albanian popular culture, as well as the instigator of an 1837 revolutionary uprising in Calabria. Even institutional or government-sponsored publications were used in creative, if not downright subversive, ways. This was the case of the governmental organ *Giornale del Regno delle Due Sicilie*, especially of its "Appendice." But the most influential of the institutional publications was the government-funded *Annali civili del Regno delle Due Sicilie*, founded in 1833 by a group of young journalists close to the established reformist circles. The *Annali* counted among its collaborators some of the best and most influential writers, civil servants, and administrators of the period, including Afan de Rivera and Ceva Grimaldi, and it coordinated the efforts of various economic and cultural associations. Locally, it was supplemented by the journals of the Economic Societies that proliferated in the 1830s and 1840s.

Another, rather unexpected, vehicle of progressive opinion was the clergy. Although the Church had certainly not become a champion of modernity, nevertheless liberalism had won some followers among the provincial clergy. Many priests were members of Economic Societies (described below) and other similar associations; many were teachers in the agrarian academies and schools. There were, as well, projects to establish chairs of agriculture and schools of practical agronomy in the seminaries. Many parish priests actively encouraged innovation: an arch-priest in Abruzzi, Tommaso Vicentini, ordered his penitent parishioners to plant trees in numbers corresponding to their sins.

Associationism played a crucial role in the forging of progressive opinion. Economic Societies, which began as government instruments but developed into autonomous loci of reformist activity, are especially interesting in this regard (see de Lorenzo 1987, 1991; Petrusewicz 1991). Instituted by Murat in 1810, re-established by Ferdinand I in 1817, the societies flourished in the 1830s and 1840s. With fourteen of them in Southern Italy and a couple in Sicily, they constituted the largest network of their kind in the Italian peninsula. Gathering and dis-seminating information and statistics, they stimulated innovation. Most importantly, they set up schools, academic chairs, and scholarships, promoting both vocational and general education. And they touched a significant number of people. Not only did each Society recruit approximately two hundred members (ordinary, honorary, and corresponding); their plenary meetings were attended by the entire local élite, delegates from other associations, and visiting scholars and celebrities. In a variety of *comizi*, or small town meetings, the Societies brought together professionals, entrepreneurial farmers, and artisans with landowners, judges, civil servants, and university professors. Associationism thus facilitated a certain mixing of classes, which was unthinkable in a salon, providing yet another vehicle for the dis-semination of reformers' ideas. Doing so, they helped to crystallize already existing opinion, the *dejà là*, in Arlette Farge's terms (1992). Not surprisingly, the network, the *trafila*, would be mobilized during the revolution of 1848–9.

In other words, during the period 1815 to 1848, several *foci* of opinion emerged. Academies and learned societies, for the most part composed of landowners, high public functionaries, church officials, and established professionals, expressed views that were more or less conservative. The Economic Societies gathered in medium-size landowners, doctors, veterinarians, pharmacists, natural scientists, engineers, and agronomists, whose orientation was scientific and pragmatic. Romantic groups attracted aristocratic and petty-notable youth, sons of small landowners, and even artisans (Lovett 1982). These various circles of opinion were not oblivious of one another. On the contrary, they overlapped, influenced, and informed each other's discourses. Economic and political debates found their way into all the journals, including the local ones — so much so that, for example, literary reviews published long articles on political economy, statistics, and prison systems. Similarly, economic journals published articles on literature, the spirit of the times, and the psychology of the senses. Journals of all kinds commented on debates having to do with language and dialect, and reviewed grammars and dictionaries like the new *Vocabolario della Crusca* or Puoti's *La Grammatica Italiana*.

The various *foci* of progressive opinion rarely dealt directly or explicitly with political issues until 1848; then it became clear that they had only been awaiting the opportunity to do so. Implicitly, though, their main interest had always been the overall condition of the country and its status *vis-à-vis* other kingdoms of the time. From their intermingling of opinions and interests, milieux and activities, there emerged a representation of the Mezzogiorno that was *modern* in various aspects. Progressive opinion considered the Kingdom of Naples to be part of the world-economy. Adopting the imperative of progress and the Europe-centered criteria of its measurement, it considered the conditions of *development* and *backwardness* not as a dichotomous opposition, but as different relative positions on a material and temporal *continuum*. In this representation, at once pessimistic and optimistic, the Two Sicilies was a backward country, but one in which progress was possible.

The country's backwardness was, however, much noted, the more so as progress was considered in relation to the wider context of agricultural and industrial development, above all in France and England. Even the United States held out some kind of standard. Carmine Antonio Lippi quoted for his readers a remark by the American president, Monroe, to the effect that "a nation . . . that is not able autonomously to satisfy its needs does not deserve the name of nation . . ." (1820: 84–5). Considered in relation to this world stage, the agrarian system of the Neapolitan Kingdom seemed to hold the whole economy back, although agriculture was argued to be the country's natural vocation. Wedded to antiquated crops, methods, and technologies, and resistant to innovation, the system was viewed as increasingly wasteful, inefficient, and even irrational. Critics lamented above all the persistence of ill-defined and confused property relations.

The conditions of manufacturing and industry hardly fared better. Enterprises born during the *decennio* had survived, but barely, and new industries were encountering many obstacles. The Kingdom shipped out raw wool, cotton, silk, hemp, flax, olive oil, and soda, not only because its customs policies favored the export of "primary products," but also because it lacked processing industries. Meanwhile, the state of the transportation infrastructure was, in the words of a civil servant, "the really great misfortune of the Kingdom;" Afan de Rivera lamented the Kingdom's delay in canal building, while Giuseppe Zurlo regretted the deterioration of old Roman and French roads and public works. There was a correspondingly sparse presence of banks and credit institutions, which discouraged investment and enterprise. Neapolitan banks were virtually absent outside Naples, and the Banco delle Due Sicilie, although praised for its innovative policies, was devoted mostly to financing public works and the government's annual purchase of a safety supply of grain (the *annona*). Last but not least, there was the "social question," which in the South was synonymous with the general condition of the peasantry: poverty, poor health, insecurity of land tenure and contracts, and widespread illiteracy.

In some respects this list resembles the older catalog of evils, but there is a fundamental difference – the absence of feudalism, formerly always topping the column as the arch-enemy of progress and the main structural cause of "la miseria pubblica." For feudalism had been abolished by a bill in 1806. The main prerequisite for advancement having been fulfilled, interpretations of the new backwardness focused instead on a range of conditions: retardation in the process of industrialization, the inadequacy of public education, flawed legislation, and the unequal distribution of public and private funds. Also discussed were the cost of wars and of the upkeep of foreign troops, erroneous government policies, corruption at the Court or the influence of the *camarilla*, and a pattern of dishonest and inefficient law enforcement. These conditions, however, did not denote "la miseria."[3] The new backwardness was grave, but contingent.

At the same time, possible remedies were the subject of lively and interesting debates. All agreed on the importance of education and good government. In fact, the reform of education engaged the energies of the best intellects of the kingdom, such as Cuoco and De Sanctis, just as the "administrative revolution" of the 1830s involved the best legal scholars of the time – for example, Giuseppe De Thomasis, leader of the new *amministrativisti*, who advocated local autonomy and communal self-administration. Other questions remained debatable: What role should the government play in furthering progress? What was the utility and impact of public works? Should land be further privatized and to what degree? How rapidly and extensively should the Kingdom commit itself to industrialization? What were the comparative advantages of centralized control versus municipal autonomy? Was total freedom of trade appropriate or even possible for a "late-comer" to industrial development? These debates reveal an intellectual maturity and creative tension that confirm the idea of a hybrid representation of the South.

Hybridity appeared in the art of the period, too. On the one hand, the Kingdom of the Two Sicilies was represented as rural and traditional, with barefoot peasants in front of their huts. On the other, it was pictured as industrial and modern. Silvano Fergola's railroads, stations, and suspended iron bridges, and Giuseppe De Nittis' and Luigi Fergola's industrial landscapes with factory chimneys, are reminiscent of the subject-matter that prevailed under the July Monarchy in France. Both Louis Philippe and Ferdinand were perceived as modernizers and patrons of the arts. Mario Borgoni's large fresco "Partenope che ricompensa le arti e le industrie napoletane," today in the Naples Camera di Commercio, is a homage to the modernizing King.

In other words, the Kingdom's overall image was not entirely bleak. The opinion that the country was endowed with enough natural resources and people to permit an economic take-off was based not only on a mythology of southern wealth, but on such well-informed pragmatists as Afan de Rivera. It seemed further confirmed by the steady growth of the population. And government policies, however cautious, were moving in the right direction, enabling the country to participate in the *Zeitgeist* of progress, so compelling at the time. In the words of the editors of *Il Progresso*, it was "an epoch during which it pleased the Supreme Being to allow that all of the passions which he had placed in the depths of human hearts should ferment again; to desire that a vast and total regeneration occur in the activities of the spirit, in the ardor of the sentiments, in the customs and ways of life . . ." (1833: II(4): 208). Naples' backwardness was not a permanent condition, but merely a lagging status *vis-à-vis* more advanced countries. Anticipating the diagnosis of twentieth-century economic historian, Alexandr Gerschenkron (1962), backwardness was held to be a question of relative position on a scale of comparative progress. England and France were far ahead, presenting those behind them with a picture of their future (not free of flaws); Lombardy, Tuscany, and Prussia were ahead, although less distantly so; and Ireland was more or less at the same point as the Kingdom; while Russia and Poland had the farthest to go. For Naples to catch up would require energy and effort; but the government was in general doing the right thing – building railroads, constructing roads to connect the two seas, encouraging manufactures, modernizing prisons, and loosening some tariff regulations.

Thus conceived, southern "retardation" did not constitute a "Question." Intellectuals were severe in criticizing their country, but they had no inferiority complex. They even saw some advantages to relative backwardness. Industrializing later, perhaps their country could avoid some of the vexing social conflicts that were haunting England and France. We can ask: had the lively intellectual and reformist climate of the period leading up to 1848 continued until the Unification of Italy, would the "Question" have been construed in the same terms? In the following pages I will speculate on the impact that the defeat of 1848, and the changed context of the period 1849–1860, had on the southern intellectuals. We will see the respects in which the "Southern Question" may have had, after all, its roots in the South. It was, I will suggest, a representation constructed in exile, both external and "internal," and by intellectuals who were once again defeated and discouraged.

Although the Sicilian and Neapolitan revolutions of January 1848 were the first to erupt, they were part of a more general European trend, which the King of Naples was no more able to resist than was his uncle in France (Sperber 1994). In other words, the Neapolitan revolution had more in common with urban revolutions of the same year in Paris, Vienna, and Berlin than with the previous southern ones of 1799 and 1820. Benedetto Croce remarked that the revolution of 1820 was dominated by old men, veterans of 1799, the soldiers and administrators of the "decade," and it was pervaded with eighteenth-century rationalism. That of 1848, by contrast, was a revolution of youth formed in the age of romanticism. The barricades of the streets of Naples were manned by the pupils of De Sanctis, Puoti, and Scialoia, who were filled with the ideas they had learned from Hegel, Chateaubriand, de Stael, Lamartine, and Hugo. It was a revolution of intellectuals, according to the well-known interpretation of Lewis Namier (1946); but not only of intellectuals. "[E]very honest heart was there with good faith, seated at the joyful banquet of January 29, 1848," wrote the novelist Francesco Mastriani (1994 [1863]: 164) — intellectuals and students, artisans and peasants, and returning exiles. The air of Naples was excited and festive; with the theaters closed, unemployed singers sang popular and revolutionary songs in the middle of the streets (Miller 1984). "I will always recall that Spring of 1848," wrote Giuseppe Sodano, a former monk, writer, and historian and in that year the president of the Circolo del Progresso, "Those unforgettable days when we were free . . . whoever did not see those days, never saw anything truly great and sublime" (quoted in Zenobi 1959: 92). Many, like Sodano, looked back with nostalgia and emotion. De Sanctis tenderly evoked the mood in a letter to Giuseppe Montanelli: "it was for us all poetry, the inspiration of our revolution" (1956 [1855]: 213).

The revolution quickly fulfilled the dreams of the Neapolitan reformers. With its new constitution and parliaments, they thought that the Kingdom had finally joined the community of civilized nations. The government of 3 April was composed, in the words of De Sanctis (1961 [1888]: 231), of "the most respected men of the land." Historian Carlo Troya was its president and jurist Raffaele Conforti its Minister of Internal Affairs. The Ministers of Foreign Affairs and Public Education were Luigi Dragonetti and Paolo Emilio Imbriani, respectively. Antonio Scialoia became Minister of Agriculture, Industry, and Commerce. Troya was editor of the conservative *Il Tempo*, but Dragonetti and Conforti were democrats, and Imbriani and Scialoia confirmed liberals. These men had had years of experience in public life, and were less naive and better prepared than their predecessors of 1799 and 1820. Theirs was a moderate government, sincerely opposed to absolutism and determined to carry out reforms. It granted amnesty for all political offences, abolished the Ministry of Police, took popular education away from the Bishops, and decreed the establishment of schools in even the smallest villages.

The prevailing mood was conciliatory. The orientation of both the government and the public was moderate, neither republican nor rabidly anti-Bourbon. Aside from a few committed republicans, such as Ricciardi, or the future devotee of Cavour, Giuseppe La Farina, the leaders felt that constitutional monarchy was the best guarantee of the stability necessary for progress. They believed that the Bourbons and Ferdinand could continue to be trusted with the task of governing. On the popular level, peasant movements were less frightening than they had been in 1799, both because in the intervening years some ties had been established between the *popolo* and the liberals, and because the peasants had become less loyalist, ceasing to view the Bourbons as their protectors against landlord greed. The landlords, for their part, having spent many years discussing the peasant question, had come to accept the necessity of some kind of land reform. In an interesting recent study, Enrica Di Ciommo, challenging the interpretation of Federico Chabod and Rosario Romeo, shows that there existed in the South both a peasant structure susceptible to revolutionary mobilization *and* a growing willingness, at least on the part of democrats, to confront the agrarian question (Di Ciommo 1993: 298–9).

There were, of course, many tensions in those spring months: the *de facto* secession of Sicily, the armed "extremist" mobilization in Calabria. But the election of 18 April confirmed the commitment to the revolution of both the *Libertà e Progresso* liberals and the *Giustizia e Progresso* radicals. The events of 15 May – it is still debatable whether they should be seen as a provocation, an insurrection, or a *coup d'état* – divided opinion, but not as sharply as the June Days in Paris. In Paris, as both Marx and Tocqueville agree, the great divide was class, and the workers had against them the National Guard, the bourgeoisie, the students, and the *provinceaux* who rushed to the capital. In Naples, on 15 May, the revolution was defended in the streets and on the barricades by the National Guard, and bourgeois protagonists fought alongside students, artisans, and peasants. Even the provinces rose in defense, with the Calabrians coming to Naples, conspicuous in their costumes, in a reverse evocation of 1799. Many democratic members of the parliament favored armed insurrection; others signed the *Atto di destituzione della monarchia* (the Act of Monarchical Destitution). It may be more appropriate to compare 15 May to the 2 December *coup* in France: like Louis Napoleon, Ferdinand dissolved the parliament, called for new elections with limited suffrage, and expelled the radicals and democrats from their positions, arresting many and forcing others underground.

As in the South of France, a part of the rural population thereafter continued to defend the revolution. In Calabria the resistance lasted into the autumn; here the fighters were joined by a faction of the defeated parliament, led by Ricciardi and the Calabrian left. Once again, on 13 November, notwithstanding the restricted suffrage, an election returned many radicals and revolutionaries, confirming the widespread desire to resist. The break between the "country" and the "Bourbons," between "us" and "them," was complete.

There followed the "*spergiuro*." In March 1849, Ferdinand abolished the parliament and abrogated the constitution. Repression followed: mass arrests, intimidations, assassinations, endless trials, heavy prison sentences, and years of purges. Although less bloody than in 1799 – death sentences were rarely followed by executions – the post-'48 repression lasted longer and was more pervasive. While show-trials were going on in Naples – against, for example, members of *Unità italiana*, Carlo Poerio, the "44," who included Scialoia and Spaventa, and the "40 defaulters" – thousands were arrested and tried throughout the country for having engaged in "bad conduct." Arrests and convictions cut across class barriers: noblemen, intellectuals, petty bourgeois, and artisans met each other in jail.

As Giuseppe La Farina put it in a letter to Cavour (quoted in Moe 1992: 79), Ferdinand II proceeded to erect a sort of a "Chinese Wall" around his kingdom, as if he wanted to erase even the memory of the liberal efforts. The movement of people, ideas, and goods came under strict control. The Ministry of the Police was resurrected, instituting a repressive police state. Both civil and ecclesiastical authorities introduced strict censorship policies. "Loyal subjects" were encouraged to inform on their colleagues and friends, and spies infested the provinces in search of revolutionary groups. Conditions in prisons were terrible, as the whole of Europe was to learn from William Gladstone's *Two Letters to the Earl of Aberdeen*, published in 1851 after he visited Carlo Poerio and Michele Pironti in jail. Prohibitive customs duties were imposed on imported books, and protective tariff barriers were raised. The latter went far beyond any real or supposed needs of the economy, reflecting primarily the political choice of autarky and seclusion.

The result of such policies was a forcibly prolonged period of isolation and depression. Even the most cautious attempts at reform were halted, with Ferdinand interpreting his ministers' recommendations in that line as a criticism of his rule. Public works projects were all but abandoned, and education reverted to the Church, which also recaptured primary responsibility for social services. In 1854 nearly half of all state expenditure was devoted to the army. Entrepreneurial energies were suffocated and trade diminished, both because of the stiffened tariffs and because foreign investors shunned this police state, whose reputation was now at its lowest, especially after Gladstone's *Letters*. The only groups to benefit were the police, the army, and the higher echelons of the Church. To some extent, however, the condition of the peasantry improved, because Ferdinand, in a design similar to that of his Viennese relative Franz Josef, partially addressed the question of land, and eased the fiscal pressures on the rural population by abolishing the hated mill-tax.

Among the losers, the intelligentsia held the place of honor. They were the main victims of repression: imprisoned, silenced, or forced into exile. For the third time in half a century, the Italian South lost a significant portion of its intelligentsia, and this time for more than a decade. Many of those who stayed went into, to use an anachronism, "internal exile." They removed themselves from public life, both because they were banned from many jobs, and to avoid the humiliation and intellectual prostitution that staying in circulation required. Attorneys, university professors, civil servants, even the director of the Pompeii excavations, lost their positions. Officers of various associations were required to take an oath that they did not and would not belong to any secret society. Endless background checks were run on the political, religious, and moral conduct of candidates for government employment, with the predictable result of a shortage of qualified personnel. Even conservatives, such as Luigi Maria Greco, preferred a retreat in the Accademia Cosentina to carrying out a "police job." Most of the journals that had flourished in the previous decades – *Il Calabrese rigenerato, Il Progresso, Charivari, Mondo vecchio Mondo nuovo* – folded or were shut by the censor. The meetings of the Learned Societies became abstract and tedious. There were a few among the prominent intellectuals who collaborated, such as Giustino Fortunato, the Prince of Ischitella, and Lodovico Bianchini, who became the Minister of Police. There were also a few servile or "loyal" scholars who, denouncing the "errors and fallacies of Mr. Gladstone," rejected these "undeserved accusations launched by a foreign pen" (Accademia Cosentina, *Atti*). In general, however, "internal exile" meant silence or at least self-censorship – discoursing only on subjects that were neutral and safe.

At the same time, there were many who chose, or were forced into, "external exile." Some were part of Guglielmo Pepe's expeditionary force against Austria, who refused to return when Ferdinand issued a recall; others evaded arrest and fled the country, in legendary flights aboard fishing boats that spirited them to Malta or Corfu in the darkness of night; still others escaped from prisons or pre-empted deportation. In one way or another, the *fior fiore* of the country's intelligentsia found itself in exile. The most popular havens were Piedmont, France, Switzerland, England, and Tuscany. Many *émigrés* joined struggles elsewhere – in defense of the Roman Republic, for the independence of Albania, against Louis Napoleon's *coup*, with the liberals of Neuchâtel. At the time of the Risorgimento, many would sign up with Garibaldi's *Mille*. In their peregrinations, the exiles made new political and personal contacts while consolidating old ones. But their contacts with their homeland were few, as travel back was unlikely and correspondence controlled. Thus the two groups of *émigrés*, internal and external, began to grow apart.

The events of 1848 were a watershed in the history of the Mezzogiorno. Significant changes took place in politics, economy, and culture on the one hand, and in the image of the Neapolitan Kingdom on the other. More and more, the image seemed to constitute the reality, as suggested by the frequent repetition of words such as backward, run down, despotic, savage, uncivilized. Of particular interest is how the exiles, in just these years, contributed to the new representation, expressing their pessimism through publications, correspondence, and debates among themselves. In the emerging discourse, they characterized their country as an unhappy wreck, ruled by an illegitimate government made up of mindless tyrants, perjurers, and traitors. Signs of barbarization were manifest in the arrests, the conditions of the prisons, the terror disseminated by general Nunziante in Calabria, the obsessive censorship, and police rule – all topics of the utmost concern. The Kingdom's stagnant economy, triumphant illiteracy, abdication of power to the Church, pitiful state of public health, and rural poverty completed the picture. Although conditions were in fact degenerating, this litany reflected the experience of the exiles as much as that of the Kingdom. Angry, bitter, and homesick, their life was hard. Nor could they help but admire the political and economic advances of the host countries in which they were living. Their sense of shame for their own country deepened accordingly (see Moe 1994; Petrusewicz n.d.).

In the exiles' writings, the backwardness of the South ceased to indicate its relative position on the scale of progress, assuming instead the more sinister meaning of an opposition to progress, a counter-position of barbarism to civilization. Their South was becoming the alterity of Europe. When, in his 1851 "Introduction" to Gladstone's *Letters*, Massari spoke of the "great battle of civilization against *barbarie*, wisdom against ignorance, virtue against vice, innocence against calumny" the terms "*barbarie*, ignorance, vice, and calumny" referred to the Bourbon tyranny, while the South, the *pays réel*, stood for "civilization, wisdom, virtue, and innocence" (Massari 1851: 11). But already a few years later, Francesco Trinchera could write of a kingdom that appears like a desert, with "no sign of a civilized life, no civil institution, no educational establishment, private or public, no roads . . . no commerce, no art, no industry . . .;" a desert inhabited by a *popolo* degraded, ignorant, and cruel, with no sense of either God or law (Anonymous [Trinchera] 1855: 26). And from there, it was but a short step toward making hopelessness an integral part of southern history, or "fatalism" a leitmotif of the southern "character." The eternally primitive nature of the South's institutions, the incompetence and selfishness of its absentee landowners, the greed and arbitrariness of its administrators, the grip of the Church, the weakness of the intellectuals, the passivity of the *popolo*, mired in poverty and ignorance, crime and violence – all had become articulated as indelible themes. To put it bluntly, even before encountering the prejudice of the Piedmontese makers of Italy, the Southern Question had been born.

Notes

1. See, as a representative example, the journal *Meridiana* published in Rome since 1988. For an English-language review of recent literature, see Lyttelton (1991); Davis (1994); Moe (1992); and Dickie (1992). It is interesting to note that in this effort of revision, the economists lag behind, "deconstructing" the Southern Question by breaking it up into many smaller questions, like so many pieces of a puzzle, which, when put back together, reproduce the original image

of backwardness. See, for example, Bottazzi (1990), who divides the Question into the sub-questions of: industrialization (or lack thereof); unemployment; growing criminality; urban areas (in decay); and a moral-political-administrative dimension (incapable, inefficient, and corrupt). The global picture that emerges replicates the original Southern Question.

2. At that time Vincenzo Cuoco's *Historical Essay on the Neapolitan Revolution of 1799* was not yet widely read in the Kingdom. It would not come out in Naples until 1861, and there is no evidence of any wide diffusion of the 1800, 1806, or 1820 Milanese editions.

3. The Duke of Ventignano, well known in reformist political circles, felt a need to define *miseria pubblica*, publishing a book on the subject in 1833.

References

Anonymous [Trinchera di Ostumi, Francesco] (1855) *La Quistione Napolitana: Ferdinando Borbone e Luciano Murat*. Publisher unknown.

Bottazzi, Gianfranco (1990) "Il Sud del Sud. I divari interni al Mezzogiorno e il rovesciamento delle gerarchie spaziali," *Meridiana* **10**: 141–79.

Colletta, Pietro (1967 [1834]) *Storia del Reame di Napoli*, ed. E. Barelli. Milan: Rizzoli.

Cuoco, Vincenzo (1913 [1800]) *Saggio storico sulla rivoluzione napoletana del 1799*. Bari: Laterza.

Davis, John (1994) "Remapping Italy's Path to the Twentieth Century," *Journal of Modern History* **66**: 291–320.

De Cesare, Raffaele (1969 [1873]) *La fine di un regno*. Milan: Longanesi.

De Lorenzo, Renata (1987) *Istituzioni e territorio nell'Ottocento borbonico*. Avellino: Pergola.

—— (1991) Gruppi dirigenti e associazionismo borbonico: le Società economiche. In G. M. Galanti, ed., *Dal comunitarismo pastorale all' individualismo agrario*. Istituto storico, Giuseppe Maria Galanti, *Atti*.

De Rosa, Luigi (1993) *Il Mezzogiorno agli inizi della Restaurazione*. Bari: Laterza.

De Sanctis, Francesco (1956 [1855]) *Epistolario (1836–1856)*, ed. Giovanni Ferretti and Muzio Mazzocchi Alemanni. Turin: Einaudi.

—— (1961 [1888]) *La giovinezza; memorie postume seguite da testimonianze biografiche di amici e discepoli*, ed. Gennaro Savarese. Turin: Einaudi.

Di Ciommo, Enrica (1993) *La nazione possibile: Mezzogiorno e questione nazionale nel 1848*. Milan: Franco Angeli.

Dickie, John (1992) "A Word at War: The Italian Army and Brigandage, 1860–1870," *History Workshop Journal* **33**: 1–24.

Farge, Arlette (1992) *Dire et ne pas dire. L'opinion publique au XVIIIme siècle*. Paris: Seuil.

Gerschenkron, Alexandr (1962) *Economic Backwardness in Historical Perspective: A Book of Essays*. Cambridge, MA: Harvard University Press.

Lippi, Carmine Antonio (1820) *Prime idèe concernenti il miglioramento delle nostre istituzioni*. Naples.

Lovett, Clara (1982) *The Democratic Movement in Italy, 1830–1876*. Cambridge, MA: Harvard University Press.

Lyttleton, Adrian (1991) "A New Past for the Mezzogiorno; New Approaches to the History of Southern Italy," *Times Literary Supplement*, October 4.

Massari, Giuseppe (1851) *Il Signore Gladstone ed il governo napoletano. Raccolta di scritti intorno alla questione napoletana*. Introduction to the Italian edition of William Gladstone, *Lettere al Lord Aberdeen*. Turin: Tipografia A. Pons e C.

Mastriani, Francesco (1994 [1863]) *I Vermi: le classi pericolose in Napoli*. Naples: Luca Torre.

Miller, Marion (1984) "The Italian Revolutions and Regional Popular Culture." Unpublished paper.

Moe, Nelson (1992) "'Altro che Italia!'. Il Sud dei piemontesi (1860–61)." *Meridiana* **15**: 53–89.

—— (1994) "Representing the South in Post-Unification Italy, *c.* 1860–1880." Unpublished dissertation, Johns Hopkins University.

Namier, Lewis (1946) *1848: the Revolution of the Intellectuals*. London: Oxford University Press.

Pepe, Guglielmo (1846) *Memorie della giovanezza*. Paris: Libreria Europea di Baudry.

Petrusewicz, Marta (1991) "Agromania: innovatori agrari nelle periferie europée dell'Ottocento." In Pietro Bevilacqua, ed., *Storia dell'agricoltura italiana*, Vol. III. Venice: Marsilio.

—— (n.d.) *Come il Meridione divenne una Questione: rappresentazioni del Sud prima e dopo il Quarantotto*. Soveria Manelli: Rubettino (in press).

Picone Petrusa, Mariaantonietta (1993) "Tradizione e crisi dei 'generi': collezionismo ed esposizioni nella pittura napoletana tra 1799 e 1860." In *La pittura Napoletana dell'Ottocento*. Naples: Tullio Pronti.

Ricciardi, Giuseppe (1860) *The Autobiography of an Italian Rebel*. London: Bradbury and Evans.

Sereni, Emilio (1974) *Capitalismo e mercato nazionale in Italia*. Rome: Editori Riuniti.

Settembrini, Luigi (1934 [1893]) *Ricordanze della mia vita*, ed. Adolfo Omodeo. Bari: Laterza.

Sperber, Jonathan (1994) *The European Revolutions, 1848–1851*. Cambridge and New York: Cambridge University Press.

Ventignano, Duca di (1833) *Della miseria pubblica, sue cause ed effetti applicati allo stato attuale del Regno citeriore di Napoli*. Naples: Tipografia Flautina.

Villari, Pasquale (1919 [1888]) *La giovinezza di Francesco de Sanctis, frammento autobiografico*. Naples: A. Morano.

—— (1961 [1888]) Introduction and Postscript to De Sanctis, Francesco, *La giovinezza; memorie postume seguite da testimonianze biografiche di amici e discepoli*, ed. Gennaro Savarese. Turin: Einaudi.

Zazo, Alfredo (1920) *Il Giornalismo a Napoli nella prima meta del secolo XIX*. Naples: Giannini.

—— (1927) *L'istruzione pubblica e privata nel Napoletano (1767–1860)*. Città di Castello: "Il Solco."

Zenobi, Giuseppe (1959) *Il triumviro Aurelio Saliceti*. Teramo.

2

The Emergence of the Southern Question in Villari, Franchetti, and Sonnino
Nelson Moe

During the second half of the 1870s, Pasquale Villari, Leopoldo Franchetti, and Sidney Sonnino elaborated a new vision of southern Italy. Their writings articulated for the first time the regional specificity of the social, political, and economic conditions of the South, inaugurating both the Southern Question and the field of *meridionalismo*. While these three men were pioneers in setting the terms of a question and a field "that situates the South at the center of its analysis and, even more importantly, at the center of national political life" (Barbagallo 1979: 7), it is important to note that their work formed part of a broader cultural trend. Over the course of the 1870s, the South increasingly attracted the attention of folklorists, visual artists, and writers, most notably Giovanni Verga. What marks this decade is the proliferation of discursive and pictorial representations of the South in a variety of fields. While this essay does not explore the relations between the emergence of *meridionalismo* and the representation of the South in these other domains, this is the broader context in which the Meridionalist writings of Villari, Franchetti, and Sonnino can be framed.[1]

The Southern Question in Villari's *Lettere meridionali*

With *Le lettere meridionali*, Pasquale Villari helped to establish a new conceptual framework within which to think about the South in the context of post-unification Italy. Before turning to these *Letters*, it is worth noting that Villari fostered an interest in the South in other ways both before and after the publication of the *Lettere meridionali* in 1875. Already in his 1872 essay, "La scuola e la questione sociale in Italia," he had called upon writers to visit the popular quarters of Naples and "describe them minutely, depict the life and moral conditions of those people, and denounce them to the civilized world as an Italian crime;"[2] and it was just such urgings, along with the impact of the *Letters* themselves, that had some part in prompting the likes of Franchetti, Sonnino, Jessie White Mario, Renato Fucini, Matilde Serao, Giustino Fortunato, Pasquale Turiello, and, later, Gaetano Salvemini to produce, between the mid-1870s and the mid-1880s, an extraordinarily rich and varied body of literature about the social conditions of the South.[3]

A Neapolitan exile in Florence (see Petrusewicz, this volume), Villari was, then, an "agitator" who stirred a wide range of thinkers into investigating the South (Salvadori 1976: 38). But it was certainly the *Letters* themselves that had the greatest impact on élites of the day. As Pasquale Turiello commented in 1877:

> If, a few years from now, our professors of sociology and economy also refer to the conditions of the Neapolitan and Sicilian peasant . . . that will probably be due to a set of letters published in *L'Opinione* in 1875, written by Pasquale Villari, on the social conditions of the Neapolitan and Sicilian peasants. For it was then . . . that a small group of Italians interested in our social problems came into existence; and the question, which even impartial observers had previously ignored, suddenly seemed to take on a capital importance.[4]

Villari first published his *Letters* in *L'Opinione*, the influential journal of the Right, which, in Chabod's words, "in part expressed the frame of mind of the governing moderates and in part contributed to its formation" (Chabod 1996: 329). However obvious it may seem, the first point to make about Villari's text is that it is written in the form of letters, addressed to the journal's editor Giacomo Dina. A contemporary of Villari's from Turin, Dina played an important role in almost three decades of Italian political history and in a sense personified that restricted group of liberal élites who were the effective addressees of Villari's *Letters*.[5]

In a moment we shall examine the particular set of concepts, figures, and rhetorical strategies through which Villari represents the South to the readers of *L'Opinione*. What is crucial to bear in mind at the outset is the critical thrust of these texts; they in fact constitute a polemic against his very readership, the liberal élites who had directed and shaped the process of Italian unification over the previous decade and a half. Villari had already voiced his disillusionment with the contemporary Italian state and society in his groundbreaking essay, "Di chi è la colpa," of 1866. There, after the humiliating defeats of Custoza and Lissa at the hands of the Austrians, he argued that it was time for Italy to wake up to the fact that

> in the very bosom of the nation there is an enemy more powerful than Austria, and it is our colossal ignorance, it is the illiterate multitudes, the unthinking burocrats, the ignorant teachers, the childish politicians, the impossible diplomats, the incompetent generals, the unskilled worker, the patriarchal farmer, and the rhetoric that eats away at our soul. It is not the quadrilateral of Mantua and Verona that stopped our progress: it is the quadrilateral of seventeen million illiterates and five million rhetoricians (in Villari 1885: 303–4).

Villari takes aim here at a wide range of "domestic" problems. But over the course of the next ten years, and particularly after the Paris Commune helped to sensitize élites to the Social Question, Villari's focus became sharper on two fronts. On the one hand, he formulated an increasingly pointed critique of the manner in which Italy's élites had governed the country since unification; on the other hand, he focused on that problem which at some level summed up the most urgent issues facing the nation: the social conditions of Southern Italy. In the first case, the fundamental problem consisted of the liberal élites' isolation from the people, in itself not an original theme in Risorgimento thought.[6] Villari's approach to it, however, is unique. On the floor of parliament in 1876, Villari spoke of it in these terms:

> We, my dear colleagues, brought about a revolution, which was largely the work of an intelligent, educated, and disinterested bourgeoisie . . . The people were in such conditions as not to be able to participate in the revolution, and were in a sense therefore dragged along by us. But precisely because we stood alone in this effort, because we alone were intent on completing the creation of a free Italy, even though we wished to do what was best for the nation as a whole, we found ourselves, without knowing it or wanting it, isolated in a closed circle, and we almost came to think that our little world was the whole world, forgetting that outside our narrow circle there is a vastly numerous class, to which Italy has never given a thought, and which it must finally take into consideration (p. 397).

A year later, in the noted essay "Ciò che gli stranieri non osservano in Italia," he described the problem similarly. Again he granted that none of the country's politicians had lost any of their patriotic spirit or "deliberately lost sight of the common good": "but all of society found itself in the hands of an extremely limited group of people which, closed up in an all too narrow sphere, naturally came to believe that its world was the whole world, and that there were no interests which differed from those which it saw and felt" (pp. 243–4). Both of these statements vividly express the élites' isolation from the people in terms of an inability to see beyond their "closed circle" and "narrow sphere." What is particularly noteworthy about the first quotation is the tension it expresses between "Italy," understood as "our narrow circle," and "the nation as a whole." His statement that "Italy has never given a thought" to the people highlights the latter's effective exclusion from the former, just as he charges "Italy" with the task of broadening its perspective to include that "vastly numerous class" that up till now it has ignored.

Now in Villari's *Lettere meridionali*, it is precisely the South that comes to represent those people, problems, and "interests" that have been forgotten or ignored by the country's élites, sequestered in their narrow sphere of command and privilege. But if, on the one hand, the South desperately needs the political attention and material assistance of Italy's ruling class, the ruling class, in Villari's profoundly moral view of the problem (Salvadori 1976: 34), also has need of the South. For Villari insists that the restrictive vision of the country's élites, which was a political necessity during the struggle to unite Italy, has, in the context of post-unification Italy, resulted in a state of moral bankruptcy. As in the passage from "Di chi è la colpa" of 1866 cited above, the problem is formulated here in terms of the waning of those "external," heroic struggles of the Risorgimento and the consequent need "to turn all our attention inward."[7] But here the emphasis on the void in the "heart of each citizen" is much more pronounced.[8] In this new "prosaic" age (Croce 1963: 2) in which the statesman's highest aim is to balance the budget and the scholar's to obtain steady employment, it is the liberation of the suffering masses, and the masses of the South in particular, that could "give us back our lost ideal."[9]

But just how is it that the South comes to perform this function in Villari's moral geography of the nation? In the following discussion I want to examine the way Villari elaborates what will prove to be a defining feature of Meridionalist discourse from this point forward: the exceptional nature of the South, its peculiarity and radical difference with respect to the rest of Italy and, indeed, modern European civilization as a whole. As we shall see, Villari's discourse vacillates between the desire to affirm the South's common bonds with the rest of Italy, which springs from the unitary imperative that Villari shares with all the early Meridionalists, and an insistence on a peculiarity that ends up transforming the South into a *regio dissimilitudinis*, a place unlike any other, irreconcilable to the modalities of modern society.

What is striking about the *Southern Letters*, then, is that the South does not initially appear to be their main theme. In the prefatory remarks the author wrote for the various editions of the *Letters* (the opening of the first letter, and the prefaces to the 1878 and 1885 editions), Villari describes the *Letters'* main concerns in the following manner: in 1875 he introduces them as an investigation into "the state of the poorest classes, especially in the southern provinces" (p. 1); in the preface to the 1878 edition he comments that "the writings that I have collected in this volume regard more or less the same question," which is to say the miserable plight of the multitudes, "and above all those that live from agriculture" (p. xxvi; in this preface, it is worth noting, no mention of the South is made whatsoever); and in the preface to the second edition of 1885, Villari writes of "two questions" of principal concern – "the miserable state of our masses in certain cities, above all in Naples; the no less miserable conditions of our peasants in many parts of Italy" (p. vii). Finally, we must recall the book's title itself, *Lettere meridionali ed altri scritti sulla questione sociale in Italia.*

In Villari's presentation, the *Southern Letters*, then, are about the miserable conditions of both the rural and urban masses and more generally – as the book's title indicates – about the "social question," where the South is singled out as a regional case of special importance. The South's problems are thus situated in a general, national context and, as we will see more clearly below, this is one of the central premises of Villari's enterprise. Yet if Villari's presentation of the *Letters'* themes serves to orient our reading towards problems of a national scope, the titles of the individual letters suggest the importance of the local context. "*Camorra*," "Mafia," "Brigandage," are all phenomena that are typically and (except in the case of brigandage) exclusively southern. And this tension between the general and specific, the national and local, runs throughout the *Letters*. While Villari presents his concerns in a national framework, his actual descriptions, observations, and analyses underscore the southern specificity of these problems.

This interplay between the national and regional is immediately evident in the first letter, dedicated to the *camorra* and the conditions of the masses in Naples. At the beginning of his discussion, Naples is introduced as that city, "among many, in which the low plebs find themselves, I won't say in the greatest misery, because that is not what is worst, but in the greatest abandon, in the most grievous degradation and dejection" (pp. 3–4). Naples is therefore introduced as a special case of the "miserable state of the masses" in various Italian cities. The highly charged rhetoric he employs and the vividness of his descriptions tend however to undermine the proposition that these conditions can also be found elsewhere, albeit to a lesser degree; each detail, name, anecdote, story, communicates the peculiarity of this place and its problems. The *camorra*, as he writes, may well be "the logical, natural, necessary consequence of a certain social condition" (p. 1) that exists in other parts of the country. But his noted descriptions of the Neapolitan slums and of the string-makers leave us with the impression that these conditions are somehow *uniquely* Neapolitan. Quoting a letter from an architect in Naples,[10] he writes

> These slums . . . generally have an entryway, without any opening on to the street, and a little courtyard, both utterly filthy, which open on to an immense quantity of terrible dwellings, much worse than kennels in fact. All of them, but especially those on the ground-floor, lack air and light and are extremely humid. In these slums several thousand people live piled on top of one another, so degraded by misery that they seem more brutes than men. In those dens, into which you can't enter because of the stench of the garbage that's been piled up there for ages, one often sees no more than a pile of straw, destined to be the bed of an entire family, male and female all together. Latrines of course are non-existent, for the streets and courtyards suffice for those needs (p. 5).

This is only the first of a number of scenes of "la miseria" in the *Letters* – "ever varied, brutal, and horrible" – that serve the explicit purpose of shocking his readers out of their state of indifference to the plight of the masses, an attitude that Villari elsewhere calls "incredible."[11] What is clear at this point is that before the descriptive power of these "lurid kennels, these terrible grottoes, and degraded inhabitants," these "unhappy, degraded people" that crawl out into the sunlight "like ants" (p. 7), the general category of the "social question in Italy" recedes into the background. With each passing description Naples appears more exceptional, if not a case unto itself: "in no other country on the earth do the terrible consequences of Malthus's theory appear more clearly" (p. 12). It is therefore the scene of the string-makers' caves that remains imprinted in the reader's imagination (p. 6),[12] or that of the poor widow who, in her cold, darkened den, bangs a rock against the wall in a desperate attempt to frighten the rats away from her sleeping children.[13]

Villari, in fact, seems to recognize this problem at some level for, at the end of the letter, he attempts to reframe his discussion of Naples and the *camorra* at the general level. He writes that he will cite an example from the North "in order to show that the ill is general and in order to dispel the impression that I wish to take all my examples from the South of Italy" (p. 14). But this very move serves to underscore the force of the former examples by comparison with the latter. The series of statistics he cites regarding poverty in Venice lacks even a brief description of the specific conditions of the Venetian poor, and thus, while the reader may take him at his word — "the ill is general" — the ill one remembers is that of Naples.

In his first *Southern Letter* on the *camorra*, Villari thus raises not so much the "question of the cities" as the "question of Naples," unique and incomparable.[14] Something similar occurs in the following letter dedicated to the "ills that afflict Sicily," above all the mafia. Here too Villari suggests that the ills of the region constitute examples of a more general social – and, in this case, agrarian – question. Yet, to an even greater extent than in the previous letter, what is salient in Villari's account is the singular aspects of these ills and, more generally, the peculiarity of the Sicilian Question.

In the first place, Villari addresses the problem of working conditions in the Sicilian sulfur mines, suggesting that they are representative of those in other areas and industries. But the overall effect of his discussion is quite the opposite. To begin with, sulfur is Sicily's major industry, and closely tied up with the island's economic identity; it is, in some way, typically Sicilian. At the same time, he underscores the particularity of the Sicilian sulfur mines, noting that while other countries with mining industries have sought to protect miners and especially child workers, no such thing has happened in Sicily. Finally, as with his account of the Neapolitan slums, he depicts the working conditions in the mines in a sensational fashion, confronting the reader with scenes of unforgettable human degradation and suffering:

These human beings are subjected to a form of labor which, described day in, day out, seems ever more cruel, if not impossible. Hundreds of boys and girls descend along steep embankments and rickety ladders, stuck into soil which is crumbling or saturated with water. Having reached the bottom of the mine, they are loaded with rocks, which they must then carry upwards on their backs, slipping on that steep and treacherous earth at the risk of falling and dying an instant death. The older approach the top sending out horrendous screams; the children arrive in tears (pp. 18–19).

In the case of the mafia, the particularity of Sicily – and of the mafia as a synechdocal representative of it – emerges with even greater clarity. Here Villari offers comparatively little in the way of graphic descriptions of human misery, entering instead into an extensive, and at times confusing, analysis of the social and economic conditions of Western Sicily that seemed to have produced the mafia. He expresses his surprise at discovering that the highest levels of criminality are to be found, not among the poor, but among the well-to-do farmers, and notes how this fact seems to "overthrow every rule of political economy and social science" (p. 24). The mafia, in short, seems to confound his analytical intent, and this difficulty results in what is probably the least persuasive and engaging part of the *Southern Letters*. His conclusion that the two great "calamities" of Western Sicily – the sulfur mines and the mafia – are generated by "the special conditions of its agriculture" (p. 32) constitutes a kind of admission that these are not problems that can be easily related to the agricultural conditions in the rest of Italy. For while he claims they are "aspects" of the Agrarian Question, they are nevertheless problems that can only be understood and remedied in terms of their specific, local conditions.

In the penultimate letter of the series, dedicated to brigandage, Villari continues to emphasize the peculiarity of the South in the manner described above. Brigandage, he writes, "is the gravest ill that we can observe in our countryside. As is well known, it is certainly the consequence of an agrarian and social question which afflicts almost all the provinces of southern Italy" (p. 38). Here Villari writes with even more extensive commentary and anecdotal description, and heightened rhetorical power. The ensuing series of descriptions of the plight of the southern Italian peasants produces the distinct impression that the South is profoundly different from the rest of the nation. In the first letter, Villari adheres more closely to his initial proposition, that the framework in which to view these problems is a general, national one. But, after the passing reference made to Venice in the first letter, the North falls by the wayside. Or rather it now appears in an antithetical position with respect to the South. Villari introduces Franchetti into his discussion – from whose study of the Neapolitan provinces he cites liberally in this letter – as one who was "grievously scandalized to see things which must have seemed impossible to him, a native of Tuscany where the peasant is not only a free and independent man, but a true associate of his master . . ." (p. 44). To the scandalized Tuscan Franchetti, the degradation of the southern peasants "calls to mind the age of slavery," in so far as the master "has the unlimited right to demand services from his peasants, and exercises it widely" (p. 46).

Here, in fact, the figure of slavery is repeated numerous times, along with other terms and tropes that emphasize the singularly abject condition of the Southern Italian peasants. For the most part, these are scandalous analogies, references (like slavery, Ireland, the Middle Ages) that are blatantly out of place (and time) with respect to contemporary Italy. Thus, reflecting on the conditions in the South under the Bourbons and how, since unification, the state of the peasants has remained unchanged, if not worsened (p. 45), Villari writes: "America has shown by its example that in many cases the enslavement of the negroes harmed the slave's master most of all, because he was thereby corrupted by the unjust dominion that he exercised. Shouldn't an unlimited dominion not over blacks, but over men of the same race, corrupt as well?" (p. 43). And in the final letter, dedicated to "The Remedies," Villari describes the relations between landlord and peasant in a similar vein:

> The landlord finds himself isolated in the middle of an army of peasants. The submission of the latter is immense . . . But all this is not the result of affection or esteem. He could kneel down before his master with the same feeling with which the Indian worships the tempest or lightening. The day that this charm were broken, the peasant would rise up to avenge himself ferociously with long-repressed hatred, with his brutal passions. Some times, in fact, one has seen hordes of slaves transformed into hordes of cannibals (p. 57).

The overall effect of these repeated analogies is of course to emphasize the South's deviation from the norm of social justice and good government, which, while occasionally associated with Prussia, England, and Tuscany, generally functions as an unstated term of comparison in the text. Villari writes of the "marvel" "the foreigner" feels upon finding no middle class in southern Italian cities as an intermediary between landowners and peasants (p. 42), and this sense of marvel, accompanied by outrage, characterizes Villari's rhetoric throughout. The South is thus, above all, remarkable, extraordinary, exceptional. Towards the end of the final letter Villari stresses – as he had at the end of the first – that Southern Italy is not the only part of the country "in which the peasants suffer unjustly" (p. 63). On this occasion he in fact provides a page and a half of descriptions and details from the Veneto and Lombardy, which create an effective link between conditions in the South and other parts of Italy. But it nevertheless represents only a brief parenthesis in the letter, and at its conclusion Villari reasserts the difference between North and South in quantitative terms: "The ill exists in many provinces, but in the provinces of southern Italy its dimensions are much greater" (p. 65).

As I noted at the beginning of this discussion, Villari represents the South in the *Letters* not only as a problem for the people of the South but as a matter of capital importance to the élites of the nation. Isolated in their "narrow sphere," the élites *need* the South, or – more precisely – need to concern themselves with the South, in order to "reawaken in us that moral life without which a nation has no purpose, no true existence" (p. 67). Yet, as we have seen, Villari's attempt to make the Southern Question seem a national problem was undermined at some level by the power of his own representations, which tended to situate the ills of the South in a remote region of unlikeness with respect to the rest of Italy. In the concluding statement of the *Letters*, Villari addresses this problem head on, formulating it as an imagined objection, which, he writes, "some, out of patriotism, don't make, but which they nevertheless harbor in their hearts":

> Fortunately, they say to themselves, not all of Italy is in the same condition as the Southern Provinces. If the peasants and poor are in such a terrible condition *down there*, if the educated do not fulfill their obligations, ignoring and failing to improve this state of affairs, tough luck for them; they'll just have to remain in their semi-barbarous state a while longer. In central and northern Italy we will be, as we are, civilized (p. 69).

This imaginary objection touches on precisely that problem of regional peculiarity examined earlier. For Villari's imagined dissenter, the South's problems are specifically and exclusively southern; and, perhaps most importantly, they are *down there*, far from the civilized regions of central–northern Italy. The Southern Question is not our national problem, but theirs.

Not surprisingly, Villari responds to this objection by reiterating the unitary, national perspective he had announced at the beginning. But he does so in a striking fashion that merits quoting in its entirety:

> Let's forget the fact that many problems, as I stated earlier, plague central and northern Italy as well. And let's assume, for the sake of argument, that Italy is in fact divided in the way my uncharitable opponents insist. But if they wished to draw such a conclusion from this state of affairs they should have thought about it before, leaving intact the Great Wall of China which the Bourbons had constructed [between northern and southern Italy]. After the unification and liberation of Italy, everything has gotten mixed together in the army, the navy, the judicial system, the administration, etc. The guilt of the more civilized provinces is equal to the guilt of the more educated and well-to-do classes that abandon the more ignorant and derelict classes of one and the same society to their own destiny. And the consequences are the same. Today the peasant who goes to die in the countryside around Rome, or who suffers from hunger in his own village, and the poor man who wastes away in the hovels of Naples can say to us and to you: After the

unification of Italy, you've got no way out – either turn us into civilized people, or we'll turn you into barbarians. And we men of the Mezzogiorno have the right to say to those of central and northern Italy: Your indifference and our indifference would be equally immoral and guilty (p. 70).

How then does Villari counter the impression that the South's problems are somehow separate from the North, an impression that, we have seen, he himself helped to create? The pre-unification division between northern and southern Italy has been replaced, he argues, by a commingling of people from the two regions in the nation's various public institutions. This point, it would seem, could be readily acknowledged by all sides. But it evidently does not go far enough, for while it has northerners and southerners working together in the same institutions, it still leaves the two parts of the country – and their problems – where they were: in different places, with a fault line running between them. Villari thus offers a more thoroughgoing reconceptualization of the relationship through an analogy that replaces the horizontal and geographical concept of North/South with the vertical concept of a single hierarchical society: the North is to the South as the "more educated and well-to-do classes" are to the "more ignorant and derelict." North and South are, then, highly differentiated, but in such a way that one recognizes the relationship between the two in terms of the supposed obligations the upper classes feel towards the lower classes *of their own society*. The substitution for a geographical conceptualization of social difference of a political one enables him to argue for a northern obligation towards the southerners that otherwise would not be felt.

Having done this, all that remains for Villari to do is provide a more dramatic expression of this newly conceived relationship. And what more effective way to do this than by letting this underclass, through a form of rhetorical ventriloquism, appeal to the nation's élites? Yet this formulation contains something more than just an appeal for social justice; it is in fact a threat: "either turn us into civilized people, or we'll turn you into barbarians."

There are two things about this formulation, and about this final passage more generally, that I would like to consider briefly in conclusion. In the first place, it recapitulates the gist of the *Letters* as a whole, which is to say it articulates the differentiation between the two regions *in the spirit of national unity*. The educated, affluent, civilized North must help the ignorant, derelict, barbaric South. In the second place, it is interesting to note where Villari situates himself in this new geopolitical schema of a "more educated and affluent" North and a "more ignorant and derelict" South. On the one hand he places himself among the southern élites ("we men of the Mezzogiorno"). On the other hand, the text's pronouns graphically represent the fact that he and the southern élites like him occupy an intermediary, and somewhat shifty, position *vis-à-vis* these two worlds. The underclasses of the

South can apostrophize "us" (the élites of the South) and "you" (the élites of the North) as the common object of their threat. But if the southern élites are joined with those of the North as the addressee in the first clause, in the clause that follows they are separated. Here, instead, "we men of the South" charge "those of central and northern Italy" – and themselves as well – with the moral responsibility of helping the southern people.

In this interplay of pronouns, the role of Villari, the Neapolitan-Florentine, as intermediary between the southern and northern élites and as representative of the southern masses to both is evident. What this means is that the novelty of Villari's *Lettere meridionali* may therefore lie not only in their launching of a new analytical field but in their inauguration of a new intellectual function: that, precisely, of the Meridionalist, the writer, from northern or southern Italy, who endeavors to provide a representation of the South to the nation's élites, especially in the North. In the following section on Franchetti and Sonnino, we shall see the important role this northern point of reference plays in each of these authors' visions of the South and Sicily in particular.

Franchetti's Sicily

If, as Leopoldo Franchetti once said, Pasquale Villari was the "revered master of the Southern Question" (Jannazzo 1986: 23), Franchetti and his close collaborator Sidney Sonnino were no mere epigoni. Both men were profoundly indebted to Villari's "lesson": the *Southern Letters* were one of the sources of inspiration for their groundbreaking investigation of Sicily in 1876; and *Rassegna settimanale*, the main journal of Meridionalist discussion that Franchetti and Sonnino edited between 1878 and 1882, was Villari's brainchild. They themselves were original thinkers, however, and with respect to Villari's *Lettere meridionali* the investigations of Franchetti and Sonnino in fact "represent a more advanced and in-depth phase of study of the socio-economic reality of the South" (R. Villari 1979: 72).

In this section I focus on Franchetti's 1876 study, *Condizioni politiche e amministrative della Sicilia* (Franchetti 1985). I should stress, however, that because their Meridionalist work was of such a profoundly collaborative nature, on many occasions I refer to Franchetti and Sonnino together in this essay: their first studies were published in a single volume in 1875 (Franchetti's *Condizioni economiche e amministrative delle provincie napoletane* and Sonnino's *La mezzeria in Toscana*); their second, more famous pair of studies, comprising Franchetti's *Condizioni politiche e amministrative della Sicilia* and Sonnino's *I contadini in Sicilia*, was conceived, researched, and published together as *La Sicilia nel 1876*; and, finally, between 1878 and 1882 they co-edited *Rassegna settimanale*. My focus on Franchetti's 1876 study is partly motivated by the fact that his investigation is of a more sociological nature than the technical, agrarian-economic analysis of Sonnino. At the same time, Franchetti's study was a more influential text than Sonnino's, a "foundational work" through which the Southern Question "began to enter into the consciousness of scholars and politicians, if not of the more general public" (Gatto 1950: 229). Most importantly, the geopolitical vision that Franchetti formulates in this text constitutes one of the most powerful conceptualizations of the difference and division between North and South ever written.

Let us begin with a brief consideration of Franchetti's earlier study of the continental South, which marks out many of the themes and problems that will be articulated with greater rigor and rhetorical force in his 1876 study of Sicily. Started in the autumn of 1873 and published a few months after Villari's *Lettere meridionali* in the summer of 1875, Franchetti's study of the "economic and administrative condition of the Neapolitan provinces" manifests a number of affinities with Villari's text (at one level, of course, there is a direct link between them, in so far as Villari cites passages from Franchetti's 1875 study, as we saw in our discussion of the *Southern Letters*). In the opening lines, Franchetti announces that he has "called things by their real names and used harsh expressions where they seemed justified" (1985: 3). Like Villari, Franchetti thus adopts a critical attitude to the southern reality under investigation, seeking to bring to light unseemly realities previously ignored or hidden from the ken of the country's élites. Franchetti then makes a move that, as we saw, was central to the conclusion of Villari's *Letters*: he issues a patriotic appeal to the common destiny of all Italians, claiming that the problems of the South are not those of southerners alone: "We are all Italians, their disgraces are our disgraces, we are weak with their weakness" (1985: 3). Like Villari, Franchetti attempts to "nationalize" the problems of the South, dissolving the force of regional difference in an equation of theirs is ours, they are us.

Certain differences between the two texts, however, are also readily apparent. In the first place, the subtitle of Franchetti's work, "travel notes," reminds us that the writer is a foreign observer. Franchetti in fact raises this point in the passage cited above, where he writes that he would be "profoundly saddened" if his southern readers, acting out of local pride, rejected his harsh assessment of the conditions in the South simply because he was a "foreigner." It is just this expression of local interest that prompts the unitarian statement cited above ("We are all Italians"), which is an attempt to efface the difference between local and foreigner, southerner and northerner, which threatens to distort the reception of his text.

Yet, as in Villari, this disclaimer of regional difference functions as a rhetorical frame that is at odds with the emphasis on regional particularity within the text. Here, too, what quickly emerges is the singular negativity of the conditions in these provinces. But whereas Villari, the Neapolitan, tried to render the South through a kind of impassioned identification with it, most clearly reflected in his attempt to give voice to the southern masses at the conclusion of the *Letters*, Franchetti articulates a South that is clearly foreign to him, the representative of a different and superior civilization. With greater analytical rigor, Franchetti artic- ulates a more systematic contrast between his world and that of the southern provinces, whereas the morally outraged Villari managed to acknowledge a certain human truth to the South. Franchetti instead represents the South as a perverse realm of social disorder and moral degradation in which human existence cannot be conceived of according to the standard measure of European civilization.[15] We see this, for example, in Franchetti's observations on the nature of the relations between peasants and landlords in Abruzzi and Molise: "Truly, if one thinks about these facts, which appear contradictory to the man accustomed to civilization, they all seem equally typical of the state of primitives; a state of barbarism, ignorant of all the relations and laws that keep society together as a whole, from the laws of the family to that of public safety" (1985: 18). In another passage, the use of the foreigner's perspective, and the corresponding sense of incredulity, is even more explicit.

At the sight of this desolation, the foreigner is tempted to think that in that country some great disaster occurs every year after the harvest, some invasion, some conquest that robs them of the fruits of the whole year's labor and prevents them from putting anything aside so as to improve the fields, so as to eliminate the fever; or that for centuries and centuries the bad harvests have followed upon one another without respite and have left just enough for the landlords and workers to eat and plant again; or that the country is inhabited by a special category of men which, in the midst of cultivated lands, has preserved the improvidence of the savages of the American plains and which, having eaten well or poorly, does not feel that desire which is common to all men to improve their condition (1985: 50).

Thus, while Franchetti's image of the South resembles Villari's in its negativity, the contrast between the South and the "more advanced provinces" (1985: 33) of Italy is more marked in Franchetti's text.

Before concluding this brief consideration of Franchetti's first study, it is also worth noting that the contrastive effect we have been discussing was further accentuated by its publication together with Sonnino's study of share-cropping in Tuscany. Sonnino's *Mezzeria in Toscana* amounted to an encomium of the Tuscan share-cropping system, which, in his view, was one of the most humane, successful forms of agriculture that could be imagined. The contrast between the disastrous conditions in the South and the "privileged position" of Tuscany was striking, and Sonnino himself seized upon this point in a sort of preview of their findings published shortly before the appearance of their joint volume in the spring of

1875.[16] Nor was this effect apparently lost on one young southern reader, Giustino Fortunato. Many years later, Fortunato recalled the profound impact these texts had upon him precisely in terms of this contrast, noting that they were "two texts published in a single volume, with the manifest intention of bringing together descriptions of two states of affairs as different from one another as the effects of the same contract in the particular conditions of the two regions are varied" (1927: 163–4).

I now turn to Franchetti and Sonnino's *Sicilia nel 1876*, focusing on the contribution of the former, *Condizioni politiche e amministrative della Sicilia*. Franchetti's earlier study and the study of Sicily are akin to one another in a number of ways, but, as we shall see below, the study of Sicily is composed with considerably more clarity of focus and rhetorical force. Most importantly, it takes the contrastive vision of the earlier study to much greater extremes, constituting, in fact, one of the most powerful conceptualizations of the difference and division between North and South ever written.

Like the preface to Franchetti's earlier study, the joint preface to *La Sicilia nel 1876* announces the authors' commitment to telling the whole, unvarnished truth about Sicily. Franchetti reaffirms this point at the beginning of his own contribution with an epigraph from Machiavelli's *Prince*, which states: "There is no other way to ward off adulation than to let people know that they won't offend you if they tell you the truth."[17] The reference to the *Prince* is not a matter of indifference: Franchetti's study is itself a treatise of statecraft, an analysis of the social and political conditions in Sicily and a diagnosis of how to remedy its ills aimed, as he writes later, at the "educated class of central and northern Italy and those few people from southern Italy who are aware of the conditions of their country" (Franchetti and Sonnino 1974: 238). The polemical edge of their investigation is apparent here as well, for they suggest that the country's élites have ignored if not suppressed the harsh truth about Sicily in the past, subscribing to "that stupid sense of shame which often makes us Italians hide our ills so as to seem greater than or different from what we are" (p. vi).[18]

The polemical spirit of the exposé therefore animates *La Sicilia nel 1876*, and, as we shall see below, surprise and shock are key elements of the text's rhetorical construction. At the same time, Franchetti articulates his study in another narrative mode that occupies a central place in the history of representations of the South: that of the travel journal. *La Sicilia nel 1876* is, after all, based on the journey Franchetti, Sonnino, and their friend Enea Cavalieri took to Sicily, and for Franchetti the travel narrative is evidently one of the most rhetorically effective ways to represent the experience of discovery that plays such an important role in his study.[19] This experience is generally framed in terms of sociological analysis, but, as the following passages show, this is not the purely dispassionate account of the positivist social investigator. A more imaginative and, in some sense, romantic perspective also comes into play, a certain enchantment with the new and foreign:

> The train sets off again, and the traveler is subtly overcome by the feeling experienced by one who finds himself in the middle of mysterious and unknown things; it seems that the valleys that open on the road, winding and then hiding themselves behind a rise, must hide strange things, never seen before (p. 20).
>
> Then the newly arrived traveler feels overcome by a sense of profound isolation. It seems to him that the nightmare of some mysterious and malicious power weighs on the bare and monotonous countryside, a power against which there is no help or defense beyond himself and the companions that have come with him from across the sea, and he suddenly feels overcome by a profound sense of affection for the carbine that he's carrying across his saddle (pp. 21–2).

Later in the text, the narrative device of the journey will be replaced by the more disembodied, scientific perspective of the social investigator.[20] But the general sense of being an outside observer from the mainland permeates the study and, as we shall see below, shapes Franchetti's representation of the Sicilian social reality. This is particularly evident in the opening pages of the study.

Franchetti begins by recounting the traveler's "first impression" upon arrival in Palermo. This, he writes, "is one of the most pleasant that can be imagined" (p. 3). He lists the delightful climate and surroundings "celebrated in every language," the splendor of the city and the hospitality of its citizens, the neighboring country-side that manifests signs of an "advanced civilization," all producing in the traveler a state of "enchantment." But – so begins the second paragraph – if the traveler stays a while, "the colors change, the aspect of everything is transformed" (p. 4). After hearing a few stories about violent crimes, "all that scent of orange and lemon flowers starts to smell like a corpse" (p. 4). The sunny commonplaces and first impressions of the island quickly yield to the grim facts of life in Sicily.[21]

For the next two hundred pages the reader is presented with an unremittingly dire portrait of the social and political conditions on the island. The island's ruling class is composed of that people in Europe that is "most passionately ambitious for domination, the quickest to take offense, the most ruthless in its struggles for power, influence and profit, the most implacable in its hates, most ferocious in vendettas" (p. 8); the oppressed peasants live in destitute conditions that call to mind "the times in which the Sicilian countryside was tilled by hordes of slaves" (p. 21); bands of brigands, bandits, and *mafiosi* maraude across the island, virtually unchecked by the forces of law and order, who, in turn, are like "an army encamped in a hostile country" (p. 13). A "nightmare of mysterious and malign power" seems indeed to weigh upon everything, bathing in a sinister light not just the Sicilian landscape, but its human reality as well.

As Renda notes, a spirit of desolation pervades all Franchetti's observations and analyses in *Condizioni politiche e amministrative della Sicilia* (see 1984: 73), as the following statement suggests: "The sight of the conditions on the entire island, irrespective of the particular province, is profoundly disturbing" (p. 56). And while Franchetti by no means renounces claims to objectivity, neither does he attempt to suppress the subjective dimension of his encounter with Sicily. On the contrary, the representation of his experience of alienation from it constitutes one of the main ways of representing the difference between the civilization of Sicily and the mainland more generally. This is an important point that we shall return to below. For the moment, let us briefly examine what Franchetti considers to be the two characteristics that typify life on the island: the omnipresence of violence; and the predominance of private interests over the public good.

Violence, as we saw, was what first caught the attention of Franchetti's traveler at the beginning of the study; and it accompanies him throughout. As much as the sheer frequency of murders, kidnapping, cattle rustling, etc., what strikes Franchetti most is the Sicilians' attitudes towards it. Acts of violence, for them, are not exceptional, but rather part of "the normal state of things" (p. 5), "necessary and normal although harmful, like the heavy rains that make the year's harvest rot in their fields" (p. 221).

Such violence reveals, in turn, the governing principle of life on the island: the predominance of private authority over social, or public, authority. It is this single phenomenon, Franchetti writes in the penultimate section, that "sums up" all the others described and analysed in the book (p. 220). From it follows the fact that in Sicily "violence can be freely employed by whoever has the means to do so, the *res publica* is exploited by the few, the rights recognized by Italian civil law are ineffectual against private force" (p. 220). It is a world, in short, in which might makes right, where "there is no place for whoever doesn't have fangs and claws" (p. 12).

These are the quintessential characteristics of the Sicilian social order according to Franchetti. What we now need to consider is how Franchetti represents these aspects of life in Sicily, and Sicily more generally, as different from what one finds on the mainland. This is a crucial point, for it is precisely the representation of Sicily's difference that constitutes one of the text's most powerful and lasting rhetorical effects.

Through a variety of rhetorical devices Franchetti makes it clear that the way of life in Sicily differs from that of the mainland author and his implied readership. I should mention at this point that Franchetti establishes a form of identity between himself and his reader as co-"continentals" from the beginning by creating two basic perspectives in the text: that of the traveler-observer and that of the Sicilians. The first perspective is generally articulated as an indefinite third-person ("one") that embraces both author and reader as the subject that observes, analyses, and experiences the Sicilian world; the Sicilians are quite simply the "other," the objects of observation and analysis.[22] We will see more clearly below the way Franchetti actually deprives the Sicilians of their political agency; but for the moment let us consider how they are rendered socially and culturally "other" in the text.

Franchetti's study is strewn with various indications of curiosity, surprise, perplexity, confusion, fear, all of which serve to underscore the cultural distance between the traveler and the Sicilians under observation. Such indications range from the use of qualifiers like "strange," "disturbing," and even "monstrous," to more extended representations of the experience of cultural difference. In the first pages of the study, for example, Franchetti stages the discrepancy between the traveler's expectations about violence and the way things work in Sicily. One would expect people to be arrested for these crimes, but they are not (pp. 4–5); one would expect people to feel angry about these incidents, but they are not (p. 7); one would infer from their frequency that Sicily was undergoing some revolution or other terrible cataclysm, but it is not (p. 11). In each case the difference between the foreign culture of Sicily and that of the mainland is underscored through the discrepancy between continental expectation and Sicilian reality.

The frequent use of questions and other indications of perplexity has a similar effect. Certain pages in fact amount to little more than catalogues of questions that express the traveler's inability to orient himself in this strange world, asking, in effect, how could this be possible? "How could these criminals acquire such a sway over men's minds? The mind searches at length in vain to solve this problem . . . What is the reason for the landowners' lack of organization . . .? . . . the mind seeks in vain a criterion that can guide it in the judgment of the facts" (p. 31). Sicily thus constitutes a cognitive challenge, a socio-political reality that, in fact, "throws into disarray all the concepts of government and the public good that one has formed in regularly constituted countries" (p. 35).

All these qualifiers, questions, and observations are so many ways of driving home what, at some level, is the fundamental point of Franchetti's study: that Sicily is different, radically different, from the mainland. And while the traveler's conceptual framework may be momentarily "thrown into disarray" by certain aspects of Sicily, it comes out of this cultural encounter quite intact of course, every bit the unwavering standard against which Sicily and the rest of the world can be judged. Sicily is therefore not just different but, as the last comment cited above makes perfectly clear, *irregular*.

What is striking about this insistent, normative assertion of cultural difference is that Franchetti and Sonnino had claimed in the preface that the phenomena under investigation "have their first origin in the laws of nature," and that they consequently had no intention "judging or condemning anyone" (p. v). By the same token, Franchetti stresses in the conclusion that the phenomena he describes "have nothing abnormal about them, but are rather the necessary manifestations of the social state of the island" (p. 237). He even grants, with an air of tolerance, that this is "one state of affairs like another," which existed in Europe for many centuries and continues to exist in many countries still today. Sicily is, in a word, medieval, behind on the time-line of historical progress with respect to the "more advanced parts" of the country, and, if left to its own devices, would probably follow in the footsteps of the rest of modern Europe (p. 220).[23]

The key problem, however, is that Sicily does not exist in isolation, but rather forms part of the *modern* kingdom of Italy. Its "abnormality" derives from its position in this context. What is abnormal in Sicily is thus "the intrusion of a different civilization that seeks to impose itself and throws the play of natural forces into disarray, which otherwise would have resulted in the regular development of Sicilian society" (p. 237). Franchetti thus makes clear a point that had been implicit throughout the study: that Sicily and the mainland, North and South, are homogeneous entities, such that Sicily's union with the mainland perforce constitutes an "intrusion," the rupturing of the hermetic seal that had previously protected "medieval" Sicily from modern civilization. Set against one another in this fashion, however, there can be no compromise or fusion between them.

> The coexistence of Sicilian civilization and that of central and northern Italy in the same nation is incompatibile with the prosperity of the nation and, in the long run, with its very existence, for it produces a weakness that renders it vulnerable to disintegration at the slightest push from outside. One of these two civilizations must therefore disappear in those parts of it which are incompatible with the other. And we believe that for any Sicilian of good faith and moderate intelligence there can be no doubt as to which of the two must make room for the other (p. 237).

Now, as one would expect, such a unilaterally negative conceptualization of Sicily has certain ramifications with regard to the prospect of governing it; and it is not surprising that, in order to formulate the specific political relationship between Sicily and the mainland, Franchetti draws upon the repertoire of medical imagery that was frequently employed to represent the South, particularly in moments of heightened social unrest and political conflict.[24] In their joint preface, Franchetti and Sonnino had in fact referred to the "diseased phenomena" that Sicily manifests; and over the course of the study the conceptualization of the relationship between northern observer and Sicily as that of doctor and sick patient is implicit throughout. In the last two sections of the study, Franchetti elaborates upon the medical metaphor extensively.

As we saw above, Sicily constitutes an abnormal part of the Italian nation. In the penultimate section, titled – like Villari's last *Letter* – "The Remedies," Franchetti makes it clear that Sicily "must be considered a morbid phenomenon, a form of disorder such that Italy has the duty to suppress it as quickly as possible" (p. 221). Who shall spearhead this radical transformation of Sicilian society? Obviously not the Sicilians, for whom such a state of affairs is normal. They cannot participate in this effort, "for it is precisely their way of feeling and seeing that constitutes the illness to be cured" (p. 221). Franchetti acknowledges that it is important to ask the Sicilians their opinions on the matter –

> but these views, these opinions, should be taken as phenomena, as symptoms of capital importance for the person who aims to discover the nature and process of the illness, not as directive norms for its cure. For a doctor, the patient's complaints of thirst are often a reason not to give him something to drink. Often the sensations about which the patient complains most bitterly are for the doctor a sign that his remedies are working and, vice versa, an apparent improvement a sign that the disease is worsening, and death approaching (p. 221).

Consequently, if the Italian state "wishes to cure the ills of Sicily, it must avail itself of the elements that the Nation provides, to the exclusion of the Sicilians themselves" (pp. 222–3).[25]

The North, then, is invested with all the authority commonly associated with a doctor, while Sicily is reduced to the figure of sick patient, wholly ignorant of its own conditions and consequently unable to make decisions on its own behalf.[26] Sicily is quarantined off from the community of Italians, denied all political agency. The problem, however, as Franchetti notes in the concluding section of his study, is that the ruling élites of central–northern Italy have been remiss in their medical duties. This part of the nation has lacked

> the sense of its duties and its mission towards Sicily and the southern provinces in general. We have received those little sisters of ours who, without a thought for the future, trustingly threw themselves into our arms. They were emaciated, starving, covered with sores, and we should have cared for them lovingly, nourished them, sought by every means, even with fire where necessary, to give them back their health. Instead, without even taking a look at their wounds, we put them to work, the hard, tiring labor of making Italy. We asked for men and money from them, and we gave them a two-bit freedom in return, imported from abroad, and we said to them: grow and multiply. And then after fifteen years we're surprised to see that the wounds have become gangrenous and threaten to infect Italy (p. 238).

This passage introduces a number of important new elements. In the first place, Franchetti clarifies an issue that had remained in the shadows throughout the study: the relationship between Sicily and continental southern Italy. Franchetti had restricted his focus to Sicily over the course of his analysis, or, to be more precise, had restricted his comparisons to those between Sicily and central–northern Italy, effectively blotting out the continental South. If one were to draw up a map of Italy based on Franchetti's observations, it would consist of an Italian peninsula truncated somewhere below Tuscany, across from which would lie the island of Sicily. Franchetti's study is therefore written as if southern Italy did not exist, and this clearly serves to reinforce the image of Sicily's insularity and isolation from mainland civilization. Here, without any further explanation, continental Southern Italy comes to form part of that same downtrodden world.

A second important feature of this passage is Franchetti's addition of a gendered, human element to his representation of Sicily and the South, which infuses the medical imagery of doctor–patient with a sense of familial pathos and big-brotherly protectiveness. At the same time, in the last line of the passage the North loses its doctorly detachment and immunity, becoming instead a part of the same diseased organism. And it is with precisely this view of the problem that Franchetti makes his final appeal in the closing lines of the text.

> Certainly, Italy will be able to survive a long time in the same conditions in which it has lived for the past fifteen years. There are many organic diseases that do not lead to an immediate death. But in a weakened organism, full of germs of decomposition, those same causes that in a healthy body would produce barely noticeable effects, generate a total breakdown. And if this should happen, the first to suffer cruelly would be the members of that class that is unable to understand the responsibility and duties towards the rest of the nation that are imposed upon it by the fact that it alone profits from the liberty of Italy (pp. 237–9).

Sicily is then an anomaly, a holdover from the Middle Ages that threatens the modernity of the mainland with its violence, clientelism, and disregard for the law. It is in short a negation of the bourgeois civilization of the mainland (cf. Mazzamuto 1975: 44–5). Sicily and the mainland are therefore, as I noted earlier, not only different from one another but utterly distinct and, in a sense, antagonistically opposed to one another. What this means is that Franchetti not only represents "Sicily in 1876" but, if you will, "the North in 1876" as well; these two geopolitical blocks are defined in antithetical relation to one another. The North, in other words, becomes, through this contrastive process, more modern, more European, more governed by law and order, than ever before. This is not to say that Franchetti ignores the fact that conditions in many areas of the North can be improved upon. He himself notes that "the social conditions of northern and central Italy leave much to be desired in every respect" (p. 237). But under the pressure of unification, Italy paradoxically splits in two. In Franchetti's text, the imaginary geography of Italy is subjected to a process of polarization of unprecedented force. Only Giustino Fortunato's stark vision of two Italies, distinguished from one another by fundamentally different natural, geographical conditions, would rival and in some sense surpass Franchetti's in argumentative and rhetorical persuasiveness.[27] But Fortunato would not elaborate this dualistic vision in writing until the end of the century. During the 1870s, which is to say at the beginnings of the Meridionalist problematic, it was Franchetti's study that constituted the most rigorous and rhetorically charged elaboration of two distinct Italies, that shaped the conceptual framework within which the country's élites viewed Sicily and the South more generally from that point forward.

Notes

1. I investigate this broader context in my forthcoming book, *Imagining the South: Italy between Europe and Africa*, from which parts of the present essay are drawn.
2. Villari 1885: 173. Henceforth in this section I will refer to the revised 1885 edition of *Le lettere meridionali* only by the page number. *Le lettere meridionali* were first published in book form in 1878 by Le Monnier of Florence. Unless otherwise noted, all translations in this essay are mine.
3. See Salvadori 1976: 37–8; Galasso 1978: 16; Palermo 1974: 67–9; and – with regard to Villari's influence on Salvemini – Garin 1962: 106–9.
4. Turiello 1980: 23n1. Five years later, Turiello wrote at the beginning of *Governo e governati*: "For me, as for others, it was Villari's *Lettere napoletane* [*sic*] – the most widely read book of all [on the South] and the most effective for the authority of its author – that inspired me to pursue these studies" (p. 23). Forty years later, Giustino Fortunato spoke in turn of "the happy year in which Villari's *Lettere meridionali* suddenly called the public's attention to what was and still is our greatest domestic problem" (Fortunato 1927: 164).
5. On Dina's career in Italian politics and journalism, see Chiala 1896–1903, as well as the entry for Dina in the *Dizionario biografico* 1991.
6. Ippolito Nievo, for example, had incisively addressed this problem in his "Frammento sulla rivoluzione nazionale," written in 1859 but not published until 1929 (Nievo 1952). Closer to the historical moment and cultural milieu in which Villari was writing, fellow Neapolitan Angelo Camillo De Meis also took up the question in his *Il Sovrano* of 1868 (De Meis 1927). On the problematic of élites and people more generally in the Risorgimento, see Asor Rosa 1979: 13–48 and, with specific reference to *Il Sovrano*, 1975: 873–8; Colummi Camerino 1975: 5–80; and Gramsci 1971: 44–120, where the issue is central to his interpretation of the Risorgimento.

7. In 1885: 67. This need for Italy to "look inside its own breast" was also the note on which De Sanctis had concluded his *Storia della letteratura italiana* five years earlier (De Sanctis 1991: 846).

8. Echoing the imagery of the "too narrow sphere," Villari also describes the experience in terms of asphyxiation: "It's as if we lack the air to breathe" (p. 69).

9. In 1885: 68–9. For a discussion of the more general disillusionment – or *deprecatio temporum* – expressed by many of the country's élites at this time, see Asor Rosa's important observations in 1975: 821–39.

10. Villari's *Letters* are in fact largely composed of various letters and reports that Villari received from correspondents in Naples and Sicily (among them his sister, Virginia [see Jeuland-Meynaud 1973: 185]); and it is striking with respect to the positivist rhetoric of eyewitness observation that informs the *Letters* – Villari speaks of the necessity of "seeing it with your own eyes" – that the most compelling accounts on the whole are those provided by others.

11. In 1885: 65. Shortly after composing this letter on the *camorra*, Villari wrote to his sister: "If you only knew how indifferent the House is to all social questions – the Left as much or more than the Right – you would understand how terribly difficult it is to speak about such things. No one wants to hear a word of it" (quoted in Cicalese 1979: 133).

12. An 1878 review of Jessie White Mario's *La miseria in Napoli* published in *Nuova antologia* begins: "The impression produced throughout Italy in 1875 by Villari's description of the caves of the so-called cord-makers in his *Lettere meridionali* has not yet faded" (Baer 1878: 330).

13. In 1885: 8–9. Bulferetti also notes this aspect of the *Southern Letters*, observing that it is not their conceptual content but rather their powerful "veristic descriptions" that grab the reader (Bulferetti 1951: 91–2).

14. Contarino notes with respect to the new literature on the "Neapolitan Question" initiated by Villari, and then Jessie White Mario and Renato Fucini, that despite the ideological differences existing among them, "it is striking that what is prevalent in all of them is the idea of Naples's uniqueness as a case of urban underdevelopment" (1989: 669).

15. Jannazzo, in his introduction to *Condizioni economiche*, highlights Franchetti's profoundly European cultural vision (Franchetti 1985: vii–xv).

16. The article, titled "Delle condizioni dei contadini in Italia," was published in the Florentine journal, *La Nazione*, on 12 April 1875, and can now be found in Sonnino 1972: 155–61.

17. Franchetti and Sonnino 1974: vi. Unless otherwise indicated, page references in this section refer to the first volume of this text. As noted above, the original title of the work was *La Sicilia nel 1876*.

18. It is also important to remember that Franchetti and Sonnino conceived of their study, at least in its final stages, as a counter-investigation to the parliamentary inquiry into the conditions in Sicily that was being conducted at around the same time as theirs. As they note at the end of the preface, the commission's final report was released shortly before the publication of their study and, while they express agreement with certain "partial" assessments made by the commission, they dissent from its "general judgments." In a letter to Enea Cavalieri written some time after the book's publication, Franchetti recalls how the authors rushed to publish their studies in time for the parliamentary discussion of the commission's report. For a comparative discussion of the two inquiries, see Renda 1984: 68–88.

19. Mazzamuto recalls the extensive tradition of travel writing on Sicily of which Franchetti was at least partially aware, and makes an argument for a number of links between *Condizioni politiche e amministrative della Sicilia* and Paolo Balsamo's *Il Giornale del viaggio fatto in Sicilia e particolarmente nella contea di Modica* (1808) (1975: 42–4).

20. Dickie provides an astute analysis of the relationship between these two perspectives in his chapter on Villari and Franchetti (1993).

21. Franchetti's demystification of the commonplaces of sunny Sicily can be usefully considered alongside that contemporary counter-discourse produced by Mastriani, Serao, Di Giacomo, *et al.* aimed at undoing what Serao termed the *rettorichetta* of picturesque Naples (see Giammattei 1987: 388–90).

22. Franchetti and Sonnino's various Sicilian hosts are one exception, to whom Franchetti expresses his gratitude in a section titled "Hospitality" (p. 22).

23. The "medievalism" of the South was a familiar trope in post-unification Italian culture. Speaking of Basilicata in a parliamentary discussion of brigandage in 1863, deputy Stefano Castagnola exclaimed: "It's the Middle Ages right under our eyes!" (cited in Villari 1885: 40).

24. See Moe 1992 for a discussion of the use of such medical imagery during the early 1860s.

25. It is important to note that Sonnino, at the conclusion of his study, adopts a much more inclusive view of the role Sicilians should play in the transformation of conditions on the island, nor is the influence of the North viewed in such a univocally positive light: "Left to its own devices, Sicily would find a solution: numerous facts demonstrate this, and it is rendered certain by the intelligence and energy of its population, as well as the immense richness of its resources. A social transformation would necessarily occur, either through the prudent collaboration of its affluent class, or through the effects of some violent revolution. But we Italians of other provinces prevent this from happening. We have legalized the existing oppression; and we guarantee the impunity of the oppressors" (Franchetti and Sonnino 1974, 2: 263). Speaking

of the corruption of the affluent classes he similarly stresses, "I'm talking about three-quarters of Italy, not just Sicily" (p. 265).

26. It was above all this analogy that outraged the first Sicilian readers of *La Sicilia nel 1876* and that Luigi Capuana later termed the "original sin" of their study – that of traveling to Sicily "like doctors to the bed of a sick patient, with the preconception that the sickness of that poor devil was something unusual, complicated, rebellious to the analyses and cures of science" (see Capuana 1892: 18–19; De Mattai 1963: 118–19; Brancato 1975: 10–11).

27. See above all his famous 1904 essay, "La questione meridionale e la riforma tributaria" (Fortunato 1973: 539–41).

References

Asor Rosa, Alberto (1975) *Storia d'Italia*, ed. Ruggiero Romano and Corrado Vivanti. Vol. 4, Part 2: *La Cultura. Dall'Unità a oggi.* Turin: Einaudi.

—— (1979) *Scrittori e popolo. Il populismo nella letteratura italiana contemporanea.* Rome: Savelli.

Baer, Costantino (1878) "La Miseria in Napoli." *Nuova antologia*, 2nd ser., **9** (15 May): 328–40.

Barbagallo, Francesco (1979) "Introduzione." In Pasquale Villari, *Le lettere meridionali ed altri scritti sulla questione sociale in Italia*, pp. 5–19. Naples: Guida.

Brancato, Francesco (1975) " La Sicilia e l'inchiesta del Franchetti e Sonnino." *Nuovi Quaderni del Meridione* **51–52**: 3–16.

Bulferetti, Luigi (1951) *Le ideologie socialistiche in Italia nell'età del positivismo evoluzionistico (1870–1892).* Florence: Le Monnier.

Capuana, Luigi (1892) *La Sicilia e il brigantaggio.* Rome: Stabilimento Tipografico Italiano.

Chabod, Federico (1996) *Italian Foreign Policy. The Statecraft of the Founders.* Princeton: Princeton University Press.

Chiala, Luigi (1896–1903) *Giacomo Dina e l'opera sua nelle vicende del Risorgimento italiano*, 3 vols. Turin: Roux Frassati.

Cicalese, Maria Luisa (1979) *Note per un profilo di Pasquale Villari.* Rome: Istituto Storico Italiano per l'Età Moderna e Contemporanea.

Colummi Camerino, Marinella (1975) *Idillio e Propaganda nella letteratura sociale del Risorgimento.* Naples: Liguori.

Contarino, Rosario (1989) *Letteratura italiana*, Vol 7. Part 3: *Storia e geografia: L'età contemporanea.* Napoli, ed. Alberto Asor Rosa, pp. 653–710. Turin: Einaudi.

Croce, Benedetto (1963) *A History of Italy 1871–1915.* New York: Russell and Russell.

De Mattei, Rodolfo (1963) "L'inchiesta siciliana di Franchetti e Sonnino." *Annali del Mezzogiorno* **3**: 113–47.

De Meis, Angelo Camillo (1927) *Il Sovrano. Saggio di filosofia politica con riferenza all'Italia*, ed. Benedetto Croce. Bari: Laterza.

De Sanctis, Francesco (1991) *Storia della letteratura italiana*, ed. Niccolò Gallo. Milan: Arnoldo Mondadori.

Dickie, John (1993) "The Other Italy, 1860–1900." Ph.D. dissertation, Sussex University, UK.

Dizionario biografico degli italiani (1991) Vol. 40. Rome: Istituto dell'Enciclopedia Italiana.

Fortunato, Giustino (1900) "Corrispondenze napoletane alla 'Rassegna settimanale'." In *Scritti vari*, pp. 309–67. Trani: Vecchi.

—— (1927) *Pagine e ricordi parlamentari*, Vol. 2. Florence: Vallecchi.

—— (1973) *Il Mezzogiorno e lo Stato italiano*, Vol. 1. Florence: Vallecchi.

Franchetti, Leopoldo (1985) *Condizioni economiche e amministrative delle provincie napoletane. Appunti di viaggio – Diario del viaggio*, ed. Antonio Jannazzo. Bari: Laterza.

Franchetti, Leopoldo, and Sidney Sonnino (1974) *Inchiesta in Sicilia* [originally *La Sicilia nel 1876*], 2 vols. Florence: Vallecchi.

Galasso, Giuseppe (1978) *Passato e presente del meridionalismo*, Vol. 1: *Genesi e sviluppi*. Naples: Guida.

Garin, Eugenio (1962) *La cultura italiana tra '800 e '900*. Bari: Laterza.

Gatto, Simone (1950) "Attualità di un'inchiesta del 1876 sulla Sicilia." *Belfagor* **5.2**: 229–33.

Giammattei, Emma (1987) "La letteratura 1860–1970: il 'grande romanzo' di Napoli." In *Napoli*, ed. Giuseppe Galasso, pp. 383–412. Bari: Laterza.

Gramsci, Antonio (1971) *Selections from the Prison Notebooks*, ed. Quintin Hoare and Geoffrey Nowell Smith. New York: International Publishers.

Jannazzo, Antonio (1986) *Sonnino meridionalista*. Bari: Laterza.

Jeuland-Meynaud, Maryse (1973) *La ville de Naples après l'annexion (1860–1915). Essai d'interprétation historique et littéraire*. N.p.: Editions de l'Université de Provence.

Mario, Jessie White (1877) *La miseria in Napoli*. Florence: Le Monnier.

Mazzamuto, Pietro (1975) "La Sicilia di Franchetti e Sonnino e i suoi stereotipi socio-letterari." *Nuovi Quaderni del Meridione* **51–52**: 36–67.

Moe, Nelson (1992) "'Altro che Italia!'. Il Sud dei piemontesi (1860–61)." *Meridiana. Rivista di storia e scienze sociali* **15**: 53–89.

Nievo, Ippolito (1952) *Opere*, ed. Sergio Romagnoli. Milan–Naples: Ricciardi.

Palermo, Antonio (1974) *Da Mastriani a Viviani. Per una storia della letteratura a Napoli fra Otto e Novecento*. Naples: Liguori.

Renda, Francesco (1984) *Storia della Sicilia dal 1860 al 1870*, Vol. 1. Palermo: Sellerio.

Salvadori, Massimo L (1976) *Il mito del buongoverno. La questione meridionale da Cavour a Gramsci*. Turin: Einaudi.

Sonnino, Sidney (1972) *Scritti e discorsi extraparlamentari 1870–1902*, 2 vols, ed. Benjamin F. Brown. Bari: Laterza.

Turiello, Pasquale (1980) *Governo e governati in Italia*, ed. Piero Bevilacqua. Turin: Einaudi.

Villari, Pasquale (1878) *Le lettere meridionali ed altri scritti sulla questione sociale in Italia*. Florence: Le Monnier.

——(1885) *Le lettere meridionali ed altri scritti sulla questione sociale in Italia*, Seconda edizione, riveduta e molto accresciuta dall'Autore. Turin: Fratelli Bocca.

Villari, Rosario (1979) *Mezzogiorno e democrazia*. Bari: Laterza.

3

How Many Italies? Representing the South in Official Statistics

Silvana Patriarca

In the introduction to a collection of essays significantly titled *Mezzogiorno senza meridionalismo*, Giuseppe Giarrizzo has recently recalled the circumstances in which a *meridionalista* discourse first emerged. The first articulation of the "Southern Question" was the work of some representatives of the Historic Right who were reacting to the defeat of their party in the southern regions in the elections of 1874, a defeat that paved the way for the Historic Left to attain power in 1876. Far from being a realization of the socio-economic "backwardness" of the South, the descriptions and denunciations of the conditions of the South produced by conservative reformers such as Pasquale Villari, Leopoldo Franchetti, and Sidney Sonnino in the mid-1870s would essentially represent a political indictment of the southern élites (too corrupt, in their views, to be able to ensure a good government of the country). According to Giarrizzo, there was indeed no perception of a fundamental economic and social dualism of North and South in the 1860s and early 1870s; this perception appeared only later, and was then read back into this earlier period (Giarrizzo 1992: xv). The Southern Question in its beginning would thus be a largely political construct. In this discourse the South was a symbol, a signifier whose referent is to be found essentially in the politics of its makers.

Partly out of a polemical stance against the straitjacket that *meridionalismo* has often represented for the South itself, Giarrizzo provides an essentially political reading of the emergence of the Southern Question in the mid-1870s,[1] an emergence that other scholars have linked to a wider set of intellectual and political developments that shaped Italian society in the early 1870s. Among the conditions that made possible the articulation of the Southern Question at that time we must recall not only the realization of the weakness of the new nation and the mood of disappointment over the poor performance of Italy in the international arena, but especially the new sensitivity of sectors of the Italian élites to the "social question" after the great fear generated by the episode of the Paris Commune (Salvadori 1960: 41; Villari 1961; Arfé 1962). This sensitivity in turn was spurred by the diffusion of a genuine interest and at times enthusiasm for positivism and empirical social investigation on the part of intellectuals and segments of the political élites (Asor Rosa 1975: 913–14; Moe 1994).

Yet Giarrizzo's reading deserves attention because it points to an issue – that of the genesis of the idea of a North–South dualism and of the specific and changing content of this dualism – that it is important to explore more deeply in order to understand the meaning of the Southern Question fully in its discursive dimension. Thanks in particular to some recent studies, it is well known how the South was often represented in the early 1860s, when it appeared as the Other of the Italian nation, as "Africa," a less "civilized" if not wholly primitive land whose inhabitants needed to be brought to order and ruled by a more "civilized" North (Dickie 1992; Moe 1992; Petraccone 1994). Old stereotypes informed the letters and accounts that functionaries, military men, and other individuals involved in the business of government in the South (mostly northerners, but also southerners) sent to their correspondents. This representation coexisted with the idea held throughout the 1860s that the South was a naturally rich land that only corrupt political institutions had ruined – a belief fostered by a scant knowledge about the South and by the forward-looking attitudes of the mostly northern élites (Salvadori 1960: 28 ff.; Villari 1961: 69–70; Ragionieri 1967: 81 ff.). But were political passions, stereotypes, and myths all there was in the image of the South that circulated in the first years of existence of the new state?

Needless to say, this is a rhetorical question, which would appear to demand a reference to the reality behind the representation. In what follows, however, I will not invoke this reality, but will focus my attention on what today's social scientists would call "hard data," i.e. quantitative information, and treat them as a representation. Following what was already common practice elsewhere, the new Italian state immediately after its establishment began to assemble a "positive" and "scientific" knowledge of the new country and of its various components through the collection and publication of statistics.[2] Thus from the 1860s on, the national élites came to know the South not only through the accounts of military men and politicians, but also through that state knowledge *par excellence*, namely statistics. Statistics was then considered a "governmental science" and a method that produced what was believed to be an objective and scientific evaluation of the level of "civilization" of a country. It constituted an actual institution of the new state, recognized as such by its makers, and it even functioned, as Raffaele Romanelli has observed, as the "official ideology of the state and its apparatus" (Romanelli 1980: 769). But statistics in the plural – in the sense of the actual numbers – were also the most authoritative mode of knowing and representing the social world in an era in which an important segment of the national élites hailed positivism as their new faith. Members of parliament frequently referred to official statistics in their debates and arguments; teachers in secondary schools and university professors used these numbers in their manuals and courses;

publicists popularized them in journals and writings that had the function of "making the country known to itself."

It is the image of the South constructed through the authoritative practice of statistics that we must examine in order to understand more fully whether and to what extent the South appeared as a distinct socio-economic reality, if not an altogether distinct "civilization," in the 1860s and early 1870s, a reality that stood out in contrast to the rest of the country. Was there a South in Italian official statistics before the articulation of the Southern Question? What did the state statisticians read into their numbers? In what way have statistics contributed to the "dualization" of Italy, to the definition of the image of the "two Italies" that since its appearance has maintained a central place not only in Italian political and scholarly debates but also in the collective self-representation of the country? These are the questions that I shall try to approach in this essay by looking primarily at official publications and focusing in particular on the period 1861–1875. I shall also examine how some social observers external to the state apparatus used these numbers in the later part of the century to articulate the paradigm of the "two Italies," and finally I shall conclude by looking at some more recent, and somehow paradoxical, developments in the representation of the country constructed and diffused through the means of official statistics.

Before the Southern Question: The South in the Statistics of the 1860s and Early 1870s[3]

The most important statistics of the first decade of existence of the new state were undoubtedly those on population. Demographic data occupied a fundamental role in the symptomatology of the national "body." The census formed the "basis of any statistical and economic inquiry," and the study of population movements was supposed to reveal the "laws according to which the nation preserves or renovates itself," as we read in the introduction to the first volume of the series (MAIC 1864a: viii). Together these investigations constituted the review of the "vital forces" of the nation. Moreover, as state statisticians faced severe difficulties in collecting quantitative data on the economy, demographic data served as the principal indicator of the condition of the country.[4] The other kinds of quantitative data that the Milanese Pietro Maestri, the head of the Divisione (later called Direzione) di statistica generale from 1862 to 1871, and his collaborators were able to collect and publish concerned mostly the working of state and local institutions (for example the finances of communes and provinces) and of all those institutions and practices that characterized a modern state, such as elections, schools, savings banks, mutual aid societies, and so on. The new state made a conscious effort to spread the knowledge gathered by the statistical service. About a thousand copies of each publication were distributed free (ISTAT 1936: 38). "Popular" editions of these works were also published, such as the one on the census results containing Maestri's own introductions to the data (MAIC 1867a), and the *Annuario statistico italiano* (1864) edited by Maestri and by another Milanese, Cesare Correnti, then member of the Giunta centrale di statistica (the central advisory committee on statistics) as well as a center-left member of parliament.

Needless to say, these men were not statisticians in the modern sense of the word. Maestri held a degree in medicine from the University of Pavia; Correnti had received a degree in law from the same university. Both had been illustrious participants in the struggle for national independence, to which they had also contributed on the cultural front with works of empirico-statistical investigation. The democratic and federalist leanings of Maestri were well known – although after 1861 he chose to be involved almost exclusively with his work at the Direzione. Correnti was a politically more moderate figure, who held several government positions in the governments of the Historic Right before contributing to the rise to power of the Historic Left. Both believed in the fundamental role of statistical knowledge for the building of liberal institutions; both had been and still were in favor of a less centralized state.[5]

The official publications containing the statistics collected by the Direzione were always introduced by detailed analyses entitled "general considerations" (probably written by Maestri, though unsigned) aiming to define the patterns, extract the meanings, and provide an explanation of the numerical results. Most importantly, they constructed and proposed a specific reading of the national territory. In what follows I will examine in detail the statisticians' own analyses of the data collected to see what the numbers revealed to them – or, better, to see how they made the numbers "speak." As Pasquale Villani has observed, in contrast with the more technical and "neutral" tone that characterized the comments to the data in later years, these analyses were candid about the beliefs and convictions of their authors (Villani 1978: 885–6). They allow us to see clearly their expect-ations and biases, the schemes that ordered their approach to the figures, but also to have a sense of what they discovered outside of these schemes, of the kind of negotiation taking place between official interpreters and the mass of data, which were supposed to provide, as Maestri observed, "a description of the people made by the people themselves" (MAIC 1865: xxii).

The three volumes on the census of 1861, published in 1864–6, provided an overall picture of the population. Volume 1 classified the population on the basis of its territorial distribution by communes, districts, provinces, and *compartimenti* (compartments) (MAIC 1864b). Volume 2 presented its age distribution, sex structure, domestic status, and literacy, and gave information on the electorate (MAIC 1865). Volume 3 showed the distribution of the population by occupation, language, origins, and religion (MAIC 1866a). In the tables accompanying the comments, probably written by Maestri, figures were aggregated and compared by compartments, by provinces, and by urban and rural communes (defined as having more or less than 6,000 inhabitants). The deployment of these various units of observation and reporting was very uneven. It was the grid of the compartments, always arranged "geographically" from the northern to the southern ones, that dominated the analysis of the data as a whole. Data aggregated by provinces episodically accompanied the aggregation by compartments and were always listed in alphabetical order. The reporting of data by urban and rural communes was more frequent than that by provinces, but less common than that by compartments.

Elsewhere I have discussed in detail the genesis of the compartments, the predecessors of today's "regions" (Patriarca 1996). Maestri introduced them in 1864 (they were not actual administrative units like the provinces). While in the census volumes the compartments were closely modeled after the old states (with the Kingdom of the Two Sicilies significantly divided into "Provincie Napoletane" and Sicily), the new compartments introduced in 1864 exhibited more variations (for example the "Provincie Napoletane" were replaced by five smaller sub-divisions). As a supporter of Cattaneo's federalistic views and thus of forms of regional devolution, Maestri maintained that his compartments would provide a more "homogeneous and proportionate partition of population and territory" than the existing uneven partition by provinces, since they reproduced the "territorial divisions based on the nature of the soil and on the laws of economic convenience" (MAIC 1864c: vi). Not only did they make more sense from an administrative and political standpoint; they would also provide a better tool for comparison.

"North" and "South" did not appear as reporting units in the official statistical publications of the 1860s (in fact they began to appear regularly, as we will see, only in recent times); however, in the comments themselves compartments were sometimes aggregated to form larger units: northern, central and southern Italy, or *alta* (higher, namely northern) and *bassa* (lower, namely southern) *Italia* were the most common. These were fairly conventional partitions of the peninsula used by geographers and statisticians in earlier times. The boundaries of these larger units, however, were quite mobile and opinions about them varied. For example the Tuscan economist and statesman Luigi Serristori in his *Saggio statistico dell' Italia* (1833) observed that Italy could be divided into two parts, one including the continental part of the Kingdom of Sardinia-Piedmont, Lombardy-Venetia, the Duchies of Parma and Modena and the part of the Papal territory corresponding to the Emilia, and the other including all the rest of the peninsula and the islands. Distinctive geographies, climates, agricultural products, and patterns of popular mores, he claimed, characterized the two areas. In his *Corografia fisica, storica e statistica dell' Italia e delle sue isole* (1845) another Tuscan, the geographer and statistician Attilio Zuccagni Orlandini, divided Italy into four parts (Northern,

Central, Southern, and the Islands) claiming that the Italian peninsula let itself easily be divided in such a fashion along "natural" lines (vol. 1: 123). Now these subdivisions were bound to assume new meanings in the context of a politically unified Italy and in connection with the statisticians' desire to find the "laws" of the new national society, laws that found expression in statistical averages and rates (and for some consisted in them) and could help to identify the causes of social growth and decline. The search for social laws, reflecting the increasing influence in postunification Italy of Adolphe Quetelet's conception of statistics as a "numerical social science of laws" (Porter 1986: 41) and not just a descriptive enterprise, introduced a naturalistic, if not deterministic, outlook that had been generally absent in previous works.

The introduction to the first volume of the census stressed how the distribution of communes by size and of population densities showed the existence of distinct patterns of settlement in various areas of the country. While Sicily and the "Provincie Napoletane" had the highest percentages of their populations living in agglomerations with more than 6,000 inhabitants, and Lombardy and Sardinia in agglomerations with fewer than 6,000, in the rest of Italy, and especially in present-day Emilia-Romagna and in central Italy, the majority of the population was scattered in the countryside. These distinctive patterns of settlement bore a relation to distinctive patterns of landownership in the various areas (MAIC 1864b: xxi–xxvi).

The same attention to regional variation was expressed also in the analysis of people's occupations and their various kinds of "industry." The preference for, indeed the idealization of small landownership and of sharecropping – an essential component of that paternalistically progressive ideology shared by many Risorgimento figures (Villani 1978: 891–3) – made Maestri contrast areas with higher percentages of peasant owners, such as Piedmont and Liguria, with the "southern provinces," i.e. "Naples" and Sicily, but also with those areas in the northern regions where laborers had to sell their labor on a daily basis (MAIC 1867a: 84–5). As for manufacturing industry, Maestri distrusted the census results, which showed higher percentages of people so occupied in the "Neapolitan and Sicilian provinces", and attributed them to the concentration of the southern population in towns, where they were more easily identified as "industrial" "for whatever little they did in the arts or crafts" ("per poco che vi esercitassero qualche arte o mestiere") (MAIC 1867a: 90). Clearly other areas of the country were more industrialized: "The parts of Italy which are most industrious are exactly those which have the richest agriculture" (MAIC 1867a: 90).[6]

Although there was no South as a <u>unit of reporting</u>, existing ideas about the former Kingdom of Two Sicilies as a whole and about its population directed the gaze of the commentator – favored in particular by that broad unit used in the first census's volumes, the "Provincie Napoletane." However, the existence of distinct patterns neatly opposing northern and southern compartments was emphasized only in a couple of places: with respect to the life cycle of individuals, where a distinction was made between "sturdy boreal [i.e. northern] generations" and "precocious southern natures" (MAIC 1865: vii) and with respect to the sex ratio, about which it was observed that "the smaller number of men, compared to women" in southern Italy was "a normal condition" accentuated by emigration and the "scourge of brigandage" (MAIC 1864b: xxviii). There were considerable differences also with regards to levels of literacy and the composition of the electorate, but enough variety could be found outside the "Provincie Napoletane" to make impossible the construction of an image of the nation along a simple North–South opposition.

The analysis of other statistical reports seems to support this evaluation. Let us look at those on the numbers of births, marriages, and deaths, which attracted more anxious scrutiny than the census, since they were supposed to reflect a changing current situation, and not a state of things that had been inherited from the past. In the belief that the positive effects of the new political order should very soon make their appearance, the principal interpretative effort in the volumes on population movements aimed at determining whether, and where, the population increased or decreased. The same units of reporting and comparison used in the volumes on the census, namely urban and rural communes, and, more importantly, the compartments, framed the analysis of the data; the provinces had virtually disappeared, with a couple of exceptions.[7]

The comparison between city and countryside, urban and rural communes, did not seem to yield the expected results. To the question whether it was an urban or a rural environment that was more conducive to population growth there were no clear answers. The first data on population movements seemed to point to a lesser "vitality" of the urban populations. However, this was in part an "artificial" result, an outcome of the higher mortality rate to be found among the poor of the countryside who went to the cities to find relief in hospitals and other institutions (MAIC 1864a: xxv). Both in the countryside and in the cities, high birth rates were accompanied by high levels of mortality, and especially by high infant mortality. Thus Maestri had to admit that "in Italy among both the populations of urban communes and those of rural municipalities, mortality reaches a proportion that has few examples elsewhere; to the point that the very increase of inhabitants is to be considered not as the effect of long life, but rather as the result of a larger number of births over deaths . . ." (MAIC 1864a: xxvi). Italy as a whole, the official commentator regretfully concluded, seemed unable to preserve its "vital forces." In the following years, the comparison of the annual natural increase in rural and urban communes showed the former consistently above the latter, a result that was at the same time cause for surprise (as it ran against developments observed in other countries), and for some satisfaction, since the rural communes remained "a rich reservoir of forces for themselves and for the larger urban agglomerations . . ." (MAIC 1866b: lxix). Yet, in the absence of data on emigration from the countryside to the cities, these results did not mean much, and the overall comparison between the vitality of rural and urban communes was abandoned after 1869.

It was, however, the grid of the compartments that was privileged in the assessment and comparison of the overall levels of "vitality" of the population. As summary results and indicators were all presented by compartments, these clearly offered the organizing frame for making sense of the figures. Maestri chose six demographic indicators (reduced to five in 1865) to determine synthetically the compartments' rank on a kind of "ladder of vitality": the ratio of births to deaths, the fertility of marriages, population growth (replaced, for no specified reason, in 1863 by *male* population growth), mean and probable length of life (replaced by "longevity" in 1865) and "premature" deaths (of people less than fifteen years old). With a few exceptions, the southern compartments appeared consistently placed in the lowest positions. Initially, the commentator related the differences observed among compartments to the political conditions existing in those areas prior to unification and – in the rare case a positive change occurred in a compartment – to the revitalizing impact of Unification. The well-marked territorial diversity revealed by these figures was considered a relic of the past, a relic that – it was his repeated wish – would disappear through the provisions of the new liberal institutions and the consequent revitalization of the economy.[8] The historical explanation, however, grew less adequate in view of the stability of the pattern that emerged through the years; and it was finally abandoned after 1866. No alternative explanation took its place. Indeed the comments on the results of ranking – results that discredited the early optimistic expectations regarding the impact of liberal institutions – became increasingly laconic; and as a result also of flaws in the accuracy of the measurements employed as indicators themselves, ranking was abandoned in 1870.

Besides presenting and analysing demographic data, the volumes on population movements also reported the anthropometric data on conscripts collected by army doctors.[9] The statisticians used these data as indicators of the physical appearance and health of the population. Starting in 1863, they drew a picture of the bodily characteristics of the population based on the percentages of rejections of conscripts on account of insufficient height or illness and deformity. The results of these investigations showed that relatively taller people were more numerous in the northern regions and Tuscany, while relatively shorter heights characterized the southern population (MAIC 1864c: xl). Heights followed a "*topographical law*, so to speak, which can be represented through a curve. This curve, reaching its peak in central Italy and precisely in Tuscany, slopes down on both sides in such a way that the slope is slightest northwards and maximum southwards [my emphasis]" (ibid.: xli). These results would later be interpreted by positivist anthropology as evidence that two "races" inhabited the Italian nation. In the 1860s and early 1870s, however, the state statisticians did not speculate on how these results should be explained. Moreover, the data on the rejections of conscripts due to health problems showed a somewhat compensating pattern: people in bad health conditions were more numerous among the taller inhabitants of the northern and central regions (Lombardy surpassed all other areas in this respect), while, with the exception of Sicily, healthier bodies were more numerous among the shorter inhabitants of the southern compartments.

Another kind of data seemed to offer starker evidence of the existence of a cleavage between two distinctive parts of Italy. These were the data on "violent deaths," namely deaths by accident, suicides, and homicides, which began to be published in the volume on vital statistics of 1864. This investigation was conceived as a first step towards the creation of a much desired corpus of medical statistics, but also had a direct relevance for measuring levels of "civilization" within the national community, as it allowed for assessing the "different attitudes and moral predispositions of [the Italian] people" (MAIC 1866b: lvi). "Some of these deaths," Maestri maintained, were "the consequence of little-advanced civilization, while others, unfortunately, must be considered the result of passions and dangers to which modern progress exposes us" (ibid.). The statistics on homicides exhibited a clear geographical pattern. The data for 1866 showed the Kingdom divided into two distinct parts; in one of them the homicide rate was almost five times higher than in the other:

> With regard to the number of homicides Italy *can be divided topographically into two distinct parts*, of which the first one includes the Northern and Western provinces (Piedmont, Lombardy, Emilia, Liguria, and Tuscany) and the second one the Eastern and Southern ones (the Marches, Umbria, Neapolitan Provinces, Sicily, and Sardinia). In the former, homicides are relatively less numerous (on average 5.23 per 100,000 people); in the latter, this ratio reaches 23.64 per 100,000." [my emphasis] (MAIC 1868: xxviii).

But three years later, the boundaries of the area with a higher homicide rate had slightly changed. Marche and Umbria were now included within the area defined by a lower number of homicides (MAIC 1871: xvi). It is important to observe that in reality not all the areas included in the "Neapolitan Provinces" exhibited the same high rates of victims of homicide. For example Apulia and Basilicata often had lower rates than Umbria, a fact that the construction of a general average for the whole South tended to obscure.

How was this dualistic distribution explained? The difference was immediately traced back to diverse and long-standing local habits determining that in "certain

Italian regions a given kind of violent, accidental or voluntary death is either very frequent, or altogether absent" (MAIC 1866b: lvi). Yet it was not only a matter of local peculiarities originating in generic local habits. In the commentary on the data for 1867 the two distinct parts had become "very distinct." This was a cause of some worry for Maestri, who added emphatically (after quoting from a patriotic poem emphasizing the cultural unity of Italians) that "it is three centuries of bad foreign and local dominations, of religious prejudices and baneful civil and economic theories that reflect and explain these strange figures [cotesta stranezza di cifre]" (MAIC 1869: xxiv). History again, more than cultural traditions, explained the regional differentials of violent crime rates, in the same way that it also explained the very high percentages of illiteracy in the southern regions.[10]

We have focused so far on the interpretation of demographic statistics. But the territorial frame also organized the reading of other kinds of statistics: for example those on elections and the electorate, scrutinized in order to measure the greater or smaller "political vitality" of the various parts of Italy. In the effort to consider the question "in general and in large masses," two distinct areas were identified: in the first one, *Italia superiore* (including Tuscany but excluding Emilia), electors *per contribuzioni* (those who met the necessary tax requirement) were dominant, while in the *Italia meridionale e media* electors *per capacità* (those who were electors by virtue of their belonging to a particular occupational category – state employees or people exercising a liberal profession) were more numerous, a distinction which the commentator linked to the "special economic conditions of the two parts of the Kingdom, namely to the more developed industrial activity and the more diffused and distributed wealth of the *settentrione* [North] and to the opposite conditions in the *mezzodi* [South]," as well as to other factors such as the level of literacy (MAIC 1867b: xxxiii). In contrast, if one examined the percentage of electors who actually voted, the Veneto and Southern Italy exhibited much higher averages than the Center and the North, thus showing the greater "diligence" of their electors, but also reflecting the advantages of a more con-centrated pattern of residence.

As for the crime statistics made available by the Ministry of Justice, the volumes published in the 1860s and early 1870s did not provide very detailed elaborations and analysis of the data. Some official commentators such as the vice-president of the tribunal of Florence, Giorgio Curcio, remarked that violent crime was more widespread in the southern regions because of the "impetuous and vivacious temperament of those populations" (Curcio 1873: 23). But, as we read in the introduction to the judicial statistics of 1869 authored by the Minister of Justice Giovanni De Falco, the "passionate desire for personal vendettas" found in some provinces "in which the moral and material progress of civil life [was] less widespread" was a phenomenon destined to disappear. It was "legitimate to hope" – the Minister went on – "that time and changing conditions will gradually eliminate the causes and the effects of these deplorable habits" (Ministero di Grazia e Giustizia 1871: viii).

If we go back now to our original question about the existence of a perception of a socio-economic dualism in Italy before the first articulation of the Southern Question, we can outline some general considerations. As I mentioned earlier, although there existed a fairly accurate knowledge of the variation in the structure of property relations in the countryside across the national territory, precise data on the economy were lacking. Quantification remained largely limited to the demographic and institutional elements we have just examined. References to a North–South opposition were not absent from the comments that made official sense of the statistics; the boundaries between these two areas, however, were not yet rigidly fixed. Undoubtedly, the comments reveal a greater sensitivity to the variety of situations in the northern and central parts of the country than in the South (which tended to be referred to as a whole, as a distinct entity even after the broad compartment "Neapolitan provinces" was replaced with five others). We could say that the southern compartments were less individualized than the others – as appears clearly in the analysis of violent deaths. In other words, an existing scheme or representation of the territory, heavily shaped by previous political arrangements, oriented the reading of the new information provided by the figures. The numbers gave not only the blessing of science, but also a concrete, "factual" body to territorial entities, making comparison more immediate. And the very statistical procedures of data aggregation tended to emphasize the larger sub-divisions of the national territory.

Even when the comparison of various statistical indicators by compartments resulted in marking the distinctiveness of the southern regions, their difference from the general mean was a quantitative difference of degree and did not yet imply a qualitative or essential opposition between North and South. The very averages for the northern areas, in any event, were not something the statisticians felt very proud of. Their faith in the virtue of good administration, their conviction that in any event change was possible, and in fact inevitable, if only the principles of good (namely liberal) government were applied, made the results appear as a temporary outcome. This belief existed in a tension with that search for the "laws" or regularities characterizing the life of the "social body" that the statisticians also tried to pursue when they analysed the figures. Indeed, the statistical idea of law tended to posit an underlying being of which means and rates were the expression. This did not fit too well with the belief in historical change effected through human intervention that also informed the outlook of the statisticians. It would take another intellectual and political climate, producing less historically minded observers, for different averages and rates to become the signs of essential differences within the "body" of the nation.

On the Making of the Paradigm of the "Two Italies"

The spread of biological evolutionism and racial determinism in the later part of the century provided this climate. In the 1890s, in the midst of social unrest and the most severe crisis yet to be experienced by the Italian state, the persistence of statistical differentials between northern and southern regions came to be read as the expression of an essential difference, a difference inscribed in the bodies and minds not only of individuals but of whole peoples and that characterized whole societies. This reading of Italian society came from the followers of Lombroso, in particular the Sicilian, Alfredo Niceforo, who was one of the first to use the expression "two Italies" for which Giustino Fortunato claimed paternity.[11]

Niceforo proclaimed his faith in statistics at the very beginning of his *L'Italia barbara contemporanea* (1898):

> Statistics — which ignorant or malicious people consider a humble handmaid to this or that opinion . . . — is in fact a truly marvelous precision instrument to investigate social phenomena. These can be placed in two great categories: those that pertain to inferior civilizations, and those that characterize superior civilizations. Statistics has this magic power: it can — through the miraculous language of its figures — indicate if a given phenomenon, expressed by numbers, belongs to one or the other civilization (p. 15).

Accordingly, he proceeded to show how northern and southern Italy exhibited different patterns of crimes (he used a distinction made by the economist and statistician Angelo Messedaglia in 1879 between a criminality distinctive of "civilization" and one distinctive of "barbarism" as epigraph to the chapter devoted to these data), levels of literacy, birth rates, suicide and mortality rates, distribution of modern industry, and modes of agriculture. In fact there was much else in the book beside numbers: claims about general features of social life in the southern regions and especially about the character of southerners (and northerners too for that matter), which had little to do with any "positive" evidence, but were the repository of stereotypes of both old and new coinage. There is no need to recall here Niceforo's vast apparatus of oppositions that defined the two "races" ("Mediterranean" southerners, by nature individualist and not inclined to life in society, and "Aryan" northerners who had a more developed social sentiment and were thus better placed to deal with the requirements of modern society; northerners more cold and thoughtful, southerners more instinctive and easily aroused, and so on): some of them have entered the "collective imaginary" of contemporary Italians.

In a new work published three years later with the purpose of responding to his critics, *Italiani del Nord e Italiani del Sud* (1901), Niceforo restated more fully his theses about the two different "races" inhabiting the Italian peninsula and more systematically subjected his descriptive material to the "discipline" of statistics. He deployed this time a much larger armory of numerical evidence both in the text and in numerous tables and bar charts at the end of each chapter: 133 numerical tables and 31 graphs, to be exact, as the subtitle specified. As a good positivist, Niceforo invited his critics to pay attention to the authority of the "long series of facts" that he had accumulated in support of his views. Now even more "indices" pointed to the alleged radical difference between the "two Italies": both fairly traditional ones such as population density and patterns of urbanization, which had been serving as indicators of "civilization" at least since the 1830s, and new ones such as the diffusion of democratic ideas as measured by the percentage of socialists in municipal councils. Niceforo was actually in trouble when attempting to show the different psychology of the two "races" with the help of numbers, and had to infer it from the different climates of the places they inhabited. But consistency was apparently not a great concern in his discourse.

It is ironic that while he spoke of two Italies, Niceforo's statistical tables in fact always reported data on three Italies: North, Center and South – with Sicily and Sardinia often apart as extreme examples of "southernness." Conveniently, most of the time the Center exhibited values that were in between those of the North and those of the South, thus appearing like a vast borderland in which the two races coexisted ("Aryans" in Tuscany and "Mediterraneans" in the rest of the area), generating medium values. However, the author did not explain the rationale for this partition, and it is very likely that he resorted to it in order to generate more contrasting averages between North and South and thus to stengthen his thesis about the two civilizations.

As Niceforo's critics were quick to point out, his "facts" were not enough to prove his racial explanations; explanations which pointed to the role of socio-historical factors in determining the conditions of the South made much more sense. To be sure, Niceforo did not completely exclude the role of socio-economic factors; but he always inscribed them within his anthropological and racial scheme of interpretation.[12] For example, when he noticed the more widespread poverty among the population of the South, he saw it as a factor that had contributed in the course of history to higher levels of "organic degeneration" and had slowed, if not paralysed, the advancement of that population. This insistence on anthropological diversity was partly functional to the politics of the anthropological school, which was strongly opposed to the centralized structure of the state and called for a federalist reform and the introduction of regional legislation. This could deal more adequately, in their view, with the profoundly different characters of the northern and southern peoples.

State statisticians did not sponsor the work of Lombroso and his followers (Pazzagli 1980: 807–8). Although they all shared a positivist outlook, a faith in "objective" science and "positive" knowledge, the simplifying biological determinism of the Lombrosians – not to mention their more than cursory treatment of numbers – never appealed to these researchers, who embraced more complex explanatory paradigms. A political contrast also opposed state statisticians and Lombrosians, since the former remained wedded to liberal and unitary views, while the latter were staunch critics of the centralized state. Questionable new "sciences" such as criminal anthropology and the biological and racial readings of Italy and its people received, however, unwitting support from the steady diffusion of statistical data on the physical characteristics of the population that was carried out by state statisticians. We have seen how in the mid-1860s Maestri and his collaborators, in the attempt to provide a detailed picture of the national population, began to publish the anthropometric data collected by army doctors in the volumes containing data on population movements. Colorful tables showing the differential distribution of the height of conscripts in the national territory were then published by the Central Statistical Office in the late 1870s and early 1880s (MAIC 1878 and 1882). These data abundantly provided very usable evidence for positivist social observers and anthropologists with a racist bent, such as Niceforo and other Lombrosians.

By calling attention to the role of statistics in the making of the "two Italies" I intend not only to point to the legitimation that certain statistical data could offer to a racist discourse, but also to question the effects of identifying differences primarily by means of statistics and by the "facts" highlighted by statistics. Official statistics establish what constitutes significant and authoritative evidence about the state of a given country or its internal subdivisions. They direct the gaze of the observer towards certain facts, those that are and can be translated into numbers. Undoubtedly many of these facts were and are revealing, and indeed are often indispensable for the tasks facing reformers and state administrations alike; but their use tends to re-enforce a classificatory and oppositional way of thinking. A recent example of this thinking may be seen in Robert Putnam's quantitative analysis of the degree of "civicness" to be found in the northern and southern regions of Italy (Putnam 1993). In late nineteenth-century Italy, the positivist method and the extensive reliance on statistics, I suggest, contributed to establish the kind of "comparativist" and non-relational approach that has characterized a large part of the debate on the Southern Question and a long tradition of studies on the South.[13]

More Than Two Italies, Only One South

The image of the two Italies that dominates the work of late nineteenth-century criminal anthropologists and *meridionalisti à la* Fortunato did not have at the time an equivalent in the units of reporting used in official statistics (although, as we have seen, references to the larger subdivisions of Italy – northern, central, and southern – appeared in the introductions to various statistical publications). How and when did "North" and "South" begin to appear as stable units of reporting? The volumes of the statistical yearbook series, which began to be published in 1878, have always maintained as principal units the same ones I described earlier (of course with some variations in their boundaries mostly due to changes in the national frontiers), namely compartments or regions and, in a subordinate role, provinces (MAIC 1878–1995).[14] During the fascist period one can find some scattered references to the larger subdivisions (North, Center, South),[15] but it is not until the period after the Second World War that these appear as stable units of reporting in the official statistical yearbooks.

A partition of Italy into the conventional four sections (northern, central, southern, and islands) appeared in the yearbook covering the period 1944–8 – but disappeared again in 1951. It was in 1958 that some of the tables in the yearbooks began to exhibit three statistical *ripartizioni* (subdivisions): the first one corresponding to the North-West, the second one to the North-East and Center (excluding the southern provinces of Lazio), and the third one to the South plus the islands and southern Lazio. This division, which replaced a previous one by agrarian regions, was used only in the tables on the physical characteristics of the territory, in some graphs, and, starting in 1960, in the tables on territorial economic accounting (in this case all of Lazio was included in the second *ripartizione*). According to the statisticians themselves, this new tripartite division was introduced mainly to serve a disaggregated study of national accounting (Istituto centrale di statistica 1960: xi–xv). The three areas had distinct economic profiles: the North-West was the most industrialized, the North-East and Center had a strong agriculture and an incipient industrial base, and the South was mostly agricultural. This division, with some variation, has constituted the basis for the image of the "three Italies" popularized by sociologist Arnaldo Bagnasco in his tripartite model of the economic development of the Italian peninsula (Bagnasco 1993).

The three statistical *ripartizioni* introduced in 1958 reflected also the renewed political interest in the South in the period after the Second World War, when it became the object of a special intervention and a recipient of special state funding through the institution of the Cassa per il Mezzogiorno. The monitoring of change in the South *vis-à-vis* the other parts of the country then became a priority for planners. Institutions such as the Associazione per lo sviluppo dell' industria nel Mezzogiorno (SVIMEZ), created in 1947, started to produce quantitative research and publications of statistical data focusing on the North–South division (SVIMEZ 1954, 1961, 1978). In the yearbooks, however, only in 1979 were two new units of reporting added for almost all data (they appear at the bottom of each table after the regional and national totals), namely "North–Center" and "Mezzogiorno," in some cases subdivided into, respectively, North-West, North-East, Center, and

Southern Italy and Islands. The specific rationale for this innovation is unknown, but it is ironic that the distinction North–South was stabilized and generalized in official statistical publications at about the time when historians and social scientists increasingly tended to reject the category of the South as a single unit of observation and analysis and proceeded to disaggregate it into its multiple components.[16]

In this essay I have not intended to deny the existence of actual differences between regions in Italy – that would clearly amount to an absurd position. Nor have I argued that the lines that divide the territory of a state are just the inventions of administrators and statisticians. In fact, they often have deep roots in complex historical events and processes – one may mention, as an obvious case for comparison with Italy, the South of the United States.[17] But these divisions tend to become naturalized and taken for granted instead of being properly historicized and subjected to questioning. While a nation like Italy is certainly not a homogeneous reality, its regional division is often taken to be a kind of indisputable truth, vulgarized to the level of a cliché. Yet, like the nation, the region too, and the macroregion, far from being natural entities, have a history. So do their statistics. This chapter is intended to be a contribution to a rethinking and a more critical reconstruction of these connected histories, one that takes into consideration the contribution of representations in the making of realities.

Acknowledgments

I would like to express my gratitude to Paolo Macry and to the members of the conference on the Italian Southern Question for their useful criticism and suggestions.

Notes

1. He is not alone in this: see also an old work by Procacci 1956, and more recently Donzelli 1990: 46–7.
2. I should make clear here that by the term knowledge I mean a practice that is itself partly "constitutive" of reality rather than a mere discovery of things "out there" (although it is useful to preserve the idea of discovery in order to point out the presence of gaps between the expectations of the investigators and what they come to see by applying certain methods of investigation). The reference here is of course M. Foucault, especially the works of his early period (Foucault 1972, 1973).

3. Some paragraphs in the next two sections of this essay have already appeared in a slightly modified version in Chapter 5 and the epilogue of my book (Patriarca 1996). I am grateful to Cambridge University Press for permission to reprint them here.

4. In 1862 an attempt to take a census of "manufacturing industry" failed completely (the attempt was not repeated until 1911); some data on agricultural production were collected by the prefects, but no agricultural census was taken before 1930.

5. On Correnti see *Dizionario Biografico degli Italiani*, s.v. There are no recent biographies of Maestri. On his work as a "statistician" see Patriarca 1996. For more details on his politics see Della Peruta 1990.

6. Maestri had some acquaintance with the topic as the author of a detailed study on manufacturing industry in the Italian states published in the Piedmontese *Rivista contemporanea* in 1858, and reproduced or summarized also in other journals.

7. Provinces were used as reporting units in the commentary only in the case of literacy rates (measured by the signatures of spouses) and for examining the relation between variations in grain prices and variations in the number of marriages and deaths. Several demographic measures reported by provinces can be found also in tables at the end of the volume on population movements for 1864 (MAIC 1866b).

8. For example, commenting upon the data on illiteracy, Maestri observed how they "were not the fruit of the new civil institutions, but on the contrary the result of a state of things which fortunately does not exist any longer" adding that "the second Italian census will find the state of public education improved" (MAIC 1865: xxvi).

9. On these studies see Farolfi 1979.

10. Significantly, the urban–rural comparison used, as we saw, in the analysis of demographic data did not appear at all in the comments on this kind of "moral statistics" – a sign that, in spite of the fairly frequent episodes of urban unrest, cities were not perceived as a particular threat to the social and political order (nor were they growing enough at the time to be perceived as such).

11. See his letter to F. Severini (27 March 1911) cited in Romano 1945: 80, note 15.

12. On this see also Farolfi 1984: 1209, and Teti 1993.

13. On the predominance of the comparativist approach see also Galasso 1991: 2.

14. I limited my systematic perusal to this series and to the volumes of the censuses because they have the largest circulation. I did a less comprehensive check of other series (such as the population movement volumes), which confirmed the conclusions I reached for the former.

15. See for example the yearbook of 1933. Also the introductions to the censuses published in the 1930s aggregated some data by these larger subdivisions.

16. The results of this new trend are visible in particular in the work of that group of scholars which in the mid-1980s founded the Istituto per lo studio della società meridionale (IMES) and created the journal *Meridiana*. In an article (published in this journal) that is one of the most lucid contributions to the rethinking of the Southern Question to appear in recent years, Carmine Donzelli has significantly questioned the excessive reliance of researchers on the South as a unit of analysis and their forgetting that it is one "statistical aggregate" among several possible ones (1990: 23, note 6). On this new historiographic trend see also J. Davis, "The Peculiarities of the South Reconsidered" (Chapter 9 in this volume).

17. The matrix of the unit of reporting called South in the official statistics of the US is to be found in the secessionist states (although the correspondence is only partial, as Barbara Fields has made me notice). Regional units of statistical reporting called "geographical divisions" appear, however, already before the Civil War. A comparison (as suggested by one of the anonymous readers) of the characteristics and functioning of the "discourse of the South" in the history of both countries (the US and Italy) could be of great interest.

References

Arfé, Gaetano (1962) "Il problema della diversità e degli squilibri regionali nella cultura politica italiana dalla caduta della Destra all' avvento del Fascismo." In *Gli squilibri regionali e l'articolazione dell' intervento pubblico. Atti del Convegno di studio Torino–Saint Vincent 3–7 Settembre 1961*, pp. 93–130. Milan: Lerici.

Bagnasco, Arnaldo (1977) *Tre Italie. La problematica territoriale dello sviluppo italiano*. Bologna: Il Mulino.

Curcio, Giorgio (1873) *Della statistica giudiziaria civile e criminale nel Regno d' Italia*. Rome: Tipografia Barbera.

Della Peruta, Franco (1990) "Contributo all'epistolario di Pietro Maestri." In Giovanni Spadolini *et al., Saggi mazziniani: dedicati a Emilia Morelli*, pp. 60–104. Genova: La Quercia.

Dickie, John (1992) "A Word at War: The Italian Army and Brigandage 1860–1870." *History Workshop* **33**: 2–24.

Donzelli, Carmine (1990) "Mezzogiorno tra 'questione' e purgatorio. Opinione comune, immagine scientifica, strategie di ricerca." *Meridiana* **9**: 46–7.

Farolfi, Benedetto (1979) "Dall' antropometria militare alla storia del corpo." *Quaderni storici* **14**: 1056–91.

—— (1984) "Antropometria militare e antropologia della devianza 1876–1908." In *Storia d'Italia, Annali 7: Malattia e medicina*, pp. 1181–1219. Turin: Einaudi.

Foucault, Michel (1972) *The Archeology of Knowledge*. New York: Random House.

—— (1973) *The Order of Things. An Archeology of the Human Sciences*. New York: Random House.

Galasso, Giuseppe (1991) "Nota introduttiva." In David Abulafia, *Le due Italie. Relazioni economiche fra il regno normanno di Sicilia e i comuni settentrionali*, pp. 1–4. Napoli: Guida.

Giarrizzo, Giuseppe (1992*) Mezzogiorno senza meridionalismo. La Sicilia, lo sviluppo, il potere*. Venice: Marsilio.

ISTAT (Istituto Centrale di Statistica del Regno d'Italia) (1936) *Decennale 1926 IV–1936 XIV*. Rome: Istituto Poligrafico dello Stato.

Istituto Centrale di Statistica (1960) "Primi studi sui conti economici territoriali." *Annali di statistica*, 8th series, **12**: xi–xv.

MAIC (Ministero di Agricoltura, Industria e Commercio) (1864a) *Statistica del Regno d'Italia. Popolazione. Movimento dello Stato civile nell' anno 1862*. Florence: Tipografia Tofani.

—— (1864b) *Statistica del Regno d'Italia. Popolazione. Censimento generale (31 dicembre 1861)*, Vol. 1. Turin: Tipografia Letteraria.

—— (1864c) *Statistica del Regno d'Italia. Popolazione. Movimento dello Stato civile nell' anno 1863*. Florence: Tipografia Tofani.

—— (1865) *Statistica del Regno d'Italia. Popolazione. Censimento generale (31 dicembre 1861)*, Vol. 2. Turin: Tipografia Letteraria.

—— (1866a) *Statistica del Regno d'Italia. Popolazione. Censimento generale (31 dicembre 1861)*, Vol. 3. Florence: Tipografia Tofani.

—— (1866b) *Statistica del Regno d'Italia. Popolazione. Movimento dello Stato civile nell'anno 1864*. Florence: Tipografia Tofani.

—— (1867a) *Statistica del Regno d'Italia. Popolazione. Parte I. Censimento generale (31 dicembre 1861)*. Florence: Barbera.

—— (1867b) *Statistica del Regno d'Italia. Elezioni politiche e amministrative. Anni 1865–66*. Florence: Tipografia Tofani.

—— (1868) *Statistica del Regno d' Italia. Morti violente. Anno 1866*. Florence: Tipografia Tofani.

—— (1869) *Statistica del Regno d' Italia. Morti violente. Anno 1867*. Florence: Tipografia Tofani.

—— (1871) *Statistica del Regno d' Italia. Morti violente. Anno 1870*. Milan: Tipografia Reale.

—— (1878) *Carte e diagramma di demografia italiana*. Rome: Virano e Teano.

—— (1878–1995) *Annuario Statistico Italiano*. Rome.

—— (1882) *Atlante statistico del Regno d' Italia. Diagrammi di demografia italiana*. Rome: Tipografia Elzeviriana.

Ministero di Grazia e Giustizia (1871) *Statistica giudiziaria penale del Regno d' Italia per l'anno 1869 e ragguagli comparativi con alcuni anni anteriori.* Florence: Stamperia Reale.

Moe, Nelson (1992) "'Altro che Italia': il Sud dei Piemontesi (1860–61)." *Meridiana* **15**: 53–89.

—— (1994) "Representing the South in Post-Unification Italy *ca* 1860–1880," Ph.D. dissertation. Baltimore: Johns Hopkins University.

Niceforo, Alfredo (1898) *L'Italia barbara contemporanea. Studi e appunti.* Milan–Palermo: Sandron.

—— (1901) *Italiani del Nord e Italiani del Sud (Con 133 tavole numeriche e 31 tavole grafiche).* Turin: Fratelli Bocca.

Patriarca, Silvana (1996) *Numbers and Nationhood. Writing Statistics in Nineteenth-Century Italy.* Cambridge, UK: Cambridge University Press.

Pazzagli, Carlo (1980) "Statistica 'investigatrice' e scienze 'positive' nell' Italia dei primi decenni unitari." *Quaderni Storici* **45**: 779–822.

Petraccone, Claudia (1994) "Nord e Sud: le due civiltà." *Studi storici* **35**: 511–41.

Porter, Theodore M. (1986)*The Rise of Statistical Thinking 1820–1900.* Princeton, NJ: Princeton University Press.

Procacci, Giuliano (1956) *Le elezioni del 1874 e l'opposizione meridionale.* Milan: Feltrinelli.

Putnam, Robert (1993) *Making Democracy Work. Civic Traditions in Modern Italy.* Princeton, NJ: Princeton University Press.

Ragionieri, Ernesto (1967) *Politica e amministrazione nella storia dell'Italia unita.* Bari: Laterza.

Romanelli, Raffaele (1980) "La nuova Italia e la misurazione dei fatti sociali. Una premessa." *Quaderni storici* **15**: 765–78.

Romano, Salvatore F. (1945) *Storia della questione meridionale.* Palermo: Pantea.

Salvadori, Massimo (1960) *Il mito del buongoverno. La questione meridionale da Cavour a Gramsci.* Turin: Einaudi.

Serristori, Luigi (1833) *Saggio statistico dell' Italia.* Vienna: Tipografia Mechitaristica.

SVIMEZ (Associazione per lo sviluppo dell'industria nel Mezzogiorno) (1954) *Statistiche sul Mezzogiorno d'Italia 1861–1953.* Rome: SVIMEZ.

—— (1961) *Un secolo di statistiche italiane: nord e sud 1861–1961.* Rome: SVIMEZ.

—— (1978) *Un quarto di secolo nelle statistiche nord–sud 1951–1976.* Milan: Giuffré.

Teti, Vincenzo (1993) *La razza maledetta. Origini del pregiudizio antimeridionale.* Roma: Manifestolibri.

Villani, Pasquale (1978) "Gruppi sociali e classe dirigente all'indomani dell'Unità."

In *Storia d'Italia. Annali I. Dal feudalesimo al capitalismo*, pp. 881–978. Turin: Einaudi.

Villari, Rosario, ed. (1961) *Il Sud nella storia d'Italia. Antologia della questione meridionale*. Bari: Laterza.

Zuccagni Orlandini, Attilio (1845) *Corografia fisica, storica e statistica dell' Italia e delle sue isole*, Vol. 1. Florence: Presso gli editori.

—4—

Biology or Environment? Race and Southern "Deviancy" in the Writings of Italian Criminologists, 1880–1920

Mary Gibson

> The Mafia is a Sicilian variant of the ancient *Camorra*, a variant shaped perhaps by a more tenacious adherence to secrecy, typical of the Semitic race (Lombroso 1896–7, Vol. 1: 621).
>
> It is to the African and Eastern elements (except the Greeks), that Italy owes, fundamentally, the greater frequency of homicides in Calabria, Sicily and Sardinia, while the least occur where the Nordic races predominate (Lombardy) (Lombroso 1896–7, Vol. 3: 30).

In these two propositions from his famous work, *Criminal Man*, Cesare Lombroso identified race as fundamental to the etiology of crime in Southern Italy. Renowned internationally as the father of the Italian school of scientific, or "positivist," criminology, Lombroso and his ideas were familiar to many outside of his own academic specialty and beyond the borders of Italy. The first edition of *Criminal Man*, published in 1876, had caused such an uproar that it became the main topic of intense debate at a series of international meetings in the new field of criminology and had been translated into French, the common language of all European intellectuals, by 1887.[1] Within Italy, the book was reissued five times within twenty years, each edition larger and more comprehensive than the last. By the 1880s, Lombroso's house in Turin became an intellectual salon for not only criminologists but leading writers and political thinkers, such as Gaetano Mosca, Achille Loria, Robert Michels, and Anna Kuliscioff, and even for foreigners such as Max Nordau, Ellen Key, and Max Weber (Dolza 1990: 53). Tireless in his mission to popularize his ideas, Lombroso published over a thousand articles during his life in at least seventy journals, many of them, like *Nuova antologia*, aimed at the general educated public (Villa 1985: 283).

Lombroso's assertion that race shaped social behavior, in this case deviant behavior, was of course not original or exceptional in late nineteenth-century Europe. Nations involved in imperialist ventures like the "scramble for Africa" partially justified their wars as civilizing missions of whites directed towards inferior black, brown, and yellow populations. Within Europe, Jews were increasingly defined as a race rather than a religious group and were denounced as foreign enemies bent on undermining the nation state, whether France or Germany. At the same time northern Europeans began to classify themselves as "Aryans," racially superior to and more pure than their shorter and darker neighbors to the south and east. And the new theorists of degeneration warned that even homogeneous "races" such as the French were threatened with biological and mental weakening from alcoholism, syphilis, tuberculosis, and other "social diseases."

In Italy, race was used in a slightly different way: to explain persistent differences within the nation, especially divergences between the North and the South.[2] Such a project seems self-defeating in the light of the strenuous attempts by the government in Rome to unify and centralize governance of the peninsula and make "new Italians" out of the subjects of the patchwork of old-regime states that had disappeared as recently as 1860. Yet even after the triumphant conclusion of the Risorgimento with Garibaldi's campaign, extreme differences seemed to persist between the North and South, with the South plagued by a plethora of problems such as illiteracy, poverty, disease, and crime. To many modern, anti-clerical scientists like Lombroso, who had been trained as a physician, the answer to the "Southern Question" was race.

While Lombroso and many of his fellow positivist criminologists made race central to their analysis of southern "deviancy," the term itself posed special problems for Italian thinkers. First, archeological research had revealed such a variety of peoples migrating to the Italian peninsula throughout its long history that every writer rejected the idea of one "Italian" race as ridiculous. How could one identify the races in Italy? The distinction between white and black, employed in colonial ventures, was not useful, nor was the northern European tendency to trace the origin of a nation to a pure "Aryan" stock. Were the labels that turned up in archeological research, such as Umbrians, Ligurians, Latins, and Etruscans, applicable to different races? What about the more recent migrations of Greeks, north Africans, and Albanians to the South? Could different groups be lumped together as an Italic or Mediterranean race? Having admitted the existence of more than one race in Italy, criminologists were logically forced to criticize the German passion for pure races. Could race mixing be invigorating rather than enervating and a signal of mongrelization and decline? If so, was race mixing useful only among "whites"? Not only their generally positive evaluation of race mixing, but also anti-German sentiment among many Italian intellectuals assured that they would never blindly follow the most extreme northern racial theorists.

A second set of complications in the application of race to behavior arose from the personal biographies of positivist criminologists. Most notably, Lombroso himself was Jewish and was sensitive to the new racial anti-Semitism in northern and eastern Europe that questioned the patriotism and threatened the civil and political rights of Jews. In criticizing anti-Semitism, Lombroso de-emphasized the hereditary nature of race in a manner that contradicted many of his other writings on Southern Italy. Ambiguities also arose from the adherence of Lombroso and most of his positivist colleagues to socialism and their humanitarian impulse to improve the living conditions of the poor, whether in the North or South. Thus their writings often exhibited a tension between the biological determinism of racial analysis and a naive but often sincere desire for social reform and progress.

The following analysis of the writings of Lombroso and other members of the positivist school, such as Enrico Ferri, Alfredo Niceforo, and Guiseppe Sergi, will outline the contours of Italian racial theory at the turn of the twentieth century. While our focus will be on the differences between Northern and Southern Italy, we must include criminologists' views of Africans, Jews, and Aryans the better to comprehend their reasoning on matters of race. The chapter will conclude with the arguments of one of the few criminologists who opposed this reasoning, Napoleone Colajanni.

Positivist Criminology

While positivist criminology – or, as it was also called, "criminal anthropology" – is today identified almost solely with the name of Lombroso, he functioned as the nucleus of an extensive group of disciples and students. Trained in diverse professions, such as medicine, law, and anthropology, they collaborated with him in publishing the results of their research in the *Archives of Criminal Anthropology, Psychiatry, and Legal Medicine*, founded in 1881. This "positivist school" rejected the older "classical school" of penology, founded in the eighteenth century by Cesare Beccaria, that had sought to devise a scale of punishment proportionate to the severity of the crime. Instead, Lombroso and his colleagues shifted the focus from the crime to the criminal, arguing that punishments should be fashioned to fit the character of the accused. Thus even the perpetrator of a misdemeanor should be punished like a felon if his or her moral depravity constituted a threat to society.

The main task, then, of criminal anthropology was to devise a system to sort lawbreakers according to their degree of dangerousness (*pericolosità*). To accomplish this task, positivists employed a form of Social Darwinism, claiming that the most dangerous criminals were arrested in their evolutionary development. "Atavisms," or physical malformations, constituted the signs of evolutionary failure, and Lombroso labeled any individual manifesting several atavisms as a "born criminal" (*delinquente nato*). Because positivists equated biological malformations with internal moral and psychological weakness, they considered any offender marked with atavisms as a permanent threat to society and thus deserving of harsh punishment. Those criminals exhibiting few if any physical stigmata, labeled "occasional criminals," were classified as less dangerous; but this group received relatively little attention in positivist research. The counting of atavisms, through physical observation and measurement, seemed clear-cut and scientific and bolstered the claims of criminal anthropologists to be inventing the first objective criminology.

Lombroso and his colleagues found evolutionary differences not only between criminals and "honest" citizens, but also between groups based on race and gender. Like most Social Darwinism of his day, Lombroso's theory was inherently racist, since it argued that "savages" and "barbarians" in Africa, Asia, and the Americas were closer to animals than to civilized humans on the ladder of evolution. "Savages" were of course black, brown, or yellow, and this atavism of skin color marked them as permanently inferior to white Europeans. Because non-whites were close to their animal origin, their crimes were "primitive" and violent like murder, assault, kidnapping, and robbery. While it was undeniable that "civilized" Europe still had crime, positivists categorized these offenses as more sophisticated property crimes – like theft, swindling, and graft – typical of advanced societies.

Like non-whites, women as a group were assigned a lower rank on the evolutionary scale than white men. As Giuseppe Sergi pointed out, "the woman . . . remains at a level that for man is imperfection but for her is the natural state" (Sergi 1892: 8). While white men were strong, intelligent, moral, and active, female nature was clearly inferior in its weakness, emotionality, vanity, and passivity. In the writings on race analysed below, authors made few references to women. But their more general theory held that most female deviancy took the form of prostitution. Asserting that "the primitive woman was rarely a murderess, but she was always a prostitute," Lombroso expressed the common view that sexual promiscuity was the predominant trait of "savage" women. Thus when European women fell back into their evolutionary past, they reverted to sexual deviancy, while their male counterparts reverted to violence (Gibson 1982, 1990).

Cesare Lombroso

Although Lombroso took race for granted as an important impetus for behavior, he was slipshod in his definition of the term. In *Criminal Man*, he sometimes divided Europe into two large groups designated the "Germans" and the "Latins" or, alternately, the "blondes" and the "dark-haired" (Lombroso 1896–7, Vol. 3: 28, 38). In other instances he multiplied the number of races, dividing Italy into three parts, the Semitic South, the Latin Center, and the Germanic, Ligurian, Celtic, and Slavic North (Lombroso 1896–7, Vol. 3: 29). Yet on the same page he added even more categories: Umbrians, Etruscans, Oscans, Phoenicians, Albanians, and Greeks. In no case did he provide empirical data as a basis for his system of classification. His approach in a book written specifically about the South, entitled *In Calabria*, appears at first glance more scientific. Here he divided the Calabresi into two type: Semites with long heads (*dolicocefalo*), eyebrows that almost met over arched noses, and either black or dark brown eyes; and Greco-Romans with short heads (*brachicefalo*), high broad foreheads over aquiline noses, and lively, conspicuous eyes (Lombroso 1898: 53–4). The attempt to identify races based on the measurement of skulls was typical of the period throughout Europe. But even in this study, Lombroso muddied the waters by alluding at times to Albanians without defining their cranial type or explaining whether they fit into either of the two major groups.

On this scientifically unsteady base of racial classification, Lombroso built elaborate and colorful typologies of criminal behavior. At times, he would generalize about the predominance of crimes against the person in the South, or in this case, the region of Calabria: "To murder someone here with a gun . . . is considered a joke and not very serious; and everyone therefore carries a gun, and he who has two barrels is more respected" (Lombroso 1898: 95). But more often he provided a criminal geography of southern Italy by ethnic group. Thus, the areas populated by Greeks were the least criminal, at least in crimes of blood, while the Albanian regions showed high rates of vendetta and brigandage. In Sicily, brigandage was concentrated around Palermo,

> where the rapacious Berber and Semitic tribes took up an early and long-lived residence . . . When one thinks that here, as in the Arab tribes, cattle and sheep stealing is the preferred crime, it is easy to convince oneself that the blood of these people – who are acquisitive and rapacious, hospitable and cruel, intelligent but superstitious, always mobile, restless and disdainful of restraints – must have its part in . . . perpetuating brigandage (Lombroso 1896–7, Vol. 3: 27).

Such barbaric behavior was less common in eastern Sicily, like Catania, where a richer mixture of "Aryan blood" could be found (Lombroso 1896–7, Vol. 3: 27). In Sardinia, Lombroso found less homicide and more property crime than in the rest of the South, and attributed this more evolved or northern profile of deviancy to the Phoenician – rather than Arab – stock of its inhabitants (Lombroso 1896–7, Vol. 3: 33). How the Phoenicians were racially different from the Arabs was never explained.

The crudity of Lombroso's racial analysis was combined uneasily with an often more subtle psychological and social analysis of the etiology of southern crime. In *Criminal Man*, he admitted that individual temperament limited the determinism of race on behavior. Even among "the most barbarous savages" like the "hottentots" and the "kaffirs" could be found both relatively honest and industrious people and "more savage individuals who are incapable of any type of work and live on the labor of others like vagabonds" (Lombroso 1896–7: Vol. 1: 85). Perhaps more importantly for Southern Italy, he admitted that vestiges of feudalism were partially responsible for the high rates of southern crime. He pushed this idea much further in the conclusion to his study of Calabria, where he not only criticized the maldistribution of land, but argued for breaking up the large estates and redistributing the land by a "collective action of the State" (Lombroso 1898: 148–51). Disappointed with the results of the Risorgimento, in which he had believed so fervently as a youth, he sadly observed that in Calabria unification had profited only the rich, while for the poor it had added "the drawbacks of civilization to those of barbary" (Lombroso 1898: 146).

Lombroso's analysis of anti-Semitism provides an interesting counterpoint to his writings on the Italian South, since he explained Jewish behavior more in environmental than racial terms. When asked by two foreign journals to express his opinion on anti-Semitism, he hesitated, feeling "that disgust which hits even the least impatient scientist when he must study the most repulsive human secretions" (Lombroso 1894: 5). But he agreed to make an impartial study, publishing the results in Italy in 1894 under the title *Antisemitism and Modern Science*. In this book, he begins by labeling Jews as a race, but later defines them as a mixture of Semitic and Aryan blood. On the basis of his studies in Venice and Piedmont, he concluded that Jews came in all sizes, body types, and hair color, since they took on the characteristics of the peoples with whom they lived. In terms of craniology, "the Jew [is] more Aryan than Semitic," through intermixing with other Europeans (Lombroso 1894: 41). He pronounced this race mixing as quite normal, arguing that "a mosaic of the most diverse races" inhabits each European nation (Lombroso 1894: 10). Race mixing was not only normal but good, for Darwin had shown the benefits of cross fertilization in plants. Alternately, where Lombroso had found "the most complete uniformity of race, as in Abyssinia and Sardinia . . . the people demonstrated an inferior intelligence to those who had a variety of cranial forms. Therefore the Sardinians are infinitely inferior to the Sicilians," since the latter region had Norman, Greek, and Semitic blood (Lombroso 1894: 56).

Despite their mixed blood, Jews did, according to Lombroso, exhibit a constellation of distinctive traits. For instance, they tended to cloak obstinate tenacity with humility and apparent flexibility, leaving them open to the charge of duplicity. But this flaw in character was neither hereditary nor racial, but necessary for survival through the centuries in hostile environments. Similarly, he admitted that Jews had traditionally been bankers, tax collectors, and wandering traders rather than exercising "honest occupations," but environment, not blood, had driven them to this choice (Lombroso 1894: 18). As nations like Italy opened all professions to Jews, they had taken immediate advantage of the new liberty to move into the universities, the state, and the army. Thus anti-Semitism was irrational and even atavistic, "an icy wind of savage hate running through even the most civilized peoples of Europe" (Lombroso 1894: 9). Anti-Semitism would finally cease when "little by little, in five or six centuries, the Jew will disappear" through intermarriage with Christians (Lombroso 1894: 98). For Lombroso, intermarriage was just another example of healthy mixing of the races, which would also promise the end of religious fanaticism in both Jewish and Christian communities.

In contrast to the Jews, Lombroso found blacks to have a mental and emotional life almost entirely determined by biology. In a work called *White Man and Colored Man*, Lombroso argued that great inequalities mark the races, with Negroes being "the most imperfect" and whites the "most perfect." (Lombroso 1871: 220–1). According to his evolutionary theory, blacks represented the lowest and most primitive race, from which all others – including intermediary groups like the Semites and the Asians – had sprung under the positive influence of temperate climates. But the African had changed little for millennia, still displaying "that infantile and monkey-like manner of smiling and gesturing" (Lombroso 1871: 840). For Lombroso, this intellectual weakness sprang directly from physical inferiority: "the brain is undeveloped in the back and weighs less than ours. As for the skull which holds it, the face predominates over the forehead as [their] passions drown [their] intelligence" (Lombroso 1871: 27–8). Thus blacks were closer to monkeys than whites in language, art, and of course science.

Enrico Ferri

A defense attorney and law professor, Enrico Ferri formed part of the triumvirate of the founding fathers of positivist criminology along with Lombroso and Raffaele Garofalo. As evidenced in the title of his most famous work, *Criminal Sociology*, Ferri stressed sociological factors more than Lombroso did. Although it was Ferri who actually coined the term "born criminal," his eloquence on the importance of factors such as poverty and illiteracy in the etiology of crime persuaded Lombroso to reduce his estimate of the percentage of crime caused by atavism continually through all the various editions of *Criminal Man*. Yet Ferri believed in a small but dangerous group of born criminals and considered race an important element in their behavior. Only race could explain the wide variations in patterns of crime in areas with similar physical and social environments such as southern Italy.

Like most criminal anthropologists, Ferri claimed to base his definition of race on cephalic indices that divided peoples into long-headed and short-headed types. Asserting that the distribution of races in Europe was generally understood, he identified three main groups: the Germans, Slavs, and Greco-Latins (Ferri 1895, Vol. 1: 251). While Italy fell into the third group, he admitted that a host of subgroups could be found within the peninsula: Ligurians in the North, Umbrians and Etruscans in the Center, and Oscans in the South, with later migrations of

Germans, Celts, and Slavs into the North and Phoenicians, Arabs, Albanians, and Greeks into the South (Ferri 1895, Vol. 1: 259–60). Two of these groups – the Germans and the Slavs – corresponded to his major races, while the classification of the others was never clarified. Ferri also at times employed the broad categories of the "white race" and the "colored races" (Ferri 1895, Vol. 1: 247).

For Ferri, race was most important as the cause of serious crimes like homicide, that is, those crimes most likely to be committed by the born criminal. He agreed with other criminal anthropologists that violent crime was giving way to property crime, since "civil evolution consists in man's continuous stripping-off of the most deep and ancient traces of his animal and savage origin" (Ferri 1929, Vol. 1: 347). In a work entitled *Homicide in Criminal Anthropology,* he traced this evolution, beginning with a chapter on "Murders among animals," followed by "Homicide among primitive humanity." Asking why "inferior races" were more prone to homicide, he speculated that "the Negro does not have a bad but only an unstable character like a baby, but with the difference that it is linked with mature physical development; thus this instability is the consequence of an incomplete cerebral development" (Ferri 1895, Vol. 1: 250).

As for the differences between patterns of crime in Northern and Southern Italy, Ferri correlated these partly with economic disparities but also with the particular "racial energies and attitudes" of each region (Ferri 1929, Vol. 1: 347). Only the North had reached the modern pattern of a predominance of property crimes like theft and fraud, so that "from the provinces of Southern Italy and the islands to the northern regions one sees a progressive diminution of barbaric and violent crime" (Ferri 1929, Vol. 1: 348). Yet even the South was dotted with oases of low homicide, where Greek, Albanian, and "Longobard" blood was common (Ferri 1895, Vol. 1: 265). Elsewhere, the predominance of Semitic blood assured high rates of crimes against persons.

Like Lombroso, Ferri tempered his racial analysis with the disclaimers that individual temperament could limit racial determinism and that environment also accounted for a large amount of crime. In fact Ferri, a more committed and consistent socialist than Lombroso at the turn of the century, suggested a future in which socialism might eliminate most lawbreaking. He rejected the rosy picture painted by some of his political colleagues in which socialism would wipe out crime entirely. For Ferri, "isolated cases of acute pathology" in born criminals could never be mitigated by benign environmental change and as such would always be dangerous to social order. But when a future socialist society guaranteed work to all citizens, the "struggle for existence" would be eased and most crime would cease (Ferri 1929, Vol. 1: 351). How socialism would erase the racial stigmata of entire regions was not clear.

Interestingly, Ferri also wrote on anti-Semitism, perhaps out of deference to his friend and colleague, Lombroso. In an article published in the *Nuova rassegna* in 1893, he minimized description of Jews as a race and concentrated on a political analysis of the rise of anti-Semitism in Europe.[3] Although anti-Semitism was not new, it was a new virulence fueled by conservative governments bent on diverting attention from present injustices and the new socialist parties that promised to right these injustices. For Ferri, it was not coincidental that those nations with the strongest reform movements – Germany, Russia, and Austria – exhibited the most hysterical outbursts of anti-Semitism. As a type of Christian revivalism meant to overshadow the "supreme ideal" of socialism, anti-Semitism, according to Ferri, was becoming "a huge fire" that threatened to escape the control of its conservative creators (Ferri 1901: 538, 542). In a chilling and unwitting prognostication of the future, he warned that "if, by a neronian hypothesis, we could imagine the destruction of all the Jews of Europe," the intellectual level of the continent would decline sharply (Ferri 1901: 540). As a non-Jew, he declared his agreement with Lombroso that "anti-semitism, as an individual sentiment, represents an atavistic residual of medieval barbary and ignorance" (Ferri 1901: 541).

Alfredo Niceforo

Alfredo Niceforo represented the third generation of students who took up eagerly the tools and theories of positivist criminology, after Lombroso and Ferri respectively. In fact, he dedicated an early book entitled *Crime in Sardinia*, published at the age of twenty-one, to his "affectionate teacher Enrico Ferri," and Ferri returned the compliment in a laudatory preface. Based on a visit to the island two years earlier, this work seemed to refute Lombroso's assertion that Sardinia was the only part of the South relatively free of violent crime. Citing statistics on homicide, arson, armed robbery, kidnapping, and extortion, he claimed that Sardinia rivaled and often surpassed Sicily in these felonies. He concluded that "these statistics are terribly eloquent; they indicate – in Sardinia – a vast and acute morbid process, a cancerous erosion that corrupts the moral life of that island" (Niceforo 1897: 6).

Yet like his older colleagues, he found a variation in crime rates across geography and asserted that "the predominance of crime in certain regions is surely dependent, for the most part, on race" (Niceforo 1897: 30). Again like his colleagues, he failed to define race clearly. In one passage he divided Italy into two major groupings: the European or Celtic race that characterized Northern Italy, and the Mediterranean race, originally from Africa, that occupied the South and the Islands. Yet in Sardinia he found over four different "zones" of crime – for example vendetta in the Gallura, theft in Alghero, and slander in Bosa – and the correlation between this criminal geography and his two races is never entirely clear. He notes that Galluran women were blond and blue-eyed, so that even tourists could tell they were "perfectly celtic types" (Niceforo 1897: 32). But he is most interested in

Nuoro, which he labeled the "delinquent zone" for its high rates of armed robbery, kidnapping, extortion, vendetta and other violent crimes. Not surprisingly, he found that the inhabitants of Nuoro exhibited more "atavistic stigmata" than other Sardinians (Niceforo 1897: 21). His study of Nuorese skulls turned up some new types, which he found to correspond with those of Canary Islanders, that is, Africans.

Although Niceforo offered an unsatisfactory definition of race, he was more explicit than his colleagues in linking race to behavior. The physical atavisms common to the Nuorese corresponded to moral deficiencies, since "the moral sense . . . [is] organized by a series of molecular variations" (Niceforo 1897: 68). Thus moral, like physical, traits were inborn, and this "psychological heredity is quite stable and will not disappear . . . [even] when confronted with other models to imitate or with education; this is the psyche which is transmitted fatally from father to son, with all its accumulation of defects" (Niceforo 1897: 68).

Niceforo presented a variety of evidence that the delinquent zone of Nuoro had "atrophied on the road to civilization and [had] retained the moral ideas of primitive society" (Niceforo 1897: 41). These mountaineers, like Africans, organized "armed raids against other villages, with the same enthusiasm as primitive tribes drawn up before their symbolic totems" (Niceforo 1897: 43). Echoing Herbert Spencer, Niceforo condemned such violence as atavistic, since modern society was evolving from egoism and war to altruism and peace. Niceforo also condemned Nuoroese men for the degradation of their wives, forced to perform the "most menial work" like women in "ancient tribes" (Niceforo 1897: 54). The latter judgment takes on a bit of irony in light of Niceforo's unabashed misogyny in other writings (Gibson 1990: 23). Even the music of Nuoro showed "great similarity to savage singing. This singing is oppressive; it penetrates the brain, rasping, whirring, and boring through it with sharpness, tenacity and insistence. It is nothing but dissonant variations on a few notes" (Niceforo 1897: 51).

While Niceforo admitted that crime sprang from social as well as biological causes, he gave the former much shorter shrift in his book on Sardinia than Ferri or even Lombroso. This was also true of another work notoriously entitled *Contemporary Barbarian Italy*, in which he argued that the South represented "a real and actual social atavism" compared to the North (Niceforo 1893: 14). Citing statistics on education, industry, suicide, and crime, he sought to establish the existence of "two Italies" divided by race. Because of their discipline and educability, the Aryans of the North deserved a form of government based on liberty, while the Mediterraneans of the South "need energetic and at times dictatorial action . . . to tear them away from the shadows" of traditionalism (Niceforo 1893: 297). Niceforo thus concluded that only a highly decentralized government would allow the two Italies to devise political systems consonant with their racial differences. While Niceforo lectured in the North and abroad, he was born in Sicily and taught at the

University of Naples, making this pronouncement an example of southerners' complicity in the stigmatizing discourse on the South.

Niceforo's racial analysis takes on much more complexity and subtlety in a slightly later work entitled *The Germans: History of an Idea and a Race*. Clearly irked by the German claims to racial purity and Aryan superiority, he denied the equivalence of the terms "German" and "Aryan." Now identifying three races in Europe, the Nordic, Alpine, and Mediterranean, he argued not only that the Nordic race – blond, long-headed Aryans – could be found in many other countries, but also that only about half of Germany was Nordic. Thus Germans were wrong to equate their nation with the Aryan race. He also defended Italy from German charges of "ethnic chaos" and "extensive racial mixing," asserting that Italy had a simple racial map with one group each in the North and the South (Niceforo 1919: 74). Furthermore, he ridiculed the German notion that all great men in European history had been Aryans. In his chapter entitled "Did all Greek heroes really have blond hair?," he answered that this was "a poetic fiction," as was the absurd theory that all Renaissance geniuses, like Dante, had been German and that this Aryan blood had later been submerged in that of the lower races (Niceforo 1919: 74–5).

For our purposes, it is perhaps most interesting that Niceforo softened his stance on the determinist link between race and psychology in *The Germans*. In an attempt to deny the possibility of a superior race, he pointed out that the psychology of each people is complex, influenced by history and environment as well as race. He now pronounced it difficult to define the particular psychologies of the Nordic, Alpine, and Mediterranean peoples. Niceforo's conversion to environmentalism in the case of Aryans clearly reflected political changes in the relationship between Italy and Germany. As Germany became an overweening senior partner in the Triple Alliance and finally an enemy in the First World War, Niceforo's admiration of Aryans paled. Bristling at their claims of racial superiority, he modified a belief in biological determinism previously held to be scientifically objective.

Giuseppe Sergi

Of the generation of Lombroso, Giuseppe Sergi had fought with Giuseppe Garibaldi during the wars of unification before becoming a pioneer in the discipline of anthropology. He was appointed to the first Chair of Anthropology, at the University of Bologna, in 1880 and four years later moved to the University of Rome, where he founded the Institute of Anthropology. Known for his work on the typology of human races, he was quoted by the other positivist criminologists already discussed, although not always accurately. Sergi collaborated actively with Lombroso in the *Archives* and shared key positivist assumptions: that, for example, physical racial characteristics determined internal psychological traits. But his work on race was more careful than most of his colleagues, and he tried to sort out many myths and misconceptions about Aryans and their relation to Italy.

In the preface to his work entitled *Aryans and Italics*, published in 1898, Sergi warned that his opinions opposed common wisdom about the Aryans. He criticized the Italian reliance on linguistics and ethnography to try to classify races; in this vain endeavor, "the principal defect . . . was to try to establish ethnological rules without anthropology, which is quite a curious phenomenon" (Sergi 1898: 4). Although linguistics pointed to the unity of most Europeans based on the Indo-European roots in their languages, he believed that all these groups could be considered "neither a race nor a people" (Sergi 1898: 2–3). Italian intellectuals needed to get over their disdain for anthropology and accept the tools that it offered for solving this puzzle.

Despite his allusions to cultural practices such as burial, Sergi relied mainly on the shapes of skulls and faces to categorize race. Claiming to have compared ancient and modern skulls of groups such as Egyptians and American Indians, he concluded that "the forms of the skull are *persistent*," unchanging over many thousands of years (Sergi 1898: 102). For Sergi, this persistence of physical type was consistent with the "laws of animality," and only "extremist evolutionists" could believe that physical characteristics such as the shape of the skull could have changed in the short time since humans appeared on earth (Sergi 1898: 103). Sergi filled his book with tables of cephalic indices and photographs of skulls to underpin his classification of races in Italy. He boasted that many had praised his new system, including "a man whose powers of intuition and sharp eyes of observation are worth a thousand others, Cesare Lombroso" (Sergi 1898: 104).

On the basis of his evidence, Sergi tackled the confusing multiplicity of groups found in Italian history, such as the Italics, the Terramare people, Umbrians, Latins, Etruscans, and Ligurians. After measuring skulls from each group, he concluded that all of Italy – in fact all of Europe – was populated by two general races: the long-headed Italics and the short-headed Aryans. According to his theory, the Italics had their origins in Africa and had spread over the whole of Europe in Neolithic times. Labeled "Euroafrican" by Sergi, they varied widely in skin color because of differing climates. In the Bronze Age, the Aryans invaded Europe from the east, pushing most Italics either to the south or the north. These "Euroasians" included the Germans, Slavs, and Celts, the last two of which groups entered Northern Italy and penetrated as far as the Tiber. But the late Etruscans and the Romans were Italic, so that Italy remained a mixture of Aryans and Italics in the North while being almost homogeneously Italic in the South. Even within the North, Aryan influence varied, so that it was quite weak in Rome, but "the Po valley can consider itself predominantly Aryan" (Sergi 1898: 88). It is noteworthy that while Sergi based his classification on biological measurement, he rejected skin color as significant.

In the conclusion to his book, Sergi left his careful and closely-reasoned analysis of physical evidence to leap into ungrounded speculation about the psychological differences between Aryans and Italics. On the basis partially of anecdotes from his own trips to northern Europe, he asserted that Aryans were more socially-connected and orderly than the individualistic, anarchic Italics. During ancient Rome and the Renaissance, Italic individualism produced great military leaders and artistic geniuses, so that Italy had triumphed over the rest of Europe. But in modern times, the social solidarity of the Aryans had allowed them to create stronger institutions, such as schools, industry, and families, and thus European leadership had passed to them. Undocumented by any rigorous data, this analysis showed that Sergi was as careless as his colleagues in assuming that biology determined psychology.

Napoleone Colajanni

While Lombroso and his circle dominated criminological discourse in late nineteenth-century Italy, dissenting voices could be heard. A minority of "sociological criminologists" denied the existence of the born criminal and attributed all crime to bad environmental influences like poverty, lack of education, homelessness, unemployment, and broken families. Perhaps the most eminent figure among this group was Filippo Turati, who in 1882 attacked the biological theories of Ferri in an essay entitled "Crime and the Social Question."[4] Never a vulgar materialist, Turati admitted that "the social question is not all related to the stomach" (Turati 1962: 193). Instead, *"poverty* means lack of *education* in the widest sense of the word. It means ignorance of the rules of social intercourse, ineptness in conforming to individual interests; bad examples, honesty betrayed, weak nerves, excitability of base passions, inability to reflect, [and] permanent deficiency in satisfying vital needs" (Turati 1962: 193). For Turati, the only answer to crime was the substitution of capitalist society with one characterized by "the egalitarian diffusion . . . of wealth and education, of the joys of love and of thought."

In his essay, Turati mentioned race only in passing, as one of many physical traits that could be ameliorated by a good environment. For a detailed deconstruction of the positivist doctrine of race and crime, we must turn to another sociological criminologist, Napoleone Colajanni. A parliamentary deputy from Sicily for many years, Colajanni showed in his denunciation of biological and racial determinism a passion partially arising from a desire to defend the South from stereotypes. With a much deeper interest in criminology than Turati, Colajanni wrote a number of books on the subject during his professorship at the Universities of Palermo and Naples, including a general text, *Criminal Sociology*. More importantly for our purposes, he addressed directly the question of race and crime in *Latins and Anglo-Saxons (Inferior and Superior Races)*.

Colajanni pointed out the confusion in racial classification, despite the general agreement among anthropologists on a tripartite division into Germans, Alpines or Celts, and Mediterraneans. He quotes a variety of experts to show the myriad discrepancies among descriptions of the characteristics of even these three simple categories, as well as the existence of multiple subcategories. According to the generally-accepted scheme, Italy harbored two races, the Alpine in the North and the Mediterranean – "the cursed race" – in the South. He was amused that the Alpine race could be considered so culturally and economically superior in Northern Italy while being bemoaned as ragged, ignorant mountain folk in southern France. He was especially delighted to show that experts could not even agree on the appropriate race categorization of great men, any more than could "the inmates in an insane asylum" (Colajanni 1906: 18). For example, one racial theorist labeled Lord Byron "a real German" while another dismissed him as "a vulgar Celt" (Colajanni 1906: 18). Colajanni concluded that while pure races may have existed in the distant past, today "peoples" or better "nations" were the proper terms for groups with a collective psychology, behavior, and history.

Even if races could be identified, Colajanni rejected a key proposition in the Lombrosian analysis: the correspondence between "anatomical characteristics and psychological characteristics" (Colajanni 1906: 14). The modern world showed this correlation to be absurd, since most nations harbored a variety of races and yet all citizens felt, thought, and acted in the same way. Furthermore, no race was superior, although "anthroposociological fantasy" had assigned to Anglo-Saxons "the *character* of *characters*, the highest trait which assures their superiority: educability" (Colajanni 1906: 42–3). For Colajanni, racial theorists were like the defenders of slavery in the time of Aristotle, who believed that "men's internal nature made them *free* or *slaves*" (Colajanni 1906: 75). That slaves in Aristotle's time were from northern Europe, now considered superior, made the notion of racial hierarchy even more absurd. Surely Aryans or even Celts had not been needed to build the marvels of Agrigento, Syracuse, Segesta, and Selinunte in his own Sicily.

When turning to statistics on crime, Colajanni admitted that Italy held "very sadly, first place in violent crime" (Colajanni 1906: 99). But he refused to see the high homicide rate as "a measure exclusively of the greater *ferocity* of the Italians, especially those of the South" (Colajanni 1906: 94). Since he claimed that assault rates were higher in Germany and Scotland than Italy, violence was not inevitably linked to one race, but common in different forms to all races. Even specific types of murder, like infanticide, were higher in northern Europe than Italy. And homicide in general had declined in Sicily and Sardinia to almost one-half of what it had been twenty years previously, a rapid change incompatible with racial determinism. Even the blot of the mafia and the *camorra* in the Italian South was not unique, since bands of whites who lynched blacks similarly dishonored the United States.

Dismissing the positivist racial theory as "pseudo-scientific," Colajanni saw homicide rates "simply as an index of the level of social and intellectual evolution" reached by a society (Colajanni 1906: 97–8). For him, the denial by criminal anthropologists of the primary influence of environment and education on crime constituted "a real madness" (Colajanni 1906: 158).

Conclusion

Even by the standards of their day, positivist criminologists failed to develop a racial theory worthy of the designation "scientific." As our analysis of the writings of Lombroso, Ferri, Niceforo, and Sergi illustrates, no consensus existed even on a general classification of race. Lombroso categorized Italians as Latins and Semites, Ferri as Greco-Latins, Niceforo as Mediterraneans, and Sergi as Aryans and Italics. Furthermore, each writer except Sergi contradicted himself within his own writings, referring to smaller groups like Umbrians, Greeks, or Phoenicians that seemed to lie outside the larger categories. Only Sergi was careful about defining his racial groups, while the others were so cavalier in their racial classification that they even misused Sergi's categories.

Confusion in racial classification arose partially from incomplete or unpersuasive data. Sometimes positivists substituted skin color (white and black) or language (Albanian or Greek) for rigorous empirical evidence of fundamental physical differences. The most persuasive data, the cephalic indices, were used consistently only by Sergi, while the other writers supplied them for some categories and not for others. Yet, the cephalic index, with only two categories of long-headed and short-headed, was too blunt a tool to create the detailed racial maps of the South proposed by Lombroso, Ferri, and Niceforo. Without a clear definition, race shifted between biological, cultural, and political categories in their writings.

Perhaps even more disturbing was the assumption, central to criminal anthropology, that biology determined psychology and morality. While the cephalic indices might have correctly distinguished inherited physical differences among humans, this type of data did not prove that the shape of the skull had any effect on morality. Of our writers, only Niceforo explicitly addressed this connection by asserting that thought is a function of molecules. This assertion proved inadequate when positivists admitted that the environment also influenced criminological behavior. Except for Ferri, who at least differentiated between violent crime springing from race and property crime arising from social influences, most writers never attempted to explain the interplay of race and environment in the etiology of crime.

Curiously, the weight of race or environment in the crime equation seemed to shift depending on the groups studied. This becomes especially clear in the writings of Lombroso and Ferri on anti-Semitism or of Niceforo on the Aryans. Here, environmentalism almost triumphed over the authors' usual racial analysis as they pursued their political aims of defending Jews or criticizing Germany. On the other hand, blacks were compared to monkeys, both incapable of escaping biological instincts. Implicitly, positivists constructed a sliding scale, with heredity at one end and environment at the other: Africans and other "savages" were placed near the pole of heredity, while Jews, and, after the rise of a threatening Germany, Aryans were placed near the pole of environment. Southerners in Italy were assigned a place near the pole of heredity, but with a slight shift toward environment. Thus prejudices or political passions underpinned a supposedly scientific analysis of racial determinism.

The illogic of racial reasoning among criminal anthropologists did not vitiate its importance at the turn of the century. In many ways, the positivist analysis simply clothed common sense, or common prejudices, in pseudo-scientific garb and was therefore readily accepted. Not loath to popularize their theories, the proponents of racial determinism were tireless in offering lectures and articles for the general educated public. Perhaps more importantly, Lombroso and his colleagues trained many students who later held important posts in the bureaucracies of the police and prisons, and possibly in Italy's African Colonies as well. Only further research can establish how these racial theories were translated in the everyday practice of the criminal justice and colonial systems. Surely such theories created an atmosphere conducive to Benito Mussolini's later racial repression, which ignored earlier interpretations of Jews or the interplay of heredity and environment. Even in the postwar era, while the names of criminal anthropologists are not remembered, sadly their notion of southern racial inferiority persists.

Notes

1. See Renzo Villa (1985: 283–8) for a comprehensive bibliography of Lombroso's writings. Lombroso's theory was the main topic of discussion at both the first and second Congresses of Criminal Anthropology, held respectively in Rome in 1885 and Paris in 1889.
2. No biographer of Lombroso, including Villa, has focused on his racial theories. Emilana Noether was the first to treat the general question in her unpublished paper, "Race is Destiny: Latin Decadence in *Fin-De-Siècle* Italian Positivist Thought."
3. Ferri's article "L'antisemitismo" was reprinted in *Studi sulla criminalità* (Ferri 1901).

4. Reprinted in 1962, Filippo Turati's "Il delitto e la questione sociale" was originally serialized in *La Plebe* in 1882 and appeared in book form in 1883.

References

Colajanni, Napoleone (1906) *Latini e anglo-sassoni (Razze inferiori e razze superiori)*, 2nd edition. Rome and Naples: Rivista popolare.
Dolza, Delfina (1990) *Essere figlie di Lombroso: Due donne intellettuali tra '800 e '900*. Milan: Franco Angeli.
Ferri, Enrico (1895) *L'omicidio nell'antropologia criminale*. Turin: Bocca.
—— (1901) *Studi sulla criminalità*. Turin: Bocca.
—— (1929) *Sociologia criminale*, 5th edition. Turin: UTET.
Gibson, Mary (1982) "The 'Female Offender' and the Italian School of Criminal Anthropology," *Journal of European Studies* 12: 155–65.
—— (1990) "On the Insensitivity of Women: Science and the Woman Question in Liberal Italy," *Journal of Women's History* 2: 11–41.
Lombroso, Cesare (1871) *L'uomo bianco e l'uomo di colore: Lettere sull'origine e le varietà delle razze umane*. Padua: F. Sacchetto.
—— (1894) *L'antisemitismo e le scienze moderne*. Turin: Roux.
—— (1896–7) *L'uomo delinquente in rapporto all'antropologia, alla giuris-prudenza ed alle discipline carcerarie*, 5th edition. Turin: Bocca.
—— (1898) *In Calabria (1862–1897)*. Catania: Niccolò Giannotta.
Niceforo, Alfredo (1893) *L'Italia barbara contemporanea*. Milan: Sandron.
—— (1897) *La delinquenza in Sardegna*. Palermo: Sandron.
—— (1919) *Les Germains: Histoire d'un idée ed d'une race*, 2nd edition. Paris: Bossard.
Noether, Emiliana (n.d.) "Race is Destiny: Latin Decadence in *Fin-De-Siècle* Italian Positivist Thought." Unpublished paper.
Sergi, Giuseppe (1892) "Sensibilità femminile," *Archivio di antropologia criminale, psichiatria, e medicina legale* 13: 1–8.
—— (1898) *Arii e italici*. Turin: Bocca.
Turati, Filippo (1962 [1882]) "Il delitto e la questione sociale." In Luigi Cortesi, ed., *Turati giovane: Scapigliatura, positivismo, marxismo*, pp. 158–236. Milan: Editore Avanti!.
Villa, Renzo (1985) *Il deviante e i suoi segni: Lombroso e la nascita dell'anthropologia criminale*. Milan: Franco Angeli.

Homo Siculus: Essentialism in the Writing of Giovanni Verga, Giuseppe Tomasi Di Lampedusa, and Leonardo Sciascia
Frank Rosengarten

Introduction

The purpose of this essay is to shed critical light on the forms of essentialism and fatalism that inhere in the writing of three Sicilian novelists, Giovanni Verga, Giuseppe Tomasi di Lampedusa, and Leonardo Sciascia. I shall be looking at the two twentieth-century novelists mainly through the prism of their nineteenth-century predecessor, in order to highlight themes present in Verga that will be taken up again but in rather different ways, by Sciascia and Lampedusa.

In *Orientalism*, Edward Said has familiarized us with the cluster of cultural prejudices and historical preconceptions that govern the thinking of many people in the West who, especially since the beginning of the nineteenth century, and for a variety of political and psychological reasons, have seen the vast geopolitical area known as the Orient, and the subdivision of the Orient called the Near East, in essentialist terms. Said argues rather persuasively that, for the stratum of Western intellectuals and policy-makers (politicians, colonial administrators, professors, publishers, etc.) who were responsible for shaping a serviceable conception of the East for imperial purposes, it was convenient and advantageous to construct an a-historical typology of the Eastern mind and of the Eastern way of being. Such a typology, with its array of unchanging traits and habits of mind, served the interests of the colonizing countries, for it made of the observed peoples and nations, the studied object, "another being with regard to whom the studying subject is transcendent" (Said 1979: 97). Among the common traits attributed to the East was (and is) its fatalism, its renunciation of will, what Michael Herzfeld calls its "passive and total resignation" to whatever events the shifting sands of historical circumstance might bring about (Herzfeld 1987: 36).

But, as this essay hopes to show, such essentialism and fatalism also manifest themselves in the ways in which some intellectuals and writers view their own societies. Following Said's lead, Nelson Moe provides ample documentation to show that deeply prejudicial attitudes have long characterized the mind-set of many northern Italians, and of some privileged southerners as well, with respect to the southern regions of their country, and that "fatalism" has been one of the key terms in the geopolitical lexicon of educated Italians writing about the South. *Meridionalismo,* Moe argues (1992), like Orientalism, is a widespread phenomenon, a cluster of value-judgments that make the South seem like an irredeemable victim of its cultural and political backwardness, itself the result of a "history" that has been transmuted into an essential "nature" no longer amenable to reform and change. In any event, as applied to Sicilian reality, essentialism, often combined with fatalism and pessimism, is on full display in the writings discussed below.

Verga's novels *I Malavoglia* (1974 [1881]) and especially *Mastro Don Gesualdo* (1979 [1889]) will be the main focus of my analysis. As for Lampedusa and Sciascia, I have limited my remarks to *The Leopard* (1967 [1958]) and to *Pirandello e la Sicilia* (1961), a group of essays in which Sciascia expounds his interpretation of Sicilian history and culture. The translations of passages from the original Italian texts of Lampedusa and Sciascia are my own, but in the case of Verga I will be citing English translations of *Mastro Don Gesualdo* (1979) by Giovanni Cecchetti and of *I Malavoglia* (*The House by the Medlar Tree*, 1955) by Eric Mosbacher. Cecchetti's translation, although occasionally somewhat stilted, is nonetheless an enormously earthy, rough-hewn version that has had a strong impact on me. It was Cecchetti's translation even more that Verga's original Italian that helped me to understand more clearly why D. H. Lawrence found Verga's writing to be so congenial to his own literary tastes and proclivities.[1] Mosbacher is less successful, yet for the purposes of this essay, it seems to me that his translation also provides a window through which to view certain aspects of Verga's vision of life.

Verga's *Mastro Gesualdo* and *I Malavoglia*

"Vision" is an important word in my critical vocabulary with regard to Verga, so let me attempt to explain what I mean by it.

The question at issue is the extent to which one thinks Verga adhered to the canons of realism and *verismo.* Put another way, one might ask whether Verga's descriptive techniques and his unflinching revelations of human greed, misery, and suffering are ends in themselves, or whether they are meant to point to something beyond — a force, a higher power, a law of necessity transcending human volition. Robert Dombroski, for example, in *Properties of Writing* (1994: 23–43), contrasts Verga's world-view with that of Manzoni, arguing that, unlike Manzoni, Verga "held the materialist belief that human nature was determined by social existence and that morality was essentially a socio-cultural phenomenon integrally connected to the life processes of particular social groups and societies." Dombroski situates Verga in the current of nineteenth-century thought that accepted both "naturalism's valorization of cause–effect progression" and the principles of positivist inquiry, which he sees as pervasive in *I Malavoglia*. While conceding Verga's "thoroughly pessimistic view of humanity as victim of nature and history and his pervading sense of life as a desperate struggle toward death," he believes that the truth value of Verga's narratives consists essentially "not in metaphysics or theology . . . but in the material determinants of specific sociocultural systems." Like Dombroski, Romano Luperini, in *Interpretazioni di Verga* (1976: 7–34) also insists on Verga's materialism, which he counterposes to the long critical tradition, of which Croce was a prime exponent, that privileged "the lyrical and nostalgic" aspects of Verga's style, thus minimizing the scientific side of his literary temperament. Idealist critics, Luperini argues, have stressed idyllic moments and landscapes in Verga's stories and novels to the exclusion of other motifs rooted in the real economic, social, and political history of the period.

This "materialist" reading of Verga is convincing as far as it goes, since there is nothing in his work that suggests belief in a personal God or in the existence of a supernatural realm in regard to which the events of this world are necessarily preparatory and subordinate. But I do think that it is possible to recognize the tragic and visionary foundation of Verga's world-view without falling into exclusively "lyrical and nostalgic" readings of his work. In other words, I do not share the view that Verga's work "contains no deep, symbolic level of meaning; rather, like ethnographic narrative, it pays attention mainly to descriptive surface. Its meaning is of a more comparative and abstract nature, allegorical rather than symbolical or representational" (Dombroski 1994: 24).

Now, we may be dealing here with semantic problems, but it is my view that Verga's descriptive passages (in both *I Malavoglia* and *Mastro Don Gesualdo*) very often call attention to themselves in such a way as to suggest something beyond, some other level or dimension of reality that these passages serve to evoke. It is in this context that I think Verga's fatalistic "materialism" and his pessimism emerge most clearly. Let me cite a few illustrative examples of what I am talking about, drawn from the Cecchetti and Mosbacher translations of *Mastro Don Gesualdo* and *I Malavoglia*.

Mastro Don Gesualdo describes a world marked by repulsion between human beings themselves and between nature and humanity. His vision of the world, although in some respects compatible with elements of Christian morality, nonetheless opposes itself resolutely to the concept of universal love animating Christianity. The novel presents us with a Hobbesian view of human life in a state of nature as "solitary, poor, nasty, brutish and short," and with a conception of the non-human animal and vegetative worlds that mocks the idea of a beneficent nature that one finds in the writings of Jean-Jacques Rousseau and in some of the English romantic poets. Verga is as subversive of all optimistic and providentially inspired notions of human betterment and progress as Leopardi, and just as fearless as the poet from Recanati in his way of confronting the problem of evil.

The human workaday world as depicted by Verga in *Mastro Don Gesualdo* is one in which alienation, distrust, treachery, and voracious appetite predominate. A poignant example of this appears at the end of the novel, when Gesualdo, afflicted by a fatal cancer, finally lets himself know what he had always suspected, that Isabella is not his biological daughter and that she finds him repulsive. His yearning for a moment of closeness with her encounters an insuperable barrier between them that not even the imminence of his death can overcome. Isabella's resistance to him is impenetrable and absolute:

> He wanted to tell her other things, he wanted to ask her other questions, at that point — opening his heart to her as if to a father confessor, and reading into hers. But she kept her head bent as if she had guessed, the Trao's obstinate wrinkle between her brow, drawing backward, shutting herself up inside herself, haughty — with her own troubles and her own secret. And he then felt himself become a Motta again, just as she was a Trao — suspicious, hostile, made from another mold. He relaxed his arms, and said no more (Verga 1979: 327).

With the exception of Gesualdo's youthful emotional and sexual bond with Diodata, not a single human relationship depicted in *Mastro Don Gesualdo* is exempt from a corrosive mistrust and lurking treachery. The consolation of family life that still survives in *I Malavoglia* has now been entirely displaced by acquisitiveness, petty ambition, scheming for political advantage, and envy. Parent and child, husband and wife, worker and employer, rich and poor, aristocrat and bourgeois citizen, are divided as if by an abyss of tormented misunderstanding, of which the alienation between Gesualdo and Isabella is but one supreme example in a hierarchy of emotional pain. Yet this alienation would not be as final and definitive in its exemplification of a dystopic vision of life if it were not accompanied by the imagery with which Verga evokes the omnipresence of death, and the highly suggestive way in which he conveys his sense of nature and its impact on the human and animal worlds.

Death, or the imminence and foreshadowing of death, is present from the very beginning of the narrative, and grows ever more ominous and pervasive as the story proceeds. The Trao family, the pathetic yet still proud and disdainful representatives of a fading aristocratic class, have nothing of the grandeur of Lampedusa's Don Fabrizio, but their vocation for death is every bit as profound as his. Bianca Trao, Gesualdo's wife, is repeatedly described as being "pale as a dead woman," a "specter" whose presence disturbs and obsesses her husband. Her brother Diego too is "pale as a dead body." His sickness and actual death occur early in the story. Verga pictures him looking at his sister from his death-bed, as he responds to her offer to bring him some broth: "At first the sick man signaled no with his head, looking into the air as he was lying on his back. Then he turned his head, staring at her with his greedy eyes from the depths of his sockets, which seemed empty, sooty" (Verga 1979: 94).

Verga's death scenes are part of a tapestry dominated by the motifs of violence, devouring mouths, and mean hatred masked by subtle innuendoes and threats. The human aspect of this world is in no essential way removed or different from its animal aspect. There is a basic equality between them, they almost seem to need and complement each other. One of the first descriptions of Gesualdo, which coexists and contrasts uneasily with his humanitarian impulses, comes from the mouth of the Notary, who addresses a member of the nobility, Baron Zacco, who has "ugly ghostlike eyes." After recounting the high points of Gesualdo's impressive mastery of entrepreneurship in the areas of land speculation and construction, he notes: "The more you eat the hungrier you get . . . He's quite hungry . . . and he's got good teeth too, I'm telling you." When Gesualdo shows his anger, it is anger comparable to that of an "enraged bull." When his father Nunzio, who looks upon his son with a mixture of fear and envy, shouts to him across a field at the site of a collapsed bridge on property belonging to Gesualdo, the shout becomes "a cry that the gusts of wind tore from his mouth and then shredded in the distance." The canon-priest Lupi (names are significant in Verga, as they are for many other nineteenth-century novelists) is depicted in the process of persuading Gesualdo to marry out of his class; he proffers his advice "looking straight at Gesualdo with his sharp little rat's eyes that seemed to pierce him like two pins, his blade-shaped face sliding away on all sides." The Baroness Rubiera, afraid for her inept son Nino, who is the real father of Gesualdo's daughter Isabella, expresses her alarm by referring to the young man's enemies as "snakes, that's what they are! Nothing but criminals! They're going to eat up that degenerate son of mine in one bite!"

Images of cutting, slashing, and devouring appear throughout the novel, at times in the least suspected places. Even inanimate objects can devour their victims. Bianca falls ill, undermined by inherited weaknesses of body and soul, and retreats to her bed, where she lingers for a long time, inconclusively: "She was like one of those caged birds that try out the songs for the spring they'll never see. The bed was eating up her flesh; the fever consumed her with a slow fire." Then Gesualdo succumbs to a fatal disease. The description of his ordeal, like other similar passages, conveys a feeling that there is more than meets the eye in the poor man's suffering, that something is operative here that suggests a fate common to men and animals inhering in Verga's dystopic universe: "Don Gesualdo, sick, yellow, his mouth always bitter, had lost his sleep and his appetite; he had cramps in his stomach, like mad dogs biting inside him." The same image appears later, at the same time that Don Gesualdo's house is being sacked and looted by a mob of self-styled "revolutionaries" getting even with the rich who have exploited them. "There was a dog in his belly devouring his liver – the rabid dog of Saint Vitus the martyr that made him a martyr too."

No segment of Sicilian society as portrayed in *Mastro Don Gesualdo* is exempt from Verga's implacable indictment of a social world that has lost its bearings, no longer able to balance means with ends, to accommodate personal with social interests, to reconcile natural impulses of the self with humane concern for the selves of others. Just as Manzoni had in *I promessi sposi* presented the established institutions of Italian society in the seventeenth century against a backdrop of pervasive greed, violence and petty ambition, so Verga, but in an even more pitiless manner, utterly subverts the common optimistic assumptions of liberal society during the Risorgimento, at least as these are embodied in representative characters from the early 1820s to the revolutionary movements of 1848. Take the new medical science, for example, which was hailed in the past century as a portent of unlimited progress. Gesualdo has summoned the best doctors from Palermo to his side. He awaits their decision. One of the physicians present mutters some encouraging words about his prospects for recovery. Then his superior intervenes:

Doctor Muscio, more cruel, blurted straight out the only remedy they could try: the extirpation of the tumor – quite a case, the kind of surgery that would do anybody credit. He showed the ways and the means, getting excited over the proposal accompanying his words with gestures, already smelling blood, his eyes burning in his large face that turned all purple – as if he were about to roll up his sleeves and begin; so much so that the patient opened his eyes and his mouth wide, and instinctively pulled away; and the women, frightened, broke into moaning and sobbing (Verga 1979: 309).

The natural elements are as cruel and devouring as the human beings depicted by Verga in this novel of Sicilian life. The sun, source of all life, inflicts terrible punishment on the pitiful humans who toil beneath its sovereign and unrelenting light. One of the most suggestive scenes of the novel occurs in the first section, where Verga blends description of the Sicilian landscape with a human encounter that one cannot help but interpret as symbolic of a fate looming over this enterprising hero of the time with a special intensity, but that spares no one from its encompassing grasp. Gesualdo is making his away across a ravine, close to his home town:

Still grumbling, he went off at the mule's pace under the boiling sun – a sun that split rocks now, and made the stubble pop as if it were on fire. In the ravine, between the two mountains, it felt like a furnace; and the town on top of the hill, climbing above the precipices, scattered among enormous cliffs, undermined by caverns that left it as if suspended in air – blackish, rusty, looking abandoned, without a shadow, with all the windows opened wide in the torrid heat, like so many black holes, and the crosses of the bell towers swaying in the misty sky. Even the mule, covered with sweat, panted up the steep road. On the way Don Gesualdo met a poor old man, loaded with sheaves, exhausted, who began to grumble:

"Oh, where are you going, sir, at this time? . . . You have so much money, and you give your soul to the devil!" (Verga 1979: 54).

Verga's landscapes in the novels and in most of his short stories have been characterized as "idyllic" and "pastoral" but this is misleading. The landscapes are as charged with fateful power as any other aspect of what I would like to call his "visionary realism." To think of Verga only as a social realist interested in the material conditions of life and their effect on human beings is to deprive him of an essential component of his art, just as to single out the visionary at the expense of the realistic imperatives of Verga's writing would be one-sided and unsatisfactory.

Despite an evident desire to situate his narrative in a clearly defined historical framework, and his interest in the political ideals that contributed to the Risorgimento, Verga treats the political movements of Risorgimento Sicily in much the same way that Lampedusa treats the period from 1860 to 1900 in *The Leopard*, namely in such a way as to make them appear at best opportunistic, at worst fraudulent. One has the impression from Verga's account of events that the liberation of Sicily would do nothing for the common people of the island except give them temporary but illusory hope that they would be freer under a new order than under the present corrupt regime.

I trust that what I have said thus far makes it clear why I feel more in tune with what Alberto Asor Rosa has to say about Verga's world-view – in the passage cited just below – than with Dombroski and Luperini. In the context of a discussion of Verga's "populism", Asor Rosa writes:

Behind the proletarians of *I Malavoglia* and the novellas there is a vision of a more metaphysical than historical character, a moral attitude that is more ontological than this-worldly, an indignation and a pessimism more universal than human. Verga does not assign to the common people a "privileged" place in the great story of suffering. What fascinates the writer is not the suffering of subaltern groups considered as having its own laws and manifestations, but rather the cyclical inexorable reconfirmation of a law common to all classes, to all human beings, to all living creatures: from the miserable donkey of the story "Rosso Malpelo," to the fishermen of *I Malavoglia*, to the aspiring bourgeois Mastro Don Gesualdo, right up to the characters imagined but not realized of the last novels of the "ciclo dei vinti", the cycle of the vanquished (Asor Rosa 1976: 187; my translation).

Such an interpretation is certainly borne out on the theoretical level by Verga's famous preface to *I Malavoglia*, written in 1881 to introduce his cycle of novels.

It is borne out also, I believe, by an attentive textual analysis of Verga's novels and short stories.

Before making a few remarks about *I Malavoglia*, a word should be said about the possibility of a Christian reading of *Mastro Don Gesualdo*. I think that such a reading has much to recommend it, not to be sure in relation to a supernatural and theistic faith, but rather in relation to the essential moral content and trajectory of Verga's work, where one can observe in action such Christian (in some instances specifically Catholic) ideas as sacrifice, confession, spiritual struggle, and martyrdom. I do not think that the names Gesualdo and Diodata are coincidental in *Mastro Don Gesualdo*. The first four letters of Gesualdo's name and all the letters in Diodata's name evoke the spiritual core of Christian belief. One can sense in *I Malavoglia* and *Mastro Gesualdo* what Giacomo Debenedetti, in *Verga e il naturalismo* (1976), calls a "Christian inheritance" requiring acceptance of suffering and resignation to one's allotted station in life. It should be remembered that both young 'Ntoni in *I Malavoglia* and the protagonist of *Mastro Don Gesualdo* are in a sense punished for their rejection of the order of things in which they found themselves at birth. It would seem that Verga joined certain fundamental aspects of Christianity with a pre-Christian conception of fate in which punishment is imposed on human beings who defy the law of necessity that governs the world's events. In Greek classical theater, violations of prescribed natural and social laws combined with inherent flaws in the characters of the transgressors are what bring about tragic dénouements. Much the same procedure is noticeable in Verga. If we add to this literary and religious tradition the "iron laws" of nineteenth-century science and positivism, which certainly influenced Verga, we can readily understand why fatalism plays such a significant role in his narratives. Classical and Christian myths live on in this disciple of nineteenth-century naturalism and scientism.

The colors of Verga's narrative in *I Malavoglia* are softer and gentler than those of *Mastro Don Gesualdo*, and the writing more lyrical, yet most of what I have said above would pertain to the earlier novel. In *Mastro Don Gesualdo*, we watch the brilliant rise and tragic decline of a man of peasant origin who becomes a prosperous businessman, destined however to suffer the grim consequences of the very virtues and impulses that had allowed him to emerge from his class. In *I Malavoglia*, young 'Ntoni suffers the fate of one who, for good and sensible reasons, rebels against the restrictions imposed on him by his patriarchal grandfather, and launches himself into the great world beyond, only to discover that this world wants nothing of what he has to offer, and that by leaving his native village he has renounced what is most precious and enduring in the human condition, namely the supportive and life-enhancing solidarity of family, friends, and community.

Other disquieting motifs we have seen at work in *Mastro Don Gesualdo* are already present in *I Malavoglia*. Disease "sucks the life out of Maruzza's eyes," as she lies in bed helpless against cholera. The village money-lender also falls victim to the plague and, although he survives, is haunted by a fear of having "his blood sucked" from him by the resentful and hate-ridden recipients of his usurious loans. Alfio's donkey is endowed with the same feeling of anger and powerlessness as his master, and his animal destiny is not really dissimilar from that of his human counterparts. In sum, *I Malavoglia* contains most of the themes and character types, and many of the same situations and relationships, that Verga will draw out with more detailed attention to the social fabric of Sicilian life in *Mastro Don Gesualdo*.

Sciascia and Lampedusa

Looking now beyond Verga to the mid-twentieth century, I have already hinted several times at themes and tendencies in Verga that reappear in the writing of Sciascia and Lampedusa.

With regard to the main subject of this essay, I would say that the specifically Sicilian component of a fatalistic world-view is more explicitly characteristic of Sciascia and Lampedusa than of Verga. In Verga's work, the language of his dialogues has a distinctively Sicilian rhythm (the famous "patina siciliana" first identified by the great Sicilian literary historian Luigi Russo), and knowledgeable readers are able to identify a host of names, places, ideas, proverbs, etc. in Verga's stories that are characteristically Sicilian. Yet despite this insular inheritance one feels that a great deal of what Verga has to say in his work could have been said just as readily about many other places and countries of the world. Probably this is because the principles of verism were applicable to the overall evolution and nature of human life in a civilization deeply influenced by the new science, by technology and industry, by the emergence of huge modern cities, and by the epoch-making discoveries of Darwin concerning the evolution of species and the biological laws of inherited traits. These laws would apply anywhere, regardless of the differences that continued to mark various societies and cultures.

For Sciascia and Lampedusa, on the other hand, who took for granted the "universal" scientific and technological changes that had taken place from the mid-nineteenth century to the middle of the twentieth, the specifically Sicilian, that is, the local and immediate cultural milieu in which they, and their fictional characters, came to consciousness, assumed much greater importance. That is to say, while Verga could let his narratives speak for themselves, Sciascia and Lampedusa felt compelled to take the measure of their native island, and of their native country, in terms that would engage the reading public in more particularly political and even polemical ways. As certain universals could be taken more or less for granted, the need to explore the particulars became more urgent. The "Southern Question" became a burning issue in Italian politics *after* the achievement of national unity, not before.

This does not mean, however, that Verga's themes and some aspects of his visionary realism did not leave their mark on the two twentieth-century writers. Let's look first at *Pirandello e la Sicilia*, where Sciascia articulates his way of interpreting Sicilian reality.

Despite his intellectual indebtedness to the eighteenth-century Enlightenment and his commitment to the radical reform of Italian society – evident in many of his novels, for example *Candido* (1977), a name consciously borrowed from the tribune of the Enlightenment, Voltaire – Sciascia seems to have adhered on a deeper level to an interpretation of Sicily not so much as the product of history as an expression of what he calls "a way of being." A way of being, we should note, not a way of life. *Pirandello e la Sicilia* begins with a quote from Americo Castro's *La Realidad histórica de España* that Sciascia makes his own. What matters for both Castro and Sciascia are not so much the causes and antecedents of the present as the attempt "to understand and evaluate Spanish and Sicilian reality." This is a reality that can be conceptualized ontologically, as being, as essentiality. "We shall refer frequently to Spanish matters," Sciascia states at the outset of *Pirandello e la Sicilia*, "because of a fundamental consideration: that if Spain is, as someone has said, more than a nation a way of being, Sicily too is a way of being."

Sciascia argues that Sicily began to acquire its essential nature only after the Arab conquest of the island in the ninth century. It is only then, he asserts, that Sicilian life could begin to be "narrated" as a distinctive and individualized socio-political entity. Yet it becomes clear as one proceeds in this book that what really fascinates Sciascia is the overall pattern of Sicilian civilization, not its historical causes; its intricate mosaic of motifs and themes, not the reasons underlying them.

The link between this way of apprehending Sicilian life and Sciascia's fictional universe is not easily identified. One might argue that his novels, especially those that directly concern the connections between the mafia and the "respectable" world of Italian politics, business, and finance, are intensely engaged "case studies" of corruption in high places that act as a stimulus to remedy the ills that beset the island within its national and international context. Yet it is my feeling that these novels (one thinks *of A ciascuno il suo* and *Il giorno della civetta*) are not likely to be translated into any kind of coherent politics. On the contrary, these books induce a feeling of renunciation, of fatalism, that Sciascia himself regards as an integral aspect of Sicilian reality and that he seems to share with his characters to some extent. To the outsider, what happens between people in his novels can only be glimpsed indirectly, tangentially, in dim outline. We know much more about life in contemporary Sicily after reading his novels, but the picture remains elusive and allusive, *sfumato.*

Sciascia describes the basic elements of the Sicilian way of being as follows. First, "an extreme form of individualism whose active components . . . are the exaltation of maleness and a captious cerebralism." These traits, he believes, are quintessentially Arabic in origin, but find a natural abode in the Sicilian social fabric. The historical origins of Sicilian reality are there, but in Sciascia's view it is history become nature. These are traits that seem unchanging and unchangeable. Second is the Sicilian sense of the inextricable unity of comedy and tragedy, unlike the Greek vision, which keeps the two masks separated. Third is the peculiarly Sicilian sense of self-love, of honor and dignity that is travestied in the criminal code of the mafia but that even in this travestied form is something that Sicilians recognize. Fourth, a deeply ingrained fatalism, which attaches itself to personal relationships, to political attitudes, to love and family ties, to friendship, indeed to every crucial aspect of life. Fifth, a cult of material possession, something different from the usual form of acquisitiveness one finds in consumerist societies. Material possessions, *la roba*, are a defense mechanism against another pervasive Sicilian trait, namely insecurity, the fear of dependency and isolation. This fear in its turn breeds a compulsive desire for exclusivity in familial and sexual relations.

Although Sciascia was a man of the Left, it is clear that his "ontological" interpretation of Sicilian life is quite different from that of such figures as Gaetano Salvemini and Antonio Gramsci, for whom Sicily must be understood as part of a complex social and historical reality rooted in class relations, labor processes, and belief systems that cannot be adequately explained in essentialist terms.

The Leopard (1958), helped along by Luchino Visconti's film starring Burt Lancaster in the role of Prince Fabrizio Salina – the protagonist through whose eyes most of the main events and characters of the novel are seen – has been translated into over thirty languages and in Italy, by 1967, in its 13th edition, had sold over half a million copies. So we are dealing here with a novel that has penetrated into mass culture, and has in some measure helped to shape our understanding of what it has meant to be a Sicilian in the nineteenth and twentieth centuries. The novel begins in 1860, at the time of Garibaldi's landing to liberate the Italian South, and ends fifty years later, in 1910, when the last heirs to the Salina dynasty, three unmarried sisters, face a lonely old age and the imminent extinction of their blood line.

My interest here is not in the considerable artistic merits of this novel, but rather in its deeply ingrained pessimism, its representation of historically significant characters and events, and above all its view of Sicilian life. Of course we have to be careful not to confuse Fabrizio's opinions with those of the author, Lampedusa, yet I suspect that the two are not far apart.

One notable feature of the book is the almost obsessive way in which the author emphasizes the protagonist's German ancestry on his mother's side (his father is a native Sicilian) and its accompanying physical, that is, biologically determined, traits: blond hair, blue eyes, a "honey-colored" complexion, and large, powerful body. There are eighteen references to these ancestral traits in the novel (in only 186 pages), which apply also to the Prince's nephew Tancredi and to several of his own children. In the very first pages, Lampedusa amuses himself and the reader with the following thumbnail sketch of the traits that distinguish Fabrizio from those of his fellow Sicilians who lack the German strain in their blood:

> But other much more uncomfortable Germanic essences fermented in the blood of this Sicilian aristocrat, in the year 1860, even if his extremely white skin and blond hair were attractive features in this milieu of olive-skinned, raven-colored people: an authoritarian temperament, a certain moral rigidity, a propensity for abstract ideas which in the flabby moral habitat of Palermo society had changed respectively into capricious arrogance, constant moral scruples and contempt for his relatives and friends, who seemed to him to be floating along adrift in the meanderings of the slow pragmatic Sicilian river.

We should note that the author specifies the year 1860, a year that, as he tells us later, was marked not only by Garibaldi's conquest of the island but also by dishonest electoral tabulations and political hypocrisy that, for this morally scrupulous half-Sicilian, half-German aristocrat, signaled an incurable corruption in the Sicilian character: the word pragmatic is clearly no compliment here; it implies a slipshod indifference to moral issues, to which the Prince eventually succumbs, to be sure, but always with the painful awareness that springs from his German blood. There can be little doubt about it in this novel: darkness is suggestive almost always of a variety of unworthy, even contemptible traits, while the blond, blue-eyed people, although also tainted by their native Sicilian roots, are handsome, proud in their bearing, idealistic yet shrewd, like Tancredi, and able to take advantage of the changes under way in Italian society for their own and their family's benefit. It is Tancredi, after all, who convinces his uncle that his joining the Garibaldian liberators had been designed precisely to protect their privileges, not to undermine them, by saying: "If we want everything to remain as it is, it is necessary that everything change."

Such ethnic and quasi-racial strains are active agents in Lampedusa's representation of Sicilian mores and the Sicilian character, which is relentlessly characterized as backward, apathetic, resigned, pragmatic in the bad sense, and doomed to endure the shame of irreparable sins. Thus the events of 1860 and of subsequent decades in the life of the newly united Italian kingdom are portrayed in an exceedingly unflattering light. It is to Lampedusa's credit that, like Verga before him, he helped to demystify and "deconstruct" a history too often uncritically exalted as progressive and part of a broadly European democratic heritage. He scrutinizes this history and finds much that is not to his liking. He does so, however, in my view, by erecting a new set of myths and mystifications to replace the old ones. I mean that Lampedusa indulges in the sort of essentialism that marks Sciascia's conception of Sicily, by having his main character, Fabrizio, comment on events and personalities in such a way as to give the reader the sense that these Sicilian traits have become by now a second nature, a virtually ineradicable assortment of habits and ways of thinking that make a mockery of the hope for progressive change.

The death of Prince Fabrizio in 1883 and the symbolic destruction in 1910 of an embalmed family dog named Bendicò are two of the more obvious signposts of decay and defeat in the novel. Lampedusa's pessimism is at once historical and characterological. Let's look briefly at the scene set in November 1860 in which a Piedmontese diplomat, *cavaliere* Aimone Chevalley di Monterzuolo, tries to persuade Fabrizio to accept an honorary seat in the Italian Senate, based on his contribution to science and to the national cause.

Fabrizio receives Chevalley in a room set aside in his vast residence for such important occasions. Above the chair destined for visiting dignitaries are miniature portraits of the Salina dynasty, including "Don Fabrizio's father, prince Paolo, dark in complexion and with lips as sensual as those of a Saracen, dressed in the black Court uniform that was striped by the ribbon of the chivalric order of San Gennaro; [and] the princess Carolina, already widowed, her extremely blond hair gathered in a tower-shaped hair-do, and her *severe* blue eyes . . .". There are those blue eyes again, *severe* blue eyes, the source, no doubt, of Prince Fabrizio's "rigid moral code."

Fabrizio refuses the Count's offer. The reason for his refusal lies mainly in his belief that a man of his class, the ruling aristocratic landowning class, cannot be expected to have the kind of political optimism required of a nation's political representatives. "In Sicily," Fabrizio observes, "it doesn't matter whether one does good or evil: the sin that we Sicilians never pardon is simply that of doing. We are old, Chevalley, very old."

A short while after this scene, to reinforce the theme of disconsolate pessimism, Lampedusa enters the mind of Chevalley as he rides back to Palermo:

> He understood the bitterness and the discomfort of don Fabrizio, he saw once again in an instant the spectacle of misery, of abjection, of black indifference that he had been witness to for a month. In the previous hours he had envied the opulence, the lordly manner of the Salina family, but now he recalled tenderly his own little vineyard, his own Monterzuolo near Casale, unattractive, mediocre, but serene and alive. And he felt pity both for the Prince without hope and for the barefoot children, for the malaria-infested women, for the not-innocent victims whose names were sent to his office every day: they were all equal, basically, comrades in misfortune segregated in the same well.

Chevalley sees the wealthy aristocrat and the poverty-stricken Sicilian women and children as equal in so far as they are all Sicilians. Class, caste, socio-economic systems, political regimes, the very stuff of history, all fade into the background, to make way once again for something called the Sicilian essence. Such a formulation probably has a powerful appeal for many people, especially when it is presented in a literary text as artfully written as *The Leopard*. Works of art, too, have a political and ideological influence in the world, which it behooves all of us to recognize and evaluate.[2]

Acknowledgments

I would like to express my appreciation to Professors Jane and Peter Schneider, for taking the initiative that led both to a memorable Conference on Southern Italy in May 1995, and to the publication of this book.

My thanks are due also to the University of California Press, for permission to cite passages from Giovanni Cecchetti's English translation of Giovanni Verga's *Mastro Don Gesualdo* (1979).

Notes

1. Lawrence saw Verga as a writer who understood passions that "stirred the blood," whether motivated by sexual desire or by violence, and who broke through the hypocritical restraints and conventions of bourgeois morality.
2. Readers interested in examining the question of the practical worldly impact of nineteenth- and twentieth-century works of fiction should see Michael Hanne, *The Power of the Story – Fiction and Political Change* (Providence and Oxford: Berghahn Books, 1994).

References

Asor Rosa, Alberto (1976) "La nuova critica marxista." In *Interpretazioni di Verga*, ed. Romano Luperini, pp. 187–205. Rome: Savelli.
Debenedetti, Giacomo (1976) *Verga e il naturalismo*. Milan: Garzanti.
Dombroski, Robert (1994) *Properties of Writing*. Baltimore: The Johns Hopkins University Press.
Herzfeld, Michael (1987) *Anthropology through the Looking-Glass – Critical Ethnography in the Margins of Europe*. Cambridge: Cambridge University Press.
Luperini, Romano, ed. (1976) *Interpretazioni di Verga*. Rome: Savelli.

Moe, Nelson (1992) "'Altro che Italia!'. Il Sud dei piedmontesi (1860–61)," *Meridiana*, 53–89.

Said, Edward (1979) *Orientalism*. New York: Vintage Books.

Sciascia, Leonardo (1961) *Pirandello e la Sicilia*. Caltanissetta-Rome: Salvatore Sciascia Editore.

—— (1977) *Candido*. Turin: Einaudi.

Tomasi di Lampedusa, Giuseppe (1958) *Il Gattopardo*. Milan: Feltrinelli.

Verga, Giovanni (1952) *I Malavoglia*. Milan: Mondadori.

—— (1955) *The House by the Medlar Tree*, trans. Eric Mosbacher. Garden City: Doubleday.

—— (1956) *Mastro Don Gesualdo*, ed. Luigi Russo. Milan: Mondadori.

—— (1979) *Mastro-Don Gesualdo*, ed. and trans. Giovanni Cecchetti. Berkeley: University of California Press.

Part II

Critical Theory from the South

—6—

The Souths of Antonio Gramsci and the Concept of Hegemony
Nadia Urbinati

Preliminary Remarks

The Southern Question was born along with the unity of Italy, out of an awareness of the limits of unity itself and a disillusionment with the leading class that had made it possible. These sentiments were shared by all the *meridionalisti*, conservative, liberal, and democratic alike (P. Villari 1868; Franchetti 1911; Caizzi 1950; Salvadori 1976). Already in 1861, in "letters" to the Milanese magazine *La perseveranza* on brigandage, the mafia, and the poverty of the southern peasants, Pasquale Villari employed the notion of the *questione meridionale* to denote the "social" and "political" problems of the South. Villari denounced the selfishness of the largerly northern "bourgeoisie," which, because of its inability to govern, had become brutal and repressive, like a colonizing force, *vis-à-vis* the South. For him, the southern problem was unquestionably related to the way in which the political unification of the country was implemented, as an "occupation" of both the local and the central government by the moderate liberals of the North (P. Villari 1878: 147).[1] A few years later another "conservative", Sidney Sonnino, declared that for southerners Italy meant nothing but repression, high taxes, and arrogant public officials (Sonnino 1972: 155–61). Subsequently to Unification, in the 1880s and 1890s, the Italian government legislated a tariff policy protecting northern industries (primarily steel and textiles) and southern wheat from foreign competition. Both northern industrialists and southern landowners supported this policy, their alliance around it constituting what is sometimes called a "historic bloc". Because the first generation of conservative *meridionalisti* distrusted the free market and liberal international exchange, they had no critique of this policy, and did not attribute the South's misery to it (Urbinati 1990: 109–47). At the turn of the century, Antonio De Viti De Marco and Francesco Saverio Nitti identified the tariff policy as the tool the North had used to industrialize at the expense of the South (Caizzi 1950: 225–34; Nitti 1987: 13–15).

The first to draw a democratic conclusion from this libertarian critique was Gaetano Salvemini, who suggested that the "subaltern classes" of the South would win emancipation only in alliance with the working class of the North. By adopting a new perspective, which was no longer moralistic but primarily political, Salvemini defined the *questione meridionale* as a national question: the South needed not simply politicians of good will and a new policy, but a new national political subject. The emancipation of the South required the democratic emancipation of the whole nation (Salvemini 1963: 71–89).[2]

Salvemini proposed federalism, universal suffrage, and an end to protectionism. These suggestions provoked one of the most important schisms within the Socialist Party (to which Salvemini belonged), whose leaders were devoted to statism and felt indifferent (even "hostile") to the extension of political rights to southern "barbarians." Salvemini left the party because of the "oligarchic deviation" and "corporate selfishness" of its Northern-oriented ideology (Caizzi 1950: 327–36; Davidson 1977: 54). The difference between the Socialists and Salvemini was essentially cultural. The Socialist Party was devoted to an "economistic" interpretation of Marxism and a fatalistic reading of the socialist transformation. The party regarded the working class as the only legitimate subject and socialism as a natural and evolutionary process, requiring neither a political strategy nor a cultural shift.

The battle over the interpretation of the Southern Question mirrored the tension between idealism and positivism that animated Italian culture during the first decades of the century (Croce 1929: 238–9; Garin 1955: 20–30; Bobbio 1986: 27–38). Idealism and positivism grew out of opposite visions of life and inspired divergent political attitudes. As Antonio Gramsci wrote in 1918, for the positivists, society was "a natural organism" ruled by fixed laws, so that human will played no role in political transformation. For the idealist Marxists, on the contrary, *being* and *knowledge* were "unified," so that social emancipation was an entirely human project to be undertaken by a tenacious rational will aiming at conscious control of sordid necessity (1994: 77–8).

It was within this atmosphere of ideological tension that Gramsci developed his political thought and his understanding of the Southern Question. Siding with the idealists against the positivists, and with Salvemini against the socialists, he developed his *meridionalist* perspective within this theoretical framework, remaining consistently idealist over the years (Garin 1974: 302–9). The Southern Question was for the Sardinian Gramsci a national question in so far as it was a question of political and cultural hegemony. Its solution required the construction of a new relationship between the intellectuals and the "people-nation," between consciousness and being.

Analysis of Gramsci's controversial notion of hegemony, and of the even more controversial interpretations attempted by scholars since the publication of Gramsci's *Notebooks*, is beyond the scope of this chapter. It is difficult, however, to avoid the temptation to trace the "troubles" in Gramsci's thought to his idealism and the resulting idea of a *positive* liberty (Femia 1981). The idealist notion of the unity of consciousness and being has different implications, depending on whether it is employed as a normative argument for social criticism or a normative imperative for social construction. On the one hand, this notion undoubtedly has strong emancipatory significance because it allows us to criticize human subordination to external authority, and to denounce a social and political order based on physical *coercion* instead of free *consensus*. Gramsci's call for individual autonomy and recognition of the equal moral dignity of all human beings rests on this premiss. "A Communist is someone who acknowledges himself to be weaker physically but not inferior intellectually and spiritually; his body may be imprisoned, but not his mind . . . what makes man is the spirit of liberty and revolt" (Germino 1990: 128). On the other hand, the notion of the unity of consciousness and being entails a society that, in order to solve the conflict between coercion and consent, encourages a harmonious order in which the individual mind adheres to the collective mind perfectly and totally (Sbarberi 1986). As Gramsci wrote in the *Notebooks*, in the society of the future, "the single individual is self-governing, without his self-governing coming into conflict with political society – but rather becoming its normal continuation, its organic complement" (1971: 268).

For the idealist philosopher, however, the critical and the constructive moments are logically related, and the work of emancipation does not end with social criticism. For this reason, some scholars have wondered whether the failure of Gramsci's political project did not in fact save it from its own likely bad consequences – although Gramsci's vision of the society of the future was anything but systematic. Indeed, it is hard to describe as totalitarian a model in which political society and civil society remain separate and in which, moreover, civil society is "complex and well-articulated" (1971: 268).[3]

Gramsci's reflections on the Southern Question confirm the many-sidedness of his political thought, widening the distance between his social criticism and his constructivist ambitions. For him the South was the home of a stubborn necessity, against which the idealist notion of cultural and moral emancipation showed all its powerful critical implications. We might conclude that Gramsci's own southerness worked as a corrective to the comprehensive and unitary character of his hegemonic ideal. In this chapter, I wish to stress that for Gramsci the Southern Question was a national question, in so far as it was a question of lack of *communication* both among the social classes of the South and between the North and the South. Thus, the Southern Question was a cultural problem, whose solution would be the conquest of individual moral autonomy by Southerners and Northerners alike, and it was a political question, whose solution would be a democratic transformation of both society and the State.

The Souths of Gramsci

Gramsci's *Mezzogiorni* were many, and many were the strategies he adopted in the tumultuous decades preceding and following the First World War (Giarrizzo 1977: 321–89). His first *Mezzogiorno*, highlighting the desire for autonomy, arose during the elections of 1913, when Gramsci 'discovered' Croce, De Viti De Marco, and Salvemini and became an assiduous reader of *La Voce* and *l'Unità*.[4] Like these second-generation *meridionalisti*, he embraced a policy of radical opposition to the ruling "bloc" of northern industrialists and southern agrarians – the bloc that had legislated the protectionist policy noted above.[5] A free-market strategy, De Vito De Marco had written, could strengthen the political alliance between southern peasants and northern proletarians, because both had the same enemy. The campaign against protectionism was perceived by the *meridionalisti* as the first southern-inspired example of a sincere non-localist policy aimed at national integration (Caizzi 1950: 217–24).

Then came the *Mezzogiorno* of the period of the war, when Gramsci began to see the relevance of the "organization" for political action. Like many of his generation, Gramsci thought that the war would create what the rural economy could not: a collective psychology and a sense of national and class belonging. Two cultural phenomena were produced by the war: first, middle-class intellectuals discovered the existence of a nation very different from their rhetorical construction, a poor and illiterate nation with no sense of belonging politically to the Italian state.[6] Second, the suffering and fear in the trenches equalized soldiers of different classes by imposing great sacrifices and discipline. In 1918, Gramsci wrote that, thanks to the war, a *mass* of "disorganized individuals" totally "removed from collective activity of any kind" had the chance to become a *people* (1958: 181). The Bolshevik revolution seemed to confirm his analysis: the war created a potentially revolutionary class by making soldiers out of peasants. According to Gramsci, the conditions in Italy and Russia "were not and are not very different" (1954: 25). Soon, however, the rise of fascism, the Popular Party's penetration of the South, and the Soviet revolution's problems in rural areas dampened his optimism (Salvadori 1970: 78).[7] Now the countryside seemed to loom like a terrible menace against the city, its culture of modernity, its industrialism, and the very possibility of the socialist revolution. The peasant, wrote Gramsci in 1920, feels "his powerlessness, his solitude, his desperate condition, and becomes a *brigand*, not a revolutionary, he becomes an assassin of the *signori*, not a fighter for communism" (1954: 317). In other words, party ideology, political alliances and a few years of war were not enough to impel the peasants to develop a class consciousness.

In the light of these crucial events, Gramsci came to realize that the revolutionary party, the Communists, had to replace the strategy of *force* with that of *consent*, turning their attention to the role to be played, even among peasants, by intellectuals. Unfortunately, the Communists of Turin "had undervalued the problems of the South like the socialists" before them, because they had treated the peasants as mere subordinate allies of the workers (Togliatti 1967: 205).[8] "Personally, I think," wrote Gramsci in 1923, "that the slogan 'Workers' and Peasants' Government' should be adapted in Italy as follows: 'Federal Republic of Workers and Peasants'" (1978: 162).

More than anything, the rise of fascism confirmed yet again the existence of a gap between the rhetoric of national unity and the real "moral and intellectual" condition of the nation. Gramsci's *Alcuni temi della quistione meridionale* (1926) ends with a fresco of the "great social disintegration" (*disgregazione*) of the South and with a splendid portrait of Piero Gobetti and Guido Dorso, two examples of the new kind of intellectual whom he envisioned.[9] Gobetti was not a Marxist, but he saw the proletariat as a legitimate political subject of the liberal struggle, and thus he encouraged an encounter between liberals and Marxists, and between the South (represented by Benedetto Croce) and the North (represented by *L'Ordine Nuovo*). The task, concluded Gramsci, was to foster the growth of an entirely new class of intellectuals like Gobetti and Dorso, able to take advantage of an even more "critical" situation and promote a new balance among social forces. It would be a long project made up of little "molecular" transformations rather than sudden, wholesale changes. "Intellectuals develop slowly, far more slowly than any other social group" (1983: 50).

Contrasting the strategies of *force* and *consent*, Gramsci linked them to two different political goals: the construction of a new State, and the transformation of an existing State. The comparison between Machiavelli and Bodin in the *Notebooks* expressed very well the rationale for his hegemonic project of transformation. Unlike Machiavelli, Bodin aimed not to construct a territorial State but to "balance the conflicting social forces" within the existing State. Whereas Machiavelli's emphasis was on the "moment of force," Bodin was interested in the "moment of consent" (1971: 142). Gramsci saw their difference as analogous to the difference between the leaders of the Risorgimento and his own vision.

A New Risorgimento

Gramsci read the hegemonic failure of the Risorgimento as a failure of its intellectuals, who had been unable to transform the dominion of force into political and cultural consent. Both the losers and the winners had failed. The democrats had failed because of their jacobinism and their unpragmatic, sentimental humanitarianism. Like Machiavelli, Carlo Cattaneo thought social unity could be achieved simply by mobilizing a national army; Giuseppe Mazzini, who understood what a great mistake it was to confuse "cultural unity with political and territorial unity," reduced the ideological task to nothing more than some "aphorisms" and "empty talk" (1992: 139, 152). To promote the "moral and intellectual unity" of the country required a *weltanschauung* – in both its theoretical and its popular form – not vague moral preaching.

Totally misunderstanding the intellectual task, the Risorgimento democrats had failed to perceive the need to implement an agrarian reform in the South, ignoring the strategic importance of winning the consent of the masses. The liberal moderates, who at least had a cultural strategy, failed in their hegemonic project because they mistrusted the masses. Accustomed to hierarchical relations, they treated Italians the way the generals of a pre-Napoleonic army treated their soldiers.[10] "The army is also an 'instrument' for a particular end, but it is made up of thinking men and not of robots who can be utilized to the limits of their mechanical and physical cohesion" (1971: 88). Piedmontese liberals who led the Risorgimento shared primary responsibility for the failure of a liberal hegemony because they had set themselves up as both intellectuals and politicians. "They said they were aiming at the creation of a modern State in Italy, and they in fact produced a bastard. They aimed at stimulating the formation of an extensive and energetic ruling class, and they did not succeed; at integrating the people into the framework of the new State, and they did not succeed" (1971: 90).

As the leaders of an earlier generation of *meridionalisti* had understood, building a liberal government necessitated the formation of public opinion. Once this project failed, the leading class was left with no instruments other than force and bureaucracy to impose a political order in the South. The vacuum left by the absence of a conservative party was filled by a demagogic nationalism that worsened "social disintegration" and made it easier for fascism to take root.

Gramsci's project began where liberal hegemony left off: with the goal of incorporating the South into the nation State.[11] But precisely because Gramsci did not consider the South to be a local problem, his *meridione* should be read as a category representing the entire nation – the "Italian people [who] did not exist as a concrete ideal, as active organization," that nation that existed simply as a figure of speech used by the rulers to manipulate popular sentiment and justify their oppressive policies. Like the South, the whole of Italian society was made up of an "enormous mass of individuals who were disorganized in all senses, innocent of the great evil and the little good that happened around them, indifferent to every ideal, estranged from every collective activity, and who refused every responsibility because they were removed from every enterprise" (1958: 181).

Gramsci's interpretation of the Southern Question as a question of national unity recalled Marx's approach to the Jewish question: as long as the nation State remained the State of the northern-centred agrarian–industrial bloc, and as long as the South remained a "great social disintegration," they were "equally incapable, the one of conferring emancipation, the other of receiving it" (Marx and Engels1978: 27). Indeed, in relation to the South, the Italian State could only adopt the attitude of a northern state, permitting the South to isolate itself from the whole and foster its corporate sentiments and interests. The emancipation of the South could only be its emancipation from itself, which would mean the emancipation of the entire nation.[12] This goal was the ideal that shaped Gramsci's research project in prison. As he wrote to his wife's sister, Tania, in 1927, he wanted to study the "formation of the public spirit in Italy" through three topics: the Southern Question, the philosophy of Benedetto Croce, and the evolution of popular literary tastes (1955: 27–8; 1973: 79). Clearly, those three topics corresponded to the "disintegrated masses," the great intellectuals and the middle-class intellectuals, respectively – in other words, folklore, philosophy, and common sense.

From a strategic point of view, common sense played the most important role, because, as Gramsci believed the war had showed, an army's effectiveness rests upon the ability of the *ufficiali* (lieutenants) to facilitate *communication* between the generals (the mind) and the soldiers (the body). The new intellectuals had to elaborate a modern humanism "able to reach right to the simplest and most uneducated classes" (1985: 211). The Protestant Reformation triumphed when the aspirations of the few became the common sense of the many, transforming a religious event into a political one. Thanks to the popularization of its tenets, the Reformation had the strength to resist Catholic armies and to form the "German nation." By the same token, liberal democracy won when the principles of the Enlightenment ceased to be the cultural property of a restricted intellectual aristocracy and became common beliefs (1971: 394). The new reformers envisaged by Gramsci would have to follow the same path, doing precisely what Italian intellectuals had never done: "going to the people" in order to understand the formation and consolidation of popular beliefs and to give the new principles, as *Capital* recites, "the solidity of a popular prejudice."

Culture and the Guilt of the Enlightenment

The growing complexity of Gramsci's *meridione* paralleled the growing complexity of his conception of culture. In the *Notebooks*, one no longer sees a homogeneous "immense countryside" (South) opposing a homogeneous "immense city" (North). The North did not mean simply modernity and urbanization; it was not free from all provincialism and superstition. The city was not necessarily more progressive than the countryside; in Italy, certainly, urbanization and industrialization did not go always and everywhere together. Gramsci's idea of culture became equally complicated; it cannot be reduced simply to a tension between modernity and backwardness, nor even to an adaptation of popular culture to the ideology of intellectuals (1971: 337).

Cultures were, for him, living bodies always subject to inner transformations, not entities to be worshipped, or homogeneous sets of meanings shared by all in the same way (1971: 418–19). Gramsci's interest in popular culture and folklore was *political* – neither the mere curiosity of the erudite, nor the nostalgic longing for a supposedly virgin world besieged by modernity (1971: 90–1).[13] Understanding popular culture meant grasping its inner diversity and the restless transformations born of its various relations with the culture of the intellectuals, past and present. Beside this idea of *gradual* transformation, the vision of sudden, epochal change appeared to him an "illusion," a sign of "the absence of a critical sense" (1992: 129). Old and new, intellectual and popular, blended to produce those complex combinations that constitute what we call a national culture.

Like Freud's contemporaneous vision of the identity of the self, Gramsci's idea of a national culture could be metaphorically compared to the city of Rome (Freud 1989: 12–17). A sufficiently learned tourist would be able to recognize the various strata that tell the story of the eternal city since the Etruscan age; she would see relics where a witless observer would see only stones. Conservation, transform-ation, sedimentation, and evolution are gradual and blended; they are the result of an endless process of mutual adaptation, as the present comes to terms with the past (1985: 417–18). The old does not disappear suddenly, but persists in new forms. Folklore and popular culture are living anachronisms, relics of the past stranded in the present and fused into a totality, like the multi-layered city of Rome. Resembling spoken language in contrast to written, folklore is "unstable and fluctuating." Far from being a "pre-history," it is a living version of existing high culture and a present-day recapitulation of past combinations of high and popular culture (1985: 194–5). Far from being passively absorbed, it is *actively* created and remodeled, even if it is formed of elements from other cultural strata and times (1971: 324). As Gramsci himself suggested, the "public spirit" he planned to study in jail was nothing but "the popular creative spirit, through its diverse phases and grades of development" (1973: 80).

This interpretation of culture affected both his notion of hegemony and his reading of the relation between city and countryside (North/South), because the interpretation allowed for a historicization of abstract categories, such as intel-lectuals and people, urbanism and ruralism. In the Italian case, wrote Gramsci in the *Notebooks*, the *typical* loses its typicality and complicates itself. Because the formation of cities preceded the industrial revolution, urbanization was not necessarily an industrial phenomenon, nor could it be identified with modernity. In Italy, therefore, one faced the paradox that "the rural type may be more progressive than the urban type." Naples, the "city of silence," was a mosaic of urban islands "submerged, pressured, crushed" by rural areas. This long-lasting conflict nurtured feelings of hatred and resentment, the very sentiments that divided intellectuals from the peasants, the middle class from the poor. For Gramsci no less than for Vincenzo Cuoco, the Enlightenment (and its intellectuals) shared primary responsibility for the fall of the Neapolitan Republic of 1799, which marked the failure of the democratic process in the South: "the countryside crushed the city with the hordes of Cardinal Ruffo because the city had completely neglected the countryside" (1992: 129–30). The main responsibility for the Southern Problem rested with the city and the intellectuals, because of their separation from popular culture and their misunderstanding of cultural phenomena. If the culture of democracy did not prevail in Italy, this failure was due not so much to the strength of the anti-modern forces (Catholicism and the Counter-Reformation) as to the deficiencies of the culture of modernity.

The two evils Gramsci identified – *separateness* and *incomprehension* – connected his analysis of southern intellectuals to his critique of the Enlightenment. The "'enlightenment' error" consisted in attributing the same method of mental assimilation and cultural elaboration to all social classes (1992: 128). This "error" grew out of the imperialistic vice of the intellectuals, encapsulated in the Cartesian view that, because truth always takes the form of clear and distinct ideas, intellectuals must foster truth by eradicating error in all its forms, in particular popular beliefs, religions, prejudices. But because intellectual processes are more complex, "the premise of an 'organic diffusion from a homogeneous center of a homogeneous way of thinking and acting' is not sufficient" (1992: 128). In so far as general principles and local knowledge stand in a relation of reciprocal influence, the cultural strategy can be neither a forced imposition of new principles ("deductivism"), nor a passive acceptance of things as they are ("empiricism").

Gramsci's observation recalls that of Alexis de Tocqueville: in Europe, intellectuals "suddenly draw general conclusions" from Descartes's method, while in America philosophy has never separated itself from people's daily lives. In Europe, democracy never became common sense, because from the beginning it took the form of a forced imposition of principles shared only by a narrow circle of *savants*. Democracy was decreed by the "authority of the masters" and left the empirical realm of everyday life generally untouched. By contrast, the Americans "have needed no books to teach them philosophic method, having found it in themselves." They were democratic in their *mores* (common sense), not in obedience to a decree of Reason (Tocqueville 1969: 430–1). Gramsci's thought revealed an affinity with that of the American pragmatists. Like them he located the Archimedean point of political action neither on the side of "deductivism" nor of "empiricism," but in the very process of their mutual interaction. Hegemonic work rested on the intellectual ability to seek the "identity underneath the apparent differentiation and contradiction and to find the substantial diversity underneath the apparent identity" (1992: 128). This epistemological premiss underlay Gramsci's idea that the relation between high culture and popular culture represented the unity of "knowing" and "feeling".

The 'Sage of Vulgar Wisdom'

The unity of "knowing" and "feeling" brings us to Gramsci's notion of *under-standing*, which, already in his youth, he identified with the Socratic "know thyself." In 1916, commenting upon Novalis' *Fragments*, Gramsci wrote that the supreme task of cultural emancipation was for the individual to learn to master herself – to become "the self of oneself" – not as an egoistic being, but as a "transcendental self" (1994: 8). "Know thyself" was an imperative of moral autonomy, in a Kantian sense. A self-mastering self could construct a dialectical relation with the outside world, which then would cease to be experienced as a reified fatal necessity. "Knowing thyself" meant knowing your condition in the world, so that your will would no longer act out of anarchical rebellion, but would express true freedom, a "passage from the 'objective' to the 'subjective'" (1975: 1244). Gramsci's notion of an "intellectual and moral reform" (hegemony) is grounded in the primacy of subjectivity (Bobbio 1968: xlv).

To clarify the political meaning of the imperative "know thyself," Gramsci used a passage from *The New Science* in which Vico traced Socrates's motto back to Solon, the "party leader of the plebeians in the first times of the aristocratic commonwealth at Athens". Solon was the "sage of vulgar wisdom," able to overcome the power of the heroes and the nobles who "believed [themselves] to be of divine origin" and "kept within their own orders all the public and private rights". Solon turned to the people and challenged them "to reflect upon themselves and to realize that they were of like human nature with the nobles and should therefore be made equal with them in civil rights". The transition from aristocracy to democracy transformed not only the subordinate classes but also the whole society: "we shall demonstrate that the plebeians of the peoples universally, beginning with Solon's reflection, changed the commonwealth from aristocratic to popular" (Vico 1948: 119–20; Gramsci 1994: 8–9).

Gramsci's intellectual was the "sage of vulgar wisdom" who could dialogue with his fellows, not in order to accept their way of being, but to incite them to become conscious of their subjectivity as "transcendental selves," as equals. The seeds of cultural emancipation were already present, even if in a disorganized and folkloric form. The difference between high culture and popular culture was a difference of degree, not of kind (1971: 199).

The "organic intellectual" can know and feel because, as Vico suggested, she is moved by the "force" of "imagination". The imagination is *dramatic fantasy*, a faculty that can vividly represent the problems and hopes of society to the mind and sentiment. Thus politics is not simply a strategic calculus, or the implementation of an abstract model. Politics is a combination of reason with an *empathetic* disposition. "In order to provide for the needs of human beings living in a city, a region, a nation, it is necessary to feel those needs; it is necessary [for the politician] to represent concretely to his fantasy those human beings as beings who live and work daily, to represent their sorrows, the sadness of a life they are forced to live. If one does not possess this power to dramatize life, one cannot guess the general and particular provisions able to harmonize life's necessities and government's availabilities" (1958: 101).

Because Italian politicians and intellectuals lacked "dramatic fantasy," their deeds were characterized by domination and arrogance. Instead of governing, they worked "to embitter the uneasiness." Their distance from the people, their rancorous contempt for the poor, made them bad politicians and bad intellectuals. "They are amateur. They do not have any sympathy for human beings. They are rhetoricians of sentimentality, not men who feel concretely. They force others to suffer needlessly in the very moment they glorify the virtue of self-sacrificing of the Italians" (1958: 101). "They are incapable of representing to themselves the suffering of others, hence they are pointlessly cruel" (1958: 104).

In the words of *Alcune note sulla questione meridionale*, rural intellectuals developed "a strong aversion for the peasant laborer whom they look on as a living machine that must be worked to the bone [. . .]: they also inherit an atavistic and instinctive feeling of crazy fear of the peasant and his destructive violence, and hence a habit of refined hypocrisy and a most refined skill in deceiving and breaking in the peasant masses" (1983: 43).

Like Gramsci himself as a prisoner, and like his fellow Sardinians, the peasants had only two options: to surrender to fatalism or to resist and rebel. Various scholars have argued that Gramsci's notion of hegemony sacrificed spontaneity to discipline and organization. But Gramsci "blessed" that spontaneous rebelliousness he had felt as a child because it saved him from a life of passive acquiescence to an inevitable destiny: "What was it that stopped me from turning into a stuffed shirt? The instinct of rebellion" (Fiori 1970: 26). He felt the same way about the peasants, the seeds of whose liberation might lie in their "instinct" for rebellion.

The words Gramsci used to describe his condition as prisoner can also be used to understand his view of the South: "When you don't have the initiative in the struggle and the struggle itself comes eventually to be identified with a series of defeats, mechanical determinism becomes a tremendous force of moral resistance," a way to maintain moral and psychological cohesion. A loser thinks "things" themselves will work on his behalf. To survive, the will to resist has to convert itself into a natural necessity. But Gramsci had no doubt that even in such extreme circumstances "fatalism is nothing other than the clothing worn by real and active will when in a weak position." His conclusion sounded like a political program: fatalism was a "cause of passivity, of idiotic self-sufficiency when it is adopted as a thought-out and coherent philosophy on the part of the intellectuals" (1971: 336–7). Intellectuals must keep alive the people's volitional instincts in order to help them "emerge from the chaos" and become the subjects of their own liberation. To know means to find the origin of power not outside ourselves, in mechanical necessity, but inside ourselves, in spiritual necessity. Gramsci was reading Marx's *Theses on Feuerbach* through Vico, like Giovanni Gentile years earlier.

Phenomenology of the Passions

In 1926, Gramsci defined the South as a "great social disintegration" (*disgregazione*): disintegration among the classes, which did not communicate with each other, and within the classes themselves, which were composed of individuals sharing the same material interests but spiritually estranged from one another. The cultural environment of social disintegration was a schism between the intellectuals as encyclopedic rhetoricians and the poor as "empty containers to be filled." The failure of the moderates of the *Risorgimento* was the outcome of a cultural distancing whose viciousness became obvious once middle-class intellectuals embraced it: "The smug little student who knows some Latin and history, the vain little lawyer who has taken advantage of his teachers' laziness and apathy to wangle himself a threadbare degree" (1994: 9). The middle-class intellectual was like a two-faced Janus, populist and democratic in his peasant soul, arrogant and reactionary in his landlord outlook (1983: 43).

Concern with cultural separateness was a constant topic of Gramsci's writings, beginning even before the *Note* of 1926 and running through his letters from prison and finally the *Notebooks*. Gramsci's treatment of this subject bore a vivid similarity to Salvemini's description of the rural *petite bourgeoisie* and recalled Aristotle's representation of the savage passions that flourish along the borderline between social classes: envy, mistrust, hypocrisy, hatred, revenge, resentment, anarchy, and sudden rebelliousness. Those very passions divided Italian society and hampered the creation of a politics of consent. The South's "great social disintegration" was a highly segregated society, where the new rich, who lived in permanent fear of losing ground, despised the very poor and envied the very rich; where the very poor hated their superiors but, overwhelmed by fear, slid toward a fatal acceptance of their condition; and where the very rich despised the members of both the other classes, and, like gods, stayed too far above them to be touched by their mean feelings and misery (1983: 42–3).

For the middle class and the landed agrarians, the peasant was a mysterious and frightening enigma, a seething cauldron of primordial passions, ignorant, rebellious, and unpredictable. He represented the *other* against which they had to defend themselves, either through religion or State repression, or both. Gramsci's politics of "knowing thyself" acquired its emancipatory strength in relation to this *moral* picture of the South.

The phenomenology of liberty and necessity, consciousness and being, that lay beneath Gramsci's Socratism permeated his own life no less than his thought. Like an invisible thread, it unified his relationship with his own body, his island, the South, and his condition as a prisoner. Each was the locus of a recalcitrant necessity against which he struggled endlessly. As he wrote to his sister-in-law about his life in prison, "What makes my suffering is the condition of uncertainty, the indeterminacy of that which will occur" (1955: 161).

His body was a dull necessity. To get it under control and correct his deformity, Gramsci had to develop an iron will, exercising "every day" with extraordinary and methodical "determination" and discipline (Fiori 1970: 19). His childhood in Sardinia, when he had struggled against hunger, humiliation, and injustice, was a terrible necessity. Like prisons, those experiences made him think of himself as locked in a permanent "war of position" against an oppressive *nature* that defied any order and rational control. To resist that "absolute and almost fatal impossibility," he donned a mask of distance and irony (1955: 29). So did the peasants he described in his writings, who fought against middle-class intellectuals (doctors, priests, lawyers) as Gramsci did against his environment: with "impassioned anger" and unpredictable rebelliousness (1971: 14).

Segregation made communication impossible and undesirable. In the South, and between the North and the South, relationships were based on reciprocal ignorance and reciprocal fear, because neither could foresee what the *other* might have done: the peasants because of their superabundance of "feeling," the intellectuals because of their arid erudition, and the Northerners because they thought of the South's "misery" as "unexplainable" (1971: 70). "The popular element 'feels' but does not always know or understand; the intellectual element 'knows' but does not always understand and in particular does not always feel" (1971: 418).

How was Gramsci to reconcile these two elements without falling into either Mazzini's humanitarian sentimentalism or an impatient jacobinism? As a student in Turin, Gramsci had been interested in understanding the practical value of the "intellectual factor," in learning why ideas had the power to make us act. His teacher directed him to the theory of the *idées-forces* of Alfred Fouillée, an earlier version of William James's "will to believe," which helped many intellectuals of Gramsci's generation escape from determinism and abstraction (Garin 1974: 356–7).

Gramsci saw two ways to overcome necessity: through a single heroic act (the "war of maneuver," or *force*) or through the slow and prosaic work of cultural reshaping (the "war of position," or *consent*). As we know, he discarded the first strategy because, according to him, it was suitable only for a less developed society. In Western countries, civil society was much more articulated and pluralistic than in contemporary Russia or eighteenth-century France, making the use of force inappropriate (Paggi 1984: 14–15). For the working classes of the West, jacobinism's moment was over. As Georges Sorel had noticed in 1919, social transformation could not be attained by implementing truths from above. "If the Church had been merely a school of philosophy preaching pure morality, it would undoubtedly have disappeared like many other groups" (Sorel 1976: 73). No élite, no charismatic leader, could create a new society by force. To use Michael Walzer's language, Gramsci's intellectual would not force the truth from outside (Walzer 1988: 90).

The struggle of the South was thus not simply a struggle for survival or for economic progress, but a struggle to liberate itself from its "tremendous" passions. To succeed it was not enough to invert the relationship between "knowing" and "feeling." As a young journalist for a radical Sardinian newspaper, Gramsci saw firsthand the powerlessness of a rebellion unable to master necessity. In 1910, the peasants had been ready to show their "startling and fearful" determination to obtain universal suffrage in local elections. To calm them down, it had been enough for the government to send eighty soldiers. Paralysed by fear of repression, their rebellious instincts were impotent (Fiori 1970: 59–60). The road toward autonomy and dignity had to lead in another direction, because the peasants' weakness lay not in their material conditions but in their lack of subjective consciousness, their inability to guide their "spontaneous" tension toward liberation (Salvadori 1970: 136). To distinguish oneself from the other, Gramsci wrote some years later, meant to attain consciousness of oneself as an independent subject, to be able not simply to will, but to have an "exact notion of one's own power" so as to know what one can will (1994: 57; Adamson 1980: 152–4).

This idealist conception of subjectivity was the seed of Gramsci's notion of *catharsis*, the passage from the purely egoistic-passional moment (economics) to the ethical-ideal moment (politics) (1971: 366). The emancipatory function of politics (the primacy of the political over the economic) stood against enslavement to biological needs in a way that echoed the Aristotelian duality between the realm of the *household* (necessity) and the *political* realm (liberty). From the former sphere paralysing passions arose; from the latter the intelligent will arose. Emancipation from "private" passions, such as fear and rage and hatred, was the precondition for political action and corresponded to the passage from a common sense that saw the "enemy" as an irreducible other (total enemy) to one that saw him as a specific antagonist (political enemy).

A Fugitive from Backwardness?

To become the intellectual who *knows* how to liberate the subordinate classes, Michael Walzer recently wrote, Gramsci had to leave behind the backwardness of common sense and learn to see things from a "universal" and external point of view. Gramsci as intellectual needed to "break as radically with the 'Sardinia' of common sense as he had done with the actual Sardinia where he was born and raised" (Walzer 1988: 95). The image of Gramsci as a "fugitive" from backwardness, seeking modernity, was first suggested in 1924 by Piero Gobetti, who described Gramsci as a man who left "the countryside in order to forget his traditions and substituted the Sardinian anachronism with a solitary and inexorable effort to grasp the modernity of urban life" (Gobetti 1969: 1003). Both Gobetti and Walzer raise a very important concern, even if what was for the former an act of heroism is for the latter a sign of a culpable estrangement.

Although appealing, however, the image of Gramsci as a fugitive from local knowledge ("his rejection of home and homeland:" Walzer 1988: 95) reduces his complexity to too sharp a dualism. Did Gramsci reject his origins? During his first years in Turin, he associated only with Sardinians, and chose to study glottology in order to deepen his knowledge of his native language. Indeed, it was this affection for his origins that kept him far from socialist circles, where a loyalty to positivism was fomenting deep anti-southern prejudices. "People usually speak of the lack of initiative of the Southerners. The fact is that capital looks always for the most safe and lucrative ways of investment" (1958: 32). An idealist Marxism was for him a way of dignifying southern identity, rather than rejecting it. Indeed, a social interpretation of Sardinian backwardness required first of all the rejection of all "scientific" theories based on a biological reading of cultural difference — among them the theory of the socialist, Lombroso (see Gibson, this volume, Chapter 4). Because the South was not "special," composed of constitutionally "different" people, the southern problem could not be solved by "special legislation" (as both conservatives and socialists were proposing). It was a "national question," a political question of "a general policy, both domestic and foreign" (1958: 31). Gramsci's idealization of modernity reflected first of all his desire to combat those prejudices and their easy diffusion within the working class, thanks to the old Italian socialist culture (1983: 31). His *città* was thus a regulative idea more than a description of an actual city (1958: 93–4).

Precisely because Gramsci never totally rejected his identity as a southerner (and as a southerner gave his first and last parliamentary speech), he was able to see the limits of the worker culture that treated the peasants of the South as obstacles to progress, as a "lead weight" for the whole nation (1983: 31; 1971: 71). Gramsci's opposition of the "universal" (the general or national) to the "corporate" should also be seen from this perspective. His promotion of a "new humanism" for all was an attempt to "deprovincialize" both the North and the South, purging the North of its racism and its egocentric localism and the South of its fatalistic resignation. Northerners — both intellectuals and common people — never felt "solidarity" with the South because of their colonizing ideology, their total "ignorance" of southern society, and their prejudices. No less than the Sardinians, the Northerners had to submerge their localism in a unitarian (or national) outlook. They did not have to deny their cultural identity, but they did need to free themselves from their selfish provincialism.

Should we see Gramsci as a "victim" of Marxist teleology? "The more advanced his theory, the more detached he is in practice from working-class backwardness" (Walzer 1988: 99). I am inclined to adopt a milder reading, because Gramsci never resolved this tension once and for all. Besides, had he embraced teleology he would not have been content with his disorganized notes; he would have constructed a system out of the sparse empirical evidences he had. He would not have felt in need of that "huge amount of material" (1973: 79). Gramsci's attitude is always in balance between spontaneity and constructivism. In prison, he grew plants. He tried constantly to "draw them up a bit to help them grow" (1973: 144). He could never solve his "uncertainty" concerning the two opposite methods of education: if he should have been "Rousseauian and let Nature, which never errs and is basically good, do what she wants," or "voluntarist, and force Nature by introducing into its evolution an expert human hand and the principle of authority" (1955: 72; 1973: 144).

Common Sense as a Common Faith

To interpret the crucial role played by common sense (and by middle-class intellectuals as *ufficiali of communication and integration*) in Gramsci's Southern Question, we should think of common sense as a medium that facilitates interaction between the two extremes, high culture and folklore.

Like the *axiomata media* of John Stuart Mill, Gramsci's common sense comprises the whole of the *maxims* through which principles are translated into moral guides for everyday life. In this sense, Gramsci wrote that every high culture and every discipline has its own folklore. In the case of judicial culture, for instance, the belief in natural rights is a form of folklore, that is, a translation of the judicial principles of the "experts" into common sense and common language. When we say that a judge should interpret the *spirit* of the law, we are asking him to adapt general principles to the shared culture of the whole society (1985: 193–4). Between these two levels, a process of reciprocal accommodation, rather than imposition on one side and passive absorption on the other, occurs. Thus Gramsci did not contradict himself when, at the very moment he accepted the leading role of intellectuals, he also insisted that between high culture and popular culture there was a difference of "quantity" not "quality" (1971: 347). Using Rawlsian language, we might say that common sense looks like a *reflective equilibrium*, or, as Gramsci himself said, "a reciprocal 'reduction' so to speak, a passage from one [principles] to the other [common sense] and vice versa," a movement back and forth between universality and common knowledge. "Recall that Immanuel Kant believed it important for his philosophical theories to agree with common sense" (1971: 199).

When Gramsci wrote that Italy needed a "public spirit" to become a unified society, he was suggesting that *communication* among social and cultural strata was needed, so that political consciousness would not exist solely among a tiny élite while the masses remained totally estranged from public life.

If we inspect Gramsci's notion of hegemony in the light of his reflections on the Southern Question, we may be legitimately tempted to extend that notion to democracy and say that his hegemonic project was inspired by the same ideal that underlay John Dewey's conception of democracy as a *common faith*. "The Italian people lack the spirit of disinterested solidarity, the love of free discussion, the desire to attain truth by purely human means offered by intelligence and reason" (1994: 37). Interpreting Gramsci's project of "moral and intellectual renovation" of Italian society from this perspective, we may conclude that his notion of hegemonic unity did not necessarily mean the repression of spontaneity and popular culture by the "missionaries" of the philosophy of praxis (Walzer 1988: 90). The movement from common sense to philosophy might be seen as a gradual (and revolving) move from a lesser to a greater level of generality in the expression of moral principles that are already shared by a political community. It is the work of intellectuals to give these principles theoretical form – not to create them. A theory of the good society has the chance to become widespread common sense in so far as it elaborates upon the notions of justice and equality that are already contained within a given culture in the form of sentiments and intuitions.

This democratic interpretation of Gramsci's hegemony can be compared to the relationship he spelled out between a dialect and a national language. "Someone who *only* speaks dialect, or understands language incompletely, necessarily has an intuition of the whole which is more or less limited and provincial" (1971: 325, italics added). The same was true of someone who spoke *only* the national language. As he wrote to his sister, not teaching her children the Sardinian tongue would mean depriving them of the possibility of understanding their whole culture, which was a blend of the local and the national. To form hegemony, therefore, does not necessarily mean to manipulate or uproot popular culture but to enable communication among the cultural levels that make up a national culture. Hegemony aims at ensuring that no social group, whether intellectuals or southern peasants, remains a "narrow province," segregated and complacent about its own isolation and diversity.

Notes

1. "The leading class takes care primarily of its own interests," while the rural working class "is suffering more than any other class." Villari proposed two solutions: first a struggle against illiteracy, second an agrarian reform. The latter had to be accomplished by encouraging the growth of a secure form of share-cropping and of smallholdings. This reference to Villari allows us to question Sidney Tarrow's thesis that Gramsci was the father of the theory of "rape" because he depicted the South as "the special victim" of the Risorgimento (Tarrow 1967: 251).

2. Both as a historian and a *meridionalista*, Salvemini was a pupil of Villari, about whom he wrote an inspiring essay on the occasion of his death in 1918 (Salvemini 1978: 57–80).

3. For a democratic and pluralist interpretation of Gramsci's hegemonic project, see Chantal Mouffe's "Hegemony and Ideology in Gramsci" (1979) and Noberto Bobbio (1977).

4. Gramsci never completely abandoned this position or totally rejected region-alism. As he wrote in 1923 in explaining the aims of the new-born newspaper *L'Unità*, to consider the Southern question a national question did not mean to think in terms of centralization: "the real tendencies of the peasant class . . . have always had in their programmes the slogan of local autonomy and decentralization" (1978: 162).

5. "Why can't one recall," wrote Gramsci in 1919, "that Sardinian miners are paid starvation wages . . .? Why should it be prohibited to recall that two-thirds of the inhabitants of Sardinia (especially women and children) go without shoes in the winter and summer . . . because the price of hide has gone sky-high due to the protective tariffs that enrich the Turin industrialists and leather manu-facturers?" (Gramsci 1968: 103–4).

6. This conviction was widespread far beyond the Communist circle. See, for instance, Carlo Rosselli's article "Wilson" (1917), quoted in Nicola Tranfaglia (1968), *Carlo Rosselli dall'interventismo a "Giustizia e Libertà"*, p. 20.

7. "In vain the Soviet government invited them [the peasants] to support the power of the workers and the peasants: they refused to give bread to the workers of the Hungarian cities and Hungary, which is a country of peasants, remained without bread" (Corvisieri 1970: 380).

8. The first criticism of the "unitarian" strategy of the Communists came from the radical *meridionalisti*, in particular Guido Dorso, who in 1925 wrote that both the Partito Popolare and the Communists could not understand and solve the Southern Problem because they "neutralized the southern action into a northern one" (R. Villari 1981: 524). As Gramsci's *Southern Question* shows,

Dorso's criticism had a deep influence on his revision of his former worker-centred Marxism.

9. The word *disgregazione* should be read as having two meanings, a moral one and a political one: as denunciation of conditions of suffering and injustice, and as the identification of the critical point from which to begin the transformation of the entire system (Badaloni 1975: 121–4; Pizzorno 1970: 114).

10. It is worth noting that the same diagnosis of the *piemontesi*'s faults was made by some conservative and radical leaders of the Risorgimento. See, for instance, Pasquale Villari, "Di chi è la colpa? o sia la pace e la guerra" (1866) in P. Villari 1868: 390, and Carlo Cattaneo, "Prefazione" of Vol. 10 of *Il Politecnico* (1860) in Cattaneo 1972, Vol. 1: 209–10.

11. Gramsci's interpretation of the Risorgimento as a "failed revolution" and a "failed agrarian revolution" was at the center of debate among historians of the 1960s and 1970s, beginning with Rosario Romeo and Federico Chabod (Davis 1979: 67–103). I personally tend to accept Alessandro Pizzorno's proposal that we consider Gramsci's interest in the Risorgimento as essentially political rather than historiographical. Gramsci's aim was to verify not a historical interpretation but a political theory; his interest was in the present and future more than in the past. His criticism of a history made of *ifs* is well known. The *ifs*, writes Pizzorno, are useful for the political leader but not for the historian, because they delineate a possible scenario for action that was not taken and ought to be taken (Pizzorno 1970: 113–14). Like Machiavelli's *Discorsi*, Gramsci's *Notebooks* is not a book of history but one of politics.

12. As Gramsci wrote in 1918, Italy's only chance of becoming a nation lay in educating Italians to become responsible citizens with a clear sense of their rights and duties. His ethical model recalled the contrast Mazzini drew between a Bentham-oriented individual and an association-oriented one, or, as Gramsci wrote, between a "capitalist-individual" and an "association-individual" (1958: 186–9).

13. An excellent analysis of Gramsci's complex notion of folklore is in Cirese 1970: 299–328.

References

Adamson, Walter L. (1980) *Hegemony and Revolution. A Study of Antonio Gramsci's Political and Cultural Theory.* Berkeley–Los Angeles–London: University of California Press.

Badaloni, Nicola (1975) *Il marxismo di Gramsci.* Turin: Einaudi.

Bobbio, Norberto (1968) "Introduction." In Rodolfo Mondolfo, *Umanesimo di Marx. Studi filosofici, 1908–1966,* pp. i–xlviii. Turin: Einaudi.

—— (1977) *Gramsci e la concezione della società civile*. Milan: Feltrinelli.

—— (1986 [1968]) *Profilo ideologico del Novecento Italiano*. Turin: Einaudi.

Caizzi, Bruno (1950) *Antologia della Questione Meridionale*. Milan: Edizioni di Comunità.

Cattaneo, Carlo (1972) *Opere scelte*, 4 vols, ed. *Delia Castelnuovo Frigessi*. Turin: Einaudi.

Cirese, Alberto M. (1970) "Concezioni del mondo, filosofia spontanea, folclore." In *Gramsci e la cultura contemporanea*, ed. Eugenio Garin, Norberto Bobbio *et al.*, pp. 299–328. Rome: Editori Riuniti.

Corvisieri, Silverio (1970) *Il biennio rosso 1919–1920 della Terza Internazionale*. Milan: Feltrinelli.

Croce, Benedetto (1929 [1928]) *A History of Italy, 1870–1915*, trans. C. M. Ady. Oxford: Clarendon Press.

Davidson, Alastair (1977) *Antonio Gramsci: Towards an Intellectual Biography*. London–New Jersey: Merlin – Humanity Press.

Davis, John A. (1979) "The South, the Risorgimento and the Origins of the 'Southern Problem'." In *Gramsci and Italy's Passive Revolution*, ed. John A. Davis, pp. 67–103. London–New York: Harper & Row.

Femia, Joseph V. (1981) *Gramsci's Political Thought: Hegemony, Consciousness, and the Revolutionary Process*. Oxford: Clarendon Press.

Fiori, Giuseppe (1970 [1966]) *Antonio Gramsci. Life of a Revolutionary*, trans.T. Nairn. London: NLB.

Franchetti, Leopoldo (1911) "Mezzo secolo di Unità nell'Italia meridionale," *La Nuova Antologia* **237**: 83–97.

Freud, Sigmund (1989 [1930]) *Civilization and Its Discontents*, ed. James Strachery. New York: Norton.

Garin, Eugenio (1955) *Cronache di filosofia italiana, 1900–1943*. Bari: Laterza.

—— (1974) *Intellettuali italiani del XX secolo*. Rome: Editori Riuniti.

Germino, Dante (1990) *Antonio Gramsci. Architect of a New Politics*. Baton Rouge and London: Louisiana State University.

Giarrizzo, Giuseppe (1970) "Il Mezzogiornno di Gramsci." In idem, *Gramsci e la cultura moderna I*, pp. 321–89.

Gobetti, Piero (1969) *Opere complete*. Turin: Einaudi.

Gramsci, Antonio (1954) *L'Ordine Nuovo, 1919–1920*. Turin: Einaudi.

—— (1955) *Lettere dal carcere*. Turin: Einaudi.

—— (1958) *Scritti Giovanili, 1914–1918*. Turin: Einaudi.

—— (1968) *Scritti 1915–1921*, ed. Sergio Caprioglio. Turin: Einaudi.

—— (1971) *Selections from The Prison Notebooks*, ed. Quintin Hoare, trans. G.N. Smith. New York: International Publishers.

—— (1973) *Letters from Prison*, ed. Lynne Lawener. New York–London: Harper & Row.

—— (1975) *Quaderni dal carcere*, ed. Valentino Gerratana. Turin: Einaudi.

—— (1978) *Selections from Political Writings (1921–1926)*, ed. Quintin Hoare. New York: International Publishers.

—— (1983 [1926, 1930]) "The Southern Question." In *The Modern Prince and Other Writings*, ed. L. Marks, pp. 28–51. New York: International Publishers.

—— (1985) *Selections from Cultural Writings*, ed. David Forgacs and Geoffrey Nowell-Smith, trans. W. Boelhower. Cambridge, MA: Harvard University Press.

—— (1992) *Prison Notebooks I*, ed. Joseph A. Buttigieg, trans. J.A. Buttigieg and A. Callari. New York: Columbia University Press.

—— (1994) *Pre-Prison Writings*, ed. Richard Bellamy, trans. V. Cox. Cambridge: Cambridge University Press.

Marx, Karl and Engels, Friedrich (1978) *The Marx–Engels Reader*, ed. Robert C. Tucker. New York and London: Norton.

Mouffe, Chantal (1979) "Hegemony and Ideology in Gramsci." In *Gramsci and Marxist Theory*, ed. C. Mouffe, pp. 168–204. London: Routledge and Kegan Paul.

Nitti, Francesco S. (1987 [1900]) "Nord e Sud dopo l'unità." In *Il Mezzogiorno in una democrazia industriale*, pp. 1–87. Rome–Bari: Laterza.

Paggi, Leonardo (1984) *Le strategie del potere in Gramsci. Tra fascismo e socialismo in un solo paese 1923–1926*. Rome: Editori Riuniti.

Pizzorno, Alessandro (1970) "Sul metodo di Gramsci: dalla storiografia alla scienza politica." In idem, *Gramsci e la cultura contemporanea*, pp. 109–26.

Salvadori, Massimo L. (1970) *Gramsci e il problema storico della democrazia*. Turin: Einaudi.

—— (1976 [1960]) *Il mito del buongoverno. La questione meridionale da Cavour a Gramsci*. Turin: Einaudi.

Salvemini, Gaetano (1963 [1898]) "La questione meridionale." In *Opere* IV, 2, pp. 71–89. Milan: Feltrinelli.

—— (1978 [1918]) "Pasquale Villari." In *Opere* VIII, pp. 57–80. Milan: Feltrinelli.

Sbarberi, Franco (1986) *Gramsci: un socialismo armonico*. Milan: Franco Angeli.

Sonnino, Sidney (1972 [1875]) "Delle condizioni dei contadini in Italia." In *Discorsi extraparlamentari I*, pp. 155–61. Bari: Laterza.

Sorel, Georges (1976) *From Georges Sorel. Essays in Socialism and Philosophy*, ed. J. L. Stanley and C. Stanley. New York: Oxford University Press.

Tarrow, Sidney G. (1967) *Peasant Communism in Southern Italy*. New Haven–London: Yale University Press.

Tocqueville, Alexis de (1969 [1835, 1840]) *Democracy in America*, ed. J. P. Mayer, trans. G. Lawrence. New York: Harper Perennial.

Togliatti, Palmiro (1967) *Gramsci*, ed. Ernesto Ragionieri. Rome: Editori Riuniti.

Tranfaglia, Nicola (1968) *Carlo Rosselli dall'interventismo a 'Giustizia e Libertà'*. Bari: Laterza.

Urbinati, Nadia (1990) *Le civili libertà. Positivismo e liberalismo nell'Italia unita.* Venice: Marsilio Editori.

Vico, Giambattista (1948) [1744] *The New Science*, trans. T. G. Bergin and M. H. Fisch. Ithaca: Cornell University Press.

Villari, Pasquale (1868) *Saggi di storia di critica e di politica.* Florence: Tipografia Cavour.

—— (1878) *Le lettere meridionali e altri scritti sulla questione sociale in Italia.* Florence: Successori Le Monnier.

Villari, Rosario (1981) *Il Sud nella storia d'Italia.* Bari: Laterza.

Walzer, Michael (1988) *The Company of Critics. Social Criticism and Political Commitment in the Twentieth Century.* New York: Basic Books

How Critical Was De Martino's "Critical Ethnocentrism" in Southern Italy?

Annalisa Di Nola

Ernesto de Martino's engagement with Marxism, evident in his works on the South of Italy, by no means exhausted his main interests. Recent critical essays on this important Neapolitan anthropologist have highlighted his concern with the concept of the loss and maintenance of "presence," that is with the possibility of constituting or preserving the "self" in the face of threatening crises (see Cherchi 1981; Cherchi and Cherchi 1987; Pasquinelli 1984). His adherence to this theme reflects his greater fascination with the existential philosophy of Heidegger, and with Kant's and Hegel's "critical" perspective, than with a Marxist approach to social research. Nevertheless, de Martino's years of scholarship on Southern Italy influenced Italian cultural anthropology to approach the Southern Question with political commitment. During the period between 1949 and 1962, when French Marxist anthropology was not yet born and the American researchers in the South of Italy were following the path indicated by Robert Redfield (1941, 1955a, b; see, for example, Banfield 1958; Friedmann 1952), de Martino showed a genuine interest in the economic and social emancipation of the people he studied.

Some of his positions are being reinvented even today, thirty years after his death. His originality of thought, however, defies easy classification. While his refusal to take problems of identity for granted places him close to some post-modern anthropologists, his firm objection to a relativistic perspective sets him far apart from them, and, in some respects, anticipates a "post-ethnic" approach (see Hollinger 1995). In this chapter, I draw attention to some debatable statements in de Martino's writings where he seems to be building an ethnocentric hierarchy of values and judging his native southern Italian society in a negative way. Considering him to be deeply ambivalent, however, I attempt to counteract this impression by accounting for these passages in the wider context of de Martino's thought. In the second, more philosophically oriented section, I thus examine the author's approach to the problem of magic, in which he utilized concepts of individual identity and objective reality that actually questioned well-established ethnocentric assumptions. I propose that his concept of culture, on which his theoretical system was founded, endowed magic with a pivotal cultural and existential function. Finally, I take up de Martino's concept of "ethnographic humanism" or "critical ethnocentrism" – one of his most original stands, in which a firm rejection of relativism is combined with a deep awareness of the historical determination and the culturally conditioned use of values and categories of judgment. A concluding section discusses the issues confronting de Martino in his more polemical and politically committed writings of the post-Second World War period, coinciding with his first investigations in Southern Italy. This attempt to give a more complete overview of de Martino's thought, to contextualize his most questionable assertions, contrasts with other treatments that consider the "southern works" separately from the rest of his opus, thus obscuring the links between his general philosophical speculation and his concrete ethnographic and historical investigations.

Questionable Extrapolations

Let us start by taking a brief look at *Sud e magia*, de Martino's 1959 study of mourning rituals in Lucania. It is stated in the preface of this book that modern civilization was born out of the choice between magic and rationality (de Martino 1980 [1959]: 8–9; 1984 [1962]). Although fascinated throughout his scientific career by the irrational, de Martino warned that submitting to its appeal meant abdicating the principles derived from our own history, in which the confrontation between magic and rationality developed in terms of a radical opposition, the two options presenting themselves as mutually exclusive and incompatible (1984 [1962]: 213). Moreover, to renounce Western values in favor of a supposed neutral relativism, or of an uncritical celebration of the "primitive" and the "mystic," would be to lose consciousness of the genesis and development of the civilization that made the anthropological endeavour possible (1984[1962];1977: 389–413). And, he believed, an inclination towards the irrational is always apt to conceal a substantial appeal to authoritarian regimes, as demonstrated by the tragic example of post-First World War Germany (1953; 1957; 1984 [1962]: 81–169).

In *Sud e magia*, de Martino defined his subject as the "ethnographic exploration of the survival of the most gross practices of ceremonial magic in Lucania, aimed at determining, for one of the most backward areas of the South, the structure of magic techniques, their psychological function, and the existential regime that favours their persistence" (1980 [1959]: 9).[1] The preface to *Morte e pianto rituale* publically thanked

> all those peasant women from Lucania who willingly . . . renewed, in front of others . . . the ritual mourning of their own dead; they themselves being instruments of an incomprehensible science, to which however they were paying a tribute of pain. For these

poor women who live in squalid villages . . . we could not separate our thanks from the warm wish that, if not they, then at least their daughters and granddaughters . . . might elevate themselves to that higher practice of mourning discipline that forms a sizeable part of the economic, social, political and cultural emancipation of our Mezzogiorno (1975 [1958]: ix).

These statements evoke a modernization approach to the southern Italian peasantry, whose magic practices and mourning rituals are presented as doomed to disappear once a higher standard of living and a more evolved cultural pattern are adopted.[2] De Martino's use of the term "survival" betrays his assumption that all the "gross" practices and beliefs that interested him had lost the integral meaning they once possessed in their original context. Although still functional in dealing with hardships, they were no longer seen by the author as embedded in a wider texture of relationships and activities in which new meanings might develop. The extent of their persistence, moreover, said something about the kind of energy that was deployed against them. "Even today," de Martino wrote, when

> the ancient seasonal crying is reduced to pale folkloric reflections, the funereal lament is still practiced in the countryside of sizeable areas of the European continent: and although it is restricted almost everywhere to the peasants and it has obviously lost the breadth and complexity of pagan mythic horizons . . . something of its ancient tragic seriousness still persists . . . This limit to the expansion of Christian customs undoubtedly poses a problem. One is tempted to say . . . that Christianity had the power to remold custom . . . in the higher strata of civil society, drawing the courts, the nobility, the lords, the wealthy urban bourgeoisie away from the pagan practice of crying for the dead, but that it could not deploy an equivalent molding energy in the countryside, where decisive progress took place not so much because of the uninterrupted civilizing action of the Church, as because of the bourgeois revolution and with it the development of the industrial age and corresponding civil progress . . . If in fact we tried to build a diachronic map of the progressive disappearance of laments among European peasants, we would see how the first to lose them were the countries and the regions that entered earlier within the orbit of the industrial revolution and of the development of an entre-preneurial urban bourgeoisie, whereas the last were those countries and regions that persisted longer in their social structure of precapitalist and semifeudal relations (1975[1958]: 354).

De Martino's views of folklore as represented by survivals that have lost their original coherence, and of the Church and the bourgeoisie as "civilizing agents," are reflected in the criteria he adopted in selecting sample villages for his Lucania study: namely, their extent of traditionalism or backwardness, their isolation or geographic distribution (1975[1958]: 74). Here he shared company with other European research traditions, for example the Finnish and other schools of folklore and linguistics (see Aarne 1928; Bartoli 1945; Bertoni 1925; Krohn 1926; Menendez Pidal 1920; Santoli 1940). Did he accept the conclusion, however, that isolation preserved the supposed purity and original essence of customs, which were progressively contaminated by more frequent culture contact? I do not think this captures the complex and relational way he thought about magic and, indeed, about the Southern Italian peasantry.

The Problem of Magic

We remain perhaps disconcerted by the way the problem of magic is posed in *Sud e magia*, but the author had already coped with it in *Il mondo magico* (1973[1948]),[3] a book that fundamentally challenged the established sense of security and stability in Western civilization, questioning what is meant by reality. Our perception of nature as an entity in itself, de Martino argued, is not a given but a historical development, in so far as science grew out of an increasing withdrawal of the projections of subjects from the objects of their research. But precisely the instruments provided by a scientific approach to natural phenomena are thoroughly inadequate when it comes to the magical world, where we encounter a reality completely interwoven with such projections (1973[1948]: 66–87, 155–62). Especially in the so-called primitive world, where a series of natural and structural circumstances render life extremely precarious and threatening, the individual is in constant danger of losing his or her "presence," that is her or his ability to be an active agent in history. In a world where "being-here" is not decided and guaranteed once and for all, one is always in the process of constituting and maintaining oneself as such, while the world itself, far from being an objective external given, cannot be thoroughly separated from the drama of the person but is, rather, entangled with it. In the context thus outlined, magic is not

> an obstacle to intelligence, to moral progress . . . The dominating interest of the magical world is . . . constituted . . . by the conquest and the reinforcement of the elementary "being-here," or "presence," of the person. Now we know that the ideology, praxis, and institutions of the magical world reveal their true meaning only [in relation to] defending, mastering, regulating the tenuous "being-here" of the person . . . As long as we persist in judging the magical world within traditional categories, we will conceal from our own eyes its characteristic drama . . . We shall deem it to have no drama, only negativity to which no history can be given (1973[1948]: 192–3).

In other words, under specific historic circumstances the Self is not a given but must fight tenaciously to establish a presence; and, by the same token, nature is not the specific objective entity well known to experimental scientists, but, rather, a culturally conditioned realm, dense with human projections. The fundamental dimension introduced by our author is a historical one, individuating a drama, a process of precarious establishment, where others had seen a plain assumption, a basic point of departure. Indeed, part of the scandal aroused by *Il mondo magico* when it first appeared was its extreme interpretation of Croce's historicism. For Croce, history developed within a clearly defined system constituted by the four eternal forms of the Spirit (Croce 1902, 1913, 1962). In questioning the eternal existence of these categories, de Martino, his student, seemed closer to Hegel who, in *The Phenomenology of Mind* (1973), had introduced a temporal dimension into the idealistic philosophy of the Spirit. Like Hegel's Spirit or Self, but unlike Croce's, the "presence" of de Martino had a beginning in time. We also see Heidegger's (1969) undeniable influence on de Martino's theory, with the difference that the philosopher's Being-here, rather than revealing the limits and finitude of a mundane existence, is interpreted as a safety valve for the individual, standing as a protective guarantee against a rather frightening loss of borders (de Martino 1973 [1948]: 190).

In distinguishing magic from the psychopathological outcomes of crises of the "presence," de Martino points out that magic is not only provoked by moments of crisis, but also, and mostly, by the reaction to crisis – by the ransom and redemption that magical institutions exact and provide as they appeal to a long-established and well-consolidated tradition of symbols and meanings. Thoroughly different from the private alienating symbolism displayed in psychopathologies, this ascending process is able to master oncoming crises suffered by individuals or whole groups, under circumstances of particular stress for the "presence" (1973 [1948]: 177–85; 1975[1958]: 24–43; 1957).

Magic is hence endowed with a very important role in de Martino's view: namely the task of reconstituting and consolidating the jeopardized "presence." It achieves its goal by enacting all its power of molding and reorganization *vis-à-vis* the chaos that could arise out of a precarious situation. When the "presence" threatens to collapse and confuse itself with a particular object or an aspect of it, to slide into a situation of mere biological passivity,[4] magic intervenes, translating that passivity into an activity, reintroducing the shaping power of culture. Magic is actually the *only* effective cultural performance allowed under such conditions.

In his later works de Martino specified better the technique adopted: cultural institutions operate through a process of de-historicization (1953–1954; 1957; 1959; 1962; 1977; see Massenzio 1985, 1986) that temporarily conceals the tension and the serious harmfulness of an unbearable historic or natural situation, submerging its negative implications in an atemporal and repetitive realm where everything is mastered and under control by means of known and meaningful procedures. In a subsequent phase, persons and objects are reintegrated in the normal course of events, the risk of a paralysing collapse having been overcome. Such is the way that ritual, ceremonies, symbolism, and culture in general function.

Culture is action – doing, forging, attributing shape and meaning to the flux of life, creating value out of what passes away despite or against us, in a way that "we risk passing with what passes"(De Martino 1975 [1958]: 18).

The perspective adopted by de Martino was inspired by Kant's criticism. Kant entrusted the possibility of a relation between object and subject to the supreme principle of the "transcendental unity of self-consciousness," a formal function able to synthesize singular elements within a totality. Although questioning their eternal givenness, de Martino attributed to the "presence", and to culture in general, those same formal, synthesizing, objectifying functions (Kant 1966; de Martino 1973 [1948]: 185–9).

Critical Ethnocentrism

It is this basic theory of culture connected to the role of the "presence" that de Martino develops in his last, posthumous work, in which he theorizes the "ethos" of "transcending life through intersubjective valorization" (1977: 667–84; see also 430–40). This "valorizing" impetus allows us to go beyond the immediacy of biological life, to transcend it through the values of community projects, historically deployed in multiple cultural forms. At stake is a discourse on the essence of humankind – analogous to arguments in Marxism on man and nature – in which the so-called "ethos of transcending" is the principle which distinguishes the human and cultural from the merely natural. Things existing *per se* are not conceivable, nor is a world of spiritual values that are not embedded in the everyday activity of transforming nature. Shared effort and use over generations constitute a reassuring and meaningful background, more or less identifiable with the anonymous and the habitual, yet leaving room for change precisely through the force of its characteristics:

> ... the given, the habitual and the obvious character of the world are possible in so far as they are faithful to the initiatives of past generations, to our own past and what is connected to it through our cultural biography ... Only through this anonymous domesticity of the world is it possible [for the single person to make] original, singularized choices ... to "restart" some aspect of the world – and he always starts it over as if he were the first ... This is only possible if all the other aspects function momentarily as background, and if this background includes an implicit human meaning, a work of humanization developed in the obvious domesticity of the environment (1977: 648).

It is difficult to understand the wider meaning of de Martino's work on Southern Italy unless we also take into account his conviction that an integral humanism[5] should inform relationships between individuals and wider human groups. From his lay humanistic perspective, the world has a human origin and destination, not a divine one; moreover, all its inhabitants strive for equal participation in cultural institutions (1976 [1961]: 21). There is, in other words, a specific "ethos of transcending" which is common to humankind in its entirety, regardless of the different ways and means by which different peoples or ethnic groups actualize their intersubjective valorization of life. Our awareness of this commonality, however, was only rendered possible as a result of the specific historical development of Western civilization. In this respect, although only in this respect, de Martino assigned supremacy to this civilization; it alone could produce the ethnographic endeavour.

> In the perspective of a "critical ethnocentrism," the western (or westernized) ethnologist assumes the history of his own culture as a unit by which to measure alien cultural histories, but . . . in the act of measuring, gains consciousness of the historic prison and of the limits of his own system, and opens himself up to the task of reforming the categories of observation he has available at the start of his research (1977: 396–7).

In other words, de Martino is not talking about a superiority of Western values in absolute terms. His claim is that the Western ethnologist cannot avoid taking a stand, making value judgments, partaking in the culture he has grown up in, as it is the only one which poses the conditions for a dialogue among different cultures within the context of the anthropological discipline. In the impossible attempt to assume a neutral stand, the Western observer inevitably and acritically projects his or her own categories on the object of study. It is, however, a critical and controlled use of those categories that de Martino promotes; a constantly tested use, involving a systematic confrontation with other cultures and a parallel questioning of the respective histories in which different cultural categories are embedded (see 1977: 389–97; 1984[1962]: 5–13, 58, 73, 283–7).

Between de Martino's philosophy of the "presence" and his epistemological stance of "critical ethnocentrism," he was far from viewing subaltern culture as intrinsically backward or stubbornly involved in an irrational and inferior value system, notwithstanding some of the passages from *Sud e magia* with which we began. Nor did he posit that cultural contact and technology transfer would cause an automatic, unidirectional change in the less developed term of comparison. It is rather a matter of reciprocal transformation, in which the supposedly more advanced civilization is challenged by the other to test its own viability and dogmatic assumptions. In the ensuing dialog, both draw upon the same "ethos of transcending," sharing equally in the dignity of culture. Both experience the same need of the "presence" to create, shape, and transform mere biological vitality into culture, overcoming the always incumbent risk of not "being-here," not acting in history. In this sense, magic is not an inferior cultural outcome with regard to Western rational attitudes and cultural products; it is instead another example of the demiurgic power of culture – a valuable effort to counteract the supreme loss threatening the very possibility of human existence.

A History of the Subaltern World

In the wake of the Second World War, the associated crisis of Western bourgeois society, and the eruption of liberation movements in the colonial world, de Martino resumed his critique of what he called the naturalist trend of anthropology, evident in both evolutionism and functionalism (1949). Apprehending the primitive (and by analogy the lower classes of complex societies) as natural people, as things or objects rather than historical subjects, these pseudo-scientific modes of classifying and describing coincided for him with the exploitation of the people studied. It was time, he declared, to historicize these subalterns, to widen our humanism by way of letting their world into history. Precisely in this context, de Martino turned to the subalterns of Southern Italy, challenging Croce's influential ethical-political history of the region, which was a history of its ruling classes and political leaders.

> Only later as a militant of the working class in the Mezzogiorno of Italy did I realize that the naturalism of traditional ethnology was linked to the very character of bourgeois society, that between the condition of existence of, for example, the day laborers in Murge and the historiographical inertia of ethnological writings there was an organic connection, and that my theoretical interest to know the primitive was born at once with my practical interest in participating in his real liberation (1949: 433).

In other words, despite the rhetorical or patronizing inflections in some of de Martino's writing, we must note the political and intellectual commitment of the author, for whom Gramsci's model of the organic intellectual, blending theory and practice, was an inspiration. The educational and technological advancement of marginal areas foreseen by Modernization theorists were a far cry from de Martino's goals. These theorists defined traditionalism as the main obstacle to development in the Mezzogiorno, but de Martino was instead interested in peasants' struggles for land reform, in their serious attempt at emancipation, in their desire to break what he, following Gramsci, understood as the key relation: dominant–dominated (not modern–traditional). His use, at least on an ideological level, of the concept of class, as well as his attention to power and domination among different strata of society, also marked his distance from the kind of ideological Manicheism implicit in Modernization theory. Insisting on a dialectical relationship between hegemonic and subaltern groups in the social reality of the South, he avoided, finally, the temptation to account for this reality in isolation.

Between the mid-1940s and the early 1950s, the intellectual and political debate surrounding Southern Italy intensified. Several revolts and land occupations occurred, provoking government repression. What began as enthusiasm on the part of the Left-wing parties gave way to disillusionment as they experienced political defeat. In the meantime, a number of applied and community studies were carried out, mainly by American sociologists and anthropologists, but also by Italian social workers and agrarian economists, which advocated the economic reform of the Mezzogiorno through capitalist industrial development. Framing this orientation was the reconstruction of the Italian state after the war and the move on the part of the United States government to shore up the position of national bourgeois élites by, among other things, making a substantial investment in programs set up to stablize and modernize the South.

Among the agrarian economists against whom de Martino reacted was Manlio Rossi-Doria (1948, 1958), the founder of the University in Portici, who had joined the Partito d'Azione in the 1940s but later drew closer to the Socialists. Rossi-Doria gave up his original theorization of the need for a substantial land reform in favor of a more conservative approach, aimed at reassessing marginal properties. And he conceived of peasant civilization as immobile and resistant to change. By contrast, de Martino's emphasis on the centuries-long interconnection between hegemonic and subaltern levels within a single history, and his Marxist recognition of the necessary alliance between peasants and workers for the transformation of existing social conditions, led him to ignore the work of Rossi-Doria, and many others, for example Guido Dorso and Danilo Dolci. Uninterested in their studies, as well as in the new sociological trend being advanced by the North Americans, he criticized what he called the traditional "economist" approach to the Mezzogiorno for overlooking cultural phenomena.

Clearly, De Martino's alignment with a Marxist approach was at odds with the dominant social science trajectory of the postwar years, yet it did not spare him from serious criticism on the part of Communist Party intellectuals who, though acknowledging the value of proletarian as against bourgeois culture, could not entertain a concept of culture that also included folklore. Perhaps they were still unfamiliar with Gramsci's as yet unpublished work when they interpreted de Martino's interest in peasant beliefs and rituals as a dangerous romantic flirtation with irrationalism and primitivism. In this respect, it is interesting to note de Martino's position on Carlo Levi, whose *Cristo si è fermato a Eboli* (1945) was also an important Left contribution to redefining the Southern Question at the end of the war. De Martino praised Levi for recognizing peasants as the bearers of a cultural tradition, but could not share his poetic view of this tradition as autonomous, isolated, enclosed in a mythic reality outside historical time and inaccessible to comprehension as well as to state intervention or political mobilization by outsiders.

In this context, we can reconsider de Martino's discussion of folkloric survivals. These materials can become documents of history, he argued, not in their present state or in isolation, but as markers that help reconstruct the religious civilization in which they existed. Sometimes they constitute a living and vital moment, organs of a functioning whole in the fullness of its social and cultural life (as shown in *Morte e pianto rituale*); at other times they are documents of a past civilization, indicating episodes of arrest in its process of expansion, mishaps that limited its will of history, forcing it, at least in certain layers of society, to tolerate, compromise, syncretize, abdicate (*Sud e magia* is exemplary). In both cases, folkloric-religious relics identified by ethnographic inquiry document a single history: that of the religious civilization of which they stand as wrecks, or of the religious civilization in which they survive or endure through a more or less deep remolding. They never indicate a *popular* religious history, opposed to, or parallel and competing with, that of the social and cultural élites. Although de Martino's use of the term "survival" might suggest otherwise, he is here rather close to the American anthropologist, Eric Wolf, whose ironically titled *Europe and the People Without History* (1982) similarly places local culture in history, and to critiques one might advance against ethnohistory as a separate historiographical discipline.

Gramsci contrasted philosophy and modern science, regarded as elaborated, coherent, and systematic conceptions of the world, with folklore as the implicit, incoherent, fragmentary conception of the subaltern classes (1975: 2311–17). Folklore, he held, is the reflection on the cultural level of the economic and political dependency of those classes; it is the servile culture of the politically servile. Reciprocally, the culture of subaltern classes cannot be understood without apprehending their relationships of political and ideological dependency, which, through cultural hegemony, subordinate and limit them. Although influenced by this view, de Martino was also critical of Gramsci's emphasis on anachronistic beliefs as obstacles to the acquisition of a mature self- and class consciousness, as if they were the debris of élite cultural production. Instead, de Martino distinguishes between traditional and progressive folklore, the latter being an outcome of the new struggles and mobilizations of the peasant movement (see de Martino 1951a, b, 1952, 1954). Yet he more often concentrated his attention on the traditional variant, neglecting an analysis of the relationships of "folkloric" traits with the social economic setting in which their changing function would become more apparent.

In a way, de Martino engages in a double battle: on the one hand he objects to the cliché of folklore as an unmodified remnant of a past civilization; on the other hand, he refuses to consider it as the product of an autonomous culture, having its own independent system of values. As a consequence he did not envision folklore in terms of resistance, a step that a number of his followers would take. Nor did he celebrate the folkloric customs he helped to draw public attention to. Although according them the dignity of culture, he used such words as "cultural misery," and "low" magical practices, to talk about crying for the dead, the evil eye, and charms (*c.* 1975; 1980[1959]: 10). This made them akin to psychological misery rather than to a curious, valuable heritage to be safeguarded. In his writing, they often evoke areas of negativity or emptiness that high culture was unable to mold, perhaps for lack of hegemonic energy, or of organic relationships in civil society (although de Martino did not use this Gramscian expression). The result is non-autonomy on the part of the person – an awareness of being constantly at risk of dispossession, of being acted upon rather than being able to act and decide, transforming critical situations into values, into culture. At best, magical practices constitute a redemption of the "presence."

De Martino's position was not without ambivalence, since he did attribute a pivotal cultural role to magic, and insisted upon the specific contribution of subaltern classes to history. Overall, however, he eschewed a naive enthusiasm for the creativity and originality of popular culture, pointing rather to the victim-ization of the people under study. We can see this in his discourse on hegemony, certainly derived from Gramsci and replete with distinctions between traditional and organic intellectuals, between the roles played by bourgeois ideology on the one hand, and the philosophy of praxis inside the revolutionary party on the other. Philosophy, Common Sense, Religion and Folklore – elements of Gramsci's delicate hierarchy – reciprocally flow into one another, constituting a variety of articulations that cannot easily be brought back to a plain dichotomy between high and low levels of culture. Yet, despite his attention to the different social and historical components of Southern Italian culture, de Martino does not always clearly distinguish among different political and ideological alignments. Thus he can sweepingly blame the hegemonic forces for not having deployed a sufficient degree of molding energy to enable the subaltern classes to participate fully in "culture," as if he were unaware that the criticism betrays a rather overt faith in the value of the "high" Western intellectual tradition, which he would like to see become the shared common property of the whole of humankind. As we have seen, however, this faith grew out of focusing on a specific aspect of élite European culture: namely, its humanistic and historicist lay view.[6]

Within the framework of a Gramscian perspective, de Martino's reproach exposes the lack of organic relationships in civil society, the historical detachment of intellectuals from the authentic needs and wishes of the masses, and their alignment instead with the dominant oppressive groups. It is not a matter of sustaining peasants in their philosophy of common sense, but of leading them to a superior conception of life, accelerating the ongoing historical process of trans-formation while keeping in touch with the conditions of their social world, their needs and aspirations (Gramsci 1975: 1384–7).

Sud e Magia, a Return

As we saw earlier, *Sud e magia* seems to start with a straightforward statement of the long-lasting and victorious battle of rationality against magic, yet the text repeatedly brings to the fore the entangled and interconnected destinies of the hegemonic and the subaltern worlds. First of all there is no room for a separate and opposed view of magic versus religion, as if they were two different stages, hierarchically arranged in the evolution of civilization. The difference between magic and religion is only a matter of degree, not of quality, for de Martino. Magic displays a narrower technical set of instruments to cope with the crises induced by dramatic existential situations. The values it discloses are few and very tightly connected to the particular crisis that needs to be resolved. Religion offers a wider technical apparatus for dealing with the so-called "crisis of the presence," its values being much more inclusive. Any attempt to explain magic on the basis of its particular characteristics is doomed to failure, in so far as it could only be an endless classification, missing the meaning that is embedded in specific historical civilizations (see 1980[1959]: 81–92; 1975[1958]: 40–3; 1957: 96). In the case of Lucania, the focus of inquiry thus became the centuries-old intertwining of Catholic and magical ideology in the Italian South, with its many contrasts and compromises over time. De Martino's reconstruction avoids an analysis of the nexus between economic and psychological misery, assuming it to be an obvious premiss. He finds it more rewarding to document the magic in southern Catholicism, with its emphasis on outward appearance and exhibitionism, even within the official liturgy. On the one hand, "low" magic introduces, however "grossly" and superficially, elements of Christianity into its practices, for example through formulae that evoke the name of Christ. On the other hand, some rituals characteristic of popular Catholicism are magically biased even when connected to wider Catholic values (1980 [1959]: 87–91).

But de Martino's analysis hints at a broader dimension in attempting to relate this regional situation to the history of élite lay culture in the Mezzogiorno in general. He wants to examine to what extent the cultural milieu of the southern Italian peasantry participated in the general movement of European élite culture away from magic toward rationality. According to him, although the Enlightenment in the eighteenth century reflected the advanced social and economic development of the European bourgeoisie, it did not exhibit the same features among its Neapolitan representatives. In the kingdom of Naples, the bourgeoisie did not have the same strength as its commercial and industrial European counterpart, and the members of enlightened circles appeared therefore much more indulgent of magical religious ritualism in their local version of Catholicism. Their polemical activity was directed, rather, to the confrontation between Church and State in the struggle for political power. This delay negatively conditioned subaltern culture by limiting its access to more fully rational attitudes.

In *Morte e pianto rituale* (1975[1958]) de Martino analyses the historical compromise between pagan dramatic mourning and Christian resignation. The symbolic image of Mary's crying is, he suggests, an intermediate formation, established during the Middle Ages and encouraging acceptance of a Christian attitude toward death. Similarly, in *La terra del rimorso* (1976 [1961]), the mythic and ritual complex represented by *tarantismo* is historically analysed as a stratified formation over time. De Martino sheds light on the historical specificity and differentiation of *tarantismo* in Puglia, and on its autonomy from similar cultural formations in other countries or regions. This autonomy and specificity, however, must be understood in relational terms; they do not indicate a deliberate, counter-cultural, or oppositional refusal of Christian values. On the contrary: *tarantismo* has always been in touch, at least for the largest portion of its history, with hegemonic culture. The exchange between the uneven levels is here particularly apparent. *Tarantismo* contributed to the development of certain élite intellectual elaborations; at the same time, élite culture was aware of its significance and remarkably influenced its trend.

According to de Martino, official Catholicism gained an especially conspicuous role in *tarantismo* during the eighteenth century, when it attempted to connect to St Paul and his specific healing power the symbol of the *taranta*, the mythic spider whose behaviour is mimicked in the course of the "pagan" ritual in order to achieve therapeutic effects. This intervention was totally disruptive of the existing folkloric custom, an intrusive hegemonic intervention that disintegrated the subaltern ideological construction. Yet, prior to the eighteenth century there was already a long history of interrelationships between this particular custom and various educated élites' literary and scholarly works (ranging from the ancient Greek myths and tragedies to the theories of natural magic following the Renaissance, to the speculation on "iatromusic" in the seventeenth century and the medical theories of enlightened Neapolitans in the eighteenth century). Clearly, *taranta* symbolism owed its liveliness to a process of cultural circulation. When enlightened opinion degraded its essence to the level of an illness, that vital connection was broken and the custom entered into its long decline.

Again, it is worth remarking that a historically oriented consideration of hegemonic–subaltern relationships implies a number of dimensions and articulations that do not easily fit in a dichotomous, unidirectional evaluation of terms such as "modern" and "backward" or, by analogy, "North" and "South."

In the end, economic and social conditions, however little they were specifically explored by de Martino, were, for him, the foundation of both the "psychological misery" of subaltern magical practices and the scant advancement in the battle for a rational lay humanistic view on the part of the élite components of Southern

Italian society. In the epilogue of *Morte e pianto rituale*, too, the crucial importance of a change in the economic and social conditions of existence for poor Lucanian peasants is very clearly expressed.

> The *ethos* of the "presence" is not a matter of grace coming down from above (even if it can appear to be so to single individuals) . . . It is attainable to the extent that it is realized in the context of social relationships . . . When this process is limited, the reality of the "presence" is weak. When only the memory of one's own failures is accumulated and one experiences only the irrationality of natural forces and the overwhelming oppression of social forces, every critical moment . . . can, given the lack of cultural forces to mobilize, stir up a crisis. The agricultural communities, and particularly the women are still subjected to precapitalist and semifeudal relations. That is why the mourning crisis takes such excessive forms, and why the techniques of lamentation are still maintained. A transformation approached exclusively on the level of religious or "moral" preaching is therefore doomed to have here a limited effectiveness (1975[1958]: 358).

This passage represents, as we can see, one more description of the loss of the "presence" and of the conditions that would render its retrieval more likely. But the mode of production is crucial in determining the precariousness of a specific existential situation and the connected deployment of a particular cultural form, able to cope with that situation. Nor is this the only place where de Martino offers an explanation of his theory of the economic as the inaugural level of the detachment of Culture from Nature, and of the economy's pivotal role in the frequency and seriousness of crises.[7] It is in any case a straightforward attempt to relate cultural forms to a mode of production, and to warn against easy remedies for poverty or backwardness, remedies such as the education or knowledge transmission so dear to Modernization theory. It is clearly implied that an effective transformation must also involve the structural level.

Conclusions

In rereading the quotations transcribed in the first pages of this essay, we can notice that what de Martino is calling for is not just a generic movement from traditional to advanced, but rather the transformation of an existential regime. What he has in mind is not so much the adoption of more modern habits as the economic, social, political, and cultural emancipation of the Mezzogiorno, according to a militant Marxist perspective. Taking into account the wider effectiveness of the industrial revolution and the educational intervention of the Church in the transformation of particular customs implies a clear notion of the embeddedness of such customs in the context of precise forces and relations of production. We can recall that de Martino's whole theorization of folklore cannot support an easy dismissal of anachronistic practices in terms of unworthy relics, but rather valorizes them as documents of history and culture. We saw that his opinions on magic show a thicker complexity than it could appear at first sight. His often declared adherence to a lay perspective, and his analysis of the absence of a qualitative difference between magic and religion, reassure us that he was not interested in celebrating the triumph of Christianity, regarded as a more evolved form of religion, even if some of the passages in *Morte e pianto rituale* might lead us to believe so.

On closer examination, the hegemony of the more advanced level was at the root of precisely that marginality that the Southern Problem used to highlight, for it acted too often to hinder a sound and up-to-date process of economic, social, and cultural development. But in any case that contact, that intertwining of destinies between the unequal levels, is not a recent outcome of modernity. It has a long, forgotten history. What is new, possibly, is the shape that such a contact could assume in contemporary society under the changed circumstances of international relationships of power.

De Martino is much more explicit and detailed when discussing his theory of the loss of the "presence" than in dealing with problems of social and economic development. Indeed, focusing mainly on cultural phenomena during his "southern period," he attacked the mounting repertoire of statistical "meridionalist" studies for their "economism." In effect, he never resolved the contradiction between his scholarly interest in the preservation of the phenomena under observation, and his political commitment to the value of transforming an unjust and oppressive social reality.

In *La terra del rimorso*, a more detached attitude toward problems of intervention led him to emphasize the importance of knowledge and consciousness as a basic stage in the formation of a new Southern awareness and reality, assigning priority to reason in the best tradition of Western thought:

Tarantismo will no doubt die "on its own" within a short time. But precisely the inertia of that "on its own" is unhealthy and deadly, because the internal law of Culture is to bring about the death of the past through the lively light of consciousness and reason. Too many things in our South die "on their own", without consciousness and reason deriving any operative merit out of it, and too many instead survive without consciousness and reason, without realizing their sharp contradictions in terms of transformation. Someone could remark that tarantismo is too minute and local a fact to stimulate such a process. But it appears "minute" and " local" only because our indifference renders it irrelevant [. . .] Pagan tarantismo, its insertion into St. Paul's cult, the break up of musical exorcism, the sick character of the chapel performances and the limits of traditional medical interpretation are today reflected in a system of inertia, intolerance, unrealized contradictions, tolerated incompatibilities. But in this chaos which is given the romantic name of "folklore", and which, at least in this case, is actually impeding history and humiliating nature, it is the task of consciousness and reason to reestablish the transforming process armed with historical knowledge (1976[1961]: 381).

Acknowledgments

For the help and the suggestions offered to me while writing this chapter, I wish to thank Clara Gallini, Allyson Purpura, Jane Schneider, Michael Sbarge, and Robert Zweig.

Notes

1. In this and the following quotations, I have translated loosely from the original.
2. For a general critical overview of "modernization theory," see Appleby 1978; Nash 1981; and Tipps 1973.
3. This work is also available in an (abridged) English edition (de Martino 1988).
4. The most extensive explanation of the meaning and function of the presence is offered in the first chapter of de Martino 1975 [1958].
5. The expression "integral humanism" is actually a term I am using for convenience, in order to cover more themes contained in de Martino's thought. He talks about an enlargement of Western civilization's self-consciousness aimed at creating a wider humanism (1973[1948]: 13). He polemically refers to the circumscribed and limited humanism of traditional culture [i.e. élite culture] (1949; 1950; 1976 [1961]: 21). He maintains the methodological need "to resolve entirely into human reasons those that in the religious experience appeared as numinous reasons" (1957: 90). He outlines it as the task of an ethnographic humanism to accomplish "the unity of what is human" in the ethnographic encounter that questions one's own culture, confronting it with alien ones (1977: 389–413). On these topics see also, in English, Saunders 1993: 875–93.
6. See above p. 162–3.
7. For his complex view of the relationships between the economic, productive level and what he later called the "ethos of transcending" see de Martino 1953; 1957; 1977: 423–39, 450–1, 649–70. Following his revision of the theory first expressed in *Il mondo magico* he recognizes the possibility of the crisis of the

"presence" as a constant risk of human civilization, which is however much more threatening when the dependence on natural conditions of existence is greater. This dependence is determined by the rudimentary level of technical means, by their destructive employment, or by exploitative social relationships, implying i.e. forms of domination. It is this oppresive economic and social situation, connected to forms of dominated consciousness – not a supposedly intrinsic stubborness and passiviity of the superstitious peasantry – that calls for a transformation, opening the way to a more complete enjoyment of cultural, not only of material, goods.

References

Aarne, Antti A. (1928) *The Types of the Folk-tale, a Classification and Bibliography. Aantti Aarne's Verzeichnis der Marchentypen*, translated and enlarged by Stith Thompson. Helsinki: Soumalainen tiedeakatemia.

Appleby, Joyce (1978) "Modernization Theory and the Formation of Modern Social Theories in England and America." *Comparative Studies in Society and History* **20** (2): 259–85.

Banfield, Edward C. (1958) *The Moral Basis of a Backward Society*. Glencoe, Ill.: Free Press.

Bartoli, Matteo Giulio (1945) *Saggi di linguistica spaziale*. Turin: V. Bona.

Bertoni, Giulio (1925) *Breviario di neolinguistica*. Modena: Società tipografica.

Cherchi, Placido (1981) "De Martino e il marxismo." *Studi bresciani* **6**: 79–102.

Cherchi, Placido and Cherchi, Maria (1987) *Ernesto De Martino. Dalla crisi della presenza alla comunità umana*. Naples: Liguori.

Croce, Benedetto (1902) *Estetica*. Bari: Laterza.

—— (1913) *Saggio sullo Hegel, seguito da altri scritti di storia della filosofia*. Bari: Laterza.

—— (1962) *La filosofia di Giambattista Vico*. Bari: Laterza.

De Martino, Ernesto (1949) "Intorno a una storia del mondo popolare subalterno." *Società* **5**: 411–35.

—— (1951a) "Il folklore." *Il calendario del popolo* **7**: 989.

—— (1951b) "Il folklore progressivo." *L'Unità*, 28 June.

—— (1952) "Gramsci e il folklore." *Il calendario del popolo* **8**: 1109.

—— (1953) "Etnologia e cultura nazionale negli ultimi 10 anni." *Società* **9**: 313–42.

—— (1953–54) "Fenomenologia religiosa e storicismo assoluto." *Studi e materiali di storia delle religioni* **24–25**: 5–21.

—— (1954) "Per un dibattito sul folklore." *Lucania* **1**: 76–8.

—— (1957) "Storicismo e irrazionalismo nella storia delle religioni." *Studi e materiali di storia delle religioni* **28**: 89–107.

—— (1973 [1948]) *Il mondo magico. Prolegomeni a una storia del magismo.* Turin: Boringhieri.

—— (1975 [1950]) "Ancora sulla storia del mondo popolare subalterno." *Società* 5: 306–9.

—— (1975 [1958]) *Morte e pianto rituale. Dal lamento funebre antico al pianto di Maria.* Turin: Boringhieri.

—— (c.1975) "Miseria psicologica e magia in Lucania (Resoconto di una indagine di sociologia religiosa)." In *Mondo popolare e magia in Lucania*, ed. Rocco Brienza, pp. 147–61. Rome–Matera: Basilicata editrice.

—— (1976 [1961]) *La terra del rimorso. Contributo a una storia religiosa del Sud.* Milan: Il Saggiatore.

—— (1977) *La fine del mondo. Contributo all'analisi delle apocalissi culturali.* Turin: Einaudi.

—— (1980 [1959]) *Sud e magia.* Milan: Feltrinelli.

—— (1980 [1962]) *Furore simbolo valore.* Milan: Feltrinelli.

—— (1984 [1962]) *Magia e civiltà.* Milan: Garzanti.

—— (1988) *Primitive magic: The Psychic Power of Shamanism and Sorcerers.* Bridport: Prism Press.

Friedmann, Frederick G. (1952) "Osservazioni sul mondo contadino dell'Italia meridionale." *Quaderni di sociologia* 2(3): 148–61.

Gramsci, Antonio (1975) *Quaderni dal carcere*, ed. Valentino Gerratana. Turin: Einaudi.

Hegel, Georg W. F. (1973) *Fenomenologia dello Spirito.* Florence: La Nuova Italia.

Heidegger, Martin (1969) *Essere e Tempo e l'essenza del fondamento.* Turin: UTET.

Hollinger, David A. (1995) *Postethnic America: Beyond Multiculturalism.* New York: Harper Collins.

Kant, Immanuel (1966) *La Critica della Ragion Pura.* Bari: Laterza.

Krohn, Kaarle L. (1926) *Die folkloristische Arbeitsmethode.* Oslo: Haschenhoug.

Levi, Carlo (1945) *Cristo si è fermato a Eboli.* Turin: Einaudi.

Massenzio, Marcello (1985) "Destorificazione istituzionale e destorificazione irrelativa in E. de Martino." *Studi e materiali di storia della religioni* 51: 197–204.

—— (1986) "Il problema della destorificazione in Ernesto de Martino. La ricerca e i suoi percorsi," ed. Clara Gallini. *La ricerca folklorica. Contributi allo studio della cultura delle classi popolari* 13: 23–30.

Menendez Pidal, Ramòn (1920) "Sobre geografia folklorica. Ensayo de un metodo." *Revista de filologia española* 7: 229–338.

Nash, June (1981) "Ethnographic Aspects of the World Capitalist System." *Annual Review of Anthropology* 10: 393–423.

Pasquinelli, Carla (1984) "Transcendenza ed ethos del lavoro. Note su 'La fine del mondo' di Ernesto de Martino." *La ricerca folklorica. Contributi allo studio della cultural delle classi popolari* 9: 29–36.

Redfield, Robert (1941) *The Folk Culture of the Yucatan.* Chicago, Ill.: The University of Chicago Press.

——(1955a) *The Little Community.* Chicago, Ill.: The University of Chicago Press.

——(1955b) *Peasant Society and Culture.* Chicago, Ill.: The University of Chicago Press.

Rossi-Doria, Manlio (1948) *Riforma agraria e azione meridionalista.* Bologna: Edizioni agricole.

——(1958) *Dieci anni di politica agraria nel mezzogiorno.* Bari: Laterza.

Santoli, Vittorio (1940) *I canti popolari italiani: Ricerchie e questioni.* Florence: Sansoni.

Saunders, George (1993) "The Ethnology of Ernesto de Martino." *American Anthropologist* 95: 874–93.

Tipps, Dean C. (1973) "Modernization Theory and the Comparative Study of Societies: A Critical Perspective." *Comparative Studies in Society and History* 15(2): 199–226.

Wolf, Eric R. (1982) *Europe and the People without History.* Berkeley: University of California Press.

The Magic of the South: Popular Religion and Elite Catholicism in Italian Ethnology

George R. Saunders

Northern Europeans have long come south to Italy for spiritual and aesthetic refreshment. Goethe, Freud, and Max Weber all discovered some sort of "spirit" in Italy that contrasted sharply with the overly rationalized, passionless instrumentality of their northern lands. Goethe, for example, spent nearly two years in Italy, from 1786 to 1788, recovering from a "terrible disease" brought on, apparently, by his service in the government of Weimar, but perhaps in part by a kind of mid-life crisis deriving from his literary work. In Italy he felt a spiritual and intellectual rebirth, a burst of new energy and excitement. His letters and journal entries from Italy express wonder and enthusiasm, generated in part by the sensual aesthetics and in part by the puzzling otherness of it all. At times, they also describe his dismay and a fair measure of disgust.[1]

Freud also, according to biographer Peter Gay, went to Italy first in 1901 after coming out of a depression, and found there a kind of spiritual inspiration. He stood fascinated in front of Michelangelo's statue of Moses, and later referred to the visit as a "high point" in his life (Gay 1988: 135). Another of his biographers, Ernest Jones, wrote this terse comment: "Then came the great visit to Rome, after which [Freud] says his pleasure in life had increased and his pleasure in martyrdom diminished" (Jones 1961: 221). Though Freud seems to have been most taken by the remains of ancient Rome, he clearly found something both marvelous and troublesome in the contemporary city. His last great reflections on the problems of the modern world, in *Civilization and Its Discontents* (1961 [1930]), open with a metaphoric association of the city of Rome and the human psyche, in both of which Freud finds the ancient and primitive coexisting with the modern and sophisticated.

Max Weber's biographers also suggest that he experienced much of his life as a struggle between the "iron cage" of rational, bureaucratized, instrumental, but soulless life (the North?) and the emotional, sensuous, aesthetic, and spiritual (the South?). At the age of 33 he suffered a major nervous breakdown that immobilized him for several years, and one of the few places he found solace was Italy (see Bendix 1960; Macrae 1974; Mitzman 1969). It may not be an accident that his best-known work, *The Protestant Ethic and the Spirit of Capitalism,* was begun shortly after his recovery. It is even worth surmising (a thoroughly unsubstantiated musing) that his conception of the connection between Protestantism and the capitalist development of the North was inspired by his observation of Catholicism in Italy.

Italy worked a kind of spiritual magic on these northern Europeans, then, but it also disturbed them. They brought their own forms of personal pathology, longing, and romanticism to the South, and seemed to find there a cultural pathology that buoyed their spirits, perhaps precisely because its "otherness" affirmed their own sense of "modernness" and refreshed them by contrast. The South healed the northerners; it compelled them with its humanity and its soul, but it nonetheless remained for them fundamentally alien. Indeed, it is striking how thoroughly "other" the Italian peninsula has been for northern Europeans and Americans. A 1962 edition of Goethe's *Italian Journey 1786–1788* is introduced by W. H. Auden and Elizabeth Mayer, and includes this observation:

> There are hundreds and thousands of Englishmen and Americans who have made an Italian journey of their own and, to many of them, their encounter with Italy, its landscape, its people, its art, has been as important an experience as it was to Goethe, so that the subject-matter of the book will interest them, irrespective of its author, and they will enjoy comparing the post-World War II Italy they know with the pre-French-Revolution Italy which Goethe saw. (Speaking for myself,[2] I am amazed at their similarity. Is there any other country in Europe where the character of the people seems to have been so little affected by political and technological change?) (Goethe 1962: viii).

Most northerners (including northern Italians) have felt little compunction about declaring the unchanging otherness of Southern Italy in particular. In discourse at least, it is an alien land, and the alien attracts and repels simultaneously.[3] The alien nature of the Italian South is reflected in part in its visual impact, its continuing agrarian character and the failures of infrastructure that impress northerners as "like the Third World." But a central component of the differentness of the Mezzogiorno has always been its religious life – the emotional character of public rituals, the sensuousness of its religious imagery, and the refusal of much of its religious belief and practice to be diluted, rationalized, and bureaucratized as one would expect of "modern" religion. Indeed, the character of popular religion led sixteenth-century Italian Jesuits to think of assignments in the South of Italy as very like missions to the New World, and they sometimes referred to the South as the "India italiana" (De Martino 1961: 22). Such conceptions persist in the twentieth century.

Italian scholars who have focused on the religious life of the South of their own country have approached it with considerably less romanticism, but with every bit as much ambivalence. The spirit of the South, particularly its religiosity and magical practices, has been seen as a form of practical wisdom, a fountain of energy for social transformation, a domain of autarky and of resistance to domination, but also as ignorant superstition, debilitating fatalism and futility, a source of social divisiveness, and an anachronism. In this chapter I want to take at face value the apparent ambivalence of two of these insider–outsider theorists, Antonio Gramsci (1891–1937) and Ernesto De Martino (1908–1965), and to treat that ambivalence as integral to understanding the place of southern supernaturalism in the larger world of Italy, Europe, and contemporary life.[4]

Antonio Gramsci was born in 1891 in Sardinia. He studied at the University of Turin, and as a young man became secretary of the Turin section of the Socialist Party. During the First World War, he left the Socialist Party for the fledgling Italian Communist Party. In the following years, Gramsci was active as a party leader, a journalist, and a political and cultural theorist. His interests spanned practical political organizational tasks, drama and popular literature, and world history. In 1926, the year of his arrest by the fascist government of Mussolini, he wrote his essays on the Southern Question. He was formally tried in Rome in 1928, and was condemned to twenty years in prison. He continued to write from prison, though necessarily in a less referenced and systematic way, and some of his most insightful writings were published as "notebooks" after his death in 1937 at the age of 46.

Ernesto De Martino was born in 1908 in Naples. He studied there under historians of religion Adolfo Omodeo and Raffaele Pettazzoni, and came into the circle of Benedetto Croce. During the Mussolini years, De Martino took an anti-fascist stance, and following the Second World War, he worked for a period as an organizer for the Socialist Party and later the Communist Party in Southern Italy. The latter experience was instrumental in focusing his ethnographic attention on Southern Italy, especially its popular religion, and he produced a number of outstanding works that have subsequently shaped the field of anthropology in Italy (Saunders 1991).

Gramsci wrote sparingly and unsystematically about popular southern religion (though he commented often about the political and cultural role of the Catholic Church). De Martino by contrast wrote extensively, creatively, and painstakingly about the religious life of the South. Both theorists, however, seemed at times confounded by popular religion, uncertain about whether to treat it with respect or overt disgust, and both struggled intellectually to figure out how it related to the future of the world that they lived and worked in. Both wanted to understand its humanity, and yet at times could not disguise their conviction of its "otherness." Both distinguished their own reactions to southern magic and religion from those of Protestant polemicists, the liberal bourgeoisie, and the economistic left. In "The Southern Question," for example, Gramsci caricatures northern bourgeois propaganda about the South: "the southerners are biologically inferior beings, semi-barbarians or complete barbarians by natural destiny . . ., lazy, incapable, criminal, barbarous" (1957: 31). Gramsci objects strenuously to such essentialist stereotypes, and yet the South remains a substantial "problem" in his work. In his calls for an alliance between the industrial proletariat (largely of the North) and the rural proletariat (largely of the South), his tone suggests considerable worry about the potential of the South to join fully as an active partner:

> The South can be described as an area of extreme social disintegration. The peasants who constitute the great majority of the population have no cohesion among themselves . . . . The society of the South is a great agrarian *bloc* consisting of three social strata: the large, amorphous, scattered peasant masses; the intellectuals of the petty and middle rural bourgeoisie; the big property owners and the top intellectuals. The southern peasants are in perpetual ferment, but as a mass they are incapable of giving a unified expression to their aspirations and their needs (1957: 42).

My goal in this chapter, then, is to interpret the work of Gramsci and De Martino in order to answer a series of interrelated questions. Firstly, what is the dynamic relationship between popular culture and élite, "high," or hegemonic culture; more specifically, to what extent do popular religion and official Catholicism represent shared systems of ideas and values? To what extent is popular religion conservative and ultimately supportive of the values of the élite, or by contrast "oppositional" to dominant culture? If it is "oppositional," is it simply a form of passive resistance, or may it in fact be "progressive," providing an ideological basis for social and cultural change? Secondly, to what extent is popular religion "historical" in the sense of affording its practitioners a place as subjects rather than objects in the movement of time and events?[5] To put this last question in another way, does popular religion relegate its practitioners to non-history, to an ahistorical "magical" practice, or does it contain at least the seeds of a consciousness that can allow people an active role in the shaping of their own historical moment?[6]

Catholicism and Hegemony: From the Top Down

Gramsci's writings deal with several aspects of the particularly fragmented character of Italian society of the nineteenth and early twentieth centuries. North and South represent in certain ways the geographical distribution of class, but not simply in the sense that the North is wealthy and powerful and the South is poor and powerless. The North is the primary home of the industrial proletariat and of such liberal bourgeoisie as has developed in Italy, while the South is the primary home of an agrarian underclass and a landowning élite. The North is a relatively secularized area, or at least liberalism has largely succeeded in pushing religion out of the public political realm. In the South, on the other hand, the disjunction between élite, official Catholicism and the religious beliefs and practices of ordinary country folk is pronounced, but in one form or another religion retains critical social relevance. This latter issue will be the focus of my analysis here, but it connects directly to the other schisms in Italian society. Indeed, Gramsci put it this way:

> But the peasant question is historically determined in Italy; it is not the "peasant and agrarian question in general". In Italy the peasant question, through the specific Italian tradition, and the specific development of Italian history, has taken two typical and particular forms – the Southern question and that of the Vatican. Winning the majority of the peasant masses thus means, for the Italian proletariat, making these two questions its own from the social point of view (Gramsci 1978: 443).

The Catholic Church thus assumes a particular importance in Gramsci's analysis of Italian society. It is, first of all, not simply a "local" religious institution, but rather the source of Italy's place in the larger world. "It should not be forgotten that from the sixteenth century onwards Italy contributed to world history especially because it was the seat of the papacy, and that Italian Catholicism was felt not only as a surrogate for the spirit of the nation and the state but also as a worldwide hegemonic institution, as an imperialistic spirit" (1985: 220–1). These are strong words, and they recall the important fact that, until the twentieth century, Italy's particular imperialism was unlike that of any other Western power. Rather than a state imperialism that used religion as a form of mystification and legitimation, Italy's was a directly religious imperialism whose international hegemonic role was "multinational" almost in the contemporary sense of being above and beyond the state. This international significance is a central factor in the Church's power in Italian domestic affairs. As Carl Boggs points out, in Gramsci's analysis the Catholic Church is the ideological buttress that sustains a unity, however fragile, in a country in which the economic, political, and cultural gaps separating élites from the poor are otherwise quite pronounced. The role of Catholicism as an official doctrine is to stress "the 'natural' (God-given) character of existing structures such as private property and the family, the importance of transcendental com- mitment over everyday ('earthly') collective action to change the world, the supposed moral virtues of poverty and weakness, and the sacrosanct nature of all forms of established authority" (Boggs 1976: 43). The struggle of the Catholic Church against the liberal reforms of the nineteenth century in Italy is well known, and the variety of hegemony Catholicism maintained was for Gramsci (rightly) quite distinct from liberalism and the associated values of Protestantism.[7] The latter were closely associated with the European bourgeoisie, of course, while Catholicism long remained the ideological base of Italy's version of the *Ancien Régime*, an agrarian-based and quasi-feudal social and political system.[8] This association in turn explains the Church's formal antagonism to the Italian state following Unification in 1861 until 1929, when it recovered its official role in Italian cultural life through the Concordat with Mussolini. Even in the years of Church–State hostility prior to the Concordat, however, Catholicism remained a dominant force in Italian ideological culture, and continued to do so well into the twentieth century.

Catholicism's ideological domination of Italian culture is a central topic of investigation for both Gramsci and De Martino. It appears to be, as Boggs suggests, a question of how the religion supports unity in a society otherwise riven by class and cultural differences – a question, that is, of "hegemony." In the introduction to *Il materialismo storico*, Luciano Gruppi summarizes Gramsci's reasoning about this process: "The dominant class in so far as it actuates its own hegemony thus knows how to realize and maintain an historical bloc of contradictory social and political forces, in its base economic and its superstructure civil and governmental, held together by ideology" (1975: xxxii). Gramsci thus emphasizes the cultural and symbolic factors as those through which subaltern groups come to be and to remain subaltern. The contradictions in the system and the gaps between groups are masked by the Catholic symbolic and ideological structure, through which rich and poor, powerful and powerless, are alike oriented to life and moved to conformity.[9]

In Gramsci's essay on "The Southern Question," there is unfortunately little comment on the Church proper. Gramsci's concern here is that in the South "the agrarian bloc" retains its particular hold on Italian society. Landed élites who derive their incomes from rents dominate southern life, unlike the industrial North, where capital and industry have displaced the agrarian bloc. But for Gramsci, such economic power is always mediated through the ideological factors that induce complicity and establish a sense of legitimacy (however tenuous). The Church, as Gramsci makes clear in other places, is the author of this ideological unity, and the intellectuals are its agents. In order for the South to progress, the ideological grip of the Church must be broken. "The proletariat will destroy the southern agrarian bloc insofar as it succeeds, through its party, in organizing increasingly significant masses of poor peasants into autonomous and independent formations. But its greater or lesser success in this necessary task will also depend upon its ability to break up the intellectual bloc that is the flexible, but extremely resistant, armour of the agrarian bloc" (Gramsci 1978: 462).

What is the character of the "intellectual bloc"? The Church attempts to provide an integralist and totalizing world view that obscures the differences between élites and the poor and creates and sustains an illusion of social justice under the hand of God and "Holy Mother Church." "The power of religions and especially of the Catholic Church has consisted and does consist in the fact that they feel strongly the need for the doctrinal unity of the whole 'religious' mass" (1957: 63). From the point of view of the Church (and of the dominant classes in general), then, a sharp break between "popular religion" and "official religion" would be a serious problem, as would, for that matter, a disjunction between "official religion" and the religious beliefs of élite intellectuals. The Church's conservatism, then, is of a particular type: it wants to hold both ends into the middle. "The Roman church has always been the most tenacious in the struggle to avoid the 'official' formulation of two religions, one for the 'intellectuals' and one for the 'simple people'" (1957: 63). Orthodoxy is essential to cultural unity, and thus magic, popular religion, extra-liturgical ritual and extra-ecclesiastical practitioners are serious threats. Gramsci is here suggesting that one revolutionary potential in popular religion is precisely the possibility of its widening the gulf between the élite and ordinary people.

Incidentally, De Martino has a similar understanding of the workings of Catholicism as a cultural force, and of "the reality that hides behind the name of 'Catholicism,'" noting that "the Catholicism of Cardinal Schuster is one thing, and the Catholicism of a day-laborer of Andria is altogether another" (De Martino 1977[1948]: 41). Like Gramsci, De Martino argues the need for "precise knowledge of the structure and the technique of the battle by the Church, of the arguments by which the Catholic faith is guaranteed, rooted in the conscience, and transformed into a collective persuasion . . ., the concrete modes of the current reactionary functions of the Church." For both theorists, the Church's strength is precisely in its ability to present itself as a universal ideology that transcends time and place, and particularly that transcends the narrow interests of class and political power. For De Martino as for Gramsci, this cultural unity needs to be disrupted and replaced by an alternative unifying ideology. De Martino thus calls for "the unification of the national culture, as Gramsci conceived of it, that is the formation of a new cultural life for the nation that will heal the rupture between high culture and the culture of the people" (1977[1951]: 145.[10]

Who specifically are the personnel involved in the creation and reproduction of politically significant (religious) ideology? As Torres notes, hegemony "is produced by the organic intellectuals of the ruling classes and is also transmitted by traditional intellectuals. For Gramsci . . . the Catholic Church is constituted as the organic intellectual of the governing class, especially under feudalism" (Torres 1992: 43). Gramsci himself identifies the particular agents whom he considers important in this process: "There are organic and traditional intellectuals, just as there are superior intellectuals and those who may be considered as being of an intermediate rank and who provide the link that binds the superior level (whether organic or traditional intellectuals) and the masses. Schoolteachers and priests who exercise parochial functions constitute this class of intermediate intellectuals" (Gramsci 1980: 342). Thus there is a high-level clergy (as well as high government officials closely allied with the Church) who are "superior" organic intellectuals, those who shape Church doctrine and relate it to political currents such as liberalism, socialism, or fascism. The intermediate organic intellectuals, at the local level, are priests and schoolteachers who propagate their own versions of these doctrines, and relate them as well to local political and cultural events.

In Southern Italy, according to Gramsci, these intermediate organic intellectuals are typically rural members of the bourgeoisie:

> In other words, the petty and medium landowner who is not a peasant, who does not work the land, who would be ashamed to be a farmer, but who wants to extract from the little land he has – leased out either for rent or on a simple share-cropping basis – the wherewithal to live fittingly; the wherewithal to send his sons to a university or seminary, and the wherewithal to provide dowries for his daughters, who must marry officers or civil functionaries of the State. From this social layer, the intellectuals derive a fierce antipathy to the working peasant (1978: 455).

This southern intellectual class differs in social situation from that of the North. Gramsci points out that priests in the North have more often been sons of artisans or peasants, sometimes with democratic sympathies and a strong sense of connection to the poor. In addition, the northern priest seems to be more concerned about moral propriety than the southern priest, "who often lives more or less openly with a woman" (1978: 455) (cf. Holmes 1989: 115 ff.). Furthermore, in the North, the priest's economic power is considerably less than in the South: "In the North, the separation of Church from State and the expropriation of ecclesiastical goods were more radical than in the South, where the parishes and convents either have preserved or have reconstituted considerable assets, both fixed and movable" (Gramsci 1978: 455). The southern priest, by contrast, appears directly to peasants as a land administrator, with whom they must negotiate rents and share-cropping agreements, as a usurer, and as "a man subject to all the ordinary passions (women and money), and who therefore, from a spiritual point of view, inspires no confidence in his discretion and impartiality" (1978: 456). Despite the lack of personal claims to moral authority, the priest remains a powerful figure: the key point of contact, the intermediary between the official doctrine of the Catholic Church, with all its moral injunctions and ideological ramifications, and the day-to-day practical, existential, and spiritual concerns of the poor in the countryside.[11]

Traditional intellectuals, on the other hand, are outside the Church in a formal sense, and constitute a class somewhat apart. Gramsci describes the role of traditional intellectuals in his discussion of Benedetto Croce (though Croce is obviously not a run-of-the-mill traditional intellectual).

> For Croce religion is a conception of reality with a morality conforming to this conception, presented in mythological form . . . . A conception of the world cannot show

itself valid to permeate all of a society and become a "faith" unless it demonstrates itself to be capable of displacing the preceding conceptions and faiths at all levels of state life. To run back to the Hegelian theory of mythological religion as a philosophy of primitive societies (the infancy of humanity) to justify confessional teaching even if only in the elementary schools, signifies nothing if not a sophisticated representation of the formula of the "religion good for the common people," and in reality to abdicate and capitulate in front of the clerical hierarchy. It cannot fail to be revealed, in addition, that a faith that doesn't succeed in translating itself into "popular" terms shows itself by that fact alone to be characteristic of a determined social group (Gramsci 1975: 229).

Thus despite his supposed independence from Catholicism, Croce's idealism is in Gramsci's view ultimately supportive of Catholic hegemony, in that it continues to bolster the national unity. Italian intellectuals, nonetheless, seem to have a habit of distancing themselves from the ordinary people, and Croce is a good example of one whom the Church was unable to control, and who thus augmented that distance. Because of the intellectuals' tendency to an idealism divorced from the practical concerns of ordinary people, then, a weakness in the historical bloc appears, a crack in the masonry. In that fissure is its potential dissolution.

Gramsci's writings pay much more attention to the character of the Italian intellectuals than to "popular religion" and ordinary people's experience, but in a few places he writes specifically about "folklore" and folk religion.[12] The most influential comments are found in four brief entries entitled "Observations on Folklore" (1985: 188–95). These contain one of the most frequently cited passages in Italian ethnology:

> Folklore should . . . be studied as a "conception of the world and life" implicit to a large extent in determinate (in time and space) strata of society and in opposition (also for the most part implicit, mechanical and objective) to "official" conceptions of the world (or in a broader sense, the conceptions of the cultured parts of historically determinate societies) that have succeeded one another in the historical process (1985: 189).

Gramsci goes on to describe the nature of popular culture:

> This conception of the world is not elaborated and systematic because, by definition, the people (the sum total of the instrumental and subaltern classes of every form of society that has so far existed) cannot possess conceptions which are elaborated, systematic and politically organized and centralized in their albeit contradictory development. It is, rather, many-sided – not only because it includes different and juxtaposed elements, but also because it is stratified, from the more crude to the less crude – if, indeed, one should not speak of a confused agglomerate of fragments of all the conceptions of the world and of life that have succeeded one another in history (1985: 189).

There are several things to note about this formulation. First, Gramsci specifically suggests that the "conceptions of the world" expressed in folk beliefs are at least implicitly "in opposition to" official conceptions, although the very notion of hegemony implies that élite culture does in fact largely overcome this "oppositional" character. Indeed, there is even the danger that popular culture can be so conservative as to be genuinely reactionary. De Martino, for example, expresses this latter concern: "Magic and superstition, mythical mentality, primitive and populist modes of opposing the world, all of this represents an immense potential of energies that can be used advantageously in an openly reactionary sense by the dominant classes, to the end of maintaining its threatened hegemony" (De Martino 1977[1949]: 58). De Martino describes particularly the ways in which German Nazism made use of folkloric notions of race and blood in order to develop support for its nationalist and militarist programs. But popular culture surely does not automatically lend itself to such co-optation. As the passage by Gramsci clearly suggests, there is an intrinsic tension between popular culture and official culture, and folklore and popular religion *may* express this tension in an oppositional form.

In the passage quoted above, Gramsci also notes the central problem of popular culture: its fragmentary, internally contradictory, and unelaborated nature. Popular culture is necessarily "bits and pieces," quilt sections not yet sewn together, some of which clash quite dramatically with others. System is a quality of official and élite cultures, including religion, and not of popular culture. Similarly, Gramsci raises in this passage the problem of the "ahistoricity" of popular culture. Folklore consists of "fragments of all the conceptions of the world and of life that have succeeded one another in history." These fragments are not necessarily relevant to the current moment, and many are survivals of various other moments. They are out of time, and their very anachronistic character makes them in some sense ahistorical. In the context of Italian social thought, this has a particular meaning.

To say that popular culture is not-historical, in the sense in which Italian historicism has conceived of this problem, is to say that it is not composed of concepts, ideas, or ideologies available to and employed by people who are active agents in the current historical moment. To be "without history" or "out of history" is to lack the consciousness essential to agency, and thus to be unable to make appropriate choices, to be unable to "act" in the moment in order to "make history," and to be, instead, a passive recipient of history as made by others. Note that Gramsci and De Martino are concerned that this is in fact often a characteristic of popular culture. Though I think that they would also have been very sympathetic to the argument of Eric Wolf (1982; see also O'Brien and Roseberry 1991) that ahistoricity is often falsely attributed to the dominated by the dominant, here they are arguing that a particular kind of ahistoricity may in fact at least sometimes be a reality for that group.

It would seem that to the extent that popular culture is "oppositional," however, it at least has the potential to overcome this ahistoricity and to return people to a place as actors in the historical moment. Still, opposition is not necessarily in and of itself productive; it is not necessarily "progressive" and not necessarily a source of agency. Popular culture may express resistance to the status quo without providing a conceptual framework for action against the historical bloc.

At any rate, for Gramsci, popular religion has this fragmented character, and the nature of the consciousness contained therein is problematic:

> Certainly, there is a 'religion of the people', especially in Catholic and Orthodox countries, which is very different from that of the intellectuals (the religious ones) and particularly from that organically set up by the ecclesiastical hierarchy . . . . Thus it is true that there is a 'morality of the people', understood as a determinate (in space and time) set of principles for practical conduct and of customs that derive from them or have produced them. Like superstition, this morality is closely tied to real religious beliefs. Imperatives exist that are much stronger, more tenacious and more effective than those of official 'morality'. In this sphere, too, one must distinguish various strata: the fossilized ones which reflect conditions of past life and are therefore conservative and reactionary, and those which consist of a series of innovations, often creative and progressive, determined spontaneously by forms and conditions of life which are in the process of developing and which are in contradiction to or simply different from the morality of the governing strata (1985: 190).

The political and ideological character of popular religion, then, is a theoretical quagmire. Since it is not a unitary thing, it cannot have a unitary valence in consciousness, or a unitary political significance. And as long as we remain at the level of theory, the importance of popular religion in "the Southern Question" remains unknown. The fragmentary nature of folklore and of popular religion, the ahistorical quality of the "survivals" of the past combined with the historicity of the oppositional elements with potential for the future, all suggest the need for a thorough and genuine analysis of "real," concrete examples of popular religion. Popular religion thus *may* contain the potential for "breaking" the hegemony in the historical bloc, and for creating new forms of consciousness on the part of subaltern groups. But it also may not. The ethnographic information necessary for such a project was clearly out of reach of the imprisoned Gramsci. De Martino made such studies a central project of his work.

Before examining that work, I should recall that for both Gramsci and De Martino, the goal of study of culture is to find ways to change it, to make it an instrument of unification of national culture through an appropriately progressive ideology. As De Martino put it,

To us this cultural life of the people oriented toward the past must certainly be of interest, not of course from a tourist's point of view nor for love of the picturesque, nor even for the erudite zeal of preserving the most archaic memories of our populace, but for the much more serious and difficult reason that to modify the tradition it is necessary to know it, and to realize the program of unification of the national culture . . . a judicious coming to terms with popular traditions is essential (De Martino 1977[1951]: 146).

Here is a key point for our time: the study of popular religion is a political act, or at least a prelude to that act. We have to understand popular religion because it is itself intrinsically political, though its politics are complex, fragmented, and contradictory. We have to understand, furthermore, so that we and those we study maintain a place in history and a realistic sense of agency.

Magic, Popular Religion, and Official Catholicism: From the Bottom Up

Ernesto De Martino wrote extensively of magic and popular religion. His earliest books, *Naturalismo e storicismo nell'etnologia* and *Il mondo magico* both concern religious phenomena, though both of these are focused on the Third World or classical Europe, with only passing attention to the ethnography of contemporary Southern Italy. The South becomes the central ethnographic situation only in *Morte e pianto rituale* (1975[1958]), *Sud e magia* (1959), and *La terra del rimorso* (1961). The picture of popular southern religion that emerges from these latter writings affirms Gramsci's notion of it as a fragmentary, disorganized, and contradictory set of beliefs and practices that connects in a sporadic and partial way with "official" Catholicism.

In the belief and practice of ordinary people, it is sometimes difficult to distinguish clearly the emic boundaries between official Catholicism and "magic." Some rituals and beliefs are essentially "officially" Catholic, and yet are transformed in minor ways for popular purposes. Catholic symbols and saints, for example, are regularly used in magical techniques that in themselves have little to do with "official" ritual, and that are performed away from the watchful eye of priests. Other Catholic elements are transformed more completely, and others still seem to have no connection at all with official Catholicism, and indeed may be at odds with it. This last is perhaps most evidently the case in the work of specialists who are clearly "shamans" rather than "priests," and who have no role in the official Church. As De Martino repeatedly points out, however, ordinary people may bring to even the most clearly orthodox Catholic practices their own very heterodox interpretations. "Popular" and "orthodox" religion, then, are unbounded, non-discrete, very fluid categories.

De Martino's ethnography of magical practices in Lucania (1959) begins with a discussion of "la fascinazione," a broad category of beliefs and practices that includes *malocchio* or "the evil eye," and *fattura,* perhaps best described as "sorcery." Fascination manifests itself in symptoms of various types, including headaches, excessive sleepiness, digestive problems, the illnesses of infants, and the failure of mothers' milk to flow. The common factor in all is the sense of being "acted on" or "dominated" by occult forces. Here De Martino's analysis seems to suggest that magic expresses the powerlessness of the rural proletariat, the sense of being at the mercy of a world that acts with its own motives and logic. The ritual practice clearly concentrates not on the active process of "fascinating" someone, but rather on the after-the-fact undoing of it.

Sometimes formulaic verses are used to cure *fascinazione,* and these often seem to mimic Catholic ritual:

Padre, Figlio e Spirito Santo	Father, Son, and Holy Spirit,
Fascinatura va' da là via	Fascination go away from there.
Va' da affascinare N.N.	Don't fascinate N.N. [name]
ca è carne battezzata.	Who is baptized meat.
Padre, Figlio e Spirito Santo	Father, Son, and Holy Spirit,
Fascinatura non scí piú nante.	Fascination don't go ahead any more.
(De Martino 1959: 16)	

De Martino notes that some of these exorcistic spells are linked to "exemplary myths of cancellation of the fascination: and the 'word' said and the 'gesture' completed in the rite are efficacious in that they repeat and reactualize the metahistorical model of cancellation" (1959: 19), as in the following example:

Duie uocchie t'hanno affise	Two eyes have fixed you
tre te vonno aità	Three want to help you
Sant'Anna, Santa Lena	Saint Anne, Saint Elena
Santa Maria Maddalena.	Saint Mary Magdalene.
Scende la Madonna	The Madonna comes down
co' le mane sante	with her holy hands
in nome del Padre Figliuolo e	in the name of the Father, Son, and
Spirito Santo.	Holy Spirit.
(1959: 19).	

Again, ritual of this sort seems anything but oppositional, and though it may provide people with a comforting "psychological" sense of control over the world, it hardly seems a consciousness with genuine potential to change their situation in the world or to challenge the hegemony of the Church or the rapaciousness of landlords.

At other times, "fascination" is used electively for purposes that would clearly find disfavor with Church officials, as when "love magic" is employed to make somebody fall in love. Women may make use of menstrual blood or pubic hair slipped into wine, coffee, or soup, in order to *legare* ("tie" – but the word itself has supernatural overtones) a man and take him away from a rival. Even in love magic, however, there are links to official Catholicism. Three drops of blood from a woman's finger, for example, can be mixed with pubic and armpit hair, dried into a powder, and carried to Church. At the ritually central moment of the Mass, during the elevation of the host, the woman murmurs:

Sanghe de Criste	Blood of Christ,
demonie, attaccame a chiste	demons, attach me to this one
Tante ca li à legà	so strongly you must tie him
ca de me non s'avî scurdà.	that he will not forget me.
(1959: 22).	

How does such behavior relate to notions of hegemony or resistance? In some vague way this practice may be "countercultural," especially with respect to gender roles, but it remains, for De Martino, an "unrealistic" solution to real-life problems, and thus its oppositional character, if there at all, is far from progressive.[13]

At the other end of the spectrum, official Catholicism also provides a kind of romantic fortune-telling service – however inadvertent – for ordinary people. At the wedding Mass, for example, if the gospel of John is read, it is an auspicious sign, while the gospel of Luke inspires genuine panic among the participants (1959: 23). In describing these beliefs, De Martino suggests that the people who hold them are gullible and that priests are duplicitous: "The couple and their relatives, at the end of the Mass, often crowd around the officiating priests and ask anxiously, 'Which Gospel came out?' And the priest, who knows the beliefs of his parishioners, to calm them responds, 'Saint John, Saint John,' even if it's not true" (1959: 24). Thus, again, though this form of love magic seems in many senses at odds with Church doctrine, it is nonetheless incorporated into a wider ideological schema in which the Church maintains its role as a legitimate and powerful authority. There seems little here to disrupt the unifying ideology propagated by the Church itself.

The second part of *Sud e magia,* entitled "Magic, Catholicism, and High Culture," is the analytic heart of the book. Here De Martino develops a theoretical explanation of some aspects of magic, focusing on its relationship to "the crisis of presence," an existential dilemma in which there is a "risk that the very individual presence may lose itself as a center of decision and of choice" (1959: 90).[14] This possibility is itself universal: it is evident in psychopathology, in great wars, in grief and mourning, and in a variety of other contexts. It is particularly likely, however, where "the immense daily power of the negative" is so evident and overwhelming. In the poor, rural zones of Southern Italy, "the precariousness of the elementary goods of life, the uncertainty of the prospects for the future, the pressure exercised over individuals by uncontrollable natural and social forces, the harshness of toil in the framework of a backward agricultural economy, the narrow memory of efficacious rational actions with which to confront realistically the critical moments of existence constitute so many conditions that favor the maintenance of magical practices" (1959: 89). Magic is thus a way of coping in the face of overwhelming social and economic marginalization. It is a cultural aspect of the class system and of an unproductive economy in a difficult ecology. In the absence of effective strategies to counter the overwhelmingly negative aspects of this environment, popular religion helps people to live with their situation. Again, this sounds like a form of mystification that ultimately supports the system and is effectively conservative.

Magic is not just bad science (or bad politics, perhaps), however, but has a larger cultural role related to its historical location as a "folkloric area of a modern civilization" (1959: 109), and particularly in its rapport with official Catholicism. Most Lucanian magical practices have analogs elsewhere in the world: the use of exuviae and the body in "sympathetic" and "imitative" rituals; the power of the spoken word in ritual contexts; the connection of harm and cure through the common belief in the power of the supernatural; the importance of "technique" and the instrumental approach. Lucanian magic thus demonstrates remarkable similarities to (an example cited) that of the Aranda of central Australia, and it would seem that magic is also in this sense ahistorical, an abstracted phenomenon that occurs everywhere. For De Martino, however, those similarities obscure more than they illuminate. "The historical sense" of Lucanian magic "manifests itself therefore only if we consider those techniques as a moment of a cultural dynamic perceptible in a single civilization, a particular society, and a definite epoch" (1959: 112). The emphasis here is on "dynamic" – magic is to be understood in *this* historical moment, not as an archaic "survival" of a past moment.

This historical sense is recognized particularly in the fact that magic forms a kind of bridge between popular culture and hegemonic culture, a meeting-place for the two, or perhaps better, a communication system between them. This bridge is evident in several ways. One of the old saws of the distinction between "magic" and "religion" is that the former is strictly instrumental and technical, while the latter is (as Croce noted) related to a system of morality and of values. The employment of the symbols of Christianity in Lucanian magic, however, opens these practices to a wider horizon, and connects them, however tenuously, to all of the values of Christianity.

> Through the connections and the shadows . . . Lucanian magic communicates therefore with the fundamental themes of the Catholic cult, with the sacramentals and the sacraments, and even with the very sacrifice of the Mass, across a continuum of moments which . . . signal a gradual approach to the heart of the Catholic religion, where the

specifically popular or in fact "southern" shadings of Catholicism in part dissolve themselves and in part become attenuated and sublimated, until finally we arrive at that which characterizes Catholicism as a particular Christian confession (1959: 120).

This latter is a system of ethics and values. Furthermore, De Martino goes on to note that the bridge connects in both directions, and official Catholicism, like all religions, continues to contain elements that are clearly magical. It is a short step, he argues, from the "extracanonical exorcism of witches and sorcerers" to the "Mass of exorcism" with its "blessings of water, of salt, prayers against Satan and the other evil spirits" and finally to "pontifical" exorcisms, that is, dedications of churches, blessing of holy oils and bells, and so forth (1959: 119–22). The question of the connection of ritual actions to value systems is crucial, and De Martino goes to some length to show, again, that the boundaries between instrumental magic and value-oriented religion are fuzzy. It is in this context that he rejects the Protestant polemics against southern Catholicism which have treated it as a form of "paganism" surviving from pre-Christian Roman ideas and practices.

However wide the gap between popular and élite conceptions of the world, then, even popular supernaturalism occurs within a thoroughly "Catholic" framework. The priest in the example above knows the meanings that his parishioners will apply to the fact that one gospel rather than another is read at the wedding Mass. No matter what approach he takes to this issue, the priest is clearly in a position of power, and knows how to use that power in the manipulation of meanings. Such power makes his wider values relevant, gives the messages of his sermons a particular impact, and constitutes the basis of his ability to act as an agent of "cultural unity" in the maintenance of the historical bloc.

By the same token, by virtue of their bridge to orthodox Catholicism, magic and popular religion do lead ordinary people into a conception of the world in which right conduct has a cosmic dimension, and in which the cosmic is a moral domain. However much one may object to the particular moral values of orthodox Catholicism, the analysis seems to imply that this bridge thus establishes the epistemological and cultural foundation for *action* oriented to political and social change. Once morality becomes a relevant issue, there is the potential to turn the judgments of such morality back on those in power themselves. If morality is relevant, then the morality of the local priest is also relevant, and can be used against him and those in power. This is a major source of the progressive potential in popular religion.

An even more interesting analysis emerges from De Martino's attempt to trace the history of *jettatura*, that is, the "evil eye," through the period of the Enlightenment. Here the particular historical moment and the collocation of the phenomenon in the southern (in this case, particularly Neapolitan) context acquire their relevance. De Martino takes up the themes of "rationalism" and "enlightenment" and their relationship to *jettatura*. Beginning in the Renaissance in Naples, he notes a trend away from the popular interpretation of the evil eye as a phenomenon involving Satan and demons, and toward a "naturalistic" and psychologized interpretation. In the latter, the evil eye would be seen as "the product of 'images' that with their charge of envy and evil depart from the eye and the glance, whence by the action of whatever such material particles or 'images' there may be, they cause for the victim distressing alterations of the body or the soul" (1959: 130). In this context, "Satan becomes the symbol of the dark side of man" (1959: 136), a decided step away from the kind of attitudes that De Martino repeatedly refers to, in this book, as "unrealistic."

Despite this movement toward a more rational, "scientific" approach, however, belief in the evil eye did not disappear. Rather, by the late eighteenth and nineteenth centuries, this belief had become more ambiguous, and had acquired a kind of facetious, almost farcical character, especially in literature. Now, De Martino considers the fact that it appears in literature at all to be in itself interesting, and he notes that the continuing reference to evil eye was particularly notable to foreigners: "In general these travelers were struck by the social extent of the belief, and did not fail to note that while in their [northern European] countries of origin the educated classes no longer participated in this 'superstition,' . . . in Naples all the classes of society were still involved in it" (1959: 158). De Martino points out that even a distinguished university professor of canonical and civil law had published a major book about it, which was widely read among the élite. This book, by Nicola Valletta, was titled *Cicalata sul fascino, volgarmente detto jetta-tura*. The title is difficult to translate, but might best be rendered something like "Idle Musings about Fascination, Popularly Called *Jettatura*." Idle chit-chat, the stuff of blow-hards, not to be taken seriously, the book appears to have been written as a kind of whimsy of Valleta's old age. De Martino notes that Valleta seems to approach the subject with a kind of dual consciousness: "the disposition . . . between serious and facetious with which even today many Italians, and above all southerners, often confront the theme of evil eye, the 'it's not true, but I believe in it' (or the 'I don't believe in it, but it's true')" attitude (De Martino 1959: 148). Furthermore, De Martino describes Valleta as "smiling" at the phenomenon, and yet this attitude highlights "above all the contrast between a superior cultural consciousness, which has learned from the Enlightenment the great theme of the rationality of the universe and of the transformative power of human labor brightened by the lamp of reason, and an inferior cultural consciousness, still not overcome, according to which, by contrast, everything goes askance with a regularity and a predictability which constitute exactly the opposite of an 'enlightened' world" (1959: 142).

Why this dual consciousness? Why the persistence of the irrational and the contradictory, even in the "cultivated classes"?[15] De Martino's explanation, in the end, is less than fully satisfying, and seems to reaffirm the essentially conservative ideological function of popular religion. To make sense of the continuing significance of the evil eye, De Martino falls back on a rather crude combination of an almost-mystical notion, "the power of the negative in the history of the South" (1959: 174), and the failure of Naples and the South to develop an industrially and commercially-oriented bourgeoisie (1959: 176). De Martino notes that the figure of the feared *jettatore* in Naples was often an upper-class public official, "by profession *letterati*, doctors, lawyers, and magistrates" (1959: 177). But remember that it was not only the poor who made such projections, so this ideology is not simply the poor's way of morally deflating the powerful. Indeed, the belief is found even at the very top of the social structure. King Ferdinand I was said to have refused for years to invite a certain De Jorio for a court audience, because he believed him to be a *jettatore*. And indeed, when he was finally persuaded to see De Jorio, Ferdinand died on the following morning, apparently convinced that his belief had been correct. And later, Ferdinand II was said to have seen two Capuchin monks eyeing him on his return from a wedding; and he died shortly afterwards, shouting on his death bed, "M'hanno jettato!" (1959: 157).

In considering this participation of the élite in popular beliefs, De Martino suggests that Naples was stuck in a non-history, and that it failed to develop genuinely rationalized systems, particularly of justice and public administration. "It was thus understandable that the ideology of the *jettatura* should enjoy particular favor precisely in an environment of this type, where the outcome requested or hoped for depended on a myriad of imponderables, and where justice and arbitrary action, law and its abuse, were inextricably confused" (1959: 178). The belief in the evil eye attributed misfortune to the moral whimsy of individual men, men who could wield their nefarious powers against the wealthy as well as the poor. Though not intrinsically a "Catholic" doctrine, it was far from contradictory to Church interests, and even such élite defenders of the faith as the Bourbon kings were believers and victims. In a quasi-feudal area where an aristocratic élite was invincible, the belief in the evil eye as a source of misfortune deflected attention from class relations themselves, assigning evil to individuals rather than to social categories. As such, it was one weapon in the armory of the élite, helping to maintain the cultural unity, obscuring the distinctions between élite Catholicism and popular religion, and between élites themselves and the poor.

But The Potential Remains

The preface to *Sud e magia* begins like this:

> The opposition between 'magic' and 'rationality' is one of the great themes of which modern civilization has been born. This opposition has its prologue in some motifs of

Greek thought and of Gospel teachings, but it is constituted as the dramatic center of modern civilization with the passage from demonological magic to the natural magic of the Renaissance, with the Protestant polemic against Catholic ritualism, with the foundation of the natural sciences and their methods, with the Enlightenment and its faith in a reforming human nature, and with the various currents of thought that are tied to the discovery of the dialectic and of historical reasoning. In this framework even the bloody epoch of the witch trials, though it appears to be a return to the demonological conceptions of medieval magic, recalls immediately this fundamental antimagical polemic that runs through the whole course of Western civilization. The modern nations which comprise the West are "modern" to the extent that they have participated seriously in this varied process in which we are still involved (De Martino 1959: 7).

For De Martino, questions of "progress" have to do with a two-sided historical movement: (1) toward increasingly "rational" solutions to human problems; and (2) toward a kind of consciousness that affords the individual greater possibility of acting as a subject rather than an object in history, of making choices that afford a measure of "presence" in the world. Popular religion, at least as found in De Martino's ethnographic studies of Southern Italy, seems to provide little basis for such progress, though it does contain that potential. As a "conception of the world," it seems most often to focus on a cosmos of supernatural whimsy, of malevolent forces activated by unseen enemies and of benevolent forces that may be (but also may not be) coerced by ritual language into helping one person against another, with little relationship to the moral status or value systems of either. It does little to suggest that choices based on values are essential to action in the world, and provides little basis for such choices themselves. It encourages people to individualize the solutions to their problems, and to deal with them in indirect ways. In all of these senses, popular religion usually inhibits the social conflict that could lead to change.

Elite Catholicism in a paradoxical way has somewhat more potential for representing progress, simply because of its claims to universal values, which bring the supernatural back to earth and affirm more directly that people's moral behavior matters. (Certainly in recent years this potential has been realized in "liberation theology" and other political-religious movements within the Catholic Church.) Still, Catholic doctrine is generally, for De Martino as for Gramsci, a reactionary and mystifying ideology, by which differences between the powerful and the poor are symbolically glossed over and legitimated, and which thus helps to create a cultural unity based on what remains essentially an irrational conception of the world. The "problem" of the relationship between élite Catholicism and ordinary people is that in fact Catholicism has been generally successful in bringing the poor into a value system promulgated by the élite. The organic intellectuals of the South, parish priests, schoolteachers, bureaucrats, and so forth, are effective agents in the creation of a genuine hegemony, however fragile it may be and however contrary to the interests of the poor.

The successes of official Catholicism are far from uniform and total, however. Popular religion has at least some elements that are oppositional, that contradict official doctrine, and that continue to emphasize the gap between the high-religious ideologues and ordinary people. This gap is a marker both of the degradation of the subaltern classes and of the possibility of their finding a kind of consciousness that could break the hegemonic bloc. The kinds of magic and popular religion that poor people use in the South seem to be, for Gramsci and De Martino, essentially unrealistic. They give a false sense of "presence" and of ability to influence the course of affairs, and they do not in fact bring the poor into history as conscious decision-makers and actors. On the other hand, to the extent that such religion emphasizes to them their own "otherness" with respect to dominant culture, it also contains the seeds of change: contradictions that are evident are the basis of a potential class consciousness and thus of social transformation. To the extent that the popular religion of the South and official Catholicism stand as two distinct and opposed systems, they represent to people the gaps between the poor and the powerful, between South and North, and they thus provide some basis for solidarity and a collective consciousness that may break the ideological unity. This is a weak potential, perhaps, but it is at least potential.[16]

Acknowledgments

This chapter and the paper on which it was based owe a great deal to the collegial friendship of Mariella Pandolfi, who continues to be a source of support and inspiration for my reading of De Martino, and whose own work (such as 1991) keeps this seminal thinker on the minds of Italianist scholars at home and abroad. I also owe a special debt in this paper to Carla Pasquinelli, whose edited book, *Antropologia culturale e questione meridionale* (1977), has been a major resource for me, and whose own introduction to the book provides a much clearer and more profound analysis than I manage here. Dorothy Zinn, who is at work on a translation of *La terra del rimorso*, has also stimulated my recent thinking about De Martino. I thank Jane Schneider for the invitation to prepare the paper for the conference, Vincenzo Padiglione for persistent friendship against all odds, Clara Gallini and Amalia Signorelli for an invitation to the special conference on "De Martino in European Culture" held in Rome and Naples in late 1995, and Lawrence University for giving me a job and continuing to pay me for eighteen years now. Much of the background work for this chapter was also completed during two recent stays in Italy, one with the help of National Science Foundation Grant BNS-9005857 (shared with Salvatore Cucchiari) and another with a summer stipend from the National Endowment for the Humanities.

Notes

1. For an excellent discussion of Goethe's observations on the Roman Carnival, see Crapanzano 1986.
2. The text does not tell us whether "myself" refers to Auden or Mayer.
3. We anthropologists are of course not immune to these ambiguous attractions, as David Kertzer reminded us in his recent paper, "Representing Italy," presented at the 1994 meeting of the American Anthropological Association.
4. The chapter by Nadia Urbinati in this volume (Chapter 6) suggests to me that, in the case of Gramsci, "ambivalence" is perhaps not the right word. Rather, his understanding of the South was complex, and changed a great deal over the course of his truncated career. My particular focus here, however, is southern popular religion, and I think that ambivalence is more appropriately descriptive in this domain than in Gramsci's more general views of the place of the South in Italian national culture.
5. The question of "subjectivity" in De Martino's work is nicely elaborated by di Nola in this volume (Chapter 7). See also my article (Saunders 1993), and Cherchi and Cherchi (1987).
6. One further note before I begin this interpretation. I emphasize from the beginning that this is an "interpretation" of ideas of these two scholars, ideas sometimes incompletely formed and sometimes contradictory, and sometimes just plain difficult for my limited and English-oriented mind to understand. Accordingly, I am aware that I more than occasionally "force" the interpretation, working from notions that "suggest themselves" to me as I read, rather than from ideas clearly articulated by Gramsci and De Martino themselves. I have also selected, for this particular essay, a particular subset of the writings of each author. For Gramsci, the set is rather eclectic, but includes his commentaries on Catholicism itself, found scattered through the *Prison Notebooks*, and also his comments on the character of "folklore." For De Martino, I will examine a number of his shorter essays, touch briefly on the magnificent *La terra del rimorso*, and concentrate on *Sud e magia*, a major text on the character of magic and popular religion in the South. An additional caveat is appropriate: like Gramsci and De Martino, I write in my "own" time and see things from the perspectives I find in that moment. The point is that though this essay takes texts by Gramsci and De Martino as its foundation, those texts are undoubtedly transformed in my interpretation of them, just as I am transformed by reading them. It's not a fair trade: I take more than I give, and at times I undoubtedly give a poor gift.
7. An excellent discussion of the Church's position with respect to the kind of intellectual culture that developed out of liberalism can be found in Leone 1985. See also Angrosino 1994.

8. The Reformation did of course make at least some headway in Italy itself, and in the nineteenth century there was a small but significant development of Protestantism, despite the continuing dominance of the Catholic Church. As elsewhere, Protestantism in Italy was particularly an urban and bourgeois phenomenon in its early stages, though it has subsequently developed a very different base. See for example Chiarini and Giorgi (1990), Maselli (1971, 1978), Mottu and Castiglione (1977), Spini (1968, 1971), and Saunders (1995).

9. Of course, sometimes the line between "force" and "cultural domination" is thin. I am reminded of Frank Snowden's account of a typical day for an Apulian agricultural day-laborer in 1905, which began literally at dawn: "Only at sunset was it permissible to down tools, and even then the men could not depart until they had knelt in compulsory prayer" (1986: 26).

10. De Martino worried that this new cultural unity might require at least a temporary "barbarianizing of culture," that is, the need for culture to be brought down to a level intelligible and meaningful to ordinary people, apparently until the people could be brought up to a higher level themselves. This notion was drawn from Gramsci (see De Martino 1977[1949]), and created considerable controversy among leftist theorists of the early postwar period (see Luporini 1977[1950]).

11. In my own research in Italy, I have often heard "priest stories" that indicate precisely the kind of tyrannical exercise of power, of questionable legitimacy, that Gramsci was concerned with. In an alpine village where I worked in the middle to late 1970s, for example, people complained that the local health service doctor refused to provide couples with any birth control information unless they first presented him with a letter from the local priest authorizing him to do so. And Pentecostal Protestants in Tuscany told me many stories of priests acting inappropriately in local affairs. One man, for example, told of his parish priest announcing from the pulpit that people could no longer – under threat of excommunication – shop at the small store owned by a woman who had recently joined one of the Protestant groups in the neighborhood. According to my informant, the woman was put out of business in a brief period.

12. See Urbinati in this volume (Chapter 6) for a deeper discussion of the relationship between high culture, "common sense," and folklore.

13. The countercultural or oppositional character of popular religion has been the focus of a great deal of attention by later Europeanist historians and anthropologists, such as Burke 1978, Christian 1972, 1984, Cirese 1971, Davis 1965, Di Nola 1976, Holmes 1989, Lanternari 1963, and Lombardi-Satriani 1974. Indeed, following Gramsci and de Martino, this was for a time a major theme of Italian anthropological studies of religion.

14. The notion of "presence" and of a "crisis of presence" runs through much of De Martino's work. A particularly good analysis of this concept can be found in the book by Cherchi and Cherchi (1987), and I have also dealt with it in a recent paper (Saunders 1995). See especially the chapter by Di Nola in this volume (Chapter 7).
15. For a good discussion of the enduring but complex character of evil eye beliefs in contemporary Italy, see Galt 1982.
16. As a postscript, it is worth noting that Italian anthropologists who have followed Gramsci and De Martino have found considerably more evidence of the realization of that potential. When De Martino himself looked for "progressive" folklore, he found a bit of it in relatively new, essentially politicized songs and festivals. Most of popular religion remained more conservative. Nonetheless, his work inspired others to search harder for elements of genuine resistance hidden in folklore, some of which might even be "progressive." Though I cannot describe this work in detail here, I refer readers to the work of Lanternari (1963, 1976), Lombardi-Satriani (1974), Padiglione (1990), Tullio-Altan (1974), and others. I have described some of this work in my papers (Saunders 1984, 1991, 1993). I am also attempting to use some of these ideas in my ethnographic research on Pentecostal Protestantism in Italy.

References

Angrosino, Michael V. (1994) "The Culture Concept and the Mission of the Roman Catholic Church." *American Anthropologist* 96: 824–32.

Bendix, Reinhard (1960) *Max Weber: An Intellectual Portrait.* New York: Doubleday Anchor.

Boggs, Carl (1976) *Gramsci's Marxism.* London: Pluto Press.

Burke, Peter (1978) *Popular Culture in Early Modern Europe.* New York: Harper Torchbooks.

Cherchi, Placido and Cherchi, Maria (1987) *Ernesto De Martino. Dalla crisi della presenza alla comunità umana.* Naples: Liguori.

Chiarini, Franco and Giorgi, Lorenza, eds. (1990) *Movimenti evangelici in Italia dall'Unità ad oggi.* Turin: Claudiana.

Christian, William A. Jr. (1972) *Person and God in a Spanish Valley.* New York: Seminar.

—— (1984) "Tapping and Defining New Power: The First Months of Vision at Ezquioga, July 1931." In *Cultural Dominance in the Mediterranean Area,* ed. A. Blok and H. Driessen, pp. 122–72. Nijmegen: University of Nijmegen.

Cirese, Alberto Maria (1971) *Cultura egemonica e culture subalterne.* Palermo: Palumbo.

Crapanzano, Vincent (1986) "Hermes' Dilemma: The Masking of Subversion in Ethnographic Description." In *Writing Culture: The Poetics and Politics of Ethnography*, ed. James Clifford and George E. Marcus, pp. 51–76. Berkeley: University of California Press.

Davis, Natalie Zemon (1965) *Society and Culture in Early Modern France*. Stanford: Stanford University Press.

De Martino, Ernesto (1941) *Naturalismo e storicismo nell'etnologia*. Bari: Laterza.

—— (1959) *Sud e magia*. Milan: Feltrinelli.

—— (1961) *La terra del rimorso. Contributo a una storia religiosa del Sud*. Milan: Il Saggiatore.

—— (1975 [1958] *Morte e pianto rituale. Dal lamento funebre antico al pianto di Maria*. Turin: Paolo Boringhieri.

—— (1977 [1948]) "Cultura e classe operaia." In *Antropologia culturale e questione meridionale. Ernesto De Martino e il dibattito sul mondo popolare subalterno negli anni 1948–1955*, ed. Carla Pasquinelli, pp. 37–46. Florence: La Nuova Italia.

—— (1977 [1949]) "Intorno a una storia del mondo popolare subalterno." In *Antropologia culturale e questione meridionale. Ernesto De Martino e il dibattito sul mondo popolare subalterno negli anni 1948–1955*, ed. Carla Pasquinelli, pp. 46–73. Florence: La Nuova Italia.

—— (1977 [1951]) "Il folklore progressivo." In *Antropologia culturale e questione meridionale. Ernesto De Martino e il dibattito sul mondo popolare subalterno negli anni 1948–1955*, ed. Carla Pasquinelli, pp. 143–6. Florence: La Nuova Italia.

Di Nola, Alfonso M. (1976) *Gli aspetti magico-religiosi di una cultura subalterna italiana*. Turin: Boringhieri.

Di Nola, Annalisa (1995) "How Critical Was De Martino's 'Critical Ethnocentrism' in Southern Italy?" Paper presented at the Wenner-Gren Foundation Conference on The Southern Question, Tarrytown, New York, May 1995 (Chapter 7 of the present book).

Freud, Sigmund (1961 [1930]) *Civilization and Its Discontents*. New York: Norton.

Galt, Anthony H. (1982) "The Evil Eye as Synthetic Image and Its Meanings on the Island of Pantelleria, Italy." *American Ethnologist* **9**: 664–81.

Gay, Peter (1988) *Freud: A Life for Our Time*. New York: Norton.

Goethe, Johann Wolfgang von (1962) *Italian Journey, 1786–1788*, trans. W. H. Auden and Elizabeth Mayer. San Francisco: North Point Press.

Gramsci, Antonio (1957) *The Modern Prince and Other Writings*. New York: International Publishers.

—— (1975) *Il materialismo storico e la filosofia di Benedetto Croce*. Turin: Riuniti.

—— (1978) *Selections from Political Writings, 1921–1926*, ed. and trans. Quinton Hoare. London: Lawrence and Wishart.

—— (1980) *Selections from the Prison Notebooks of Antonio Gramsci*, ed. and trans. Quintin Hoare & Geoffrey Nowell Smith. New York: International Publishers.

—— (1985) *Selections from the Cultural Writings*, ed. David Forgacs and Geoffrey Nowell-Smith, trans. William Boelhower. Cambridge, Mass.: Harvard University Press.

Gruppi, Luciano (1975) "Introduzione." In *Il materialismo storico e la filosofia di Benedetto Croce*, pp. xiii–xl. Turin: Riuniti.

Holmes, Douglas R. (1989) *Cultural Disenchantments: Worker Peasantries in Northeast Italy*. Princeton: Princeton University Press.

Jones, Ernest (1961 [1953]) *The Life and Work of Sigmund Freud*. New York: Basic Books.

Lanternari, Vittorio (1963) *The Religions of the Oppressed*. New York: Mentor.

—— (1976) *Crisi e ricerca d'identità. Folklore e dinamica culturale*, 2nd edn. Naples: Liguori.

Leone, Alba Rosa (1985) "La chiesa, i cattolici e le scienze dell'uomo: 1860–1960." In *L'antropologia italiana, un secolo di storia*, ed. Pietro Clemente, Alba Rosa Leone, Sandra Puccini, Carlo Rossetti, and Pier Giorgio Solinas, pp. 51–96. Rome: Laterza.

Lombardi Satriani, Luigi M. (1974) *Antropologia culturale e analisi della cultura subalterna*. Rimini: Guaraldi.

Luporini, Cesare (1977 [1950]) "Intorno alla storia del 'Mondo popolare subalterno'." In *Antropologia culturale e questione meridionale. Ernesto De Martino e il dibattito sul mondo popolare subalterno negli anni 1948–1955*, ed. Carla Pasquinelli, pp. 73–89. Florence: La Nuova Italia.

Macrae, Donald G. (1974) *Max Weber*. New York: The Viking Press.

Maselli, Domenico (1971) *Breve storia dell'altra chiesa. Storia delle chiese evangeliche in Italia*. Naples: Edizioni Centro Biblico.

—— (1978) *Libertà della parola. Storia delle chiese cristiane dei fratelli, 1886–1946*. Turin: Claudiana.

Mitzman, Arthur (1969) *The Iron Cage: An Historical Interpretation of Max Weber*. New York: Grosset and Dunlap.

Mottu, H. and Castiglione, M. (1977) *Religione popolare in un'ottica protestante. Gramsci, cultura subalterna e lotte contadine*. Turin: Claudiana.

O'Brien, Jay and Roseberry, William, eds. (1991) *Golden Ages, Dark Ages: Imagining the Past in Anthropology and History*. Berkeley: University of California.

Padiglione, Vincenzo, ed. (1990) *Le parole della fede. Forme di espressività religiosa*. Bari: Edizioni Dedalo.

Pandolfi, Mariella (1991) *Itinerari delle emozioni. Corpo e identità femminile nel sannio campano*. Milan: Franco Angeli.

Pasquinelli, Carla, ed. (1977) *Antropologia culturale e questione meridionale. Ernesto De Martino e il dibattito sul mondo popolare subalterno negli anni 1948–1955.* Florence: La Nuova Italia.

Saunders, George R. (1984) "Contemporary Italian Cultural Anthropology." *Annual Review of Anthropology* **13**: 447–66.

—— (1991) "Ernesto De Martino." In *International Dictionary of Anthropologists,* ed. Christopher Winters. New York: Garland.

—— (1993) "'Critical Ethnocentrism' and the Ethnology of Ernesto De Martino." *American Anthropologist* **95**: 875–93.

—— (1995) "The Crisis of Presence in Italian Pentecostal Conversion." *American Ethnologist* **22**: 324–40.

Snowden, Frank M. (1986) *Violence and Great Estates in the South of Italy: Apulia, 1900–1922.* Cambridge: Cambridge University Press.

Spini, Giorgio (1968) "Movimenti evangelici nell'Italia contemporanea." *Rivista storica italiana* **80** (3): 463–98.

—— (1971) *L'evangelo e il berretto frigio. Storia della Chiesa Cristiana Libera in Italia, 1870–1904.* Turin: Claudiana.

Torres, Carlos Alberto (1992) *The Church, Society, and Hegemony: A Critical Sociology of Religion in Latin America,* trans. Richard A. Young. Westport, Connecticut: Praeger.

Tullio-Altan, Carlo (1974) *I valori difficili. Inchiesta sulle tendenze ideologiche e politiche dei giovani in Italia.* Milan: Bompiani.

Urbinati, Nadia (1995) "Against Necessity: The Souths of Antonio Gramsci". Paper presented at the Wenner-Gren Foundation Conference on The Southern Question, Tarrytown, New York, May 1995 (Chapter 6 of this book).

Wolf, Eric R. (1982) *Europe and the People without History.* Berkeley: University of California Press.

Part III

Alternative Representations and Realities

Casting Off the "Southern Problem": Or the Peculiarities of the South Reconsidered[1]
John A. Davis

The New Agenda

It is hardly surprising that the South should figure as one of the central themes in the revisionist agenda around which Italian historians are currently rethinking Italy's path to the twentieth century. Central to that agenda is a questioning of the teleological assumptions that linked the collapse of liberal Italy and the rise of fascism to the failings of modernization in Italy (cf. Davis 1994, Pezzino 1993a, Romanelli 1991).

Nowhere have the assumptions of modernization theory been more influential than in the debates on the "Southern Problem". Widely as they differed over the causes, the classical interpretations of the *Meridionalisti* from the late nineteenth century onwards took as axiomatic that social backwardness was determined by the absence of economic change or growth. These assumptions were firmly embedded in images that have dominated postwar debate on the place of the South in modern Italian history. They are captured in Alexander Gerschenkron's description of Italy as an industrial *late comer*, and hence subject to highly dualistic, internally contradictory and regionally differentiated processes of economic growth. But they are also present in Antonio Gramsci's "Passive Revolution." For Gerschenkron, modernization occurred without and despite the Mezzogiorno; for Gramsci, the social and economic retardation of the Mezzogiorno blighted the opportunity for a full bourgeois revolution in Italy in the mid-nineteenth century, and remained thereafter – through the *Blocco Storico* – the principal obstacle to political and social modernization.

The debate that focused around Gramsci's thesis was, of course, closely linked to the ambitious postwar programs for reconstruction in the South. This was a project that – at least for a short season – mobilized impressive intellectual and cultural energies in the South and created many unusual political alliances (Bevilacqua 1993). But despite the vitality of these postwar debates, the South had to some extent become a prisoner of its own notoriety – not least because the immensely rich documentation provided by the classical studies of the *Meridionalisti* until only very recently continued to provide the sole documentary base for discussion. The established images of backwardness that were inherited from the past were now to be reinforced by a new vocabulary of developmental sociology that, with concepts like "amoral familism," locked the South into a time-warp of social primitivism and economic immobilism (cf. Banfield 1958).

But the South's postwar experience – viewed half a century on – has shown the premisses of these debates to be without solid foundation. Economic growth and social changes since 1947 have been dramatic, and have profoundly changed the fabric of southern society. *Bank of Italy* estimates suggest, for example, that between 1947 and 1983 production *per capita* increased threefold in the South, and reached figures comparable to those of Northern and Central Italy twenty years earlier. If the gap between North and South remained, it must be remembered that growth in Northern Italy in these years had been amongst the most dynamic in the whole of Europe (Barbagallo 1990). In the 1980s, the rapid expansion of small enterprises not only in Apulia, but also in historically poor agricultural regions like the Abruzzi and Beneventano, signaled to some that the Mezzogiorno was finally breaking out of the trap of backwardness and following the paths of belated but dynamic economic growth pioneered by the "third" Italy – Umbria, Tuscany, the Marches, and the Veneto, the regions that in the 1980s became synonymous with the new Italian entrepreneurship (Trigilia 1988, 1992).

In the event, those expectations remained short-lived, and the significance of postwar economic growth in the South still remains open to question. Southern Italy is still at the bottom of the European league in terms of *per capita* income and production, suggesting that in real terms the North–South gap may have widened. In 1989 a SVIMEZ report curtly referred to what it called "mere appearances of modernity:" a view reinforced by economists like Augusto Graziani (Barbagallo 1990).

Whatever the nature of postwar economic and social change, change there has been – and on a scale without precedent. Yet these changes have not been accompanied – and this is where modernization theory is most obviously wrong-footed – by a decline in those structural problems traditionally associated with the Mezzogiorno – poverty, unemployment, institutional and structural inertia. Indeed, until very recently, there has been notable deterioration on all these fronts, and a massive qualitative decline in the structures of civil society and the quality of life in the postwar Mezzogiorno – a deterioration that, despite improvements in living standards and public health, is evident in the appalling inadequacies of public services and infrastructures (hospitals, schools, urban planning, etc.), persistently high levels of unemployment and (both symptom and cause) the devastating growth in the closely interdependent phenomena of organized crime and political corruption.

Postwar experiences have necessarily reformulated the classical questions addressed at the South, and a new historical agenda no longer seeks to explain why there has been no economic change, but why it is that economic change has not been accompanied by more solid processes of economic growth and social and institutional modernization: a set of questions that is often summarized (not without an element of tautology) in the formula of "modernization without growth" (*modernizzazione senza sviluppo*).

Inverting the central problematic and taking not economic immobilism or backwardness, but rather a persistent failure of economic change to trigger off wider processes of growth, has had the effect of challenging the stereotypes of backwardness, and offers an opportunity to emancipate the South, at least in part, from the suffocating weight of the "Southern Problem." In his recent *Short History of Southern Italy*, Piero Bevilacqua (1993) calls for the "Southern Problem" to be cast off altogether. Identification with the Southern Problem has, Bevilacqua argues, made the history of the South synonymous with failure and backwardness in ways that have turned the historical experience of the enormously variegated southern regions and their people into a single, undifferentiated and stereotyped "Mezzogiorno" – a mere negative reflection of the North that is denied any "history" of its own.

Whether this is feasible – and whether his own work succeeds in making this neat separation – will be discussed below. But in arguing that the South's path to the twentieth century deserves to be studied in its own right and in its own terms, Bevilacqua echoes a much wider concern of the new history of the South. By shifting the focus from immobilism and backwardness to "change without growth" or "difficult modernization," the traditional parameters of what is southern come into new perspective. Rather than ask why there was no internal pressure for growth, the new agenda asks instead: why have the forces for change and growth within the South been unable to assert themselves more effectively over the last century and a half? What was the nature of these forces? Have the constraints been external or internal? It also asks whether the South's path to the twentieth century does not represent a particular pattern of capitalist development rather than the failure to attain some abstract model of modern economic growth.

That has also reopened discussion on the political role of the South, and not least the nature of the *Blocco Storico* – the alliance between reactionary southern landlordism and northern industry. Not only for Gramsci and the Left, the *Blocco Storico* has widely been seen as the corner-stone of Italian politics from the protective tariffs of the 1880s to Mussolini's agrarian autarky – indeed, for many the Christian Democrats' success in turning the South into an electoral fortress after 1949 has been seen as a continuation of the politics of the *Blocco Storico* by other means. But without backwardness and immobilism, both the concept and the politics of the *Blocco Storico* call for careful reconsideration.

This chapter will examine very briefly some of the ways in which the "new" history is redefining these central themes in the historical experience of the contemporary South and will ask to what extent it is indeed possible to study the South in terms other than those of the "Southern Problem".[2]

A Difficult Modernization?

The new agenda replaces an image of the South locked into timeless immobilism with one that highlights instead the particularly persistent, unpredictable, and unstable nature of economic change. The studies by Biagio Salvemini, Angelo Massafra, Luigi Masella, and others at the University of Bari, by Giuseppe Barone and Salvatore Lupo and others in Sicily, by Piero Bevilacqua, Augusto Placanica, and others on Calabria, and by the Neapolitan group around Pasquale Villani and Paolo Macry have clearly documented the variety of forms of economic change that were present within the nineteenth-century South (Barone 1983; Bevilacqua and Placanica 1985; Lupo 1990; Macry and Villani 1990; Masella 1983; Masella and Salvemini 1990; Massafra 1988; Salvemini 1984).

Their research brings into profile two characteristics that were hidden by the stereotype of economic immobilism: the first is the immense economic diversity of the regions that constitute the South; the second is the ubiquity, constancy, and disruptive impact of economic change in these regions.

New emphasis on the internal diversities of the South poses a fundamental question: what, if any, are the "unities" of southern history since Unification? Its political integrity vanished in 1861, while in economic terms the South constituted a number of distinct and quite separate regions, which after 1860 had in many cases less rather than more contact with one another, and whose principal economic ties and emigrant flows were directed outwards and away from the South (in the case of Sicily across the Atlantic; in the case of Apulia, north along the new railroad to Rome and central and northern Italy and along the Adriatic; while Naples lost many of its commercial and economic ties with its former provinces once it lost its status as a capital).

The "Southern Problem" in the decades after Unification was of course constructed from perceptions of common features of the South and of southerners – defective social organization, criminality, racial inferiority, and so forth. The ways in which images of the South were constructed in the nineteenth century have been revisited recently by Dickie (1992), Moe (1992) and Pick (1986). They offer an interesting reformulation in postmodernist idiom of earlier observations by Gramsci and Salvemini, but may unwittingly strengthen the notion that the South existed simply as an "otherness" that served to define identities after Unification, thereby again reducing the historical experience of the South to a series of metaphors. But rather than dwell on image-making, the new historiography is more concerned to explore and reconstruct the economic and social realities of the South after Unification and to document the conditions and experiences that were common to the South as a whole.

One answer is provided by the formula of "difficult modernization:" if the southern regions did experience economic change (and had been doing so from much earlier than Unification), they did so in circumstances and on terms that were particularly disadvantageous. The key agent of economic change was the market, but the changes that this brought were persistently uncertain and unstable, because of the extremely precarious and vulnerable terms on which the southern economies were integrated into international markets. It is easily forgotten, for example, that the southern regions – Apulia, Sicily, Campania – remained until 1914 much more closely dependent on overseas export markets than on national markets. Sicilian oranges, for example, were not sold in Milan until the twentieth century, although for decades they had been sold in huge quantities in the United States (Lupo 1990).

This perspective on economic change in the South up-ends many accepted images of the "backwardness" of southern society and economic operators. Biagio Salvemini, and most recently Alberto Banti (Salvemini 1984; Banti 1989a), have argued that the mercurial and shifting character of the markets in which southern producers found themselves operating account for the preference for a wide range of short-term, multi-sectoral, and essentially speculative investments. These can be seen as rational responses to prevailing circumstances, informed by a logic of risk-sharing in uncertain and uncontrollable markets. Rather than the embodiment of entrepreneurial "backwardness," therefore, the multiple investments of Verga's *Mastro Don Gesualdo* become instead a paradigm of entrepreneurial rationality (Iachello and Signorelli 1987).

Difficult Modernization: Modernization without Growth or Passive Modernization

The subordination of southern producers to powerful external markets, over which no effective controls could be established, can also account for the absence of more solid economic infrastructures. But if there is considerable agreement on the central importance of economic vulnerability and uncertainty in the South (although one might ask whether this was not also true of other Italian regions as well?), there is less consensus, however, over the implications of this "difficult modernization."

Did the relatively anarchical and unstable forms of economic change experienced in the South preclude the possibility of more solid processes of economic growth? Bevilacqua, for one, denies this, and insists that despite the obstacles imposed by natural constraints and by unstable markets, it is possible to identify longer-term phenomena of growth. These focused around the gradual development of small and middling peasant properties, which were vehicles for accumulation and established reservoirs of entrepreneurship that would eventually find expression in the post-1945 era (Bevilacqua 1993).

The slow and discontinuous pace of growth, Bevilacqua insists, had little to do with a lack of propensity for modern economic organization or development, but was caused by the failure of successive Italian governments after 1860 to recognize the particular requisites for economic growth in the South. One of the most striking arguments lies in the line of continuity he detects between the land reclamation program and legislation evolved by the last Bourbon governments of the early nineteenth century, Serpieri's *Bonifica Integrale,* and the original program of the postwar *Cassa per il Mezzogiorno.* The failure to implement that program, he argues, can be explained only in terms of Italy's postwar political system, which has prioritized the creation of networks of political patronage at the expense of productive investment. However, Leandra D'Antone's detailed study of irrigation projects and initiatives in Apulia suggests that the obstacles were far more complex and the earlier provisions much less effective than Bevilacqua claims (D'Antone 1990). While castigating the shortcomings of the southern ruling class in the postwar period, Bevilacqua insists that the principal constraints on economic growth in the South have been external and are located in Italy's postwar political system (Bevilacqua 1993).

Bevilacqua's "optimistic" reading of the capacity for growth in the South has been challenged, and certainly raises a number of questions. At one point, for example, he argues that the natural (geographical, physical, market) obstacles to growth in the South demanded exceptional entrepreneurial skills; but how does this square with his concerns for the shortcomings of southern entrepreneurship? And how do these concerns square with the insistence on the South's historical "industrial vocation"? Why has the growth on which he insists not been accompanied by the formation of a southern middle class with more positive attributes? His arguments have a tendency to weave between exogenous and endogenous constraints in ways that do not always avoid confusion, or distinguish clearly between endogenous obstacles (for example his critique of southern entrepreneurship and of the southern ruling classes) and exogenous forces (the state and the political system).

Others, while recognizing that prevailing economic conditions imposed a particular rationality on economic activity in the South, have also seen these conditions as a principal cause for the absence of more continuous forms of economic growth. In this view, persistent and unstable economic change has not simply conditioned – as Bevilacqua argues – particular forms of growth in the

South, but has made solid growth impossible. In this perspective, the South's path to the twentieth century is described as "modernization without growth" (*modernizzazione senza sviluppo*).

The phrase probably works better as a rhetorical flourish than as an analytical formula, because the terms are slippery and have a tendency to become interchangeable; but it seeks to capture the peculiarities of modernization in the South. One application of this explanation of the absence of institutional and social change can be found in Diego Gambetta's recent study of the economic functions of the mafia. Developing an essentially market-driven analysis, Gambetta argues that chronic economic uncertainty and insecurity, combined with weak public authority in western Sicily, created the essential institutional and economic conditions for the development of the mafia. The mafia developed and gained strength not simply as a form of organized violence, but above all because it provided the essential commodities of protection and insurance in an environment in which these could not be provided by a weak state or from within a civil society where the rule of law remained weak, and personal power and violence the norm (Gambetta 1993).

This functionalist approach brings important new insights on the economics of the mafia and can also be seen as part of a wider tendency to explain key structural features of Southern society – the relative weakness of public authority and horizontal social formations and solidarities – in the light of prevailing economic conditions. In those terms, Sicily and the South more generally can be seen as victims of Polanyi's *Great Transformation*, where the violence of change precluded the formation of those checks and controls that Polanyi identified as the keys to political and social stability. But the weakness of the argument is, of course, that it offers no adequate explanation of why the mafia historically developed in certain regions and not in others, or why and how the geography of the mafia has changed profoundly over time – and especially since the 1960s. (Gambetta does address the issue, but only to argue that "responses" in other areas were different because conditions were different.)

Gambetta's analysis would seem to confirm what Luciano Cafagna – a staunch advocate of the dualistic character of Italian economic growth (Cafagna 1989) – has described in characteristically provocative terms as "passive modernization." Arguing that there never was a real process of modernization in the Mezzogiorno, Cafagna points out that it is hardly surprising to discover that economic change occurred: how could it not? But the economic changes that did occur were almost exclusively external in origin, and the response of the southern élites was invariably "Things must change to stay the same." The attitude of the southern élites was defensive and sought wherever possible to minimize the extent and impact of what Cafagna describes as a process of "passive – as opposed to active – modernization" (Cafagna 1989).

Here we seem to be coming around full circle, and indeed Cafagna's polemical intent is to reaffirm the anti-modern outlook of the southern entrepreneurial élites. His "passive modernization" is a rewriting of Gramsci's "Passive Revolution" and the *Blocco Storico*, but his case relies heavily on contrasts between North and South that recent research has begun to question. Not only are we now more aware of the variety of economic interests that were present in the South, but a number of historians have also begun to explore the realities that lay behind stereotypes of northern capitalism and entrepreneurship (cf. Banti 1989b; Fumian 1984, 1990; Lanaro 1993).

The *Blocco Storico*

Emphasis on the variety of economic interests present in the South necessarily leads to a reconsideration of the political expression of those interests. For Salvemini, for Gramsci and for Sereni, the *Blocco Storico* – the alliance between reactionary southern landlordism and northern industrial interests that took shape around the protective tariffs of the 1880s and thereafter dominated Italy's political system until the collapse of the Liberal state – was the political reality that sat at the heart of the "Southern Problem." But as Giuseppe Barone, Luigi Masella, and Salvatore Lupo and others argued in the volume that first gave the revisionists a new agenda, the original formulation of the *Blocco Storico* locked the South into an undifferentiated backwardness that seriously underestimated not only the diversity, but also the strength of more progressive sectors and more progressive groups (Giarrizzo 1983).

It is now evident that important sections of southern producers were strongly hostile to tariff protection in the 1880s, which they knew would damage their economic interests and leave their valuable export crops vulnerable to reprisal (as indeed occurred). Re-examination of the debates that surrounded the tariff issue in the 1880s has revealed the presence of a variety of different and coherent programs for growth in the South, and has also led to a re-evaluation of the relative balance between "progressive" and more archaic sectors of the southern economy.

It has been recognized that there were a number of relatively dynamic economic sectors in the South – in particular, those linked to high value-added cash crops like olives, citrus fruits, specialized Mediterranean market-garden products, and processing industries. But it has generally been argued that these were too heavily exposed to uncertain market circumstances to survive (the impact, for example, of the agrarian crisis in the 1880s, of phylloxera on southern wine exports, of the collapse of agricultural prices during the Depression, and of fascist commercial policies in the 1930s). As a result, the economic history of the modern Mezzogiorno has long been depicted as a Manichean struggle between the "progressive" and the "backward" sectors, in which the former were the losing contender (see Sereni 1947; Rossi Doria 1948, 1958).

It is precisely this contrast between what Manlio Rossi Doria described as "the bones and the flesh" of southern agriculture that has been extensively reconsidered. A major focus here has been the *latifondo*, the vast grain-producing estates that dominated many parts of the mainland Mezzogiorno (Capitanata, the Apulian Tavoliere, the Ionian plains of Calabria, and western Sicily) and have long been considered expression and cause of the agrarian backwardness of the South.

New studies now question that image and show that in practice the *latifondo* combined extensive wheat-growing and transhumant grazing with the more intensive and hence modern production of high value-added cash crops. Whereas Emilio Sereni – like Gramsci – saw the *latifondo* as a residue of feudalism, more recent studies stress its capitalist nature and its nineteenth-century origins. Rather than relics from the feudal past, the vast latifundist estates grew out of the ashes of the *Ancien Régime* and took shape from the huge sales of Crown, Church and common lands that began in the Napoleonic period and were renewed after Unification. (For Sicily see Blok 1985; Lupo 1990; Schneider and Schneider 1976; for Apulia see Cormio 1983; for Calabria see Petrusewicz 1996.)

As a creature of the nineteenth century, and of the combination of high value-added cash crops with the more traditional extensive pasture and wheat-growing, the *latifondo* was commercially oriented, creating a "system" that permitted considerable flexibility in responding to changing market conditions. When export markets were poor, the system could fall back on the extensive sector and its own internal markets. Marta Petrusewicz, for example, stresses how the management of the vast Barracco estates in Calabria constituted a commercially oriented form of production that was rational and made highly flexible use of the resources available through a system that again sought to minimize the risks inherent in those markets (see Lupo 1990; Petrusewicz 1996).

Some critics have seen in Petrusewicz's depiction of the *latifondo* and her emphasis on its rationality and paternalism something akin to an apologia. But there are also questions about the nature of this "rationality," which seems to have remained dependent on exploitation of a captive labor force on the estates and on the maintenance of a variety of different forms of monopolies, which certainly enhanced the profitability of the enterprise, but at the same time inhibited wider forms of commercial and economic development within the vast bounds of the Barracco estates. Recognition of the rationality of the enterprise and indeed of the modernity of its management in some sectors, does not necessarily deny that the *latifondo* remained an obstacle to wider forms of economic change – by perpetuating non-economic constraints, by holding back levels of consumption and preventing the development of an internal market. Even had the functionality of the system not been undermined by the agricultural crisis (which reduced profits, increased pressure on the labor force, and ultimately exacerbated social tensions), it is difficult to see how this system could have moved beyond a defensive response to prevailing market conditions to become a force for growth.

The stress on the rationality of the management of the Barracco estates cannot, therefore, fully dispel an earlier image of the *latifondo* as an obstacle to economic growth – or at least an institution designed to respond to changing external demand and conditions. But the devastating effect of the agricultural crisis of the 1880s on the Barracco estates that Petrusewicz documents does point to what is now seen more generally as a key turning-point in the economic history of the South. Before the 1880s the southern economies offered many windows of comparative advantage that could be successfully exploited – olive oil, wines, and citrus fruits being the most obvious. But after that date, the changed structure of world markets and the changed structure of the industrial economies as they entered the Second Industrial Revolution heavily reduced those spaces.

The importance of these changes emerges sharply from Salvatore Lupo's recent and fine study of the Sicilian citrus industry from the nineteenth to the mid-twentieth century. Oranges and lemons were throughout this period Sicily's single most valuable export commodity. In documenting the rise and fall of citrus production and the citrus trade, Lupo reveals how the Sicilian producers and merchants found it increasingly difficult to remain competitive as they entered the twentieth century. Here again the latifundist and the commercial sectors were closely integrated, and Lupo shows that this did not prevent Sicilian producers from initially taking advantage of expanding US markets in the second half of the nineteenth century. But this was not accompanied by structural or organizational change: the Sicilian producers continued to rely on established factors of production, and when their export markets were challenged by rival citrus production in California and Florida they were unable to respond. They had no domestic markets to fall back on, and while they proved well able to organize effective associations for political and commercial lobbying, they were wary of introducing changes in methods of production that might reduce their own control or power, showed little interest in investing in new sectors such as processing industries, and were reluctant to enter into alliance with powerful northern banking and financial concerns for fear that this might jeopardize their autonomy. Even more important, they were unable to exert significant pressure on the government, which consistently adopted policies that damaged their interests (Lupo 1990; see also Rienzo 1996).

These characteristics are echoed in other studies of southern entrepreneurs in the Giolittian period, and call into question more than one feature of the *Blocco Storico*. Lupo's study – like the work of Giuseppe Barone, Luigi Masella, and others – indicates that economic interests in the South were more variegated than the old notion of a *Blocco Storico* allowed. But these studies also point to the failure of the southern élites to adopt more aggressively modernizing strategies –

a failure that cannot, they argue, be attributed simply to the determinism of the market-place.

The Southern Bourgeoisie

Re-examination of the role of the "visible hand", that is to say the strategies, decisions and mentalities of the southern economic operators, leads on to a wider consideration of the nature and development of the southern bourgeoisie – the class that from the time of Pasquale Villari's *Lettere Meridionali* to the present have been blamed for most, if not all, the ills of the South (what study fails to cite Salvemini's judgment on the *piccola borghesia* of Molfetta?).

Paolo Macry's important study of the impact of economic change on five Neapolitan patrician families in the nineteenth century adopts a view from above, and offers an excellent example of the uncertainties that accompanied economic change in the South. Macry's study offers even stronger evidence that the southern patrician class was dealt a devastating blow after Unification by the twin impact of the agrarian crisis and massive increases in fiscal burdens. Falling revenues and rising taxes drove these families from the patrician world of land and lineage into a new world of cash and commodities. Their fortunes varied, but sons were now more likely to inherit large debts than broad hectares, and with these changes a whole subculture of aristocratic family strategies and norms became redundant. Like the landed classes in Italy as a whole, Macry's patricians made the transition from a landed to a cash economy; yet it was a transition they made hesitatingly and haltingly, as they tried to cling to earlier aristocratic ways and values and sought to distance themselves from the bourgeois world of which they were now inseparably part (Caglioti 1955; Macry 1988a,b; Montroni 1996).

Macry's study finely pinpoints the realities and indeed the irreversible nature of economic change in the nineteenth century and charts the dramatic demise of the landed patriciate – there was to be no persistence of the *Ancien Régime* in the Mezzogiorno. But it also shows that the old order in the South passed without its being clear whose was the inheritance.

The uncertainty of the processes of social change in the South is emphasized in other studies that have focused in particular on the links between social formation and state formation. Although the rise of the professional classes began earlier, the creation of an "administrative monarchy" in the Napoleonic era marked the first clear step forward. Under the Restored Bourbon monarchy, provincial administration continued to act as an important pole for professional employment (on the period 1800–60 see especially Massafra 1988 and more recently Di Ciommo 1993); but it was Unification and the introduction of elected local government that really gave the expansion of the southern bourgeoisie its critical perch and purchase. Giuseppe Civile (1990), Gabriella Gribaudi (1990), and Paolo Pezzino (1993) have all shown how the establishment of elected local administrations created new vectors for professional employment in the South, in which new social, political, and economic networks intersected with older ties of kinship and faction.

While in many respects – in their tastes, culture, and forms of sociability – the new social forces that took shape in the South resembled their counterparts in other parts of Europe, the southern bourgeoisie was in large part (as Pezzino puts it) "born in the shadow of the processes of modernization that originated from the State" (Pezzino 1993: 32). Did this "dependency" from the start anticipate what has in the twentieth century been described as a *borghesia assistita* characterized by an *imprenditorialità assistita*? Such thoughts have led some to look again for the cultural and social reasons for the absence of more aggressive forms of modernization in the South.

Working backwards from the reasons why small enterprises failed to establish themselves in the South in the 1980s, Carlo Trigilia, for example, has argued that in the North the expansion of market capitalism in the nineteenth century resulted in collective mobilization and the development of mass political movements that brought about mechanisms for regulating and controlling the working of market forces. With collective mobilization in the North came the introduction of what Polanyi termed "social defense mechanisms," in ways that then reduced the importance of more primary social institutions such as the family and kin groups in favor of wider collective organizations. These developments in turn created the infrastructures essential for social and economic modernization (Trigilia 1988). In the South, it is argued, there was no comparable mobilization, with the result that political parties remained weak and trade unions non-existent, so that the family and the kin-groups retained their paramount function as agents of social defense. This in turn created the basis for clientist politics and the primacy of sectoral and partisan interests in ways that inhibited collective political values and organization.

As yet there has been no serious attempt to re-examine the social institutions of the South, and new discussions of the "social constraints" on growth have preferred to resurrect outworn and ahistorical cultural determinisms to explain the absence of "civic traditions" [no matter how elegantly presented, Putnam (1993) represents this direction]. Generally these excursions into the social and cultural "peculiarities" of the South have failed to take account of how far patterns of social and economic organization in the North differed from ideal-type models. The work of Banti on Emilia (1989b), and of Lanaro (1984) and Fumian (1984) on Venetian entrepreneurship, for example, reveal how little collective solidarities had to do with the success of northern capitalism in either the nineteenth or the twentieth centuries (see also Corner 1996).

The South, the State and Politics

Perhaps one of the most important features of the new southern historiography has been to revisit and revise many of those ideal stereotypes in which the North–South contrasts have for long been drawn. In challenging the notion that capitalism and Liberalism were either synonymous or interdependent in Emilia or in the Veneto, Banti, Lanaro, and others effectively removed one of the polarities on which the old "Southern Problem" depended.

How does this more brutal assessment of the processes of capitalist development in the North refocus the question of economic and social change in the South? One solution would be to invoke the pluralism of modern economic growth, and identify a particular "southern" path to the twentieth century. But thanks to the new work on both the North and the South it is becoming possible to identify real differences and distinctions. Amongst these, probably the most important lies in the relationships between state and society in the North (and Center) and in the South.

The dependence of the southern bourgeoisie on state employment has already been noted, and new research has shown the extent to which—from the beginning of the nineteenth century—the southern bourgeoisie began to "invade" the State, causing a peculiar blurring of public and private power (Aliberti 1987; Davis 1994; Pezzino 1987; Spagnoletti 1985). Was this unique to the South? It is important to distinguish carefully here. Northern/Central Italy—especially Tuscany, Piedmont, Lombardy, and the Veneto—provides endless examples of the survival of forms of private power and influence that remained almost untouched by the presence or the realities of the State until 1900 or beyond. There were crucial consequences—in the Veneto, for example, a paternalistic order to which the State remained external existed into the twentieth century, leaving the landowners as *padrones quasi patres* (Lanaro 1984). In the South, on the other hand, that paternal order—which survived in Lombardy, Piedmont, and Tuscany at least until the closing decades of the nineteenth century—had collapsed much earlier. Why? The history of social relations in the South cannot be written without reference to the tensions and violence that made the South one of the principal epicenters of political upheaval, revolution, and endemic rural unrest and protest in Europe down to the middle of the nineteenth century. The tendency of the southern élites to "invade" the institutions of the State may have had economic motives, but it cannot be divorced from the wider tensions that characterized much of rural society in the South — to which both the mafia and the *camorra* can also be seen as responses.

In short, at a time when the paternalist worlds of their Venetian, Tuscan, and Lombard counterparts remained largely undisturbed, throughout the South the position of the élites was more precarious. Challenged from below and subject to profound internal transformations, the emergence of new élites in the South in the nineteenth century cannot be isolated from the uncertainties of economic change; but nor can it be separated from the equally uncertain processes of political change and social tension. This was one reason why the southern élites from the start looked to the State and its institutions for protection as well as resources. While the northern landowners could keep the State at a distance (at least until later in the century, when their authority also began to be challenged), the southern élites turned to the resources of the State to reinforce their own fragile power.

The ties of interdependence between the southern bourgeoisie and the State went far beyond material benefit, and the role of the southern intellectuals in formulating the theory of the State and in developing Italian nationalism in the nineteenth and twentieth centuries needs to be reconsidered in this light. It is also worth contrasting this strong intellectual and theoretical commitment to the State in the South to the opposition to the interference of the State that was articulated overwhelmingly in the North in the distinction made famous by Stefano Jacini between "Real Italy" and "Legal Italy" after Unification (Davis 1994; Di Ciommo 1993).

But if the southern bourgeoisie wanted a stronger state, why did the State remain weak in the South and why did the demarcations between public and private power remain particularly indistinct? Although it was an exceptional case – and exceptional within the South, it should be remembered – recent studies of the mafia offer some important indications. The persistence and the terrible increase in the power and geography of the mafia in recent decades not only constitutes a fundamental challenge to any attempt to equate economic modernization with institutional change, but has also made the mafia the subject of a serious historical analysis for the first time. The carefully documented studies by Salvatore Lupo and Paolo Pezzino have reconstructed the historical origins of the mafia in Sicily from the late nineteenth century, and revealed its organized and criminal character from the start. This is important because – over and above the economic functions examined by Gambetta – these studies show that there cannot be any adequate explanation of the mafia that is couched solely in terms of the subcultures and values that were peculiar to western Sicily. Nor, indeed, can the mafia be explained solely in terms of economic conditions. Nor, as Lupo argues, can the mafia be seen as a residue of the *Ancien Régime*: it was its gravedigger, the product of radical changes in the nature and composition of the Sicilian élites, at a moment when the absence of a powerful state gave opportunities for new groups (the notorious *gabelotti* and other intermediaries) to assert their power. This they did, both through the exercise of violence and through cooperation with the representatives of the new state. The mafia was a purveyor not only of protection, but also of votes and "social control" in ways that made the mafia clans from the start not only powerful brokers between state and society, but essential partners in government.

Why did the new Italian state enter into covert alliance with the mafia in ways that guaranteed its further growth? The answer would seem to be that the mafia in western Sicily offered the representatives of the new state durable allies in a region that was otherwise characterized by fragile and faction-ridden structures of notable politics. The alliance between the political representatives of the new state and mafia factions in Sicily was also replicated elsewhere in the South in other ways, and Gabriella Gribaudi's study of Eboli shows, for example, how the administrators of the new state, while bemoaning factionalism in the South, carefully worked to foster and encourage it, because it provided them with political alternatives that any factional monopoly or firmer organization of power would have precluded (Gribaudi 1990). When these political alliances are set in the context of the particular processes of political exchange that determined relations between center and periphery in Liberal Italy (Romanelli 1988, Pezzino 1987, 1993b), it becomes clear that the process of state formation in the South played on and indeed per-petuated factional rivalries and divisions.

The State can therefore be seen as an important agent of political fragmentation and disunity in the South. This is also one of the reasons why, despite the extent to which the southern élites had "invaded" the administrative structures of the State, southerners remained ill-equipped to influence economic policies or to protect wider economic interests. A good example is that of the tariffs of 1889. Both Lupo and Petrusewicz show that the southern latifundists were deeply hostile to agricultural protectionism, which they knew would devastate their valuable export trades. So why did the southerners vote for a measure that was damaging to their economic interests? They did so as a trade-off for the shelving of a program of tax reform which would have abolished the fiscal privileges the South had been conceded in 1861. Why was one interest traded for another? Because the fiscal question created greater unanimity than the tariff question, and the studies by Giuseppe Barone, Salvatore Lupo, and Francesco Barbagallo on the politics of southern agrarian, commercial, and financial interests reveal how often the highly fragile and diversified character of the southern economies precluded concerted action and encouraged the development of the "politics of exchange" in ways that left broader interests vulnerable. Some of the best examples of this vulnerability were to come from the 1920s and 1930s, when, as Lupo shows, the interests of first southern commercial exporters and then the southern landowners more gener-ally were ruinously subordinated to the needs of fascist economic policy (which traded Sicilian lemons with Hitler for coal and steel). There is no better example of this vulnerability than the attempt by the Sicilian landowners to stage a strike against the fascist internal colonization policies in 1940!

Conclusions

Where does all this take the debate on the South? The new southern history has probably been more successful in knocking down stereotypes than in exorcising the Southern Problem, and the difficulty of reformulating the history of the South *de novo* is evident in the plurality of formulae that have been adopted and indeed in the slipperiness of alternative formulations – especially *modernizzazione senza sviluppo*. Having said that, the terms of the old debate on the South have been largely transformed, while this has been accompanied by a critical rethinking of certain "models" of northern capitalism. The history of the South can now be freed, if not of the Southern Problem, at least of two sets of abstract stereotypes (Lanaro 1993). While reconfirming the weaknesses of the southern bourgeoisie and the southern entrepreneurial classes the new agenda also moves beyond the stereotypes of the *Blocco Storico* to reveal the central role that the Italian state and its political systems have played in the development of the South – a role characterized most often by exploitation of the economic and political weaknesses of the region.

This is not simply to introduce another "exogenous" interpretation: the State did not create the divisions amongst the southern élites, nor did the State create the economic diversities that divided these élites, nor indeed the region's vulnerable exposure to international markets. But if the "Southern Problem" has derived in part from factors present within the South, it has also been shaped by the processes of state formation that form part of Italian history more generally. From the time of Unification, the actions of the State have consistently fostered and exacerbated those divisions. The nineteenth-century mafia, for example, was at least in part a creation of the political system that was established after Unification – just as the more recent spread of organized crime in the South is inexplicable without the connivance of political parties and forces. More generally, Italian governments and the Italian political systems – from the tariffs of 1889, to the entry to the European War in 1915, to the revaluation of the Lira in 1927, to Mussolini's policy of economic autarky, and the debasement of the program for special investment in the South after 1950 into a gold mine of political clientism – have failed to take account of the particular economic and social needs and interests of the South. The new southern history therefore contains important messages for those in Northern Italy who in recent years who have been retailing the old stereotypes and the old untruths about the "Southern Problem".

Notes

1. A shorter version of this essay was published as "Changing Perspectives on Italy's 'Southern Problem'" in C. Levy, *Italian Regionalism: History, Identity and Politics*, Oxford: Berg, 1996.

2. No brief survey can do justice to the range, breadth, and deeply innovative character of the research that has set out to reformulate and re-address the central themes in the historical development of the South from the end of the *Ancien Régime* to the present. The new agenda has been driven forward by energetic groups of young historians at the Universities of Naples, Bari, and Catania, and developed through a series of major publishing ventures – notably the Einaudi series, *Storia delle Regioni,* which includes volumes on Calabria, Campania, Sicily, and Apulia (see Aymard and Giarrizzo 1987; Bevilacqua and Plancanica 1985; Masella and Salvemini 1990); journals such as *Studi Storici* and *Quaderni Storici* (with particular reference to recent research on the bourgeoisie); and to the new journal, *Meridiana,* which is devoted exclusively to exploring "southern" issues. Together with IMES, *Meridiana* has provided the principal forum for reformulating and programming research on the South from the early nineteenth century to the present. The "revisionist" agenda on the South has also been directed at an earlier period (see Marino 1988 and Astarita 1992 for important reconsiderations on the character of southern " feudalism").

References

Aliberti, G. (1987) *Potere e società locale nel Mezzogiorno dell'800.* Bari: Laterza.

Astaria, T. (1992) *The Continuity of Feudal Power. The Caracciolo di Brienza in Spanish Naples.* Cambridge: Cambridge University Press.

Aymard, M. & Giarrizzo, G., eds (1987) *Storia d'Italia. Le regioni dall'Unità a oggi. La Sicilia.* Turin: Einaudi.

Banfield, E.C. (1958) *The Moral Basis of a Backward Society.* Chicago: Free Press.

Banti, A. M. (1989a) "Gli imprenditori meridionali: razionalità e contesto." *Meridiana* 6: 63–89.

—— (1989b) *Terra e denaro: Una borghesia padana dell'Ottocento.* Venice: Marsilio.

Barbagallo, F. (1990) "Il Mezzogiorno come problema attuale." *Studi Storici* 31: 587–9.

Barone, G. (1983) "Stato, capitale finanziario e Mezzogiorno." In *La modernizzazione difficile: Città e campagne nel Mezzogiorno dall'età giolittiana al fascismo,* ed., G. Giarizzo. Bari: De Donato.

Bevilacqua, P. (1993) *Breve storia dell'Italia meridionale dall'Ottocento a oggi.* Rome: Donzelli.

Bevilacqua, P. and Placanica, A., eds (1985) *Storia d'Italia. Storia delle regioni dall'Unità a oggi. La Calabria.* Turin: Einaudi.

Blok, A. (1985) *The Mafia of a Sicilian Village.* Oxford: Blackwell.

Cafagna, L. (1989) *Dualismo e sviluppo nella storia d'Italia.* Venice: Marsilio.

Caglioti, D. (1995) "Associazionismo e sociabilità d'élite a Napoli, nel XIX secolo." Doctoral thesis, Scuola Superiore di Studi Storici di San Marino.

Civile, G. (1990) *Il comune rustico: Storia sociale di un paese del Mezzogiorno nell'800.* Bologna: Il Mulino.

Cormio, A. (1983) "Le campagne pugliesi nella fase di 'transizione' 1880–1914." In *La modernizzazione difficile: città e campagne nel Mezzogiorno dall'età giolittiana al fascismo,* ed. G. Giarrizzo. Bari: De Donato.

Corner, P. (1996) "Italy, the Eternal Late-Comer." In *Agriculture and Industrialization from the Eighteenth Century to the Present,* ed. P. Mathias and J. A. Davis, pp. 129–48. Oxford: Blackwell.

D'Antone, L. (1990) *Scienze e governo del territorio. Medici, ingegneri, agronomi e urbanisti nel Tavoliere di Puglia (1865–1965).* Milan: F. Angeli.

Davis, J. A. (1994) "Remapping Italy's Path to the Twentieth Century." *Journal of Modern History* **66**: 291–320.

Dickie, J. (1992) "A Word at War: the Italian Army and Brigandage." *History Workshop Journal* **33**: 1–24.

Di Ciommo, E. (1993) *La nazione possibile: Mezzogiorno e questione nazionale nel 1848.* Milan: Franco Angeli.

Fumian, C. (1984) "Proprietari, imprenditori, agronomi." In *Storia d'Italia. Le regioni dall'Unità a oggi. Il Veneto,* ed. S. Lanaro. Turin: Einaudi.

—— (1990) *La città del lavoro. Un utopia agroindustriale nel Veneto contemporaneo.* Venice: Marsilio.

Gambetta, D. (1993) *The Sicilian Mafia: The Business of Private Protection.* Cambridge, Mass.: Harvard University Press.

Giarrizzo, G., ed. (1983) *La modernizzazione difficile: città e campagne nel Mezzogiorno dall'età giolittiana al fascismo.* Bari: De Donato.

Gribaudi, G. (1990) *A Eboli: Il mondo meridionale in cent'anni di trasformazioni.* Venice: Marsilio Editori.

Iachello, E. and Signorelli, A. (1987) "Borghesie urbane nell'Ottocento." In *Storia d'Italia. Le regioni dall'Unità a oggi. La Sicilia,* ed. M. Aymard and G. Giarrizzo. Turin: Einaudi.

Lanaro, S., ed. (1984) "Il Veneto: genealogia di un modello." In *Storia d'Italia. Le regioni dall'Unità a oggi. Il Veneto,* ed. S. Lanaro. Turin: Einaudi.

—— (1993) "Le élites settentrionale." In "La questione settentrionale," Special issue of *Meridiana* **16**, January 1993.

Lupo, S. (1990) *Il Giardino degli aranci: il mondo degli agrumi nella storia del mezzogiorno*. Venice: Marsilio.

—— (1993) *Storia della mafia dalle origini ai nostri giorni*. Rome: Donzelli.

Macry, P. (1988a) *Ottocento: Famiglia, élites e patrimoni a Napoli*. Turin: Einaudi.

—— (1988b) "Le élites urbane: stratificazioni e mobilità sociale, le forme del potere locale e la cultura dei ceti emergenti." In *Il Mezzogiorno pre-unitario: economia, società e istituzioni*, ed. A. Massafra, pp. 799–820. Bari: Dedalo.

Macry, P. and Villani, P. (1990) *Storia d'Italia. Le regioni dall'Unità a oggi. La Campania*. Turin: Einaudi.

Marino, J. (1988) *Pastoral Economics in the Kingdom of Naples*. Baltimore and London: Johns Hopkins University Press.

Masella, L. (1983) "Elites politiche e potere urbano nel Mezzogiorno dall'età giolittiana all'avvento del fascismo." In *La Modernizzazione difficile: città e campagne nel Mezzogiorno dall'età giolittiana al fascismo*, ed. G. Giarrizzo. Bari: De Donato.

Masella, L. and Salvemini, B. (1990) *Storia d'Italia. Le regioni dall'Unità a oggi. La Puglia*. Turin: Einaudi.

Massafra, A., ed. (1988) *Il Mezzogiorno pre-unitario: economia, società e istituzioni*. Bari: Dedalo.

—— (1988) *Meridiana: Rivista di storia e scienze sociali*, 2 "Circuiti Politici" January 1988 (S. Lupo, L. Masella, L. Musella); 4 "Poteri locali" September 1988 (R. Romanelli, P. Pezzino, G. Civile, M. Cammelli).

Moe, Nelson (1992) "'Altro che Italia!'; Il Sud dei piemontesi (1860–61)." *Meridiana* **15**: 53–89.

Montroni, G. (1996) *Gli uomini del Re. La nobiltà napoletana nell'Ottocento*. Catanzaro: Meridiana Libri.

Petrusewicz, M. (1996) *Latifundium. Moral Economy and Material Life in a European Periphery*, trans. Judith C. Green. Ann Arbor: University of Michigan Press.

Pezzino, P. (1987) "Mezzogiorno e potere locale." *Rivista di storia contemporanea* **4**.

—— (1990) *Una certa recipocità di favori. Mafia e modernizzazione violenta nella Sicilia post-unitaria*. Milan: Franco Angeli.

—— (1993a) *Il paradiso abitato dai diavoli: società, élites, istituzioni nel Mezzogiorno contemporaneo*. Milan: Franco Angeli.

—— (1993b) *La congiura dei Pugnalatori: un caso politico-giudiziario alle origini della mafia*. Venice: Marsilio.

Pick, D. (1986) "The Faces of Anarchy: Lombroso and the Politics of Criminal Science in Post-Unification Italy." *History Workshop* **21**: 60–86.

Putnam, Robert D. (1993) *Making Democracy Work: Civic Traditions in Modern Italy*. Princeton: Princeton University Press.

Rienzo, M.G. (1996) "L'esordio della Banca di Calabria nel tessuto economico napoletano. Il percorso di un'oligarchia finanziaria in età liberale." *Società e Storia* **69**(1): 71–93.

Romanelli, R. (1988) *Il commando impossibile. Stato e società nell'Italia Liberale.* Bologna: Il Mulino.

—— (1991) "Political Debates, Social History and the Italian Bourgeoisie: Changing Perspectives in Historical Research." *Journal of Modern History* **63**(4): 717–38.

Salvemini, B. (1984) "Note sul concetto di Ottocento meridionale." *Società e storia* **26**: 917–45.

Schneider, J.and P. (1976) *Culture and Political Economy in Western Sicily.* New York: Academic Press.

Sereni, E. (1947) *Il capitalismo nelle campagne 1860–1900.* Turin: Einaudi.

Spagnoletti, A. (1985) "Il controllo degli intendenti sulle amministrazioni locali nel Regno di Napoli." In *L'Amministrazione nella storia moderna*, Vol. 1. Milan: Giuffré.

Trigilia, C. (1988) "Le condizioni non-economiche dello sviluppo: problemi di ricerca sul Mezzogiorno di oggi." *Meridiana* **2**: 167–87.

—— (1992) *Sviluppo senza autonomia: effetti perversi delle politiche nel Mezzogiorno.* Bologna: Il Mulino.

—10—

"Virtuous Clientelism": The Southern Question Resolved?

Simona Piattoni

Much has changed in Italy in recent times, but the "Southern Question" still remains central to Italian political and economic life. Even though the institutions that had been created after the war to promote southern development have been dismantled and the parties that championed state intervention in the South have disappeared, it is commonly believed that an economic, political, and possibly cultural gap between North and South still exists. Such a gap today finds its expression in new concerns and a new language.

The economic debate on "dualism," the economic catchword of the postwar period, has been mostly replaced by a debate on "globalization," but the underlying idea that some parts of the country do worse, and are likely to keep doing worse, than others in the context of the world economy is still widespread. At the political level, too, the North–South gap persists in a new guise. It once took the form of a different modality of vote: the relative prevalence of an "opinion" and "membership" vote in the North and of an "exchange" vote in the South (Parisi and Pasquino 1977). Today the political gap is arguably expressed by the electoral successes of the Lombard League in the North and the revival of Alleanza Nazionale (the former Movimento Sociale Italiano, or neo-fascist party) in the South. That these parties, which on many social and economic issues take opposite stands, had to accept an uneasy cohabitation in the Berlusconi government of 1994 is a sign, at the same time, of the existence of the gap and of the difficulty of closing it.

While the "Southern Question" remains unresolved, the scholarly debate on it has somewhat subsided, perhaps for want of new ideas as well as a widespread sense of disillusionment. For many years, the debate has centered around a few unchallenged propositions that, I believe, have pushed scholarly reflection into an intellectual cul-de-sac: that the economic gap is a reflection of a deeper socio-cultural gap, and that a clientelistic form of politics has been instrumental in preserving this gap despite state efforts to engineer an economic catch-up. Under-lying these common contentions are the equally unchallenged assumptions that, despite its evident internal differentiation, the South can be treated as one relatively homogeneous area and that the North–South disparity is still more significant than any intra-South (or intra-North) difference.

This chapter reviews these assumptions as they have appeared in the work of political scientists, particularly in the United States, who, it might be said, have played a significant role in shaping the postwar construction of the Italian South as uniformly backward and irredeemably clientelistic. Intra-South differences, on the contrary, are significant and, if studied in detail, may direct our attention to the factors that can explain the economic success of some southern regions and the disappointing, if not utterly dismaying, situation of others. Insistence on the supposedly deep-seated social and cultural differences between North and South fossilizes the debate around the wrong conceptual categories and, given the structural and slow-changing nature of these traits, fosters a sense of false impotence.

In highlighting the political dimension of the "Southern Question," which resulted from the failure of both national and local political elites to unify the country over and above the diplomatic and administrative levels, I will argue that, far from being an intractable problem that owes its resilience to structural and cultural causes, the "Southern Question" can be resolved through politics. Politics, rather than being deleterious for southern development, has played a fundamental role in ensuring the development of some southern regions.[1] Indeed, I will argue that the "Southern Question" as it has been traditionally understood – as the existence of a sizeable economic gap between North and South, much greater than any difference internal to these two areas – is already on its way to resolution, as is suggested by data demonstrating that some southern regions have made so much progress as to be able to (symbolically) "pull themselves out of the South."[2]

The key to the success of these regions, this chapter contends, is to be found in their local political classes.[3] This is a fairly contentious statement in the case of the Italian South, where politics is commonly depicted in very negative terms. In what follows, I first review the depiction of southern politics in the hegemonic literature of American political science, concentrating on the all-important concept of clientelism. I then reinterpret this concept as strategic behavior on the part of both patrons and clients rather than as a syndrome that epitomizes all the evils of the South. Finally, I sketch out a typology of clientelistic politics that shows how similar practices can be used to rather different ends, producing different results. While the evidence that supports the contention that clientelism can be instrumental to economic development is available elsewhere (Piattoni 1996, 1997), I will develop here the same argument in theoretical terms. I will conclude by speculating on the possibility that the feedback effect of economic development on local politics could lead to the replacement of clientelism with a more "civic" style of politics.

Political Institutions and Economic Development

It is commonly believed that underlying the "Southern Question" are structural and cultural factors that, although having their roots in historical events and human choices, have proved surprisingly resilient and self-reinforcing. Although crucial in the past, historical contingency and human agency seem to have lost their power in current times. Politics has either been seen as a reflection of these cultural and structural factors, and therefore devoid of any explanatory power, or as a mere intervening variable or reinforcing factor. Such an understanding actually gained new popularity in 1992 as the state abandoned its forty-plus-year commitment to reducing the North–South economic gap.

After the war, the "Southern Question" had been tackled with unprecedented energy and optimism. A vast program of state subsidies and direct public action, known as the "Extraordinary Intervention," was set in motion in order to help the South industrialize. Traditional obstacles to agricultural progress were, meanwhile, being removed through the Agrarian Reform. These policies were met by disappointing (if not counterproductive) results, and were therefore interpreted as either naive in their expectation that deep-seated discrepancies could be reversed in the space of few years, or flawed by bad design and implementation, or again as thwarted by perverse political interests.[4] Economic statistics on per capita income, degree of industrialization, worker productivity, per capita savings, and so on, were regularly released throughout the postwar period, almost as "war bulletins" on the "southern development front." While their official goal was to document progress and guide future policies, they often lent themselves to being interpreted as indicators of the cultural differences between North and South (for example, the lower productivity of southern workers was said to index "laziness," the lower rate of saving to be a sign of "profligacy").

In 1992, the intractability of the problem and its cultural character were supposedly exposed (once again) by the declared failure of the development effort, and the Extraordinary Intervention was terminated. Politically, this new (indeed, old) interpretation went hand in hand with the new political resolution of the North to rid itself of the southern "ballast." Because the "Southern Question" was presented as a structural problem that could not be addressed through public intervention, the option of resolving it by severing the political union that kept the two halves of the country together suddenly became politically feasible. The northern secessionist project acquired increased legitimacy by adding on to the structural reading of the "Southern Question" the aggravating factor of the inefficiency and corruptness of the southern political class.[5] In other words, efforts at closing the North–South gap were considered not only meaningless, since the gap had deep structural causes that could not be reversed, but also harmful, because these very efforts had become a breeding ground for greater corruption.

Of course, this more "cultural" reading of the "Southern Question" was hardly new. One of the most influential postwar attempts at a cultural explanation for southern underdevelopment was the 1958 publication of American political scientist Edward Banfield's *The Moral Basis of a Backward Society*. This work was nothing less than a theoretical treatise on the external and internal conditions for the existence of diffuse distrust in Southern Italy. External circumstances – the extreme uncertainty of the economic context – and mental attitudes – the generalized assumption that each individual will act to maximize the material, short-run advantage of the nuclear family – explained why the inhabitants of Montegrano, the town he selected as prototypical of the entire South, did not engage in collaborative enterprises. Lacking the social capital of trust, they forfeited the opportunity to learn the virtues of collective action, that is to enter into a self-reinforcng "virtuous circle" of shared values and economic progress.

The same "amoral familist" ethos that characterized Montegrano's peasants in their economic and social dealings also affected the way in which they saw politics and acted in their political capacity. The Montegranesi, Banfield argued, were politically passive, unstable in their partisan preferences, and incapable of working through their representatives to improve their material lot. Their mistrust of public authorities and their belief in the corruptness of all public officials induced them to avoid involvement in politics as much as possible and, at most, to use their vote as a token in exchange for personal favors. Thus was it explained how clientelism could grow even in the most politically barren environment of Montegrano.

Thirty-five years later, another American political scientist, Robert Putnam, proferred a similar analysis, in the form of a broadly researched comparative study of regional government performance called *Making Democracy Work: Civic Traditions in Modern Italy* (1993). According to Putnam, southerners' lack of trust in one another, and their incapacity for engaging in collective enterprises – and conversely the mutual trust of the Northerners and their capacity for such enterprises – can be traced back to the solutions that were devised in the twelfth century to the endemic problem of securing external borders and ensuring law and order within them. While in the South the Norman kings took care of external and internal enemies, but also imposed their centralized control on all forms of social and economic activity, in the North the citizens themselves provided for their external and internal security and regulated their social and economic inter-actions. Consequently, while southerners learned the importance of tending to the solidity of their ties to power in order to secure their physical and economic survival, northerners accumulated collaborative enterprises and a stock of mutual trust that characterizes the way they interact with power to this day. Clientelism is thus contrasted to civicness as the hallmarks of politics in the two halves of the country.

That distrust and cynicism inhibit collective action both in the economic and in the political spheres is a widely accepted contention. Healthy and dynamic societies are assumed to develop collective structures to regulate social and political interactions. The diffusion of collective structures of interaction, alongside the dyadic structures that prevail in the private sphere, ensures that, in their public dealings, individuals learn to base their behavior on deferred rewards and general principles rather than on immediate rewards. Political scientists Luigi Graziano (1974) and Sidney Tarrow (1967) have further developed this point.

But how exactly do social and political structures of exchange influence economic development? The paradox of the market is that, in order to function, it needs something that it cannot generate. That something is trust. Market exchanges, says Graziano, are typically dyadic, for goods and services are exchanged immediately and personally. As such, they contain in themselves all the incentives for their successful execution and do not need – nor do they tend to generate – more general and impersonal principles than the satisfaction of the actors' preferences. Yet, although each exchange taken in isolation may be so regulated, in the aggregate the market needs structures and principles that it cannot generate and that it must borrow from the social and the political spheres. These structures and principles, according to "transaction cost" economists, are meant to avoid those opportunistic behaviors that would eventually jeopardize the good functioning of market relations.

From the political institutions the market borrows the solution of its "capital" problem: the effective enforcement of property rights and the law of contracts. The state, by socializing the costs of the credible enforcement of contracts, makes transactions among economic actors possible (North 1990). While this is a primary requirement for the functioning of the market, it is often not enough. High levels of economic development can be reached only by those societies in which economic actors succeed in establishing trust relations among themselves and in engaging in collaborative enterprises, whose boundaries are flexible and subject to continuous renegotiation (Sabel 1993). In this second task, political institutions are flanked by social and cultural institutions, which facilitate communication among economic actors and often provide a first test-case for future economic interactions. Hence, political and social institutions "square the market's circle" and allow it to bring about economic development.

Given this frame of reference, it is a short step to conclude that the different natures of social and political institutions in the North and the South of Italy explain the different economic development of the two halves of the country. The cynicism and disaffection that characterize State–citizen relations in the South, and the clientelistic mode of interaction between voters and politicians there, are traced back to the fragmented nature of the southern social structure. As Tarrow wrote in 1967,

Clientelismo is a pattern of political integration that is linked directly to the inflexibility, disjunctiveness and fragmentation of the stratification system of the Mezzogiorno; it is characteristic of fragmented systems passing from a traditional to a modern organization of social roles. Hence politics is nonideological, broad functional interests cannot be expressed and access to authority can expand only through the further vertical extension of clientele links. One reaches the structure of authority not by merging one's demands with parallel demands of others, but by linking oneself to a hierarchical chain of personal acquaintance that reaches power holders at the higher level (Tarrow 1967: 74–5).

For both Tarrow and Graziano, the incomplete transition of the South to capitalism is cause as well as consequence of the persistence of particularistic relationships in all spheres of social life. The incapacity of the southerners to form categorical associations to further their common interests and, even more, their cynical rejection of secondary associations as "illegitimate and corrupt" resulted in what Graziano called a "totalitarian conception and practice of power" (Graziano 1974: 358). This amounts to conceiving social conflict as a struggle amongst factions and demanding from the State private protection and selective access to the spoils of government. No one in the South seems to know what the "common good" is. Rather, joining in a clientele remains the sole antidote against the exclusive and discriminatory use of authority. As the provision of collective goods is unproductive from the point of view of gaining political influence, so the argument goes, all state functions – including justice, taxation, and defense – are performed in a discriminatory way.

Clientelism is thus the way in which southerners are integrated into the political system. Even after the Second World War, when universal suffrage was introduced and veritable mass political parties emerged, clientelist politics did not give way to principled politics in the South. Rather, clientelism was reinterpreted and updated. As the new political leaders enjoyed no personal or social prestige independently of the party, they had to engage in "mass patronage." "Clientelism of the notables" became "clientelism of the bureaucracy."

[A]s political power shifts from prestigious individuals to party organizations without a corresponding rise in political ideology, patronage must take the place of personal loyalty as a basis of affiliation. But it is patronage channeled through an organization rather than through a chain of individuals. It is the mass patronage of the modern state and mass party, distributed within the framework of a progressive program for economic development (Tarrow 1967: 325–7).

According to these authors, then, just as they do according to Banfield and later Putnam, social structures and cultural values determine politics. The socially fragmented and ideologically totalitarian environment of the South managed to stifle southern economic development in the postwar period. Clientelism caused underdevelopment by preserving and strengthening vertical links at the expense of horizontal ones, by stifling the formation of an organized opposition to power, by encouraging instead its cooptation through patronage, and by inhibiting the accumulation of trust and breeding cynicism (see also Gambetta 1988). Moreover, clientelism also negatively affected policy-making. Decisions guided by clientelistic criteria normally failed to meet economic rationality standards and thus led to sub-optimal results. Additionally, as policies were decided and implemented in order to gain electoral support, they were not just sub-optimal, but outright wasteful. Indeed, since the power base of the political leaders lay in their mediating role between the State and the citizenry, policy decisions could even be harmful, as they were aimed at reproducing the objective conditions for the mediating role of the politicians (Gribaudi 1980).

It is my argument that at the heart of the political science literature on the Italian South are two assumptions that render these studies unable to explain the recent economic success of some southern areas. The first is that, although the importance of political institutions for economic development is widely acknowledged, the performance of these institutions is explained by structural and cultural factors that are basically unaffected by human action. Thus any real independent effect of politics on development is in practice negated. The second common assumption is that the initially somewhat different structural and cultural features of Northern and Southern Italy managed to perpetuate themselves by igniting self-reinforcing processes that put the two regions on increasingly divergent paths. Consequently, the possibility that they might start to converge again or might simply tread different (and internally differentiated) paths is ruled out.

In the following section, an alternative argument regarding the role of local political classes in economic development will be proposed.[6] I will argue that, by looking at clientelism on its own terms, that is, as a political strategy for gaining and maintaining power, it becomes possible to identify a variety of "styles of clientelistic government" that, although superficially similar, nevertheless operate according to rather different logics and produce widely different results in terms of economic development. I will ground my proposal in the political equilibria that characterized the "first Italian republic."

Styles of Clientelistic Politics

Why do regions characterized by similar cultural values, social structures, and political institutions achieve different levels of development? Why do their political classes express different styles of government? These questions cannot be posed, let alone answered, if one believes, as Banfield and Putnam do, that the causes of the "Southern Question" are cultural and that the South is, all in all, fairly homogeneous. It is only by focusing on intra-South differences and their evolution through time that one begins to appreciate the political origins of the "Southern Question."[7] The larger study on which this chapter is based shows that the different degrees of success with which different southern regions managed to weather the crisis of the 1980s and early 1990s, sustaining the growth spurt of the 1970s, depended on the ability of their respective local political classes to help the local economy tackle the necessary restructuring (Piattoni 1996). This differential ability, in turn, resulted from the different strategies implemented by these classes in order to maintain their power. In other words, superficially similar clientelistic systems may in reality generate different types of politics, with important consequences for economic processes.

Patronage can be defined as an "informal contractual relationship between persons of unequal status and power, which imposes reciprocal obligations of a different kind on each of the parties" (Silverman 1965: 296). The contract is never formally drawn and the obligations never fully specified. Generally speaking, these relationships aim at a large and unspecified series of performances of mutual assistance. The patron–client relationship presupposes the availability of alternative, fully legitimate channels of access to desired resources, for example, markets. By entering patron–client relations, the clients give up access to markets except through the mediation of the patrons, because of the supposedly lower benefits or higher costs that direct access would entail.

> The client 'buys' protection against the exigencies of the markets or of nature or of the arbitrariness or weakness of the center or against the demands of other powerful groups or individuals. The price he pays for it is not just a specific service, but the acceptance of the patron's control of the client's access to markets and public goods, as well as of his ability to convert fully some of his resources (Eisenstadt and Roniger 1981: 281).

Historically, the clients had little actual choice, as the patrons stood "guard over the critical junctures or synapses of relationships which connect the system to the larger whole" (Wolf 1956 quoted by Silverman 1965: 294). Nowadays, this is less true. Today, in so far as they are willing to accept the mediation of the patrons to obtain resources that they could otherwise access through more legal and legitimate channels, the clients freely underwrite the "clientelist contract."

The literature on clientelism claims that the main goal of the patrons (the local politicians) is to preserve their uneven power position *vis-à-vis* their clients (the citizens) by mediating between the center and the periphery in such a way as to reproduce the dependence of the periphery on the center and, therefore, perpetuate their mediating role (Gribaudi 1980; Chubb 1982). From this assumption derive a number of behavioral consequences. First, the patrons will seek to avoid any real economic integration of the areas under their control into the national and international economy, because the introduction of market channels of access to desired resources could weaken their power. Second, the patrons will seek to prevent the formation of secondary associations among clients, as these would represent a potential threat to the personalistic and vertical relationship that links each client to his patron. The vertical and atomizing way in which the clientele system integrates each citizen into the political system through a chain of personal relationships with powerful individuals should already prevent the aggregation of political demands, defuse conflicts, and preempt the formation of an organized opposition. However, the patrons might also deploy additional tactics – most probably a mix of threat and persuasion, fear and affection – in order to keep their clients individually tied to them.

If, in order to retain their power, the patrons wilfully try to preserve the economic backwardness of the areas under their control, does this not constitute a breach of the patron–client contract? Or, in Chubb's formulation, "Given the undisputed failure of Palermo's local government not only to provide essential public services but even to guarantee the functioning of normal administrative activities, how can the unbroken electoral success of the DC in the past 30 years be explained?" (Chubb 1982: 3). Scholars of clientelism believe that, far from being contradictory, clientelist politics and economic backwardness imply one another. Given the general scarcity of resources in a situation of economic backwardness, what clients ask from their patrons is not economic development – a public good that benefits all if it benefits some – but personal material advantages. However, material advantages are also in short supply and patrons may be unable at any given moment to satisfy all the clients' requests. Moreover, as limited resources are allocated according to clientelistic criteria – that is, criteria that do not command legitimacy and are, therefore, incapable of providing an accepted justification for the existing distribution of resources – there will be no self-enforced upper limit to the demands of the clients, and inflation will ensue. As a consequence, clientelism should collapse under the weight of its own contradictions or, paraphrasing a famous expression, it will cause the "fiscal crisis of the polity." Refuting this conclusion, Chubb showed that clientelism entails not just the exchange of material favors for votes, but also the exchange of those products of the public administration (permits, licenses, authorizations, and so on) that do not cost the patrons money, but have a significant economic impact on the clients. "The essence of clientelism lies . . . in the skillful manipulation of scarcity . . . [T]he patron–client bond . . . is dependent not on a continuous stream of benefits, but rather on sustaining the expectation of rewards in the maximum number of people with the minimum payoff in concrete benefits" (Chubb 1982: 5). In this way, patrons are able to preserve their power even in the face of systematic breaches of the patron–client contract.

Given this picture of clientelism, why should a patron bother to attract investment to the area under his control? Why should he use his power to provide collective goods rather than limit himself to satisfying the clients' individual demands or manipulating resources so as to create the expectation of reward? Why should he try to create a community where individual interests once dominated? And, finally, why should he try to reinforce market mechanisms where clientelistic methods of distribution can be used? True enough, private and public investment, even of an apparent public nature, can be used for clientelistic purposes. Thus, highways may be built not because of their potential effect on economic growth, but because their construction creates numerous occasions for clientelistic exchanges. Similarly, firms may be attracted to an area not because of their impact on the local economy, but because the jobs that they create can be distributed among loyal clients. When such investments are realized in clientelism-ridden areas, it is almost automatically assumed that their justification lies not so much in their effective utility, but in their political fallout. As a consequence, it is also expected that these investments will be scarcely profitable and will soon fail. Any actual economic progress that might result from such investments should then be considered as unexpected and uncalled-for, as it would have the undesired consequence of weakening the dependence of the clients upon their patron.

Even more puzzling is the behavior of those patrons who actually seem to care for the area and people that they control, so much so as to make great efforts to build and maintain relationships of personal acquaintanceship, if not affection, with their clients. Students of clientelism have argued that an affective component is inherent in the patron–client relationship, but that the rituals through which this component is created and maintained (for example rituals of godfatherhood) are largely symbolic. Attending a handful of weddings and baptisms is a small cost if it ensures faithful electoral support from scores of relatives and friends for years to come. Similarly, attendance at village fairs, inaugural events, and local celebrations may be interpreted as skillful and inexpensive promotional activity. Again, the creation and strengthening of community ties that might derive from these activities are considered unexpected and undesired consequences, as they could give rise to collective identities and sustain collective actions that might challenge the power position of the patron.

This interpretation of clientelism is clearly too restrictive. In what follows, I propose a different approach, capable of accommodating a variety of patrons' behaviors. The model of clientelism that I will develop makes sense of the above sketched behaviors without resorting to the notion of unforeseen consequences; rather it fully integrates them into the range of strategies available to the patrons. Patron–client networks are interpreted as "strategies for the maintenance and aggrandizement of power on the part of patrons and of coping and survival on the part of the clients. They are probably never the sole strategies available . . . [O]ne may often find individuals employing a number of seemingly incompatible strategies simultaneously or *seriatim*" (Waterbury 1977: 332–3).

As already seen, it is usually held that the patrons will try to avoid the emergence of similar relations among clients and, in so far as these do emerge, they will consider them as unforeseen and undesired consequences. Yet the patrons might pursue the economic development of the area that they control, wagering that this might be the best way to preserve or increase their electoral support and, consequently, preserve or increase their power *vis-à-vis* the center. Moreover, as has been argued by Silverman (1977), it is possible that patrons, far from trying to prevent the formation of horizontal links among clients, may indeed foster the formation of a community in the name of which they can subsequently claim resources from the center. "Public patronage," that is patronage exerted with respect to groups or entire communities with the aim of providing public goods, rather than political nonsense, could in fact constitute a highly sophisticated political strategy. Similarly, it is also conceivable that the clients might create secondary associations not in order to oust the patrons and replace the clientelist system, but in order to tilt in their favor the patron–client relationship. Again Silverman (1977) suggests that clients may be interested in perpetuating the "myth" of patronage, irrespective of the real or symbolic nature of its content, as a way of drawing potential new patrons into local commitment.

Borrowing from the game-theoretical vocabulary, we might say that patron and clients are engaged in a two-level game. At the first level, patron and clients bargain over the terms of the contract that binds them. At this level, the relative power of the players is skewed in the patron's favor: it is he who decides who will have access to the resources that he controls. The clients are weak and divided as they compete against one another over access to the desired resources. At the second level of the game, however, the patron competes with similarly positioned patrons over access to those centrally managed resources that determine his political status, which he then has to allocate among his clients. At this level, the relative power of the players is skewed in the opposite direction, as the clients decide with their vote the amount of resources that each patron will obtain.[8] At this second level, the clients have the opportunity not just of choosing amongst different patrons, but of choosing between the patronage, or clientele, system and alternative systems of resource allocation. In choosing alternative systems, the clients may act in concert, and thus be particularly effective, but they may also simply express their distaste for clientelism by voting against the patrons (or not voting).

What factors determine the respective power of patrons and clients? The existence of few competing patrons will enhance the power of each one of them *vis-à-vis* the clients, while also making their claim for centrally distributed resources more likely to succeed. On the other hand, the existence of a strong opposition will give the clients greater leverage in their power game with the patrons, as well as enabling them to choose among patrons. Four main situations can be thus singled

Table 1. Types of Clientelist Government

Strength of Opposition	Number/Cohesion of Patrons	
	Few/Cohesive	Many/Divided
Strong	Virtuous clientelism	Challenged clientelism
	Collective goods	Mixed goods
	Growing legitimacy	Fluctuating legitimacy
	Sustained development	Intermittent development
	(Abruzzo)	(Campania)
Weak	Vicious clientelism	Ineffective clientelism
	No output	Individual goods
	No legitimacy	Fading legitimacy
	Economic involution	Economic stagnation
	(Sicily)	(Puglia)

out by plotting the number (or cohesiveness) of the patrons against the strength/weakness of the opposition.

To each situation correspond specific incentives that will induce the patrons to play one or another type of "clientelistic game." So, for instance, cohesive patrons will have no incentive to sustain economic development, nor to provide material goods to the individual clients, so long as they can count on the absence of available alternatives, and probably on the existence of fear, to keep clients' dissatisfaction in check (vicious clientelism). To the contrary, cohesive patrons facing strong opposition might well foster economic development and deliver actual goods in order to maintain their position (virtuous clientelism). In both cases patrons are powerful; but in the first they can afford to disregard the clients' demands and resort to symbolic tactics, whereas in the second they are induced by the opposition to use their power to attract resources from the center and to allocate them effectively in the periphery. Divided patrons, meanwhile, will lack the power *vis-à-vis* the center to attract resources and the power *vis-à-vis* the periphery to enforce any given distribution. Their actions will probably cross-check one another, leading to insignificant or contradictory results. Either they will be engaged in petty squabbling among themselves, when faced by a weak opposition (ineffective clientelism), or challenged and eventually overthrown, when faced by a strong one (challenged clientelism).

The incentives entailed by any given situation, however, are not all. External shocks may propel clientelist systems from box to box, just as patrons may adopt strategies and clients create pressures capable of forcing such movement. The latest patron of the Abruzzo, the Christian Democrat Remo Gaspari, succeeded in eliminating competing patrons and achieved full leadership within the local party and control over the entire region, thus becoming hegemonic. Conversely, after an external shock deprived Puglia of its charismatic leader, the Christian Democrat

Aldo Moro, the remaining patrons failed to recompose their internal quarrels and regain cohesiveness, thus allowing prospective patrons to gain some power and complicate the regional political landscape.

Moreover, the Abruzzo's leader used his hegemonic power to support the opposition – the Communist Party – against the up-and-coming patrons – members of the Socialist Party. Although this meant that he could not dominate the opposition uncontested, it also weakened his potential competitors. In contrast, the low-equilibrium point reached by Puglia's political system induced local leaders to act simply in order to maintain the status quo. However, if one patron had gained hegemonic power over his competitors, or if the opposition had gained sudden strength, this region would have looked quite different.

Clientelist systems, then, are determined by the incentives inherent in each situation, by the creative choices of the patrons but also by the reactions of the clients. The Abruzzo's citizens seemed uninterested in simply changing the identity of the patrons and, contrary to what has happened in other regions, kept voting either for the existing patrons or for the opposition, thus helping maintain the system of incentives associated with "virtuous clientelism." Even when at the central level an alliance between the Christian Democratic Party and the Socialist Party suggested an overture to competing patrons, Abruzzo's voters either reconfirmed their trust in the traditional patrons by voting for representatives from the hegemonic faction of the DC, or signalled their wish to change the system altogether by voting PCI. Puglia's voters, on the other hand, expressed their dissatisfaction with their traditional patrons by supporting competing patrons even before centrally agreed-upon formulas granted greater power to the PSI. Their behavior thus resulted in governmental stalemate and decision-making gridlock, two typical elements of "ineffective clientelism."

That different styles of clientelism have profoundly different effects on economic development is empirically demonstrated elsewhere (Piattoni 1996, 1997). Here I would like to offer a theoretical argument in line with the discussion produced above about the role of politics in economic development. It was argued above that economic development can thrive only where exchanges of a complex kind can be safely carried out and are indeed encouraged. For that to be possible, political institutions must provide a framework in which economic cooperation is feasible and rewarding. In more technical terms, political institutions must secure the credible enforcement of contracts. The qualification "credible" is crucial and has a double meaning. On the one hand, enforcement must be credible in the sense that each party must be sure that the enforcing agency will not, at some point, side with the other party. The punishment of opportunistic behavior must be impartially administered. On the other hand, the enforcer himself must be credible in the sense that he will not take advantage of his superior position to extract undue resources from the contracting parties (Weingast 1995).

In the light of this discussion it is clear why conventional clientelism cannot be the hotbed of development. The conventional patron cannot fulfill the function of enforcer of contracts precisely because he is not credible in either sense. The clients cannot be sure at all times that their patron may not be indeed favoring some clients over others, and will therefore avoid being trapped in contractual relations in which they might end up losing. At the same time, the clients cannot be sure that the patron is not taking advantage of his position of power to keep for himself too large a share of the resources that he should be channeling to the clients or that he is not exacting too high a price for his services as enforcer. There is one exception to this rule: the "virtuous patron."

Only a "virtuous patron" will be interested in, and will be capable of, credibly enforcing contracts and promoting economic development. Precisely because he is trying to build a reputation for himself that will allow him to be hegemonic at the local level, the "virtuous patron" will have an interest in enforcing contracts impartially. If he did not, he would be shown to be the patron of only some of the clients, and leave room to other patrons to compete for the protection of the neglected clients. He will also be capable of enforcing contracts because, being hegemonic, he will control the local political system and administrative apparatus and will thus ensure the coordinated effort of all levels of the representative government and public administration. Secondly, because the opposition is strong and vocal, he will also eschew using his hegemonic power to appropriate too large a portion of the resources attracted from the center or to exact too high a price for his intermediation. The same incentives that prompt him to produce public instead of selective goods will also restrain him from exploiting his power position.

These highly abstract concepts acquire an extraordinary realism when one looks at the developmental needs of southern regional economies. Both big and small firms in the South ail under the chronic undersupply of material and immaterial public goods — infrastructures and cooperation. Large firms often produce at lower levels of productivity than those of which they are technically capable because the surrounding economic and social infrastructures cannot provide them with what they need to function at top levels. The infrastructures that were built in the South to promote the investment of large firms served in some instances more the selective interests of the southern contractors than the interests of the investing firm and the community at large. Also, the conflicts that inevitably surrounded the crisis-induced restructuring of many large firms in the South were sometimes effectively intermediated and other times aggravated by the local political classes. The fate of the southern "growth poles" depended in large part on how effectively the local authorities mediated these conflicts (Piattoni 1996: 161–237).

The small southern firms, too, need both material and immaterial public goods to grow and prosper. Physical and informational infrastructures are crucial if small southern firms are to emancipate themselves from the condition of subcontractors of northern firms. These infrastructures must be accessible to all the potentially competing firms if they are to be effective. Lack of coordination and trust, which inevitably afflicts the relations among firms constantly struggling to keep their heads above the water, will easily wreck such common projects except in the event of the presence of an external and impartial actor – of an elected or administrative nature – that acts as arbiter and coordinator. Also, the fate of the southern "areas of specialized production" during the crisis of the late 1980s depended on the effective intermediation of inter-firm conflicts (Piattoni 1996: 238–303).

Conclusions

This chapter has argued that as the "Southern Question" has its roots in politics, so it can be resolved through politics. To "solve" the "Southern Question" would mean, in the light of the most common interpretation, to narrow the economic differentials between the northern and southern regions to the point where no area could be assumed to be more backward simply because it was southern. Only then would economic differentials lose their political load and cease to constitute the basis for secessionist political projects.

That the "Southern Question" is not only solvable but indeed already on its way to resolution was argued on the basis of a comparison between the economic performance of Abruzzo and Puglia in the 1970s and 1980s (the analysis itself was not presented in this essay). The chapter also proposed that different economic performances can ultimately be attributed to the different political strategies of local élites. A typology was presented to show that different clientelistic styles of government yield profoundly different economic and political results. In this concluding section I would like to suggest the possibility that economic development can feed back to politics, contributing to the replacement of clientelism by a more "civic" style of politics.

What can start as a particularly sophisticated strategy for keeping and expanding personal political power at the local level may in fact generate material and immaterial conditions for its supersession. If through "virtuous clientelism" a backward region does indeed develop, the generalized welfare that it produces will make the clients more independent from their patrons and therefore freer to choose between clientelism and civic politics. Moreover, because development is a public good (that potentially benefits all if it is to benefit some), it will send the powerful message that the economic advancement of each individual must not necessarily occur at the expense of someone else (which is the logical premiss on which clientelism is based), but that advancement can be collectively enjoyed. Past choices, both on the part of the patrons and on the part of the clients who supported the "virtuous" patrons, will thus be validated and will probably be confirmed. The process, initially set in motion by a free choice of the local patrons, could therefore feed on itself and lead to the waning of the clientelistic mode altogether (or to emptying it of its substance while leaving in place its rituals).[9] Although once isolated and atomized clients demanded selective goods for their exclusive individual benefit, now a community would demand a share of the national resources (which it increasingly contributes to producing) to be used for the public good.[10]

Historical contingency and human action do not cease to exert their effect at any given time. The creative choices of political agents can change what, at any given time, may appear as structural and cultural features. To argue otherwise, especially in relation to the Italian "Southern Question", runs the risk of unknowingly serving particular political projects.[11]

Notes

1. This paper is based on a larger research project that studied the pattern of industrialization of four provinces in two southern regions in order to capture the internal differentiation of the South and highlight the fundamental link between politics and economics (Piattoni 1996, 1997). The second and third sections have appeared in similar form in Piattoni 1997. The shift to a lower unit of analysis – the province instead of the whole South – is instrumental to the change in focus. It is only by blurring the intra-South differences that sweeping socially or culturally deterministic arguments can be advanced. And once the North–South gap is emphasized over and above equally deep intra-South (and intra-North) differences, the solution of the "Southern Question" cannot but appear exceedingly difficult and distant. By changing the unit of analysis, we not merely throw into due relief the independent, and often positive role, of politics for economic development, but also see successful cases next to disappointing or dismal ones.

2. That is the case, for example, with the Abruzzo, which, in the 1970s and 1980s, experienced a sustained rate of economic growth, thus achieving, at the end of this period, levels of per capita income and industrialization not far from the national average. The case of Puglia makes for a telling contrast. Although similarly positioned at the beginning of the 1970s, this region ended up with a stagnant level of income and a much lower level of industrialization. Such divergent behavior emerges even more clearly when selected provinces within these regions are compared (Piattoni 1996).

3. For a similar argument, see Mutti (1994).

4. Many harbor doubts as to the real objectives of the Agrarian Reform and the

Extraordinary Intervention, seeing them rather as carefully designed instruments of partisan penetration in the South through clientelistic exchanges. While it is undeniable that they largely turned out to be precisely that, I prefer to consider this aspect as a partially unplanned outcome that ran against the best intentions of many publicly spirited personalities.

5. Ironically, the unveiling of diffused corruption in the North of the country was interpreted as a sign of how deeply the North had been "infected" by southern ills. The South was either directly blamed for exporting to the North its corrupt style of politics or, at the very least, for encouraging under-the-table bargains in order to keep together two politically incompatible areas.

6. By "political class" I mean both the national representatives elected from the provinces under examination and the regional and local representatives.

7. In his review of Putnam's book, Tarrow draws attention to the "the effect of the pattern of state-building on indigenous civic capacities" (Tarrow 1996: 394) and, consequently, on the mode of political integration of the South's citizenry into the national political system. He also underscores how "Every regime that governed southern Italy from the Norman establishment of a centralized monarchy in the twelfth century to the unified government which took over there in 1861 was foreign and governed with a logic of colonial exploitation" (Tarrow 1996: 394). Political clientelism as well as economic backwardness were, therefore, politically created. For a similar interpretaion see also Piattoni (1995).

8. Assuming, as was certainly the case in Italy at least until 1994, that resources are allocated among patrons according to the size of their clientele. This point, which will not be developed further here, is a well-documented feature of the political equilibria that characterized the "first Italian republic." Between 1948 and 1994, government posts and administrative jobs were allocated among the governing parties according to the size of their internal factions. The local leaders of the governing factions are the "patrons" to whom this chapter refers. For a full development of this point, see Piattoni (1996: 129–60).

9. I would like to emphasize that there is nothing automatic about this self-reinforcing process. At any moment contextual circumstances and the free choice of the political actors could stop it or reverse it.

10. Is it far-fetched to suggest that the "commonwealth" on which civic politics is allegedly based could emerge in precisely this way? And does not often public-spiritedness at the local level coexist with parochialism and selfishness at the national level?

11. As Tarrow remarks, Putnam's book became enormously popular with the Italian media, and its author was unknowingly enlisted as "an ally in the game of trashing the South, a game which became fashionable with the rise of the separatist Northern League in the early 1990s" (Tarrow 1996: 389).

References

Banfield, Edward (1958) *The Moral Basis of A Backward Society.* New York: The Free Press.

Chubb, Judith (1982) *Patronage, Power and Poverty in Southern Italy. A Tale of Two Cities.* Cambridge: Cambridge University Press.

Eisenstadt, Shmuel and Roniger, Luis (1981) "The Study of Patron–Client Relations and Recent Developments in Sociological Theory." In *Political Clientelism, Patronage and Development,* ed. S. N. Eisenstadt and René Lemarchand. Beverly Hills: Sage.

Gambetta, Diego, ed. (1988) *Trust. Making and Breaking Cooperative Relations.* Oxford: Blackwell.

Graziano, Luigi, ed. (1974) *Clientelismo e mutamento politico.* Milan: Angeli.

Gribaudi, Gabriella (1980) *Mediatori. Antropologia del potere democristiano nel Mezzogiorno.* Turin: Rosenberg and Sellier.

Mutti, Antonio (1994) "Il particolarismo come risorsa. Politica ed economia nello sviluppo abruzzese." *Rassegna Italiana di Sociologia* **35** (4), December.

North, Douglass (1990) *Institutions, Institutional Change and Economic Performance.* Cambridge: Cambridge University Press.

Parisi, Arturo and Pasquino, Gianfranco (1977) "Relazioni partiti–elettori e tipi di voto." In *Continuità e mutamento elettorale in Italia,* ed. A. Parisi and G. Pasquino. Bologna: Il Mulino.

Piattoni, Simona (1995) "Review of *Making Democracy Work. Civic Traditions in Modern Italy.*" *Journal of Modern Italian Studies* 1: 160–5.

—— (1996) "Local Political Classes and Economic Development. The Cases of Abruzzo and Puglia in the 1970s and 1980s." Ph.D. dissertation, MIT.

—— (1997) "Local Political Classes and Economic Development. The Cases of Abruzzo and Puglia in the 1970s and 1980s." In *The Political Economy of Regionalism,* ed. Michael Keating and Sean Loughlin. London: Frank Cass.

Putnam, Robert (1993) *Making Democracy Work. Civic Traditions in Modern Italy.* Princeton: Princeton University Press.

Sabel, Charles (1993) "Constitutional Ordering in Historical Context." In *Games in Hierarchies and Networks,* ed. Fritz Scharpf. Frankfurt: Campus.

Silverman, Sydel (1965) "Patronage and Community–National Relationships in Central Italy." *Ethnology* 4(2), April. (Reprinted in Steffen Schmidt *et al.,* eds, *Friends, Followers and Factions. A Reader in Political Clientelism,* Berkeley: University of California Press, 1977.)

—— (1977) "Patronage as Myth." In *Patrons and Clients in Mediterranean Societies,* ed. Ernest Gellner and John Waterbury. London: Duckworth.

Tarrow, Sidney (1967) *Peasant Communism in Southern Italy.* New Haven: Yale University Press.

—— (1996) "Making Social Science Work across Space and Time: A Critical Reflection on Robert Putnam's *Making Democracy Work." American Political Science Review* 90(2).

Waterbury, John (1977) "An Attempt to Put Patrons and Clients in their Place." In *Patrons and Clients in Mediterranean Societies,* ed. Ernest Gellner and John Waterbury. London: Duckworth.

Weingast, Barry (1995) "The Economic Role of Political Institutions: Market-Preserving Federalism and Economic Development." *Journal of Law, Economics and Organization,* 11, Spring.

Wolf, Eric R. (1956) "Aspects of Group Relations in a Complex Society: Mexico," *American Anthropologist* 58: 1065–78.

–11–

Il Caso Sciascia: Dilemmas of the Antimafia Movement in Sicily

Peter Schneider and Jane Schneider

Among the ways that the "Southern Question" discourse in Italy stigmatizes the regions south of Rome is by drawing attention to their reputation for organized crime and political clientelism. The recent anti-crime and anti-corruption efforts of the Italian judiciary, however, demonstrate unequivocally what has long been suspected: that leaders of the national political regime that governed Italy from the end of the Second World War until the fall of the Berlin Wall not only tolerated mafia, *camorra*, and *'ndranghetta*; but, largely as a clientelistic trade-off for safe electoral majorities, these leaders were also in various ways complicitous with organized crime. Thanks in no small part to this complicity, by the late 1970s criminal organizations had vastly expanded both their role in the global narcotics traffic and their presence in Northern Italy.

By the same token, if organized crime is not an exclusive property of the Mezzogiorno, opposition to mafia, *camorra*, and *'ndranghetta* is hardly unique to the North. Taking what is perhaps the most stigmatized case, that of Sicily, we can discover local and regional antimafia traditions that are as old as the mafia itself. These traditions, however, are not of a piece. In part because the national discourse on Southern Italy tends to criminalize the whole of Sicily for having been the original home of the mafia, it is hard for Sicilians to sustain a thorough and consistent antimafia stance without turning their backs on, or appearing to reject, their own roots. Diverse strands of antimafia activism reflect changing approaches to this problem.

This chapter focuses on a particularly revealing polemical exchange of the 1980s between the Sicilian writer, Leonardo Sciascia, and several representatives of a new social movement, the *Movimento Antimafia*, that emerged then, in response to the dramatic increase in mafia violence associated with narcotics trafficking, and to mafia political hubris. This polemic illustrates the complexities involved in seeking liberation from the mafia without embracing the almost racialized categorization of Sicilians that permeates the national discourse on the South.

The Chronology

On 3 September 1982, Carabiniere General Carlo Alberto dalla Chiesa and his wife Emmanuela Setti Carraro were ambushed on the streets of Palermo and killed. After leading a successful effort on the part of the State to suppress ultra-left terrorism in mainland Italy in the 1970s, dalla Chiesa had been sent to Palermo to act as a "super-prefect," charged with organizing and coordinating the government's campaign against the mafia. Before his death he had begun to complain, first privately to the competent authorities, and then publicly, that he had in fact received little of the support from either the State or the Palermo authorities that he needed to accomplish his mission. A little over three months after the assassination, Nando dalla Chiesa, the General's son, writing in *la Repubblica* (19 December 1982), accused his fellow intellectuals, especially Sicilian intellectuals, of promoting a *pax mafiosa* by failing to attend to the political, legal, economic, and moral implications of a system that could tolerate the monstrous crimes of which his father was only the most recent victim. (Nando dalla Chiesa is professor of Sociology at the Boccone of Milan, and was already then the author of a book on the mafia, published in 1976.)

The Sicilian novelist, literary critic, and political essayist Leonardo Sciascia surprised many by entering the polemic with an attack on dalla Chiesa — father and son — in an article in *l'Espresso* (20 February 1983) headlined "Even generals make mistakes; and even the dead can be wrong." General dalla Chiesa was ingenuous, he said, for failing to understand that the mafia, having been transformed into a criminal multinational similar to terrorism, had entered a new relationship with state power and with local customs (traditions, ways of being Sicilian). The old rules for *convivenza* (convenient coexistence) no longer applied, and state power had to be understood as shadowy, occult, Pirandellian. Attempting to confront the mafia with direct action, imagining it could quickly be reined in, would only lead to an abuse of power by the State. In his earlier campaign against terrorism, Sciascia argued, General dalla Chiesa had already acquired too much power. The special laws he sought guaranteeing protection to *mafiosi* who collaborated with the authorities could violate the spirit of the constitution, undermining in particular its commitment to civil liberties. The allocation of extraordinary powers and special measures in order to meet the mafia emergency put the shadow of a "police state" on the horizon (see also Ambroise 1989).

In response, Nando dalla Chiesa accused Sciascia of "playing the mafia's game" (*fare il gioco della mafia*), by making his father out to be an aspiring dictator. Sciascia, he argued, held a view of the mafia that was "psychological" and "quasi-racist" for implying that only Sicilians can understand (and, perhaps, combat) the phenomenon. According to dalla Chiesa, Sciascia had reduced his (Nando's) accusations against the silence of the intellectuals to "the fruit of anti-sicilianism."

It was no surprise, therefore, to learn that members of the corrupt political class in Palermo – the Christian Democratic leader Salvo Lima, for example – had cited Sciascia with approval. These comments appeared in an interview with Giovanni Valentini, *la Repubblica*, 20–21 February 1983, entitled, *Sciascia, perché tanto veleno?* ("Why so much venom?"). In 1984, Nando published a book about his father's career and assassination, *Delitto Imperfetto*. An appendix reprints most of the articles that constitute the exchange of polemics, including Valentini's interview and Sciascia's vitriolic response in *l'Espresso* (6 March 1983), which he titled *Un dalla Chiesa piccolo piccolo*.

Between the time of the dalla Chiesa assassination in 1982 and 1986, nearly 15,000 men were denounced throughout Italy for "association of a mafia type," with some 707 investigated by the instructional magistrates and 460 being brought to a trial in Palermo that lasted from February 1986 to December 1987. The dramatic trial, known as the *maxi-processo*, took place in a specially constructed high-security bunker courthouse built inside the walls of the nineteenth-century Ucciardone Prison, to which over three thousand police, military, and judicial personnel were assigned. In all, the State's hand was strengthened by evidence from *mafiosi* who had turned "State's witness" – a virtually unprecedented break-through, for which the Sicilian magistrate Giovanni Falcone received much credit. Accompanying these developments were the election, in Palermo, of a militantly antimafia mayor, Leoluca Orlando, and the emergence of the *Coordinamento Antimafia*, an umbrella organization of social movement activists whose mobilization in the regional capital produced a new expression: "the Palermo Spring."

Then, in January 1987, Sciascia fired another salvo. Invited by *Corriere della Sera* to review Christopher Duggan's book on Cesare Mori, the fascist prefect whom Mussolini had assigned to "clean up the mafia" in Sicily (see Duggan 1986), he used the occasion to mount an attack on what he labeled the "antimafia professionals" (*professionisti dell'antimafia*). Establishing his own antimafia credentials, Sciascia began by quoting extensively from his early "mafia novels," *Il Giorno della Civetta* (1961a) and *Al Ciascuno il Suo* (1966). In those days, he noted, it was blessed to ignore the mafia; today it is blessed to talk about it all the time. The current "flood of rhetoric" is an improvement over past indifference, but it contains a confused "racial resentment" regarding Sicily and Sicilians, as if Sicily could not be pardoned for its sins, even though it also produced such luminaries as Verga, Pirandello, the painter Gattuso . . . (and, by implication, Sciascia himself).

The review also referred to the vastness and pain of the mafia problem, and the complicated ways that ordinary people are caught up in it. This is not mystification, claimed Sciascia. One can understand the mafia, but it would take more time, and a more nuanced analysis, than the antimafia *professionisti* seem prepared to give. Most important, they are naive about the clear risks to democracy inherent in such a project. Sciascia sounded offended that others would believe that the mafia could be subdued – that they would not allow for doubts or dissent, almost as if it were the eve of the dictatorship in 1927!

In Sicily, the review went on, the mafia had earlier "played the role of fascism" by impeding the diffusion of socialist organization. Nevertheless, Mussolini had been able to mobilize the island's landowners and mineowners around the idea of eliminating the criminal element. Mori set about this in an authoritarian way; his strong sense of duty and belief in the legitimacy of the State seemed to justify his assumption of draconian powers. Sciascia noted that few people objected, because of the involvement of the dominant class. Antimafia in that context was an instrument of conservative forces seeking to achieve superior power and restore public order. Anyone who dissented was labeled *mafioso*.

Now, Sciascia wrote, we already have a warning that this could happen again. Take, for example, "a mayor" who begins to exhibit himself on TV, and to make appearances in the schools, as a crusader against the mafia. He spends so much time in self-display that he neglects the city's problems: water, sanitation, road-maintenance, and so forth. People outside his administration may criticize him, but insiders who question or challenge his policies can expect to be smeared as *mafioso*, and possibly removed from office. Although Sciascia insisted this was just a hypothetical example, his words were clearly aimed at the mayor of Palermo, Orlando. Making matters worse, he attacked the Sicilian magistrate, Paolo Borsellino, who, he said, was promoted out of the line of seniority because he dealt with mafia crimes. Nothing better enhanced a magistrate's career than bringing a *mafioso* to trial; others were held back because they lacked this opportunity.

Sciascia's attack on Borsellino created a storm of shocked protest, as Borsellino was second only to Falcone in public esteem among the judges of the antimafia pool. On 14 January, the author retracted his accusation in part, telling reporters that he did not mean to impugn judge Borsellino's qualifications, only the modality of his promotion. But he added that the antimafia activists' reaction had proved his earlier point. He recalled again Mori's suppressions – Mussolini's "quick solution" to the problem of public order in Sicily. It is surely significant that he was also at the time publishing *Porte Aperte* (1986b), a novel about a Palermo magistrate under fascism who refused to bend to political pressure and inflict the death penalty in the case of a convicted wife-murderer, because the accused had in fact been aggrieved by his wife in collusion with officials of the fascist hierarchy. Joseph Farrell perceptively comments that the Borsellino affair ". . . disconcerted those who had expected of Sciascia opposition to the mafia by any means, but had a certain logic and even predictability for those who had also been attentive to his own rigorous cult of pure principle in matters of law" (1995: 11).

By 1987, several developments were conspiring to bring about a waning of activists' commitment to the new antimafia movement – a return to "normalcy" that would endure until the terrible killings of both Falcone and Borsellino in the summer of 1992. Among these were the heating up of a national campaign for civil liberties (the *garantista* campaign), supported by Sciascia, which portrayed indicted and imprisoned *mafiosi* as victims of an outmoded criminal justice system; the virtual abandonment of local antimafia priests by the archbishop of Palermo, who retreated from his earlier outspokenly courageous stand against the mafia; and a reversal in the editorial stance of the only viable Palermo daily, *Il Giornale di Sicilia*, which even went so far as to re-publish *I Beati Paoli* – the popular novel that many consider an ideological charter myth for the mafia – in full-color comic strip form. In Palermo during the summer of 1987 we encountered many persons of antimafia persuasion for whom Sciascia's January review was a betrayal that both contributed to, and symbolized, this shift of ground. According to his critics, among them Eugenio Scalfari, the editor of *La Repubblica*, Sciascia bore some responsibility for the new level of tension. The author himself never publicly acknowledged this accusation, however. Ill and living in northern Italy, he died on 20 November 1989.

A few years later, on 11 December 1993, "il caso Sciascia" reappeared in the "Culture" section of *La Repubblica*, embedded in a review by Pino Arlacchi, the renowned antimafia sociologist, of Sebastiano Vassali's novel, *IlCigno*. In the review, Arlacchi praised the novel for representing a late-nineteenth-century crime of politics and mafia in a way that "does not indulge in a magnification of the power of mafia," and for treating the theme of *sicilianismo* as an ideology in defense of mafia interests. This, he suggests, is liberating – an improvement on the Sicilian skepticism that renders mafia as "destiny." By contrast, Arlacchi tells us that he was disillusioned by a recent re-reading of Sciascia's *Il Giorno della Civetta* and *A Ciascuno il Suo* when compared to his memory of their effect on him when he was younger. On re-reading, the writer's "commitment to the antimafia cause" (*impegno antimafia*), as expressed in those works, seemed less clear.

The reverberations continued. Ten days later, on 21 December, Nicola Tranfaglia, also a social scientist, defended Sciascia for having spoken out about the mafia in the 1950s and 1960s when others were silent, when the commonplace definition of the phenomenon was folkloric. Certainly, in those days no one else had the courage to explore the mafia's political and financial support system in print. Nevertheless, Tranfaglia conceded, Sciascia had erred in his response to the killing of dalla Chiesa. And his *Corriere della Sera* attack on Borsellino was a grave error indeed. It revealed in him residues of *sicilianismo* – an intellectual "mentality" linked to Pirandello and the Sicilian literary tradition. Arlacchi responded along similar lines on 23 December.

Antimafia, Sciascia-style

There were many reasons to be unsettled by Sciascia's growing animosity toward the leading exponents of the antimafia movement after 1982. Prime among them was his reputation as a courageous and committed critic of the mafia during his younger years, and his identification with the regional Communist Party – then considered almost unique among Sicily's institutions for its rhetoric of resistance to mafia power. Born in 1921, Sciascia grew up in Racalmuto, in the sulfur-mining zone of south central Sicily, where the exploitation of mineworkers, and their unjust treatment by domineering bosses, were notorious. Although of humble origins, his parents were not the poorest of the poor, his grandfather having risen from a low-skill hauler of sulfur to become a mine supervisor. Yet Sciascia, who was for a while an elementary school teacher, and who held a degree from a teacher training institute (*scuola magistrale*), attended but did not complete a university course, and retained a keen sense of empathy for those who struggled to revindicate their rights to decent, humane treatment and to a livelihood. In his 1961 book, *Pirandello e la Sicilia*, he went out of his way to emphasize the connections between the mafia and power – the power of Sicily's baronial class of mineowners and *latifundisti*, and of their offshoots and allies who served as parliamentary deputies and high officials of the national state.

The early mystery novels developed this understanding. Revolving around unsolved crimes, their villains are not so much *mafiosi* as the *onorevoli* and *manutengoli* (notables) who use the mafia for their own ends. Sciascia's descriptions of their machinations display his keen interest in the conspiratorial habits of the politically powerful. Unlikely to plan their projects in open meetings or corporate boardrooms, these élites indulge in face-to-face, collusory conversations in the informal settings of the café, the hunting expedition, the club. Some of the plots were modeled on, or were likely to evoke, real instances of criminal conspiracy, and took much courage to publish. The assassination in *Il Giorno della Civetta,* for example, had an analog in the killing of Accursio Miraglia, a trade union leader, in the town of Sciacca, after the war. The epilogue of this book alludes to the political pressures that prevented the author from ending it as he had wished.

Both *Pirandello e la Sicilia* and the early novels broke new ground in writing about the mafia, for as Sciascia himself noted, it was then much more common to evade questions of power. Some observers, like Giuseppe Alessi, president of the Sicilian Region, reduced the phenomenon to a litany of "sporadic, delinquent facts," claiming that it was an offense to Sicily to admit the existence of an "*associazione per delinquere*" with precise links to public institutions." According to Sciascia, Alessi, who was a penal lawyer living between Caltanissetta and Palermo, must have known the proportions of the mafia and the collusion between it and the ruling class, but he chose to minimize these aspects before northern journalists (1961b: 163–4). Equally egregious, Giuseppe Longo, writing in the *Osservatore politico letterario*, had masked the problem of conspiratorial power by using the word "atmosphere," as if the mafia were a down-home aspect of Sicilian life, as quotidian as the unrelenting summer sun (1961b: 164).

Perhaps needless to say, Sciascia rejected out of hand the nineteenth-century racial theory of "southern" criminality, which, he flatly said, enlightened nothing. In *Pirandello e la Sicilia* he reminded his readers of Colajanni's restatement of what the problems of the South really were: a centuries-long history of abuse by landlords and bad government (1961b: 167). Given these problems, the mafia made them worse. One could call it an "atmosphere" if one wanted, but only with the qualification that its guns were pointed in a particular direction – at sindicalists or peasant union organizers. "Tell me against whom you shoot," Sciascia offered, "and I will tell you who you are" (1961b: 165). Although there were exceptions, for the most part the Sicilian mafia "defended the property of the *latifondo* from peasant hunger." One could, indeed, define the mafia as "an association for crime with the aim of illegally enriching its members and posing itself as an element of mediation between property and labor." Parasitic, imposed by means of violence, the mediation benefited the *padroni*; it was only "accepted" by the laborers (in America) and "endured" by them in Sicily (1961b: 168).

Echoing the position of left intellectuals, above all Communist Party leaders, Sciascia further proposed an inverse relation between workers' consciousness and mafia presence. Where no class consciousness existed, the mafia substituted for the *sindicato*. Where there was a *sindicato*, the mafia fought it as a "*sotto* [underground] police force". Moreover, wherever the mafia held sway, electoral practices could not be immune to crime or the corruption of public power (1961b: 169).

But Sciascia's relationship to the Communist Party was not without complexity. Elected to the Palermo City Council as an "independent on the Party ticket" in the mid-1970s, he became disillusioned by the regional leaders' acceptance of the national pursuit of a "historic compromise" with the Christian Democrats. And, accusing his Communist colleagues on the Council of ignoring drastic problems of water and sewage, transportation and housing, he soon resigned. Then, after the March 1978 kidnapping of the Christian Democratic Prime Minister Aldo Moro, Sciascia disputed the national Communist Party position that the State should refuse to negotiate with Moro's Red Brigade captors (see Sciascia 1987a). Nevertheless, his position on the mafia was close enough to the official pronouncements of the Party that his challenge to Nando dalla Chiesa (a PCI member at the time of his father's assassination) seemed altogether unlikely, and shocking to many.

Intellectual Generations

If Sciascia's credentials as an "opponent" of the mafia seemed well enough grounded in the context of the 1960s and 1970s — we remember him well for contributing to our own understanding of mafia's "political shield" in those years (Schneider and Schneider 1976) — the intellectual cohort to which he belonged was giving way to a new generation by the time of dalla Chiesa's murder in 1982. In the mix of antimafia leaders who emerged during the Palermo Spring, hardly any were without a university education. More than this, most had earned their degrees during the heady days of the late 1960s and early 1970s when Italian universities, the University of Palermo among them, participated in a Europe-wide movement of students and workers confronting old structures of power. Not only were they products of higher education during a remarkably transformative moment; some of the most outspoken leaders had pursued their studies outside Italy — for example, the antimafia mayor Orlando had studied in Heidelberg. Priests in the forefront of the movement traced their intellectual formation to the relatively progressive atmosphere of the Gregorian Institute in Rome, following Vatican II. Nando dalla Chiesa, of course, was not a southerner but a Milanese, although he had lived in Sicily during his father's earlier tenure there, from 1966 to 1973, attending Palermo's best-known middle-class *liceo*, the Garibaldi, and meeting there the person he later married.

Many differences separated the antimafia leaders of the Palermo Spring from Sciascia. Not only were they, for the most part, university-educated magistrates, politicians, teachers, professionals — Sciascia once glossed them as "sociologists of assault" — and he a former high-school teacher and self-trained intellectual; they thought and wrote at a time when many of the older verities were falling away. In an interview with us in 1988, dalla Chiesa put it this way: the "old" antimafia was part of the struggle of classes whose locus was agrarian and whose combative arm consisted of the Left parties and unions; the "new" one is urban and has a predominantly "moral and cultural" agenda that is furthered through the activities of "pure citizens" — ideologically disinterested members of civil society. Exponents of the old version such as Sciascia were "anti-State": from their perspective, the State and the *Carabinieri* (in which dalla Chiesa's father was a General) were too much involved in the exploitation of Sicily to ever be a part of the solution. The new antimafia, by contrast, viewed *pezzi dello stato* (elements of the state), above all its reformed or reforming police, *Carabinieri*, and judiciary, as spearheading changes with which society had to keep up. A first step in keeping up would be to defeat the fatalist outlook of pessimists like Sciascia (see also Arlacchi and dalla Chiesa 1987: 109–41).

There was as well a difference in outlook regarding the collusive "pieces" of the State. Feeling empowered, the "young Turks" of the 1980s antimafia movement were prepared to go beyond Sciascia's literary mode of exposing what they began to call the "third level" of power – the level of conspiracy and accommodation between mafia and public officials that the novelist had brilliantly outlined without ever naming names. Sciascia, in fact, was highly skeptical of such naming; the heroes of the early novels who attempted to get to the bottom (or, as it were, the top) of things were drawn as rather naive characters, almost asking to be made the victims they became. Tellingly, the new generation of investigating magistrates and police were considerably more determined than comparable figures in these novels.

Like Renato Candida, a police officer in the province of Agrigento during the 1960s, Sciascia was convinced of the impossibility of "turning" a *mafioso* into a witness for the State (see Candida 1956). The reverse was more likely: a poorly equipped, pre-modern police force, according to Candida, was too easily drawn into the mafia ambience. In *Pirandello e la Sicilia*, Sciascia elaborated on the duplicitous role of the informer or confidant by describing the dynamic of mafia extortion in reverse. First a *mafioso*, sucked in by the police, begins to betray his companions; but they, finding out, supply *dis*information carefully prepared by the mafia. In the end, the police become participants in a factional dispute. Even the fascist system of exiling *mafiosi* worked only to help certain factions get rid of their enemies, *assisted* by the police (1961b: 175–8). Deeply cynical on this point, Sciascia hardly anticipated the singular success of Falcone and Borsellino in exploiting the phenomenon of the *mafioso pentito*.

Sciascia had actually criticized Candida for naming names, for his political denunciations. Electoral collusion is an old story, he chided in *Pirandello e la Sicilia*; we have known about it ever since the Franchetti report of the 1870s (1961b: 178–9). Unfortunately for the reformer, the mechanisms of collusion are indirect. Members of the dominant class rarely need to directly order a murder or a *minaccia*. They need only be allied to *mafiosi* for violent acts to materialize. Nor are the alliances easy to impede. Articulated through networks of friends of friends, they seemed to most to pose no moral problem. In this sense, the mafia was truly a *force* – an enormous problem not only on the *latifundium*, but throughout society.

In part, Sciascia believed that there would be less violence if things were left alone. Indeed, he saw *mafiosi* as shunning acts of violence when they could (1961b: 46–4). His discussion of *La Nana*, the nineteenth-century novel by the Sicilian writer, Emmanuele Navarro della Miraglia, reveals this point of view. As Sciascia notes, critics had long been puzzled that this book, whose descriptive passages seemed so authentic, ended in an "un-Sicilian" way, without a pistol or knife. Rosolino Cacioppo, the protagonist, was, after all, a *borgese* – a member of the "middle peasant" stratum so imbued with mafia culture. Given that his bride-to-be had been violated by the son of a landowner, was it not imperative for him to draw blood in return? On the contrary, Sciascia argued, in Sicily there was a historical condition of sexual vassalage *vis-à-vis* the feudal lord, the *rentier*, the overseer, leading to a certain "moral and sentimental situation, a social comportment, in which sexual violation was accepted in order to save appearances . . .". It seems paradoxical, he noted, "but bloody crimes of honor are rarely verified in the *ambito mafioso*" (1961: 47–9). Nor is such violence a major theme in Sciascia's novels.

This is not to suggest that Sciascia harbored a romantic view of the mafia; quite the contrary. He gave no credence to its mythologized claim of Robin Hood-like beginnings. Yet he, through some of his leading characters, wants us to understand how a *mafioso* could be respected, as in the discourses on masculinity in *Il Giorno della Civetta*. There, it will be recalled, a *mafioso* is described (albeit with an overtone of irony) as "a good man, an exemplary father, an untiring worker. He's got rich, certainly he has, but by his own efforts . . . Certain men inspire respect: for their qualities, their *savoir-faire*, their frankness, their flair for cordial relations, for friendship . . . [they have above all] a sense of justice . . . naturally, instinctively . . . which makes them inspire respect" (1964 [1961]: 62–3).

In the same novel, Sciascia has the *mafioso* divide humanity into five categories: "men, half-men, pigmies, arse-crawlers – if you'll excuse the expression – and quackers," and then flatter his listener, a police captain, by calling him "a man" (1964 [1961]: 102–3). Interviewed in 1979, the novelist drew attention to the 1961 eulogy for a small-town *mafioso*, Francesco Di Cristina, in which his family extolled him as a "true man" – imposing, respectful, an "enemy of all injustices" (Sciascia 1979: 27–8). Such intimations of respect for individual *mafiosi* are anathema to the new antimafia leaders, among whom only a few, most notably the magistrate Falcone, engage *mafiosi* in their everyday language, the Sicilian dialect, in his case shunning the criticism that anything short of correct Italian in taking depositions is an invitation to collusion and a "procedural error."

Far from respecting *mafiosi* or their families, the new antimafia activists advocate a policy of *spaccatura*: decisively breaking with anyone whose social network includes *mafiosi*, their friends, or their protectors, or who, for whatever reason, seems disinclined to abandon "compromising" social or political connections. Outside the corral are people who owe their employment to a patron's favor, who seek such a favor on behalf of someone else, or whose former involvements with the governing parties, or party factions, taint them in some way. Restructuring is not a "question of ideology", one activist leader told us in 1987, adopting the polarizing language of inclusion and exclusion: it is a question of "acceptable and unacceptable people". Many citizens, including not a few of antimafia persuasion, have found these criminalizing formulae unnecessarily rigid, though on the surface they are beyond reproach. Particularly for people of limited means – the unpropertied classes of town and country whom Sciascia presumed to speak for – disrupting clientelistic arrangements and promoting *spaccatura* can threaten, or be perceived to threaten, everyday ways of getting by.

Contrary to Sciascia's "fatalism" or caution, the antimafia leaders of the 1980s believed their struggle would be efficacious. A thoroughgoing break with compromises of the past could, for example, result in Palermo's becoming a premier city of Europe, attractive to foreign and North Italian investors as well as to tourists. Moreover, although the earliest *pentiti* such as Tommasso Buscetta were reluctant to expose a "third level" of political complicity, activists imagined prosecutions reaching deep into the Italian government – a projection that has already been realized with the spectacular indictment of the former prime minister, Giulio Andreotti. Some of the new antimafia leaders, looking ahead in this way, condemned Sciascia's caution as a cover for mafia crimes. His retorts were equally disparaging: by labeling all manner of powerful persons *mafioso* and "unacceptable," he argued, the new leaders hoped to have them removed so as to take their place; or, by not allowing for doubts, dissent, and criticism, these leaders were evoking fascism, an end to liberty. Sciascia's goal, he said, was to interpret the nuances. The "sociologists," by contrast, assigned people to categories of good and bad.

Sciascia, the 1980s Antimafia, and the Southern Question

Optimistic about the strategy of *spaccatura*, antimafia activists of the 1980s foresaw a future in which the public sphere of "civil society" would be much enlarged. Concepts like "equal rights before the law," transparency, and democracy appeared repeatedly in their discourse. These concepts are universalistic; they harken back to the Liberal nationalisms of France and England, and ultimately to the Enlightenment. Their European frame of reference is evident in the movement's quest for, and anticipation of, European Community investment. One sees it too in Palermo's monument to the victims of the mafia, erected by friends and colleagues of Nando dalla Chiesa after his father's murder. Starkly abstract, it is surrounded by a lawn (a *prato inglese*) that remains green through Sicily's arid summers only by dint of constant watering.

Sciascia was also cognizant of the modular nationalism of the liberal state that Italian statemakers had borrowed from France and England in the nineteenth century, and into which the southern regions, as "internal colonies," were, with difficulty, inserted. Far from steeping himself in archaic Sicilian, he made splendid use of the Italian language to render Sicilian ideas. He also loved Paris, and proclaimed himself a "Child of the Enlightenment." As such he followed in the footsteps of other Sicilian writers who had this dual footing – Navarro della Miraglia, author of *La Nana*, for example. Like Pirandello and Verga, the better-known writers who had lived as expatriates in Northern Italy, he saw himself mediating between the mystery or non-reason of Sicily and the reason of cosmopolitan Europe. Also like them, he harbored deep reservations about the extent to which a culture of reason could be imposed on Sicily from without. As he himself put it, one had to go to Paris to breathe this different air (see Padovani 1979: viii–ix).

If anything, when applied to Sicily, Sciascia's commitment to a model of Enlightenment rationality only nurtured his Pirandellian suspicion of appearances, so evident in the detective novels (see Farrell 1995: 60–100). This is because he believed that reason can prevail over passion only if we are able to suspend our initial gut-reaction to events. Appearances are always deceptive, and people are always capable of betraying their own apparent political identities and allegiances. Little wonder that Sciascia was chronically suspicious of the "professional activists" and "assault sociologists" of the antimafia movement. These activists, meanwhile, see Enlightenment culture growing and flourishing not only among urban, middle-class Sicilians like themselves, but in a broader arena. Enthusiastically promoting programs of cultural re-education in Sicily's schools and parishes, they hope to reach the popular classes as well. It is ironic that the same deep-rooted skepticism of appearances that so troubled Sciascia, the chronic doubt about the intentions of allies and potential allies in the struggle for reform, has accompanied these activists' practice of *spaccatura* – the complicated triage made necessary by their project of separating the good from the bad (see Schneider and Schneider 1994, 1997).

Another distinction we might explore concerns women, who have played a decisive role in antimafia activism – as participants, as leaders, as a majority presence at many demonstrations and events. Sciascia was no doubt uncomfortable with their public presence, as he may have been with the messages of gender equality and feminist legitimation that often accompany the discourse about civil society and democracy. His position on women appears to have been traditionally misogynist, prompting Nando dalla Chiesa to describe him as *molto maschio Siciliano*. According to the 1979 interview, life experience had taught Sciascia that Sicilian women "judge men according to their ability to make money," applying a pressure that even the most honest have difficulty resisting. "Many disgraceful events, many tragedies of the South, come to us through women," he proposed. "How many crimes of honor were provoked, instigated or encouraged by women [who] are at one blow capable of the worst nefariousness in order to repair the oppressions they themselves suffered in their youth." The recourse had by southern women to a "frightening social conformity" was "an element of the violence, of the dishonesty, and of the abuse of power in southern society" (1979: 13–14). By contrast, the 1980s antimafia movement is marked by images of gender balance, and well articulated with Sicilian feminism. If it has fallen short of its goal of reaching out to "mafia women" – the wives, daughters, and mothers of *mafiosi* – this is because most such women are themselves suspected of being active participants in mafia power (see Schneider and Schneider 1994; Siebert 1994).

While contemporary antimafia activists see emergent social groups — women, the middle classes — as carriers of Enlightenment culture in Sicily, Sciascia's analyses betray, instead, an essentialist understanding of culture as pervading all classes and groups, permitting of no alternative formulation. *Pirandello e la Sicilia* represents an early attempt to outline what he called "the inner world" of Sicilians, or the *realtà Siciliana*. Américo Castro, in his history of Spain, presented Spain as more than a nation — as a *modo di essere*, a way of being. So too, for Sicily. And this *modo* is very close to the *essere spagnolo*. As in Spain, it began with an Arab conquest. This almost mythic past was superseded by conquering Normans, whose Court plunged Sicily into "history." There followed five centuries during which the island was the center of encounters between the dynamic forces of the times: papacy and empire, Christianity and Islam, Latin and Germanic cultures, city-states and nation-states (1961b: 9–11). In Sciascia's view, the period of the Normans was creative; a benign state emerged, there was an interior unity. It matters, he argued, failing to connect culture with power, whether state institutions coincide or not with the *vita stessa dei popoli* — that is, if they express the interior lives of a people. "A people, like an individual, carries with it its own (undifferentiated) manner of being" (1961b: 11).

Sciascia's interpretation of peasant struggle is strikingly consistent with this essentialization of Sicily. Citing Gramsci, he proposed that the Sicilian popular masses were more (politically) advanced than in the rest of the Mezzogiorno; but their progress had assumed a typically Sicilian form. Socialism in Sicily has a whole tradition of its own, a "particular development," he wrote (1961b: 13). For example the *Fasci* uprising of the 1890s resembled anarchism more than socialism, anarchism being equated with an "individual revolution, an end in itself." According to Sciascia, not only the *fasci* but their rebel forerunners in 1848 and 1860 articulated class solidarity with personal instincts and sentiments, producing the vengeful cry of "death to the *galantuomini*, down with the upper classes." All too often the result was a bloody repression, as in Verga's tragic and stupendous example of the revolt against the Brontes in *Libertà* (1961b: 13–14).

Sciascia interpreted this litany as an effort to vindicate the misery caused by the propertied classes. "Sicily was a bomb prepared over centuries, which the *fasci* and the socialist agitators ignited." At the same time, he understood Sicilian brigandage as a "savage and brutal protest of misery against ancient and secular injustice" (1961b: 14). The mafia had its origins in protest and the *vendetta di classe* — origins which, however, became remote and vague with later organizational development. Overall, Sciascia argued, in Sicily it is hard to separate the elements of political or civil unrest from the acts of particular individuals or groups who behave like the mafia — possibly an Arab-derived word that he translated as "hidden," or "meeting in a hidden place." Garibaldi's success in bringing Sicily into the new Italy during the Risorgimento was owed to *consorterie mafiose*, and to the private, individual resentments of particular notables. The revolt for Sicilian autonomy following the Second World War was similar, being driven at once by a social force and by private "brigandage" (1961b: 15).

For Sciascia, the "essential character" of Sicilians is an "exasperated form of individualism." Both Pirandello and Gramsci had grasped this "ideology," which fed on the twin sentiments of *amicizia* (friendship) and *invidia* (envy), leading to the generic form of political-electoral behavior known as *clientelismo*. The same was true of Spain and Southern Italy. In Naples, the heads of the *clientele* were lawyers; in Sicily they were the princes of the land and the sulfur mines. Although clientelism served private interests, it did not do so in the manner of the *Confindustria*, Northern Italy's association of manufacturers. Private interests in Sicily were oriented toward preserving the *roba* of the individual, not for investment, but as a patrimony to leave behind. The rhythm of accumulation was the rhythm of death. Death, then, was the definitive *contrasegno* – the synthesis of the way of being Sicilian (1961b: 22–6).

A history of extraordinary insecurity was the fundamental process underlying the attachment to *roba*. One's effects were never safe; and this became an obsession for Sicilians. Little *questioni rurali* having to do with property lines and rights of access easily passed from the *perito catastale* to the *perito balistico* (from administrative to violent solutions) as people sought to defend their turf on their own (1961b: 24). The reason was "not for avarice but for apprehension" – a sentiment that was also projected on to family members. Just as the boundaries of a plot of land could be invaded by a neighbor and its produce robbed, family members might be violated by an outsider. In *Il Giorno della Civetta*, Sciascia has the police captain muse that for Sicilians the family is more "a dramatic juridical contract or bond than . . . a natural association based on affection. The family is the Sicilian's State", which makes the political State "extraneous to them, merely a *de facto* entity based on force . . .". Within the family, moreover, "the Sicilian can cross the frontier of his own natural tragic solitude and fit into a communal life where relationships are governed by hair-splitting contractual ties . . . In imagination he may be carried away by the idea of the State and may even rise to being Prime Minister; but the precise and definite code of his rights and duties will remain within the family, whence the step towards victorious solitude (that is, ultimate security) is shorter" (1964 [1961]: 95).

Whatever the gaps around gender issues separating Sciascia from the leadership of the antimafia struggle of the 1980s, there was a wide, perhaps unbridgeable distance between his appreciation of, and their contempt for, the "ways of being Sicilian" that he identified. Intensified, perhaps, among *mafiosi*, these ways were, for him, also present in society at large, influencing the inner domains of family, kinship, community, reciprocal obligation, and, through these, the structures of a clientelistic public life. Sciascia lamented that while Menendez Pidal had theorized these sentiments in his "Introduction to the History of Spain," referring to them as an element of *remora* or "delay" in Spanish civilization, an analogous treatment had yet to be developed for Sicily (1961: 177–8). Instead there was only the outsider's view of rampant and vile corruption – a history of lack. Consistent with such a view, the pursuit of *spaccatura* on the part of the new antimafia, well-meaning as it appeared on the surface, was to Sciascia a noxious and alien solvent of sentiments and social relations that were a source of good, however much they also nourished evil. Sciascia might have predicted that, as the policy of *spaccatura* unfolded, some at least of its proponents would risk stigmatizing Sicily's rural and urban lower classes for, precisely, their Sicilian ways (Schneider and Schneider 1994; 1997).

Sciascia grew up under Fascism, but did not have to participate in the obligatory fascist youth training program because an uncle, who was a *fascist* official, was able to arrange his exemption. To an interviewer in 1979, he said, "in Sicily the family, in its vast ramifications, has this function: to protect, to privilege its members respecting the duties that society and the state impose on everyone. It is the taproot of the mafia, I well know. But for once I also profited by it" (1979: 7). A committed anti-fascist (if an ambivalent anti-modernist), Sciascia's comment was intended in the moral sense. We heard it again, in a slightly altered form, from a lawyer-friend, in 1996. "In Germany," he said, "you would send your mother to Auschwitz but here you would keep her hidden, and tell the authorities that you never had a mother." In addition to Sciascia's immobilizing Sicilianism, this tendency to elide the difference between fascism or Nazism and antimafia is deeply troubling to the present-day martyrs and followers of the cause. A few of them, indeed, would draw a parallel between the escalated mafia violence of the 1970s and 1980s and the Nazi regime.

References

Ambroise, Claude (1989) "Cronologia." In *A Futura Memoria,* ed. L. Sciascia, pp. 165–88. Milan: Bompiani.

Arlacchi, Pino and dalla Chiesa, Nando (1987) *La Palude e la Città: Si Puo Sconfiggere La Mafia.* Milan: Arnaldo Mondadori Editore.

Candida, Renato (1956) *Questa Mafia.* Caltanisetta: Salvatore Sciascia.

Dalla Chiesa, Nando (1976) *Il Potere Mafioso. Economia e Ideologia.* Milan: Mazzotta.

—— (1984) *Delitto Imperfetto; il Generale, la Mafia, la Società Italiana.* Milan: Arnoldo Mondadori Editore.

Duggan, Christopher (1986) *La Mafia durante il Fascismo.* Soveria Mannelli: Rubbettino.

Farrell, Joseph (1995) *Leonardo Sciascia.* Edinburgh: Edinburgh University Press.

Padovani, Marcelle (1979) "Presentazione." In *La Sicilia come Metafora; Intervista di Marcelle Padovani,* ed. L. Sciascia, pp. vii–xiv. Milan: Mondadori.

Schneider, Jane and Schneider, Peter, (1976) *Culture and Political Economy in Western Sicily.* New York: Academic Press.

—— (1994) "Mafia, Antimafia, and the Question of Sicilian Culture", *Politics and Society* **22**, 237–58.

—— (1997) "From Peasant Wars to Urban Wars: The Antimafia Movement in Palermo." In *Between History and Histories; Making Silences and Commemorations,* ed. Gerald Sider and Gavin Smith. Toronto: University of Toronto Press.

Sciascia, Leonardo (1961a) *Il Giorno della Civetta.* Milan: Einaudi.

—— (1961b) *Pirandello e la Sicilia.* Caltanissetta: Salvatore Sciascia Editore.

—— (1964) *Mafia Vendetta.* New York: Alfred A. Knopf. Trans. Archibald Colquhoun and Arthur Oliver from *Il Giorno della Civetta.* Milan: Einaudi, 1961.

—— (1966) *Al Ciascuno il Suo.* Milan: Einaudi.

—— (1979) *La Sicilia come Metafora; Intervista di Marcelle Padovani.* Milan: Mondadori.

—— (1987a) *The Moro Affair,* and *The Mystery of Majorana.* Manchester: Carcanet Press.

—— (1987b) *Porte Aperte.* Milan: Adelphi Edizioni.

—— (1989) *A Futura Memoria (se la memoria ha un futuro).* Milan: Bompiani.

Siebert, Renate (1994) *Le Donne, La Mafia.* Milan: il Saggiatore.

–12–

Re-writing Sicily: Postmodern Perspectives
Robert Dombroski

In December 1983, a literary conference devoted to the theme of "Writing Sicily" was held in the Sicilian city of Syracuse (Siracusa). Its purpose was to examine the different ways contemporary Sicilian writers conceived of and represented their native homeland as a locus of social and existential meaning. The choice of Sicily as theme was not accidental, for among all the regions of Italy the island is believed to possess a unique cultural landscape, defined and sustained by the numerous civilizations and ethnicities it has hosted throughout the centuries.

While Sicily possesses also a varied physical landscape, it is the barren, arid interior that has summoned the greatest attention in literature, because it best conveys the sense of destruction and petrification associated with the notion of chaos often evoked to describe the essence of the region, its intangible reality, so to speak, that affects the way Sicilians feel and think.[1] "Io sono . . . figlio del Caos," Pirandello remarks in reference to his birthplace, Càvasu (Sicilian dialect form of Χάοδ, a wooded area of the Girgenti [Agrigento] countryside (Pirandello 1965: 1281). But in strict etymological conformity with the original Greek word, "chaos" for Pirandello does not mean only physical disorder, but also a negative, existential state of living in, or on the edge of, an abyss.[2]

Vincenzo Consolo, considered to be Sicily's most prominent contemporary novelist, also believes that Sicilians are the children of "chaos," for the simple reason that they have been born into a mixture of mixed things, into a history that has imitated the island's variegated landscape in producing a large assortment of races and civilizations that have never blended into a unified whole, each leaving distinct traces of itself. Sicily's malaise, the discontent, solitude, and estrangement of its inhabitants, derive in large measure, according to Consolo, from this age-old heterogeneity. Pirandello's concern with the problem of identity and the negative value he assigns to disorder are rooted in what Consolo sees as the objective condition of Sicilian life. Yet the meanings these writers invest in the concept of chaos are actually quite different, just as different as the cultural milieux in which they wrote. In Pirandello we have a *fin-de-siècle*, modernist awareness of the breakdown of order: the world shattered into a multitude of fragments, incommensurable private languages ("A me la coscienza moderna dà l'imagine d'un sogno angoscioso attraversato da rapide larve or tristi or minacciose, d'una battaglia notturna, d'una mischia disperata, in cui si agitino per un momento e subito scompajano, per riapparirne delle altre, mille bandiere, in cui le parti avversarie si sian confuse e mischiate". [Modern consciousness gives me the impression of a tormented dream full of fast moving shadows which seems at times threatening, at times melancholic; a nocturnal battle, a violent riot, in which thousands of banners are momentarily waved and then disappear, only to give way to other banners in which the adversarial factions are mixed together.] – Pirandello, *Arte e coscienza d'oggi*, 1965: 906); while in Consolo we find the attitude, characteristic of what is called postmodernism, that disorder and fragmentation play a constructive role in the shaping of a national identity or consciousness. In other words Pirandello's negative position implies that there was once order and invites the question of how chaos can be overcome (given "form"), while in Consolo, chaos, since it is an integral part of being Sicilian, demands that we search for a way to represent its complexity of practices and material conditions without subsuming them to some overarching concept of totality.

Pirandello's and Consolo's notions of chaos are extremely useful in showing how the image of Sicily and its history has passed from one that privileges ideal abstraction ("chaos" as opposed to "order" and "reason") and that is essentially linear and univocal, to one that foregrounds empirical variation, randomness, and ambiguity as the deep structures of a cultural system.[3] The transition I shall attempt to describe constitutes by analogy what is often referred to as a "paradigm shift" from global to local theorizing, from modernity to postmodernity.

It was not by accident that the literary conference referred to above was held in Syracuse, the birthplace of Elio Vittorini, one of Sicily's best-known twentieth-century novelists, and that, accordingly, it was subtitled "Vittorini ed oltre," marking at once a point of arrival and departure. For it is with Vittorini (not Pirandello) that Sicily takes on fully the characteristics of a sacred essence, of myth and memory, that underlies a sort of territorial identity that modernity in the form of fascism has sought to erase. A modernist of the political left, Vittorini was a committed Marxist strongly attached to the eighteenth-century Enlightenment myth of progress, exhibited in the story of Robinson Crusoe who, having embarked on a long journey in search of knowledge, re-creates *his* civilization on a desert island. Like Defoe's Crusoe, Vittorini too believed that it was possible to build a better world over the ruins of the past by returning to a kind of origin and starting over from scratch. Sicily was a homeland to be re-conquered; it existed in the anthropological and cultural dimension of "otherness": the same "otherness" we find at the conclusion of Silvestro's journey in *Conversazione in Sicilia*. Both end and origin, it was the place where Vittorini's protagonist could find his roots and where he could reflect on the causes of a world devastated by war, poverty, and disease. Like Crusoe, Silvestro undertook his journey in search of knowledge, authenticity, fecundity, and plenitude – all typically modernist objectives – that would guide him from political and existential chaos to a new, abundantly more humane order. Equally as important as the goal itself is the way Vittorini expresses his process of re-discovery. Silvestro's coming-of-age, which initiates his movement toward Sicily, manifests itself with a clear purpose, positing itself as a natural and ordinary event, commonsensical and familiar. The form of the text (its allusive lyrical style, modulated harmony, counterpoint, refrain, indeterminate grammatical forms, formulaic syntax, and sometimes biblical language) constitutes a technique intended to suspend the reality of everyday events within a deeper poetic dimension; as a consequence, the ideology of the text is circumscribed within a purely aesthetic realm. Vittorini makes no attempt to acknowledge his narrator's ideological positioning; he has no desire to reflect back on and question Silvestro's own experience and interpretations. As a result, the subject, or position of the subject, is solidly grounded in authorial consciousness to the extent that the voices of Vittorini-the-ideologue and Silvestro-the-traveler are thoroughly conflated. With regard to Sicily as the thematic subject of Silvestro's journey, the emphasis falls on realities that lie beneath the surface of daily life and knowledge in some unfathomable dimension: Sicily is myth and mystery, a repository of the sacred.

From this genuinely modernist station in the world, referred to as Sicily, but which – as Vittorini admits – could be Persia or Venezuela, many different itineraries are possible. Vittorini believed that literature could prefigure development and progress; he saw its function as prophetic; its hopes and desires were utopian. The Sicilian literature that develops from the late 1950s to the mid-1990s,[4] with perhaps the only major exception being Stefano D'Arrigo's *Horcynus Orca*, moves largely against the grain of Vittorinian modernism. Even such writers as Sciascia and Bonaviri, whose first novels were published by Vittorini in the prestigious Gettoni series, veered quickly away from the visions of narrative fostered by him, adopting perspectives on Sicilian life regulated by the grotesque, irony, and the fantastic. Characters and plots no longer retain the explanatory significance they once had. The protagonist in *Conversazione in Sicilia* is the novel's locus of consciousness, and thus he occupies a position of extreme cognitive and epistemological importance as the bearer of meaning; the plot, which is Silvestro's journey, is the vehicle by which the author subjects the reader to meaning, and thus controls his consciousness. Rather, in the new literature, meaning consists much less in what is presented as fact and reality than in the ways fact and reality are understood or interpreted, as the emphasis shifts from an already given reality to one that is constructed and modified through language, or better, through languages. Sciascia's later novels are a good example of what by definition can be regarded as "postmodern": that is, a perspective in which the character and the event lose their certainty as objective truths and give way to the play of interpretation. In *Todo modo* (1974), for example, interpretation and synthesis are engaged and encouraged only in the end to disappoint: what appears most reliable takes on a disturbing plural aspect. The text presents a possible world open to radically different interpretations that neither character nor reader are in a good position to choose among. Objective realities and institutionalized reason offer no guarantee whatsoever of truth. Writing takes as its subject obscurity and fantasy; while the maximum of historical exactitude coincides with the maximum of invention.

The late 1950s in Italy signal the beginning of a radical transformation in the economic and social structures of Italian society. Industrial production is intensified and geared toward mass consumption and the creation of a cultural market-place. Intellectuals become more and more aware of belonging to a workforce recruited by the culture industry to produce goods and services that are bought and sold for profit. From the standpoint of the Sicilian writer, namely from a subordinate social perspective in which capitalism is manifest not in extensive industrial and tech- nological structures but rather in traditionally based individual initiatives, the products of Italy's industrial boom are alien phenomena, ushered in to destroy the myth of a superior Mediterranean intellectual and emotional homeland cultivated by the island's middle classes to compensate for their peripheral existence. The allegorization of such a condition may be seen in the early works of Antonio Pizzuto, Sicily's best-known experimentalist novelist, who, like Gesualdo Bufalino, flowered late in life, having published his first novel, *Signorina Rosina*, in 1956, at the age of 63. Pizzuto's work constitutes an important link between Vittorini and such writers as Consolo and Bufalino, whom we shall discuss in a moment, because it thematizes the disappearance of Sicily as essence and origin. *Signorina Rosina* is noteworthy is this regard. Its title refers to a person, met early on in the narrative, who is the old, spinster aunt of the main character, Bibi. When the reader meets her, however, she is dying, and, in fact, as soon as she is introduced, she expires. Her corpse is dispatched to a burial destination 951 kilometers away. Signorina Rosina reappears at the end of the novel in the cemetery where she is buried, as an image of a good that can only be retrieved nostalgically through memory. In the space that separates the two brief experiences the reader has of Rosina, Pizzuto refers to at least six other Rosinas whom Bibi encounters in his travels. The extension of Rosina's name to different textual referents is the most important aspect of the novel's structure. It results in the reader's being unable to locate and define the person intended to serve as a focal point for meaning and understanding. Rosina, in other words, is nothing else than a desire for referentiality. The images we have of her do not coincide with a particular substance, but refer back to other signs. She is a trace of what was once a center of consciousness, but is now regarded as an arbitrary construct. As the subject of Pizzuto's narrative is decentered, so is the Sicilian landscape in which it is supposedly set. The nineteenth-century veristic ethnographic perspective, with its emphasis on the region's unique customs and language, is thoroughly eclipsed, as is the sense of homeland or maternal womb or stage of existence, conveyed so emblematically by Vittorini. Instead, Pizzuto's Sicily, like Signorina Rosina, is gone, and with it the sense of human community, symbolic practices, and ways of affirming social unity through ritual.

Some twenty-five years later, Vincenzo Consolo would write that traditional Sicilian culture no longer exists as a narratable reality. The changes brought about by Italy's postwar industrial boom have deprived local cultures of their distinct individuality and, therefore, of their history. Earlier, in 1977, Consolo had written a short narrative entitled "Paesaggio metafisico di una folla pietrificata"[5] [The Metaphysical Landscape of a Petrified Crowd], in which he allegorizes this demise:

Un urlo bestiale rompeva il silenzio nella notte di luna piena. Ed era uno svegliarsi, un origliare dietro le porte serrate, uno spiare dietro le finestre socchiuse, un porsi in salvo al centro dei crocicchi o impugnare la lama per ferire alla fronte e far sgorgare gocce di nero sangue. Il licantropo s'aggirava per l'abitato, a quattro zampe, ululando, grattando le porte, con le sue unghie adunche. Il lupo mannaro era l'incubo, lo spavento notturno, nella vecchia cultura contadina, carico di male e malefizio, contro il quale si opponevano crudeli gesti esorcistici.

[A wild cry broke the silence of a moon-lit night. It was a wakening, a listening behind locked doors, a looking out of partly opened windows, a searching for a safe place to hide, or the grabbing of a knife to stab and make drops of black blood gush forth. The werewolf stalked the village on all fours, howling, scratching the doors with his sharp claws. It was the nightmare, the nocturnal fright, of the old agrarian cultures, bearer of evil and black magic, against which cruel rites of exorcism were leveled.]

In the modern world of industrial and technological progress all the werewolves have left Sicily. But in their place has come the more terrifying beast of consumer culture:

Traversare la Sicilia interna, visitare quelle città e quei paesi un tempo vitali per umanità e cultura, carichi dunque, ancora fino a pochi anni addietro, di volontà e di speranza, luoghi che il moderno feticcio dell'accelerazione spasmodica, l'autostrada, ha tagliato fuori dallo spazio e ribattuto ancora più fuori dalla storia; visitare oggi Enna, Caltanissetta o Ragusa, visitare Caltagirone, Riesi, Palazzolo Acreide o Racalmuto più che attenderti furori, inutili ormai, ti infonde sconsolazione e pena. Sono paesi che si sono vuotati d'uomini e di significato.

[When traveling across Sicily's interior and visiting those cities and towns once so vital for humanity and civilization (Enna, Caltanissetta or Ragusa, Caltagirone, Riesi, Palazzolo Acreide or Racalmuto), instead of by now useless furies, you are filled with grief and hopelessness. Up to a few years ago, these places were full of hopes and desires. Now the super highway, that modern fetish of spasmodic acceleration, has cut them off from space, casting them even further outside of history. They are towns emptied of men and meaning.]

Consolo's *Il sorriso dell'ignoto marinaio* [*The smile of the Unknown Mariner*] (1987) was published in 1976 and immediately heralded as a monumental literary event. The novel is applauded for its extraordinary linguistic pastiche and varied intertextuality. For the practical purposes of definition it is a historical novel, but one devoid of foundation in either collective or individual memory. At the same time, it has little in common with the historical metafiction of such writers as Umberto Eco, Sebastiano Vassalli, or Roberto Pazzi. Paradoxically, it is a historical narrative without a center of consciousness or controlling perspective, whether it be the omniscience of a Manzoni, the scientific pretense of a De Roberto, the total vision of a Tomasi di Lampedusa, or the postmodern irony of the three authors just mentioned. Instead, the narrator is part of the fragments that constitute his historical account, a fragment among fragments – fragments exhibited, however, in well-calibrated sequences. Consolo believes in "history": *his* history of a Sicily deprived of history and culture, as a consequence of which he believes all the more in *his* myth, position, ideology.

The novel's protagonist is a real historical figure, Baron Enrico Pirajno di Mandralisca (1809–1864), archeologist, naturalist, philanthropist, and collector of art and rare coins. The Museo Mandralisca of Cefalù holds his collection, which includes Antonello da Messina's *Ritratto di ignoto*. He was active in government: deputy in the Camera dei Comuni in 1848, and, after the Unification, in the first parliament of the Kingdom of Italy. Mandralisca's interlocutor in the novel, Giovanni Interdonato, is also a historical figure who held numerous political appointments, culminating in 1865 in his nomination as Senator of the Kingdom of Italy. Mandralisca was an exponent of the enlightened bourgeoisie and aristocracy; Interdonato, a left democrat who was instrumental in granting amnesty to the peasants and *braccianti* who took part in a bloody revolt at Alcàra Li Fusi in May of 1860, mentioned in the novel. The novel's historical referent are the attempts, in northern Sicily in the area between Cefalù and Sant'Agata, to incite revolt after Garibaldi's landing on the Island. The history recounted is a history of libertarian dreams and desires; but it is at the same time a history that can never be known, because it is entangled in ideology and in the bad faith of intellectuals; it is the history written by those in power who tell the story in their own language. Enrico Pirajno, *barone* di Mandralisca, conscious as he is of this history, can only escape from it through his hobby, the study of mollusks, and he is forced to confess to Interdonato (the "ignoto marinaio") his incapacity to reconstruct and rewrite that history, even though he has witnessed the repression and slaughter of the Sicilian proletariat.

Re-writing Sicily: Postmodern Perspectives

The specifically "postmodern turn" that historical narrative takes in *Il sorriso dell'ignoto marinaio* consists in the following: the author constructs a plotless picture of a character of whom he is neither historian nor ideologue, but only narrator, that is inventor or re-creator. The regressive nature of things that speak for themselves (epic memory) is the diametrical opposite of rationalist and scientific historiography. The narrator can only invent history in fragments that take the form of the voices silenced by official historiography. These fragments compose the work's collective, epic memory; they are uttered in a host of registers (lyrical, documentary, dialectal, diaristic, comic, erudite) so varied that the reader can not in any way reduce them (this history) to a controlling idea (for instance, the dialectic of oppressed and oppressors [Manzoni] or the story of offended humanity [Vittorini]). Put differently, the reader is denied access to a totalizing narrative with which he /she may identify. With the multiplicity of different local narratives, we become imbricated in the same historical predicament as the narrator and character. All we learn is the existence of otherness in its myriad of forms. We also know that there is no single position which would eventually absorb all the others, although the moral and political signal underlying the narrative strategy cannot escape us.

The lesson learned from *Il sorriso dell'ignoto marinaio* is not that we cannot understand social reality, but that we are just part of it, subject to all its languages, possibilities, uncertainties. Consolo calls his novel a "romanzo chiocciola" [sea-shell novel]:

> Sùbito un murmure di onde, continuo e cavallante, una voce di mare veniva dal profondo, eco di eco che moltiplicandosi nel cammino tortuoso e ascendente per la bocca si sperdea sulla terra e per l'aere della corte, come la voce creduta prigioniera nelle chiocciole, quelle vaghissime di forma e di colore della classe Univalvi Turbinati e specie Orecchiuto o Bùcina o Galeriforme, Flauto o Corno, Umbilicato o Scaragol, Nicchio, d'un di quelle in somma *vulgo* Brogna, Tritone perticato d'in sull'apice, che i pescatori suonano per allettare i pesci o richiarmarsi nel vasto della notte mare . . . (Consolo 1987: 110).

> [At once, the sounds of the sea, the low murmur and constant lapping of the waves rose from the depths, echo upon echo which, multiplying in their ascending tortuous way up the shaft, dispersed on the ground and in the air of the courtyard, like the voice supposedly held captive in sea-shells. Those shells, splendid in form and color, of the univalve or turbinate genus, and of the auriculae, buccina, galeiform, fluted or horned, umbilicus or scaragol and mytilus species, are all, when holed in the top, capable of use as triton or shell-trumpet (as it is commonly called), and employed by fishermen to attract fish or to call to each other in the vast sea of night.][6]

Like a sea-shell, the novel echoes all the voices of Sicily in a pastiche of ancient, medieval, baroque, and peasant languages. The social and cultural effect we get from this multilingualism is a surface effect. These voices are events rather than signs or symbols of an absent origin, or an effaced ideal. Sicily returns to the literary imagination in all its complexity, but without affect; an orchestra of discordant voices, harmonized by the author in writing. The result is the balanced anarchy Consolo describes in his discussion of the baroque aesthetic: "[un] connubio di costruzione e di immagine, di struttura e ornamento, di ritmo e melodia, di ragione e fantasia, di logico e di magico, di prosa e di poesia" [a blend of form and image, structure and ornament, rhythm and melody, reason and fantasy, logic and magic, prose and poetry] (Consolo 1990: xxv).

Consolo's most recent novel, *L'olivo e l'olivastro* (1994), takes us to the heart of his baroque imagination, exemplifying both the creative potential of the fiction text and its indeterminacy. The text here is Sicily itself in all of its finite, materialized space: Sicily as intersection of dream, myth, legend, desire; a world of memories and traces; most of all, a cultural subject existing somewhere between chaos and textualization. *L'olivo e l'olivastro* are respectively the symbols of culture and nature. A battered and humiliated Ulysses, at the outer limit of his impotence and vulnerability, finds refuge between them, in a dichotomy between order and disorder. But this is literature or myth, the convention out of which Consolo ultimately guides us by introducing us to the chaos, or "balanced anarchy," it serves to replace. The layers and layers of Sicilian reality come forth to re-constitute the historical memory and identity that technology has effaced. On the one hand, the text posits a return to myth as a more authentic form of knowledge, in that it harbors a profound mistrust of Western techno-scientific culture, of a way of life bound to capitalist exploitation and its imperialistic tendencies. At the same time, Consolo's return to mythical knowledge makes no attempt to restore the "traditional" culture that modernization has effaced. Myth for Consolo means narration and, as such, it contains a dimension that is not only historical but also, in so far at it records unconscious drives, psychoanalytical. History in *L'olivo e l'olivastro* abides by the narrative model: it is a collection of stories – stories, however, that are fundamental in that they are linked to the interior life of the narrator. They form a "history" that cannot be reduced to a structural model. They are not, in other words, an allegory of one or another historical force or norm of reality. Within myth, the proof of history is borne by traces or fragments. Messina, the narrator remarks, does not exist. Only myths and legends exist. But perhaps there was a city called Messina because drawings and maps indicate the semicircle of a port,

con dentro galee che si dondolano, e mura, colli scanditi da torrenti, coronati da castelli, e case palazzi chiese porte . . . Del luogo dove si dice sia Messina non rimangono che pietre, meno di quelle d'Ilio o di Micene, rimane un prato, in direzione della contrada Paradiso su cui giacciono sparsi marmi, calcinati e rugginosi come ossa di Golgota . . .

Trace, prove d'una storia frantumata, d'una civiltà distrutta, d'uno stile umano cancellato. Deve essere dunque successo qualche cosa, sacco d'orde barbare o furia di natura (Consolo 1994: 11).

[with galleys dancing on the waves, and city walls, hills lined with streams and crowned with castles and houses villas churches gates . . . In the place where Messina is supposed to be remain only stones, fewer than those of Ilium and Mycenae, there remains a field in the direction of Paradiso on which lie scattered pieces of marble, calcified and corroded like the bones of Golgotha . . . Traces, proof of a fragmented history, of a civilization that has been destroyed, of a style of life deleted. Something therefore must have happened, a plundering by barbarian hordes or some fury of nature.]

The fury of nature is the earthquakes that leveled the city twice, in 1783 and in 1908, and that summoned visits from Goethe in 1787 and D. H. Lawrence in the 1930s. Sicily for Consolo is a landscape marked by such apocalyptic events, one that gives rise to the baroque manner that characterizes as much the island's architecture as it does Consolo's style:

Quello stile fantasioso e affollato, tortuoso e abbondante è, nella Sicilia dei continui terremoti della natura, degli infiniti rivolgimenti storici, del rischio quotidiano della perdita d'identità, come un'esigenza dell'anima contro lo smarrimento della solitudine, dell'indistinto, del deserto, contro la vertigine del nulla (Consolo 1990, xviii).

[In a Sicily, plagued by continuous earthquakes, infinite revolutions, where one runs daily the risk of losing his identity, that imaginative, mixed, tortuous, abundant style is the mind's defense against solitude, the indistinct, the desert, against the vertigo of nothingness.]

Consolo's writing is very much like the activity of the seismographic needle at the onset of the tremor he describes at the end of *L'olivo e l'olivastro*: sudden vibrations, jumps, dips, vertical leaps, zigzags, acute entanglements. It moves on different registers in an attempt to restore what has vanished from the human scene. As the needle signals the impending destruction of the Arab quarter of Mazara, the narrator begins its process of reconstruction, imagining the daily life of the Tunisians who had settled there and in other areas of Sicily in the late 1960s to undertake the back-breaking labor left behind by immigrants who left. Quoting from ancient chronicles, Consolo remembers the first landings of Arab settlers in Sicily in the year 827, evoking the beauty of Mazara, a city that in Norman times, according to al-Idrīsī, an Arab geographer at the king's court, was a model of prosperity. From then on, Mazara and all of Sicily declined into silent misery, until the 1960s, when the forces of multinational capitalism, deciding that the area was ripe for exploitation, turned it over to enterprising shipbuilders. At this point the narrative quickens, in imitation of the speed with which an entire culture was transformed:

> Mazara s'arricchì d'improviso, il denaro circolò impetuoso, cascò a valanghe, s'apirono banche, botteghe, si risvegliò la campagna, s'abbandonò la casbah, la vecchia città di tufo e di malta, se ne costruì intorno, sulla piana, una nuova di cemento e di marmo. Gli emigrati dalla costa dell'Africa occuparono le case vuote e cadenti di via del Bagno, del Turco, del Serraglio, del Serpe, s'imbarcarono sui pescherecci che razziavano il pesce nel golfo di Gabès o nel Gran Sirte, vennero usati e sfruttati, furono oggetto, nei momenti di crisi, di speculazione politica, nel montare della xenofobia, di persecuzione, di caccia, di obbligatorio rimpatrio (p. 140).

> [Mazara became suddenly rich, an avalanche of money, circulating impulsively, banks and stores opened, the rural areas awakened, the Casbah and ancient city, made out of tufa and maltha, abandoned ; around it, on the flatland, arose a new city built in cement and marble. The immigrants from the coast of Africa occupied the empty and broken-down houses in via del Bagno, del Turco, del Serraglio, del Serpe; they took out to sea in the fishing boats that sacked the waters in the gulf of Gabès or the Gran Sirte; they were used and exploited, and, in times of social crisis and political dealing, when xenophobia heightened, persecuted, hunted down and deported.]

With its newly acquired wealth, Mazara becomes a violent city. Into its slums flow immigrants from Africa in search of a better life; from here derives the racism, the beatings, the "demented fury" of contemporary Italian fascism. At this point, the narrative leaps on to a higher plane. The information it has produced has reoriented the reader to the author's mind, but there is one last bit of news that destroys the previous system of reportage: in a storm in which a fishing boat is lost: "Annegano i cinque mazaresi e i due tunisini che erano a bordo. Di questi solo dopo giorni si scopre l'identità, il nome. Sono due giovani di ventotto e venti anni, si chiamano Mounir Ben Lohbidi Mohamed e Bugawi Kemais" (p. 140) [Five boys from Mazara and two Tunisians who were aboard drowned. The names of the latter were known only after several days. They were two youths of 28 and 20, Mounir Ben Lohbidi Mohamed and Bugawi Kemais.] Adding information to information, the narration is transformed into epiphany. The drowning of the two Arab boys crystallizes first into poetry: Bugawi's body lies at the bottom of the sea, as in T. S. Eliot's *Death By Water*: "Phlebas the Phoenician, a fortnight dead,/ Forgot the cry of gulls, and the deep sea swell/and the profit and loss./ A current under sea/Picked his bones in whispers" (Eliot 1952: 46) – and then into myth: into the Ulysses of old who roams the island that was once his Ithaca, who visits his friends and family, who, guided by his son Marco, interviews Arab immigrants in the casbah, who attends the procession of San Vito. With Marco as his guide, Ulysses visits the deserted, polluted beaches, off-limits like the Montpipeau of

Villon's *Aus enfants perdus*, a malaria-ridden, Caravaggesque landscape on which they meet their death. The intuitive leap into a mythified present again reorganizes into chronicle as Ulysses and Marco fade into two young Sicilian painters, Luca and Giancarlo, who are slaughtered "da ragazzi d'inganno e ferocia, di malavita e di droga, di questa Mazara di oggi, di questa Sicilia barbarica" (p. 141) [by boys bred in the deceit and violence, in the crime and drugs of today's Mazara].

In this journey of Ulysses (the author) in search of his lost homeland (Sicily), Consolo underlines the power of literature to revive a lost culture by creating meaning out of a variegated stream of information. Acting on history from the margins of power, literature transforms multiple historical facts into myth. Homer, Aeschylus, Empedocles, Virgil, Verga, D'Annunzio, Pirandello, Vittorini, Goethe, Maupassant are all points on Consolo's map of knowledge. They give balance to the anarchy that history has spawned; force, totalization, and mastery over generalized communication. But the book for Consolo, his book, as it is primarily concerned with mortality, posits a foundation at the very same time it oscillates and disorients.

A civilization constructed from the wisdom, imagination, poetry, and hopes of a varied constituency of peoples (Greeks, Arabs, Catalans, and native Sicilians) is also the primary subject-matter of the fiction of Gesualdo Bufalino. The point of contact is somewhere between the extremes of overexposure to light (*solarità*) and darkness, between European rationalism and African magic. Bufalino's Sicily is a land formed by an excess of identities, of innumerable micro histories. Sicilians have been commanded by fate to mediate between discordant continents and cultures:

> condannati da sempre a subire sul viso, come eroi pirandelliani, il sopruso di molte maschere, tutte attendibili e tutte false, veramente noi siciliani scoraggiamo chiunque voglia racchiudere in una formula univoca la nostra franta, ricca, contraddittoria pluralità (Bufalino 1992: 1137).

> [condemned forever to wear on our faces, like Pirandellian heros, the outrage of multiple masks, all both authentic and false, we Sicilians discourage anyone who would attempt to enclose our rich, fragmented and contradictory plurality in one simple formula.]

Such reflections address the tendency, present in the greater part of writings on Sicily and Sicilians, to homogenize the island and its inhabitants into one of a number of essences ("Sicilia mafiosa," "Sicilia terra dell'onore," "Sicilia solare," etc.). Bufalino's position, like that of Consolo, is that there is no one foundation or transcendent objective order to which we can refer, but rather many, and that these entities or modes of existence are without metaphysical legitimation; instead they are created by human beings and are realized in a play of forces. Once we have understood that everyone lies, then, as Vattimo put it well, "lying becomes useless and impossible" (Vattimo 1992: 98).

Unlike Pirandello, for whom words carry a heavy metaphysical burden, Bufalino does not believe in the power of verbal art to transform reality. Peter Hainsworth has pointed out that Bufalino purposefully undermines the status of his own fiction, reveling, as he does, in dissonance and excess: "Bufalino often uses several formulations where a more sober writer would prefer one, or manufactures elaborate, sometime deliberately tasteless metaphors which seem to announce their artificiality and their emptiness rather than the power of illumination, or suddenly and wilfully switches from exalted matters and perspectives to ones that are vulgarly comic and trivial" (Hainsworth 1994: 22). Narrative itself in Bufalino's prose self-consciously succumbs to the lure of artifice, artifice that, in the tradition of *A Thousand and One Nights*, is meant to forestall death. But Bufalino has the postmodern presence of mind not to surrender to his own inventions. He is aware of the interaction between the reality of death and the lies of story-telling. Such an awareness is thematized in his most recent novel *Le mensogne della notte* (1988, in Bufalino 1992).

In the prisoners' fate of impending death, Bufalino has allegorized the writing process: a signal in the head of the watchful author that reminds him that death is near. It is a realization that is constantly reawakening amid dreams and fear; the writer is like his own prisoners who at "il primo riverbero d'umido sole" ["The first damp glimmer of sunlight"] are intent on tracing among the overhead beams of their cells the "linee di forza e di fuga, un intreccio di svincoli, botole e crepe, alla fine dei quali li attenda una felice assenza di peso, un'area dissennatezza, un sentimento di volo che nel loro idioma mentale, non scritto né detto, corrisponde all'idea, così virginea e sorgiva, di libertà" (Bufalino 1992: 567) ["lines of force and dispersion . . . a network of escape routes, hatchways, loopholes, through which they achieve a joyous weightlessness, an aerial insanity, a sensation of flight which in their unwritten, unspoken idiom corresponds, so virginal and pure, to the idea of freedom"].[7] *Le mensogne della notte* is the story of playing (writing) in the face of death. The setting is a Bourbon prison fortress situated on a remote island in a stormy sea. Four prisoners are scheduled for execution by guillotine the following day. We learn from the prison warden or governor as he peruses their dossiers that they are all political revolutionaries (Corrado Ingafù, Baron of Letojanni, Saglimbeni, a poet, Agesilaos degli Incerti, a soldier, and Narcissus Lucifora, a student). Another political prisoner, also scheduled to die, is a bandit priest called Cirillo. Although not one of their company, he orchestrates their final game, suggesting that they, following the example of the *Decameron* (a text he says he snatched from the flames) pass the night away by telling stories. At which point Bufalino, pastiching an entire tradition of foundational narratives, has the baron state his hope that from their literature might emerge some reason for their destiny; that they might deduce why they are dying and find some reason for excusing either God or themselves. That the stories would prove otherwise was certainly to be expected given the total absence of theological meaning from Bufalino's perspective and his distinctly postmodern tendency to valorize a surface or constructed reality. Bufalino's story and the stories it encompasses are preeminently metafictional, having made the reader follow the most artful and devious of courses ("vie più oblique e più scaltre" [p. 679]) to end up face to face with nothing more than unresolved tensions and dialogic oppositions, that is, to reflect on the materials of narrative themselves. At the story's end the four prisoners meet their fate, choosing death over life as informers. Every ruse was employed to get them to divulge the name of the head conspirator, the External Father, but to no avail. Deceit is played back against the deceivers, the incessant movement of "signification" can only be arrested, thematically, by death.

Le mensogne della notte contains a variety of texts that, in their appearance as "reality" or as constituitive of the world, leave the reader with little certainty of the (fictional) truth. Moreover, within these narrative emplotments that activate the cultural *mise-en-abyme* or narrative chaos so typical of Bufalino's work, we find an even more powerful and, if it were possible, more disquieting structure that stands as the novel's epilogue. It bears the heading "Carte trovate su un piccione da un cacciatore" in which we learn that Brother Cirillo, the bandit priest, presumed to have been executed, who managed the entire story-telling diversion, was an imposter and actually Consalvo De Ritis, Knight of Putigliano. The papers, written by Consalvo, include his will, naming the King as beneficiary, and a letter in which he confesses he had invented the story that behind the subversive activity of the prisoners there was a plot to overthrow the King and that the Count of Syracuse was the traitor. But more importantly, Consalvo tells the King that he became aware that the baron and his men learned of the deception and that their stories and conversations were designed purposefully to trick him: "Ne ho tratto coscienza che i quattro m'abbiano non solo raggirato ma irriso: proponendomi in ogni loro novella sciarade e subdole cifre, il cui ritornello batteva sempre sull'ambage dell'essere e dell'apparirre, secondo che in terra si svolga e squaderni l'infinita festa in costume dove balliamo . . ." (p. 684) ["This showed me that the four of them had not only tricked me, but laughed me to scorn, all their tales being offered me in the form of charades or cryptic ciphers, the ritornello of which was always based on the ambiguity of what is and what seems to be, just as the infinite fancy-dress ball of our life on earth unrolls and unravels" – p. 159]. The theme is Pirandellian, but what is not Pirandellian is Bufalino's indictment of the author's creative authority: "Apocrifi noi tutti, ma anche chi ci dirige o raffrena, chi ci accozza o divide" (p. 685) ["Apocryphal, all of us, but apocryphal also is he who urges or restrains us, who throws us together or tears us apart" – pp.160–1].

The loop of interpretation has reached its outermost limit. Consalvo's mind is operating within its own *mise-en-abyme*; he is at the end of allegory and therefore of his own writing; only silence will follow after he releases the hammer of the musket positioned between his knees. His letter to the King is Bufalino's final commentary on and a most fitting end to his own fictional operation. Through this extraordinary *fiction* and bizarre linguistic polyphony runs an ultimate nihilism that defeats the *jouissance* and closes the text with a reflection on the end of fiction. We have come a full circle from the meaning of lying to its meaninglessness. The postmodern route has been taken to its dead-end.

It is tempting to take the island fortress on which the novel's action takes place as Bufalino's Sicilian homeland, the rock on which the author is ultimately a prisoner and from which he calls forth his special resources. The prison is his own labyrinth of discordant voices, deception, and spiritual darkness; it is a Sicily devoid of all foundations; an abyss into which he not only as author stares, but is certain to plummet.

In conclusion, this postmodern vision of Sicily, deprived of essential beliefs and values, age-old customs, superstitions, primitive ritual, fierce passions and the indomitable will to both survival and destruction, which was the subject of "Sicilian" literature from Verga to Vittorini, offers neither refuge nor solace, as it once did, for the Northern reader caught in the grip of rapid industrialization. With Consolo and Bufalino, Sicily becomes a multiple reality strongly resistant to the fantasies of totality. Their works defeat the desire to be at home, to occupy a center and to be rooted in a place that expresses our identity. Their Sicilies, like any structure of thought or language, contain a perpetual deconstructive movement. As a result, the reader is frustrated because, instead of entering into a familiar and comforting place, he/she is forced to wander on the margins of a place that could be. Such a homelessness is not exile, but rather the prime condition of a new creative freedom. The traces of civilization, the otherness of the past and its unfulfilled possibilities, lurk in the postmodern consciousness as our only means of survival.

Notes

1. Vincenzo Consolo, one of the authors discussed in this essay, describes Sicily as follows: "Twenty-five thousand, four hundred and sixty square kilometers of land, one thousand nine hundred kilometers of coastline, Sicily, this triangle, this island in the middle of the Mediterranean, possesses the most varied physical geography possible in a land so small. A vast assortment of rivers, clay, lava,

tufa, rocks, chalk, minerals . . . And mountains, volcanoes, wooded highlands, burrows, caves, plains, valleys. And then a variety of woods, gardens, olive groves, grapevines, grain fields, pastures, sands, deserted expanses. In this land, nature seems to have stopped evolving and appears crystallized in the landscape from primordial chaos to amalgamation, uniformity, serene recomposition, benign peace. Yes, we believe that all of Sicily has remained for ever that physical chaos like the Girgenti countryside where Prandello saw the light of day" (Consolo 1985: 11).

2. Pirandello describes this abyss as a void that arises from introspection in his essay on humor: "In certain moments of interior silence, when our mind divests itself of all of its habitual fictions and our eyes become sharper and more penetrating, we see ourselves in life, and life in itself, as if in an arid, disquieting nakedness. We feel assailed by a strong impression, as if, in a flash, a reality different from what we normally perceive became manifest, a reality beyond the human horizon, outside the forms of human reason. Then, the entire context of human existence, as if suspended in the emptiness of our interior silence, appears to us, most plainly, devoid of meaning and purpose, and that different reality seems horrific in its impassable and mysterious crudeness, since all of our habitual fictitious emotional relations and what we imagine to be true collapse into it. The internal void is enlarged, exceeds the limits of our body to become an emptiness surrounding us, a strange emptiness, as if time and life had come to a stop, as if our interior silence became lost in the abyss of mystery" (Pirandello 1965: 152–3).

3. On the concept of "chaos" as it is used in this chapter, see Hayles 1991.

4. Published in 1975, *Horcynus Orca* is the story of a sailor whose return home at the end of the war assumes the dimensions of a Homeric epic. Back in Sicily, his experiences culminate in a life-and-death battle with a killer whale.

5. Both passages are cited by Fernando Giovale (1985: 125).

6. *The Smile of the Unknown Mariner*, translated by Joseph Farrell, Manchester: Carcanet, 1994, p. 105.

7. *Lies of the Night* translated by Patrick Creagh, New York: Atheneum, 1991, p. 8.

References

Bufalino, Gesualdo (1991) *Lies of the Night*, trans. Patrick Creagh. New York: Atheneum. 1992 "Le mensogne della notte" and "La luce e il lutto." In *Opere di Gesualdo Bufalino*, ed. Maria Corti and Francesca Caputo. Milan: Bompiani.

Consolo, Vincenzo (1977) "Paesaggio meto-fisico di una folla pietrificata." *Corriere della sera*. October 17.

—— (1987) *Il sorriso dell'ignoto marinaio*. Milan: Mondadori.

—— (1990) "Introduction" to *Il barocco in Sicilia: la rinascita di Val di Noto*, ed. Vincenzo Consolo. Milan: Bompiani.

—— (1994) *L'olivo e l'olivastro*. Milan: Mondadori.

D'Arrigo, Stefano (1975) *Horcynus Orca*. Milan: Mondadori.

Eliot, T. S. (1952) *The Complete Poems and Plays*. New York: Harcourt, Brace and Co.

Giovale, Fernando (1985) "L'isola senza licantropi: 'regressione' e 'illuminazione' nella scrittura di Vincenzo Consolo." In *Scrivere la Sicilia*. Elio Vittorini *et al.* Syracuse: Ediprint.

Hainsworth, Peter (1994) "Gesualdo Bufalino." In *The New Italian Novel*, ed. Zygmunt G. Barànski and Lino Pertile. Edinburgh: Edinburgh University Press.

Hayles, N. Katherine (1991) *Chaos and Order: Complex Dynamics in Literature and Science*. Chicago and London: University of Chicago Press.

Pirandello, Luigi (1965) *Saggi, poesie, scritti varii*, ed. Manlio Lo Vecchio-Musti. Milan: Mondadori.

Pizzuto, Antonio (1959) *Signorina Rosina*. Milan: Lerici.

Sciascia, Leonardo (1974) *Todo modo*. Turin: Einaudi.

Vattimo, Gianni (1992) *The Transparent Society*. Baltimore and London: Johns Hopkins University Press.

Part IV

Conclusions

—13—

Contemplating the Palm Tree Line
Michael Blim

Wandering in a Parma piazza, his investigation of three Sicilian mafia murders undone by unnamed higher-ups, Captain Bellodi, Leonardo Sciascia's protagonist in *Il Giorno della Civetta*, encounters an old school friend curious about the carabiniere's recently ended southern sojourn. "You have to go to Sicily to realize just how incredible Italy is," Bellodi responds. For Bellodi, Sicily was the end of Italy – the place where finally Italy no longer made any sense.

For former school chum Brescianelli, Sicily signifies something more sinister, more contagious for life as he and the northern-born carabiniere knew it:

> Maybe the whole of Italy is becoming a sort of Sicily. When I read about the scandals of that regional government of theirs, an idea occurred to me. Scientists say that the palm tree line, that is the climate suitable to growth of the palm, is moving north, five hundred metres, I think it was, every year . . . The palm tree line . . . I call it the coffee line, the strong black coffee line . . . It's rising like mercury in a thermometer, this palm tree line, this strong coffee line, this scandal line, rising up throughout Italy and already passed Rome . . . (Sciascia 1964: 117).

In this short passage, Sciascia reveals a bit of the South's peculiar hold on Italian imaginations. For some, like Bellodi, the South is the place where the contradictory, precariously parallel lines of Italian life finally meet, with the resultant collision creating an "incredible" form of life. For others, as Sciascia imagined in Brescianelli, the South is part contagion, part seducer – a sultry creeper bearing heat, palm trees, and strong coffee as it strangles the life of Italy one meridian at a time.

The essays collected in this volume testify to the undiminished importance of the "Southern Question" in the civic and institutional life of Italian society and to scholars who study it. As these essays demonstrate, it is a many-sided question endowed by its long and important historical lineage with a capacity to generate its own distinctive internal discourse about life and its meanings.

Three lines of inquiry present themselves as promising paths for commentary and discussion of the work in this volume. The first task is to explore the process of representing the South in the politico-cultural discourses of the past one hundred and fifty years. The second is to analyse the contributions that studies of the Italian South have made – and continue to make – in the variety of fields of knowledge that touch upon issues of culture and identity. Third, it is important to ask how one might reformulate the "Southern Question" in the light of the some of the insights presented by the preceding authors about life in the contemporary Italian South.

Representing the Italian South

Owing to the richness of the material presented in this volume and to the complexities of the subject itself, an examination of how and in what ways conceptions of the Italian South have been formed in modern imaginations is a daunting and complicated undertaking. For analytic purposes, it is important to examine these contributions along two axes. A temporal axis can aid in sorting out how the South evolved as a specific designation in the cosmological calendar of Italy, the modern nation. The second axis accounts for the politico-cultural spaces from which the various discourses about the South spring. Particular conjunctures in space and time can be observed when the image(s) of the South become distinct and highly relevant in shaping the dispositions of different sets of actors.

Becoming a Different, Abnormal South

There was a time, not so long ago, when southern Italian intellectuals considered their homeland only "normally backward," writes Petrusewicz. Before the 1849 restoration, the southern intellectuals' diagnosis and prescription for southern health matched those of their Enlightenment comrades throughout Europe: abolish feudalism, reform and activate the State, and liberalize the economy. Do these things, they thought, and progress and prosperity were within reasonable reach of the Two Sicilies and their peoples.

Instead, absolutism's last gasp in the years leading up to the Unification of Italy, Petrusewicz believes, profoundly altered the more benign view of southern society held by southern intellectuals. From their posts of exile throughout a liberalizing Europe, they saw their homeland falling behind the rest, devolving while the North evolved toward a new form of life.

Italian state-builders and their intellectual counterparts lost no time elaborating this untoward tableau of the post-Unification South. It was as if exhortations for northern development required matching denigration of a devolving(ed) South. As Moe notes, founding figures of the "Meridionalist" discourse such as Pasquale Villari and Leopoldo Franchetti treated the South not simply as backward, but as other. The South with its degraded peasantry and criminality was an impediment to the development of the new Italian nation-state, as the American South with its slavery was a fetter on the growth of the Union. The analogy is pressed to perfection, as Moe recounts: Villari dresses his fears in the best Lincoln-esque anti-slavery form by reporting a southern informant's plea that the North must civilize the South, or risk being barbarized by it.

Perhaps not surprisingly, other intellectual discourses began to trade on North–South differences. Between 1860 and 1890, Patriarca reports, statistics were progressively "re-arranged" to highlight disparities between the two regions. Discrepancies in the ordinal distributions of vital statistics and crime rates now signalled qualitative differences in the nature and quality of life between North and South. A poisonous combination of crude social evolutionism and racial stereotyping was deployed in explaining the behaviors of the passionate, vendetta-savoring Semitic peoples of the South – to borrow a label or two from Patriarca's turn-of-the-century sources.

The relatively new sciences of society played no small part in the process. As Gibson points out, the pioneering criminologist Cesare Lombroso and his followers, positivist reformers no less, exploited a certain amount of crackpot physical anthropology, mixed it with a *mélange* of folk-national ethnic prejudices, and placed regional misfortunes squarely in the hearts and genes of southern peoples. Their claims did not go unanswered, as Gibson demonstrates in a discussion of the work of southern criminologist Napoleone Colajanni.

Images of Despair

Native literary production since Unification has also served up what Rosengarten, discussing the case of the late-nineteenth-century Sicilian novelist Giovanni Verga, called a profoundly "dystopic vision" of life in the Italian South, though its character and meanings have fluctuated over time. Human relationships, Rosengarten notes in relation to Verga's work, are full of mistrust and treachery in an environment where the act of taking refuge in family life is undermined by the cravenness of the family members. In the later works of Leonardo Sciascia and Giuseppe Tomasi di Lampedusa, a more pervasive air of fatalism prevails, as the writers acknowledge implicitly that the age of science and reason has passed through Western civilization leaving the Italian South untouched and on the margins of Europe.

Though for Pirandello, Dombroski argues, the world of the South was a land of chaos, an existential abyss, younger post-Second World War southern writers find their region a kind of cultural archaeological ruin. Traces of the different cultural pasts abound, and the sources of alienation now lie in the chaotic effects of postwar capitalist development. Folk lives filled with werewolves have been replaced in the contemporary literary imagination with visions of "the more terrifying beast of consumer culture," Dombroski believes.

A Vigorous, If Ambiguous Culture of Dissent

Amidst the thorns of Southern life, there were also roses, as dissenters developed an important alternative vision of the South and of its problems. Foremost among them, of course, was Gramsci. As Urbinati notes, the Southern Question was the "National Question" for Gramsci, for he was convinced that the southern peasantry – like the northern proletariat – could not save themselves without revolutionizing Italian society.

Gramsci's attentions to the ambiguities of popular culture and its sometime capacity to support the growth of progressive consciousness and moral autonomy among ordinary people and their organic intellectuals profoundly influenced the course of dissent on the Southern Question. As Saunders shows, the special devotion to folk ritual, customs, and healing that the preeminent post-Second World War southern anthropologist Ernesto de Martino exhibited was derived in part from Gramsci's emphasis on the cultural sources of resistance among the subaltern classes of the South. De Martino follows Gramsci, however, in his relatively judgmental attitude toward folk culture, as Di Nola suggests. A confirmed anti-relativist, de Martino deplores much of the magic and folklore among Southern peoples as simply another form of "cultural misery." He laments less the loss of folk customs with the postwar transformation of the South than their loss without any accompanying greater conscious awareness and/or progressive learning.

The Italian South and the Human Sciences

Yet, as the chapters in this volume disclose, there is a strongly existential strain present in Southern Italian life and in the native intellectual tradition that it has spawned. Though the literary works discussed by Rosengarten and Dombroski are tainted by a bit of fatalism, they nonetheless convey a sense of lives where people must act, albeit chimerically or even tragically, in order to find their way in a disordered world.

Moroever, it is possible that the best case for this existentialist strain can be found in the intellectual labors of de Martino himself. The fear of loss of the sense of self, what de Martino calls "the crisis of presence," acts as an existential fulcrum in human existence. Saunders argues that, for de Martino, this sense of tilting on the edge of reality is especially dominant in the particularly precarious lives of Southern Italians. To emerge in this difficult context acting as a subject of one's history, rather than the object of another's, is the positive measure of things for de Martino.

This standpoint diminishes the tendency of human identities toward fixity, as di Nola points out. However, de Martino's insistence on social transformation as a necessary consequence of human action also lessens the degree to which actions ever are a cause of liberation. This return to the Wittgensteinian "rough ground" of real life on de Martino's part affirms the observation that one common quality of Southern Italian life is still instructing new efforts in the arts and sciences: namely, the region's profoundly agonistic character.

New research hints at changes in these time-honored dispositions. As the Schneiders show, antimafia movements throughout the southern regions mark an intellectual as well as social break with the pessimism of the past. New southern social strata are demanding the stigmatization and exclusion of the mafia and *mafiosi* and their affiliates from economic, political, and civil life. As the Schneiders argue, Leonardo Sciascia's seemingly inexplicable (he was a courageous antimafia voice in the postwar decades) and bitter attack on antimafia figures during the 1980s reveals how southern élite and popular views of what to think of and what to do about the mafia have changed dramatically. For many new southerners, social ostracism of people considered collusive and the extirpation of the mafia go hand-in-hand — an attitude that a state-wary and more fatalist Sciascia could not understand.

The South Is Changing, As Is the Question

It is hard not to think about Southern Italy as one place, after a century and a half of practice. Though revisionist historians, as Davis reports, have convincingly shown how the claim of "one South" has always been exaggerated, it is almost as if the modern intellectual apprehension of Southern Italy stopped at Eboli too. "The South" means more than it *in actuality* is: but the realization that this may be so is taking some getting used to.

As Piattoni and Davis point out, there are many Souths, and there have been for a long time. To be sure, three fateful processes in some sense began to homogenize "the South" at Unification, as Davis argues. First, nation-state formation, instrumentally supported by a historic bloc, aggregated parallel and like-minded social and political interests throughout Southern Italy between Unification and the end of the Second World War. Second, with the advent of a world agricultural crisis in the 1880s, Southern Italian agriculture neither survived intact nor recovered market strength through reform and reorganization. Instead, it languished across the board, and with it, Southern Italian economic organization and standards of living. Third, the social structure dependent upon agriculture also entered a profound crisis beginning in the 1880s, and Davis reports that there is some evidence that the middle classes that were "re-formed" from that period onward were strategically weak. These new strata were pinned in practice between the patronage of a fledgling State and the growing power of illegal criminal syndicates with whom they often symbiotically co-existed for survival.

After the Second World War, powerful forces for further homogenization of the South and for its differential treatment *vis à vis* the rest of Italy presented themselves. A new, weak, post-Fascist state needing political legitimacy in a Cold War world spent 200,000 billion lira (in 1989 lira; $133 billion in 1989 dollars) between 1951 and 1989 for economic development in a context where expenditures bore an additional, indispensable patronage value for the disbursers (Trigilia 1996). The mafia prospered, and local standards of living rose; but rapid, sustainable economic growth – especially in comparison with the booming northern two-thirds of Italy – did not occur. "The South" was rendered physically unrecognizable but also highly differentiated economically by the input of financial flows ranging from government monies and immigrant remittances to spot industrialization, agro-business recovery, and mafia growth. As Piattoni argues, there are now in fact many different paths to southern development, depending on the region in which one finds oneself.

Given that there are many "Souths" now, perhaps the wisest course for further reflection *and* reform is to acknowledge and utilize this knowledge in encouraging the development of more politically and economically autonomous, self-determining regions where civil society and concrete social differences among people are the differences that matter. The new Southern Question is how to help the many "Souths" find their way to more successful collective lives in the new millennium.

References

Sciascia, Leonardo (1964) *Mafia Vendetta*, trans. Aarchibald Colquhoun and Arthur Oliver from *Il Giorno della Civetta* (Milan: Einaudi, 1961). New York: Alfred A. Knopf.

Trigilia, Carlo (1996) "Coping with the South: A New Strategy for an Old Problem?", *Harvard Center for European Studies Occasional Paper.* Cambridge, Mass.: Harvard University, 12 pp.

Two Italies: Rhetorical Figures of Failed Nationhood

Mariella Pandolfi

The representation of Italy as a nation divided or even *manquée*, a fragile and artificial union of two divided and estranged Italies, raises questions about alterity understood in both collective and individual terms. Generally, we suppose that the consciousness of a group can be integrated through a rhetoric of alterity; insiders reinforce their own identity by constructing an external, deterritorialized "other." In the Italian historical context, however, the rhetorical construction of a South opposed, and even inimical, to the North escapes this pattern to produce a more richly complex figuration. On the one hand, southerners continue to invoke the figure of a land invaded, of centuries of foreign oppression, of the abandonment of an artistic heritage – a position which places the South in the realm of alterity to Italian nationhood. On the other hand, a reciprocal figure emerges in which this alterity must be internalized in order to imagine a territorially integral Italy.

The South, then, is represented by a double figure: on one side, the passive product of alterity externalized, and on the other side, the internalized other in an active national subject ("Italy"). But in this paradox, we can begin to see the possibility of political change. For while the rhetorical figure of externalized alterity reveals continued victimization and with it immobility, the figure of an internalized other demands the recovery of its historicity. In other words, for Italian nationhood to succeed in its project of agency and historical coherence, it must overcome the otherness of the South. And this work of overcoming is only possible through the production of a historical consciousness.

Some southerners, including intellectuals, would counter the deeply ingrained Italian motif of a rupture between a hard-working North and a poor, parasitic, and mafia-ridden South by denouncing the northern region as a capitalist wasteland with a long history of starving its own workers and peasants, as well as appropriating southern resources. But such an image masks the deep continuity of a national structure of political power in which southerners have been significant participants. Curiously, the Western press has also missed the existence of this structure, focusing rather on the presumed "instability" of the Italian political élite.

Did not the same powerful persons and groups directly and indirectly govern an Italy "presumed" to be ungovernable until the political earthquake of 1992?

Among intellectuals, Italian anthropologists have generally accepted the opposition of North and South and, for political reasons, concentrated their research efforts on the latter. Southern Italy was to them what the formerly colonized peoples of Africa, Asia, and the Americas were to the anthropologies of the former colonial powers: England, France, and the United States. Already in the seventeenth century, Jesuit missionaries had defined the Italian South as *indias de por aca* ("our own Indies"), only marginally less savage, pagan, and ripe for conversion than the *indias* of the European empires across the ocean. In treating the South as a dominated and colonized land, Gramscian anthropologists in the postwar period reiterated a similar theme, although without the stigmatizing labels of savagery and paganism. If North and South were integrated and co-dependent, this was because the South, with its large mass of undifferentiated rural peasants and tiny but powerful economic and cultural élite, served as the North's indispensable pool of subjugated and disempowered labor. Here too, the power of the rhetorical configuration of Southern Italy as continually menacing separation from a radically different North goes unremarked, subordinated to the co-dependence between southern peasants and the northern capitalist economy that Gramsci emphasized (see Gramsci 1978; Said 1995: 21–40).

Yet Gramsci's vision of territory differed from the dangerous and arrogant categorizations of some proponents of the Southern Question, and he was careful to dissociate himself from their essentialism. Such geographical determinisms, according to which the South was separate and backward, corrupt and parasitic, because of its climate, topography, agrarian regime, only legitimated the authoritarian and imperialistic stances of the North. Rather, territoriality was a political perimeter; it referred to a peripheral place subject to imperial and strategic domination by the center. It defined a category to be understood in the same way that we understand countries that have been subjected to imperial domination, imperialism being a particular mode of capitalist domination.

Italy's political landscape of the 1970s, with its corrupt links among the Vatican, political parties, the mafia, and elements of Freemasonry, is comprehensible only from a perspective that eschews the contrastive geographies of North and South. The regime that constructed this landscape fell in 1992, one of many casualties of the recent changes in the global balance of power. Significantly, moves to replace the outdated political élite with a new and forward-looking political class have been accompanied by the revived *topos* of "two Italies" — an organized and hardworking North opposed to a chaotic and dangerous South. No less than in the past, such a representation masks entrenched interests and powers. Easily discernible under the camouflaging rhetoric of efficiency, modernism, and liberal democracy, the opposition North–South repositions Southern Italy as the territorial watershed between Italy as Europeanized (or Americanized) and Italy as African.

I would like to suggest that this auto-orientalist construction of a double Italian identity was overcome only for the briefest moment when the Fascist regime proclaimed its agenda of transforming Italy into a late colonial empire. It was only during that historical fragment, that brief period of twenty years, that intellectuals and political leaders came to construct a representation of a unitary national identity. Only then did the many complex elements that composed the Italian nation come together to affirm that identity, overriding and obliterating the rhetorical strategy of an Italy divided between North and South. In the international upheavals of the 1920s, when the nation-state of Italy was in fact quite fragile, the Fascists generated the collective dream, indeed delirium, of achieving superpower status, giving birth to a national identity that had been up to then paradoxical. North and South as enemies did not figure in the everyday discourse of fascist intellectuals. An image of Italy as a utopian project, a hazy veil that hid complex differences, grew to cover the entire national territory. The Southern Question gave way to the rhetorical figure of Italy defined as the direct descendant and inheritor of Imperial Rome.

Between September 1943 and April 1945, this fiction came tumbling down like the house of cards that it was, and once again Italy found itself divided, this time by the Gothic Line.[1] On one side, the South witnessed the American landing in Sicily and the liberation of Naples, while on the other side the North writhed in agony under the last spasms of the Fascist Republic of Salo, which only ended with Mussolini's execution by partisans in April 1945 and the liberation of Rome. These eighteen months signaled the loss of a coherent representation of national homogeneity and of the possibility of an undivided national confederation; a loss that could not be recovered. There followed the emergence of the polarized discourses of Italian Marxist culture, with its rhetoric of resistance, and of Italian anti-communism, which characterizes the resistance against the Fascists as the work of traitors, only interested in settling personal scores, perpetrating massacres under the cover of an ideology of freedom, and betraying their own kin who were under arms.

In literature and cinema, if not in anthropology, one discovers the tragedy of this contradiction: the two faces of the Americans as enemy and liberator, of the Germans as friend and assassin. No wonder that the generation that lived these events has failed to transmit the memory of them to their successors. A fracture in the collective memory has been born of the yearning to mask or even erase this suffering and shame – a fracture that has blocked the process of modernization and democratization in Italy over the last fifty years. We may even suggest that the Italian love affair with the ideals of freedom and resistance, and the headstrong embrace of America, constitute a collective engagement in a cathartic ritual. And, thanks to Marshall Plan assistance, it was soon possible to construct an image of a country rising from the ashes, producing the economic miracle of the 1950s and 1960s, joining the ranks of the industrialized West, yet still unsure of belonging.

In the 1960s, the massive immigration of peasants from the South to the North transformed the urban proletariat, a process emblematic of the occasionally violent foreignness lying between North and South, as portrayed, for example, in Visconti's film "Rocco and His Brothers." The events of 1968 in Italy were produced as a unified discourse of national protest, but it must be noted that the protagonists of '68 were the children of that generation who lived through, repressed, and no longer spoke of the collective shame of the war. In other words, the impossibility of creating a representation of Italian civil society as a whole, with all its conflicts, tragedies, and paradoxes, repeatedly manifests itself as the trope of the continuous drama of Italian life, in which rhetoric and historical tragedy are blended. In the end, every crisis becomes linked to the millennium-long struggle between North and South, perceived as preventing the modernization of the nation, its full participation in European life as an equal partner, and the evolutionary transformation of the nineteenth-century nation-state into a contemporary democracy.

This narrative, it should be noted, paints a picture of Italian history on a linear canvas rather than one constructed from the contingencies of life. It is a rhetorical figure that anesthetizes civil society, activates the same cathartic ritual of the "Liberation," and impedes the emergence of more concrete and contextualized visions of history. An alternative analysis of civil society was erased the day after the Enemy was transformed into Liberator, Ally, and Savior; the day after the fascist powers – the Italians and the Germans – became defined as the enemy. This was the historical transformation of alterity from an externalized formation to an internalized one – a formation sedimented as a silent memory. Herein lies a history whose uncovering would depart from the tired mold of the opposition of North and South and the paradox of failed national identity.[2]

Notes

1. The opposition between nation and *patria* in the years between 1943 and 1945 is one of the central themes debated in contemporary Italian historiography. This is not the place to enter this debate, which goes on between historians and political theorists (see especially Galli della Loggia 1996 and Viroli 1995), except to note the absence of Italian anthropological reflection on this contemporary ideological concern.

2. Corrado Alvaro, in his novel *l'Italia Rinunzia* of 1945, tells, in emblematic fashion, of the traumatic transformation in Italy that inverted allies and enemies (Germans and Americans) in 1943 and marked the repression of national memory.

> Right from the first day of the war, a large segment of Italy looked forward to and fervently hoped for defeat. Every Italian had his ear cocked to the news from Radio Londra (the BBC), to speeches that continually repeated that the Italians and the Allies were friends at heart, that it was only necessary that Italy rid itself of the yoke of fascism for harmony and good relations to reign. Many Italians believed in Radio Londra . . . even though their sons were fighting in Africa, in the Balkans, and in Russia. If there ever was a tragic dilemma for Italians, this was it – seeing one's own son fighting for what was perceived as a foreign cause; seeing soldiers on leave listening to Radio Londra and exhorting them to desert; seeing civilian neighborhoods bombed and thinking the "enemy" was right; justifying what could rightfully be called a civil war, Italians killing Italians and destroying Italian houses. There are enough of these stories to paint a tragic picture of the moral madness a people suffer because of dictatorship. Was all this a sense of justice? A feeling of the truth? A desire for penance? It was simply the catastrophe of a people that had lied to itself (Alvaro 1986: 34–6; my translation).

In examining the same passage, Ernesto Galli della Loggia underscores Alvaro's grasp of (in his words) *questa tremenda realtà* – the fragility of the Italian collective memory at that historical moment (Galli della Loggia 1996: 8).

References

Alvaro, Corrado (1986[1945]) *l'Italia Rinunzia*. Palermo: Sellerio.

Galli della Loggia, Ernesto (1996) *La morte della patria*. Bari: Laterza.

Gramsci, Antonio (1978) "Some Aspects of the Southern Question." In *Selections from Political Writings 1921–1926*. London: Lawrence and Wishart.

Said, Edward (1995) "The Methodology of Imperialism." In *After Colonialism*, ed. Gyan Prakash, pp. 21–40. Princeton, N.J.: Princeton University Press.

Viroli, Maurizio (1995) *Per amore della patria. Patriottismo e nazionalismo nella storia*. Bari: Laterza.

Notes on Contributors

Michael Blim is Associate Professor of Anthropology in the PhD Program in Anthropology at the Graduate School of the City University of New York. He is the author of *Made in Italy: Small-Scale Industrialization and its Consequences* (1990) and the co-editor with Frances Rothstein of *Anthropology and the Global Factory: Studies of the New Industrialization in the Late Twentieth Century* (1992). Other works include articles for the Einaudi *Storia d'Italia, Politics and Society, Critique of Anthropology*, and *Identities*.

John A. Davis holds the Emiliana Pasca Noether Chair in Modern Italian History at the University of Connecticut and is a co-editor, with David I. Kertzer, of *The Journal of Modern Italian Studies*. The author of *Conflict and Control, Law and Order in Nineteenth-Century Italy* (1988), he is currently completing a book on the crisis of the *Ancien Régime* in Southern Italy and is the general editor of the forthcoming *Oxford Short History of Italy*.

Annalisa Di Nola has a degree in Humanities and Cultural Anthropology and a PhD in History of Religions from the University of Rome. She has conducted research on ancient Jewish culture, on the history and anthropology of pilgrimage in central and Southern Italy, and on the problem of interrelationships between religion and secularization in modern history, publishing several essays on these themes.

Robert S. Dombroski is Distinguished Professor of Italian and Director of Italian Doctoral Studies at the Graduate School of the City University of New York, and Distinguished Professor of Italian at the College of Staten Island (CUNY). An authority on nineteenth- and twentieth-century Italian literature, he has published on Gadda, Manzoni, Pirandello, intellectuals and fascism, Gramsci, and the modern Italian novel. His latest book, *Properties of Writing: Ideological Discourse in Modern Italian Fiction* (1994), was awarded the Modern Language Association's Howard Marraro and Aldo and Jeanne Scaglione Prizes for Italian Literary Studies.

Mary Gibson is Professor of History at John Jay College of Criminal Justice and the Graduate School of the City University of New York. Her book, *Prostitution and the State in Italy, 1860–1915*, has been published in English and Italian. She has written on the history of women, crime, and sexuality in modern Italy and is presently completing a study of Lombrosian criminology.

Nelson Moe teaches Italian cultural studies at Columbia University. He has published essays on Boccaccio, Antonio Gramsci, Federigo Tozzi, Rocco Scotellaro, and Amelia Rosselli, as well as on Neapolitan folk music and Italian film. He is currently completing a book on the representation of the South in nineteenth-century Italy.

Mariella Pandolfi is Professor of Anthropology at the University of Montreal where she teaches postmodern anthropological theory and comparative literature. She has also taught psychological anthropology at the University of Rome. Her research on feminine identity was the basis for her book *Itinerari delle emozioni. Corpo e identità feminile nel sannio campano*, an English translation of which, under the title *The Body Speaks*, is being prepared by Cambridge University Press. Her edited volume, *Perchè il corpo. Utopia, sofferenza, desiderio*, was published in 1996. She is currently working on the problem of "post-coloniality" and violence in southern Europe.

Silvana Patriarca is Associate Professor of History at Columbia University. She is the author of *Numbers and Nationhood: Writing Statistics in Nineteenth-Century Italy* (1996). Interested in the social and cultural history of Italy and in the history of the human sciences, she is presently researching the trajectory of Italian geography from liberalism to fascism, its connections with the development of Italy's colonial project and with the issue of Italian national identity.

Marta Petrusewicz was born in Warsaw and studied in Poland, Italy, and the United States. Currently Professor of History at Hunter College and the Graduate School of the City University of New York, she has also taught at the Università di Calabria and at Harvard and Princeton Universities. In addition to her book, *Latifondo. Economia morale e vita materiale in una periferia dell'Ottocento*, she has published on seventeenth-century Polish economic history, brigandage in Southern Italy, and Italy's Southern Problem. She is currently completing a manuscript on alternative ideas of progress in nineteenth-century Europe, comparing Poland, Ireland, and the Two Sicilies.

Simona Piattoni took an undergraduate degree in Economics at the Bocconi University in Milan, then completed her PhD in Political Science at the Massachusetts Institute of Technology. She now teaches Comparative Politics at the University of Tromsø in Norway. She has published articles in Italian, German, and English on the implementation of public policies, regionalism, and the role of political institutions in economic development. Her dissertation, "Local Political Classes and Economic Development; the Cases of Abruzzo and Puglia in the 1970s and 1980s," is currently being revised for publication.

Frank Rosengarten was Professor of Italian at Case Western Reserve University and at Queens College and the Graduate School of the City University of New York until his retirement in 1992. He is the author of *Vasco Pratolini: The Development of a Social Novelist* (1965); *The Italian Anti-Fascist Press, 1919–1945* (1968); and *Silvio Trentin dall'interventismo alla Resistenza* (1980). In 1994, his edited two-volume work, *Letters from Prison of Antonio Gramsci*, was published by Columbia University Press.

George Saunders is Professor of Anthropology at Lawrence University in Wisconsin. He has done extensive anthropological fieldwork in Italy, most recently on Pentecostal Protestantism in Tuscany. His publications include essays on the history of Italian anthropology, especially the work of Ernesto de Martino. Interested in how people think about "the self" in different cultures, he has furthered his comparative understanding of this problem through fieldwork projects in Venezuela and India.

Jane Schneider teaches anthropology at the Graduate School of the City University of New York and is co-author, with Peter Schneider, of two books: *Culture and Political Economy in Western Sicily* (1976), and *Festival of the Poor: Fertility Decline and the Ideology of Class in Sicily* (1996). Also interested in textile history, she co-edited, with Annette B. Weiner, *Cloth and Human Experience* (1987). Her current research focus is the Antimafia Movement in Palermo.

Peter Schneider, Professor of Sociology at Fordham University, has been engaged, with the collaboration of Jane Schneider, in a series of research projects dating from the 1960s that have charted Sicily's transformation from a predominantly agrarian society to one that is both urban and urbane. Having co-authored two books on this transformation (see entry for Jane Schneider), he is currently completing research on the changing relationship of the mafia and "antimafia" in Sicily, in preparation for a forthcoming book.

Nadia Urbinati is an Assistant Professor of Political Science at Columbia University and the author of two books: *Le civili libertà* (1990) and *Individualismo democratico* (1997). In addition she edited the first English translation of Carlo Rosselli, *Liberal Socialism* (1994) and is currently editing a collection of essays by Piero Gobetti for Yale University Press.

Index

agency, capacity for historical action, 68–9, 87,
123, 129–30, 137, 140, 150, 211–2, 240,
285
  particular problem for peasantry, 14–5,
  145–8, 166, 186–7, 282–3
  "passive revolution," concept of, 31, 153
  n.11, 205, 212
  see also collective action, fatalism, peasantry
agonism, "culture of mistrust," 1, 6–7, 12–3,
20, 211, 229–31, 258, 283
  as theme in Sicilian literature, 120–2, 126–7,
  258, 281
  as impediment to social action, 14, 18, 256
Agrarian Question, *see* land tenure system, land
  reform
amoral familism, *see* Banfield, Edward C.
antimafia movement, 2, 20, Chapter 11 *passim*;
  283
anti-Semitism, 100–1, 104–7, 114

"backwardness", *see* development
banditry, brigandage, 9, 13, 14, 55–7, 65, 83,
103, 135, 138, 257–8
Banfield, Edward C., 6, 12–3, 19, 157, 206,
228–9
binarism, *see* dualism
body types, differences of, 83–5, 90, 104,
127–8
  see also race, racism
Bossi, Umberto, 1–2, 28
  see also Lega Nord
Bufalino, Gesualdo, 20, Chapter 10, *passim*

camorra, the, 55, 56, 72 n. 11, 112, 217, 245
capitalism, global capitalism, 3, 149, Chapter 9,
  passim; 269–70, 281–2 , 285–6
Carboneria, Carbonari, see "secret societies"
Cassa per il Mezzogiorno, 28, 91, 210
  see also Extraordinary Intervention
Catholic Church, Papacy, 15–6, 124, 143, 148,
  Chapter 8, passim; 257

in Kingdom of Naples 28–30, 32, 37–8, 42,
  44–6
sale of ecclesiastical domain 29–30, 213
vis the peasantry 15–6, 159, 168–70
  see also religion
chaos, as concept in Sicilian literature, 261–2,
268, 274–5 n. 1, 275 n. 3, 281
Chatterjee, Partha, 17–8
Christian Democracy, Christian Democratic
  Party, 236–7, 247, 251
civilization, issue of belonging to, 2–3, 5–6, 10,
  15, 20, 45–6, 63, 65–71
  retrieval of ancient civilizational histories, 5,
  15, 20, 142, 269, 271
civil society, democratic culture, 1–2, Chapter
  10 *passim*
  axis of North-South contrast, 1, 6–7, 21, 216,
  288
  emergent in today's South, 2, 3, 19, 252,
  255–6, 283, 288
  in light of vastly unequal power, 17, 139–41,
  143, 145, 151, 159, 167
  see also state, "weakness" of
classes, class relations, 18, 43–4, 53–4, 64, 127,
  129
  class consciousness as problem, 14–6, 138,
  148, 166, 251
  élite class alliances, 27, 135, 138, 212
  subaltern class alliances, 14, 59–60, 135–6,
  138–9, 149, 182, 282, 286
"clean hands" anti-corruption movement, 2,
  19
clientelism, 1–3, 6–7, 12–3, 216, Chapter 10,
  passim; 254, 258
  national links, post-Unification Italy, 19,
  218–9, 241 n.7
  national links, "First Republic", 2, 210, 241
  n.8, 284, 286
  relation to organized crime, 2, 20, 126,
  218–9, 220, 250–1, 252–3, 255
  see also corruption

Index

Colajanni, Napoleone, 11, 12, 111–2, 251, 281
  see also race, racism
collective action; "failure" of, 1, 6–7, 11, 12,
    18, 20, 27, 180, 229–30
  racial theory of, 111
  see also agency
colonialism, vis the Italian South, 13–5, 27,
    135, 149, 286
  see also imperialism
Communism, Communist Party, 137, 138–9,
    152–3 n.8, 165, 179, 237, 250, 251
Consolo, Vincenzo, 20, Chapter 12 passim
constitutional monarchy, 6, 29–30, 32, 37,
    42
corruption, 47, 78, 128, 206, 234, 241 n. 5, 247
  collusion with organized crime, 2, 20, 126,
    218–9, 250–1, 252–3, 255
  see also clientelism, mafia
crime; violent crime, 1–2, 9, 10–1, 46, 47, 55,
    66, 85–8, Chapter 4, passim; 121–2, 206,
    208, 271
criminology, "criminal anthropology," 8, 10–1,
    89–90; Chapter 4, passim
Croce, Benedetto, 29, 41, 136, 138–9, 141,
    161, 164, 184–5
Cuoco, Vincenzo, 30–1, 40, 143

death, outlooks on death, 120–2, 158–9, 258,
    272
De Martino, Ernesto, 14–7, 20, Chapter 7,
    passim; Chapter 8 passim; 282–3
demographic indices, 40, 80–1, 82–4
  see also emigration, immigration
De Sanctis, Francesco, 33, 34, 35, 40, 41–2, 72
    n.7
development, underdevelopment or
    "backwardness", 1, 39, 41, 45–6, 72 n.14,
    164–5, 206, 230–1, 237–9
dualism, 5, 6–7, 10, 46, 60, 70–1, 78–9, 85–6,
    88, 164, 225

emigration, 1, 19, 83–4, 208, 269–70, 284, 288
  see also demographic indices
Enlightenment, 9, 11, 14, 20, 27, 126, 141, 143,
    193, 255–7, 262, 280
  Neapolitan Enlightenment, 30–1, 41
entrepreneurs, entrepreneurship, see middle
    class

essentialism, cultural determinism, 3, 20, 87,
    149, 227–8, 249, 257–9, 271, 286
  theme in Sicilian literature, 12, 20, 117–8,
    126–30, 271, 274
  related to racial determinism, 11, 19, 88–90,
    126–30
European Union, 1, 2–3, 7–8,
exile, experience of, 8–9, 28, 31–3, 36, 41–6
Extraordinary Intervention in the South, 1–2, 6,
    10, 28, 91–2, 206, 220, 227, 240–1 n. 4, 284,
    288
  see also Cassa per il Mezzogiorno

fascism; neo-fascism, 20–1, 114, 138–9, 158,
    179, 284, 287–8
  possible recurrance, 3, 20–1, 225, 255
  damaging to southern economy, 219, 220
  and repression of the mafia, 247–8, 253, 259
fatalism, 12, 20, 46, 118–9, 122, 124–30, 145,
    149, 252, 281, 282
  see also agency
feudalism, abolition of feudalism, 6–7, 8–9, 19,
    29–32, 40, 104, 181–3, 280
folklore, popular culture, 8, 9, 14–6, 35, 51,
    141–2, 249, 281–2
  in interaction with élite culture, 15–6, 142,
    150–1, 159–60, 165–72, Chapter 8,
    passim
  revolutionary potential of, 14–6, 142, 166,
    282
  see also peasantry
Fortunato, Giustino, 45, 51, 64, 70–71, 74 n.
    27, 88, 90
Foucault, Michel, 92 n.2
Franchetti, Leopoldo, 10, Chapter 2, passim;
    77, 135, 253, 280–1
Freud, Sigmund, 142, 177

gender, gendered representations, 1, 10–1, 17,
    69–70, 102, 107–8, 127, 129, 170, 253–4,
    256
Gerschenkron, Alexander, 41, 205
Gladstone, William, 5–6, 44–6
Goethe, Johann Wolfgang, 177, 269
Gramsci, Antonio, 13–9, 27, 127, Chapter 6
    passim; 166–7, Chapter 8 passim; 205–6,
    208, 257–8, 282, 286
Gribaudi, Gabriella, 2, 219, 232

Index

Orientalism, 5, 8, 17, 20–1, 117–8
Ortiz, Fernando, 16–7

patronage, *see* clientelism
peasantry, Southern Italian peasants, 14–5, 18,
30, 42–3, 53, 57–9, 63–5, 138–9, 145–8,
166–70, 180–2
  peasantry in India, 17–8
  revolutionary potential of, 18, 43, 145
  see also agency, folklore, land tenure system,
  poverty, revolutionaries
Pirandello, Luigi, Pirandellian, 246, 247, 249,
255–6, 261–2, 272–3, 275 n. 2, 281
Pizzorno, Alessandro, 12–3, 153 n.11
Positivism, 10–1, 77–8, 82, 85, 89–90, 101,
113, 124–5, 136
poverty, 9, 28, 52–6, 65, 89, 135, 152 n. 5
  and degradation, "*miseria*", 14, 54–6, 65,
  118, 129, 147
  and illiteracy, "ignorance", 30, 39, 45–6, 52,
  59–60, 100
  and poor health, 39, 45–6, 100, 262–3
  and underdevelopment, "backwardness", 1,
  30, 45–6, 158–9, 170, 206
  see also peasantry
"presence," philosophy of, 16, 161–3, 167–71,
172–3 n. 7, 190–1, 196, 199 n.14, 282–3
protectionism, *see* trade, economic liberalism
Protestantism, 178, 181–2, 192, 198 n. 8, n. 11
Putnam, Robert D., 6–7, 13, 19, 21, 90, 216,
228–30, 241 n. 7, n. 11

race, racism, 3, 10–1, 85, 88–90, Chapter 4,
passim; 149, 179–80, 186, 245–7, 280–1
  anti-racism, 11–2, 111–2, 149, 251, 281
  race-mixing, 100, 104–5, 109
  racial categories in literature, 127–9
  see also body types, Colajanni
regional separatism, regional nationalism, 2–3,
18
  see also Lega Nord
relativism, cultural relativism, 15, 17, 162–3,
282
religion, popular religion, 15–6, 17, 124,
166–72; Chapter 8, *passim*; 282
Restoration, of the Bourbon monarchy (1815),
8–9, 31, 215–6
revolutions, uprisings, 5, 17–8, 30–2, 37, 53,

164–5, 217–8, 257–8, 272–3
  counter-revolutions, 14, 30–2, 43–6, 143
  Neapolitan uprising (1848), 8–9, 35, 41–6
  French Revolution, 8, 29
  Paris Commune, 9, 53, 77
  Bolshevik revolution, 138
revolutionaries, images of, 14, 18, 121–2, 138,
145–6, 148, 180, 257–8
  see also peasantry
Risorgimento, Unification of Italy, 5, 6, 7, 12,
13, 59–60, 100, 109, 127, 182
  special problem for the South, 13, 52–4, 104,
  123, 135, 218–20
  failure to build consensus, 52–3, 135–6,
  139–40, 146, 153 n.11
  turning point in discourse on the South, 8–9,
  27, 77–87, 125
Romanticism, 9, 31, 34–6, 41–2, 119
Rossi Doria, Manlio, 28, 165, 213

Said, Edward, 5, 117
Salvemini, Gaetano, 51, 71 n. 3, 127, 135–6,
138, 152 n. 1, 208, 215
Sciascia, Leonardo, 11–2, 20, Chapter 5
passim; Chapter 11, *passim*; 263, 279, 281,
283
secret societies, conspiracy, *Carboneria,
Freemasonry*, 8–9, 32–5, 272–3, 286
sharecropping, smallholding, *see* land tenure
system
Silverman, Sydel, 12–13, 232, 235
Social Darwinism, 10, 108
  see also Spencer, Herbert
Social Question, the, *see* poverty
Socialism; Socialist Party, 106–7, 136, 165,
179, 237
Sonnino, Sidney, 51, 61–4, 68, 73–4 n.18, n.
25, 77, 135
Spencer, Herbert, 10, 108
statistics, 8, 10, 37, Chapter 3, *passim*; 112
state, "weakness" of in South, 19, 140, 211,
216, 218, 258, 284
  see also civil society
sulphur mines, Sicilian, 56–7, 250

Tarrow, Sidney, 13, 152 n. 1, 229–30, 241 n. 7,
n. 11
theater, 8, 29, 35–6, 124

Printed in the United States
118331LV00001B/31-48/A

9 781859 739976